A Word from Our Sponsor

A Word from Our Sponsor

Admen, Advertising, and the Golden Age of Radio

Cynthia B. Meyers

Fordham University Press | New York 2014

Fordham University Press has no responsibility for the persistence or accuracy of URLs for external or third-party Internet websites referred to in this publication and does not guarantee that any content on such websites is, or will remain, accurate or appropriate.

Fordham University Press also publishes its books in a variety of electronic formats. Some content that appears in print may not be available in electronic books.

Library of Congress Cataloging-in-Publication Data

Meyers, Cynthia B.
    A word from our sponsor : admen, advertising, and the golden age of radio / Cynthia B. Meyers.—First edition.
        pages   cm
    Includes bibliographical references and index.
    ISBN 978-0-8232-5370-8 (cloth : alk. paper)
    ISBN 978-0-8232-5371-5 (pbk. : alk. paper)
    1. Radio advertising—United States—History—20th century.   2. Radio programs—United States—History—20th century.   3. Radio broadcasting—United States—History—20th century.   4. Advertising in popular culture—United States—History—20th century.   I. Title.
    HF6146.R3M49   2014
    659.14'2097309041—dc23

                                                                    2013024364

Printed in the United States of America

16 15 14   5 4 3 2 1

First edition

Contents

Acknowledgments

I am indebted to many for their help, both material and emotional, during the long process of researching and writing *A Word from Our Sponsor.* Books like this can emerge only from communities of scholars, archivists, students, teachers, friends, and family.

I am grateful to all the staff at Fordham University Press for their professionalism and enthusiasm for this project, especially Fredric Nachbaur, Will Cerbone, and Eric Newman. I benefited much from their attentiveness, especially Eric Newman's thoughtful copy edit. I am glad to be able to include illustrations. I thank Michael Henry at the Library of American Broadcasting for locating and providing some images; Katherine J. Parkin and Kathryn Fuller-Seeley for advice; my daughter, Lina Dahbour, for her photographic assistance; and my husband, David Bywaters, for his technical assistance.

Archivists and librarians who assisted me include Michael Mashon, who shared resources from the Broadcast Pioneers Library before it became the Library of American Broadcasting at the University of Maryland, College Park; Thom LaPorte and Marion Hirsch at the John H. Hartman Center for Sales, Advertising and Marketing History, Duke Special Collections Library; Harry Miller and staff at the Wisconsin Historical Society; Roger Horowitz and Carol Ressler Lockman, who provided a research grant, and the staff at the Hagley Museum and Library; the staff at the Oral History Research Office at Columbia University; the staff at the Howard Gotlieb Archival Research Center at Boston University; Ron Simon at the Paley Center; and the staff at the New York Public Library. Archivists and staff also supplied me with materials from private and corporate archives, including Elizabeth

Draper and Howard Davis at N. W. Ayer; Mark Stroock at Young & Rubicam; Mary Muenkel at BBDO; and Elizabeth Adkins at Kraft. Fellow researchers shared material with me, including Anne Boylan, Kathryn Fuller-Seeley, Michael Mashon, and Philip F. Napoli, whose recording of his interview with Anne Hummert is a unique source.

At the College of Mount Saint Vincent my colleagues have been exemplary in their support for my scholarly pursuits; I am grateful to Frances Broderick, Brad Crownover, James Fabrizio, Vincent Fitzgerald, Charles Flynn, Ted Kafala, Guy Lometti, Sr. Patricia McGowan, Cortney Moriarty, Daniel Opler, Ron Scapp, Michelle Scollo, Br. Michael Sevastakis, Robert Williams, Jackie Zubeck, and all the students and faculty who have attended my presentations and classroom lectures on this topic.

I have shared earlier versions of this research with many scholars, in both written and presentational form, and their feedback has shaped the book in ways large and small. Anonymous reviewers of versions of this work have helped me bring out its larger significance. Michele Hilmes encouraged me throughout this long process and has done more than anyone else to bring this work to others' attention. Kathryn Fuller-Seeley likewise championed this project and encouraged my reemergence in the scholarly world. I am grateful to Thomas Schatz and other faculty at the University of Texas at Austin, including Michael Kackman, Jeffrey Meikle, Horace Newcomb, and Laura Stein, as well as Mary Desjardins, John D. Downing, Nikhil Sinha, Mark Smith, and Sharon Strover. I also benefited from comments on drafts by Anne Boylan, Cliff Doerksen, Robert Morrow, and Michael Socolow. I have deeply appreciated the support and advice of many other scholars and writers, including Noah Arcenaux, Steven Bach, James Baughman, Susan Brinson, Michael Brown, Eric Darton, Gali Einav, Evan Eisenberg, Walter Friedman, Jennifer Holt, Richard John, Michael Keith, Bill Kirkpatrick, Ralda Lee, Anna McCarthy, Tom McCourt, Robert MacDougall, Megan Mullen, Susan Ohmer, Katherine Parkin, Alisa Perren, Alex Russo, Erin Copple Smith, Leslie Schnur, Christopher Sterling, Shawn van Cour, Jennifer Wang, and David Weinstein, among many others who have welcomed me into wide-ranging discussions. Thanks also to the Old Time Radio (OTR) community members who have provided an expert audience for some of my research.

My gratitude to friends and family, near and far, who have provided encouragement over the years is difficult to reduce to a few sentences. Family members no longer here still live in my heart, and I am grateful for the love and support of my parents, siblings, cousins, and in-laws. My daughter, Lina Dahbour, and my stepchildren, William and Susan Bywaters, have enriched my life immeasurably with their creativity, intelligence, and kindness; I thank them for their bemused tolerance of my scholarly obsessions. My husband, David A. Bywaters, has not only been the source of the moral support spouses are obliged to provide, but he has also given me tremendous logistical, technical, editorial, and conceptual support, without which this book would not exist. To David I owe the deepest debt, and I hope to repay him with enduring love and esteem.

A Word from Our Sponsor

Advertising agencies produced programs

Introduction

Jack Benny: "Oh, come on in, Dennis. I'll be with you in a minute. I'm calling Mr. Duffy of Batten Barton Durstine & Osborn, my advertising agency."

Dennis Day: "Why do you need *them*?"

Jack Benny: "Well, Dennis. They put on my program for Lucky Strike. They handle all the publicity, the exploitation, the advertising, the commercials. They hire the musicians, the writers, the actors. They do *everything*!"

[a beat of silence]

Dennis Day: "Why do they need *you*?"[1]

In this 1948 broadcast, radio comedian Jack Benny, who specialized in self-deprecation, acknowledges the key role of an advertising agency in producing his show: "They do *everything*!" In fact, the majority of nationally broadcast sponsored programs on network radio during the "golden age" of radio, from roughly the late 1920s until the late 1940s, were created, produced, written, and/or managed by advertising agencies. Consider a few examples: J. Walter Thompson produced *Kraft Music Hall* (1933–49); Benton & Bowles oversaw *Maxwell House Show Boat* (1932–37); Young & Rubicam managed *Town Hall Tonight* with comedian Fred Allen for Bristol-Myers (1934–40); and Blackett-Sample-Hummert produced dozens of soap operas, including *Ma Perkins*, for Procter & Gamble (1933–56). The historian Michele Hilmes, noting that advertising agencies of the radio era resemble today's television production companies, argues that "[t]he full chronology of advertising agency involvement in radio does indeed deserve a history in itself, not least because it is virtually coterminous with commercial radio broadcasting."[2]

And yet, in popular memory and in most broadcast histories, the importance of the advertising industry's work in golden age radio is obscured, if not invisible. The reasons for this are many. One is that advertising agency staff did not receive on-air credit for their work, as in the case of J. Walter Thompson's Carroll Carroll, who went unheralded for writing clever lines for Bing Crosby on *Kraft Music Hall*.

Claim to obscurity

Cast member: "Are you all set for Christmas, Bing?"

Bing: "Yep. I made the last of my resolutions just a little while ago."

Cast member: "Resolutions? You're supposed to make resolutions on New Year's Eve."

Bing: "Oh, not me. I've got me a system. I find it's kind of tough keeping resolutions from New Year's to Christmas. So I make mine on Christmas and it's a cinch to keep 'em 'til New Year's."[3]

The lack of on-air credit was the outcome of the decision by advertising agencies and their clients—the sponsors—not to distract audiences from the product being advertised; they hoped listeners would smoothly associate the pleasing entertainment with their products, with Kraft cheese or Lucky Strike cigarettes. Drawing attention to the construction of the entertainment would undermine that association. And listeners were drawn to radio not by the producer but by the entertainment and the stars, Batten Barton Durstine & Osborn (BBDO) needed Jack Benny very much. Without the star, there would have been no show and, consequently, no audience organized to attend to the sponsor's message. Yet, despite their invisibility, advertising agencies were arguably the most important sites of radio entertainment production in the United States during the 1930s and 1940s.

non-diegetic sound

Stars attract audience

a.

Why did the advertising industry become so deeply involved in broadcast programming? The short answer is that advertising agencies were best positioned to address the needs of broadcasters (for programming) and the needs of advertisers (for reaching audiences) during a period when most programming was fully controlled by advertisers

Ad agencies = biggest deal.

and at a time of economic exigency. The longer answer is what I intend to provide in the rest of this book. Hilmes remarks:

During the formative decades of American broadcasting, as genres were invented, basic structures set in place, and the industry's cultural role extended throughout the world, the main innovation in programming took place in the offices of advertising agencies. Despite this fact, not a single book-length scholarly work has focused on the role of the advertising agency.[4]

What follows is just that book. In the course of it, I challenge conventional views about the role of advertising in culture, the integration of media industries, and the role of commercialism in broadcast history. I mean in doing so to revise how we view media industry history, especially as to the advertising industry's role in that history.

Jennifer Holt and Alisa Perren argue that media industry studies scholars must move away from the Frankfurt School approach, which assumes that media industries are monolithic, the beneficiaries of a "one-way flow of communication from a central industry out to a passive audience."[5] John Hartley and Ian Connell argue that media industries have no "fabulous" powers or shared consciousness.[6] Rather, they are made up of individual agents negotiating various social, economic, and cultural structures and constraints.[7] Media industry studies, as articulated by Holt and Perren, seek to analyze "culture and cultural production as sites of struggle, contestation, and negotiation between a broad range of stakeholders," presuming those sites to be "anything but monolithic."[8] Such studies, moving beyond the texts available to audiences, must not only construct "behind the scenes" narratives of media production but also take account of those industries in all their complexity, as made up of overlapping and intersecting fields, systems, actors, and dynamics.[9] As an example of this approach, Alexander Russo argues that radio cannot be considered a single field or object of inquiry; instead, radio "is actually the result of the 'dynamic interplay' of a system of technologies, industrial and regulatory dynamics, programming, and practices of reception and use."[10]

Likewise, advertising is not, any more than radio, a single phenomenon. It has been well analyzed as a vehicle for ideological and hegemonic values;[11] as a means for creating false needs;[12] as a mirror of

American culture;[13] as an economic force in "free" media;[14] as a functionalist method of persuasion;[15] as a form of social communication;[16] as a mediating text;[17] and as a discourse intersecting with multiple other cultural discourses.[18] Building on existing advertising history scholarship,[19] I treat advertising as a media industry deeply integrated into other media industries, especially broadcasting, which throughout most of its history has depended solely on advertising revenue. I consider differences among individuals, agencies, affinity groups, organizations, and institutions within the industry, without a knowledge of which we can hardly hope to understand the historical contingency of advertising theories and practices and the social, economic, and cultural constraints in which those entities operate. Like John Caldwell, I seek to "look over the shoulder" of advertising practitioners not to construct some "behind the scenes" story of how they work but to register all the complex and multifarious ways in which they understand their work, represent themselves to one another and to their clients, and respond to technological, social, and cultural changes.[20] In all of this, I resist simplistic models of the relations of advertising, culture, and commerce. Advertising's structuring force is its economic function, to sell—yet to be effective it must articulate contemporary cultural meanings in ways intelligible to its audiences.[21] It is therefore involved in a complex negotiation of meanings and outcomes that its makers cannot fully comprehend or predict. My aim is to map these negotiations in all their complexity.

Revisionist broadcasting histories reject the notion that commercial broadcasting was the inevitable use of radio technology.[22] Erik Barnouw, Susan Douglas, Susan Smulyan, Robert McChesney, and Kathy Newman regard commercial broadcasting's development as hotly contested.[23] Utopian aspirations for radio as a vehicle for education, democracy, and cultural "uplift" are, in the work of each of these scholars, crushed by a triumphant commercialism, although each identifies a different historical moment for this triumph.[24] Although I build on these revisionist histories, I believe, with Hilmes, that there was no one single moment of decline into commercialism: Radio was commercial from its "earliest moments."[25] Hilmes considers commercialism not as a force corrupting broadcasting but as an "avenue of access to the popular," not unlike other commercial media such as the penny press, vaudeville, and movies.[26] In his research into independent radio stations of the 1920s, Clifford Doerksen finds that broadcast commercialism "originated at a grassroots level, as a populist deviation from polite corporate practice."[27] Independent commercial stations, which broadcast "lowbrow" music such as jazz, were viewed as endangering the "cultural uplift" and educational potential of radio. Though a highbrow minority fretted about on-air advertising as a source of cultural degradation, Doerksen concludes that "[c]ommercialism triumphed in the American airwaves because most Americans did *not* object to it."[28] Russo also challenges the top-down narrative of most broadcast histories in his study of non-network radio institutions and practices throughout the radio era, enriching our understanding of the multifaceted phenomena we call commercial radio.[29] Like Hilmes, Doerksen, and Russo, I analyze commercialism not as an outside force silencing the voice of the people but as a set of beliefs, practices, and economic incentives that not only created dominant institutions but also helped build authentic popular cultural forms.

Historical research in media industries in general and in advertising in particular is made difficult by the ephemeral nature of media products. Vast numbers of media texts (such as radio programs and commercials) and the documentation of their production (such as scripts, memos, and correspondence) were discarded by their producers long before any scholar could identify and analyze their significance. Like the drunk forced to look for his lost keys under the streetlight because that is where the light is, a media industry historian must search within the constrained light of what happens to have been preserved. Thus, while CBS records are largely unavailable to scholarly researchers, NBC's, deposited at the Wisconsin Historical Society and the Library of Congress, have led historians to build NBC-predominant narratives, because that is where the streetlight is.[30] Likewise, the archival primary source materials for advertising agencies of this period are limited and fragmentary; the J. Walter Thompson papers at Duke University provide the most complete agency records, including staff meeting transcriptions, memos, house organs, and account histories, and thus figure prominently in narratives such as this one. This book is based as much as possible on this and other archival sources, including the partial agency records of BBDO; Benton & Bowles; Young & Rubicam; and N. W. Ayer, and, most important, the voluminous correspondence among NBC and agency executives. Contemporaneous trade publications fill in some of the gaps left by this partial record, particularly concerning internal industry debates. Within the pages of *Printers' Ink* and *Advertising & Selling*, as well as other magazines aimed at members of the advertising industry, we can find various and conflicting perspectives, allowing us to "look over the shoulders" of advertising practitioners when they communicate with one another rather than with consumers or clients. Advertising agents' reminiscences and oral histories, though also useful, are less reliable, in part because hindsight usually colors memory and, in the case of many admen who had labored anonymously on famous campaigns, leads to the claiming of credit whether or not it is due.[31]

In using these sources, I apply critical and interpretative methodologies that contextualize them as much as possible, with an awareness of the positions and perspectives of the writers and readers of those documents. Advertising men, as Roland Marchand notes, represented themselves one way to their clients, another to consumers: To the former, they claimed strong powers of persuasion; to the latter, they claimed only to reflect consumers' existing desires.[32] This is not to say that all advertising practitioners were liars, only that context matters in interpreting their self-representations; and so I have sought to take it into account.

A Word from Our Sponsor is structured chronologically, beginning with a brief survey of the pre-broadcasting advertising industry, moving through the rise of commercial broadcasting in the 1920s and 1930s, and ending at network radio's apogee in the late 1940s. However, some chapters are structured to analyze key advertising agencies and how they engaged in specific debates and practices. To frame this study as one focused on the *advertising industry*, in Chapter 1, "Dramatizing a Bar of Soap: The Advertising Industry before Broadcasting," I draw on existing scholarship to provide an overview of how the modern advertising industry developed, then analyze key debates within the industry. Some of these debates shape the emerging commercial radio industry, such as the difference between "hard sell" and "soft sell" advertising strategies. I also introduce recurring issues such as advertising's cultural salience, innovation in advertising, the problem of instrumentality undermining advertising's credibility, the frustrations of admen's anonymous authorship, and the demands that advertising agents wear "two faces" to service the conflicting needs of clients and audiences.

Chapter 2, "The Fourth Dimension of Advertising: The Development of Commercial Broadcasting in the 1920s," shifts focus to the origins of commercial broadcasting, which emerged with little assistance from the advertising industry. As Susan Smulyan remarks, at the time of radio's widespread adoption in the 1920s, few were sure how best to commercialize it.[33] I recount the process by which broadcasters developed the radio business model of renting airtime to advertisers, who were then responsible for filling airtime with programming in order to attract listeners. Men trained in advertising were hired by the newly established national networks to "sell" the new medium to advertisers, who were initially suspicious of that untested medium.

Once convinced they could reach consumers over the air, advertisers were unsure how to attract listeners to their messages. Chapter 3, "They Sway Millions as If by Some Magic Wand: The Advertising Industry Enters Radio in the Late 1920s," explores how and why advertising agencies became program suppliers. The advertisers, known as "sponsors" because they paid for programming that listeners received for free, needed program oversight services. They worried that Broadway producers, musical directors, stage directors, and other potential program producers would favor artistic concerns over selling. Advertising agencies offered to provide programming that would sell. However, advertising agencies at first resisted entering radio. Their traditional expertise was in print media; translating print advertising strategies to the aural and evanescent medium of radio proved a challenge. Once the demand for ad agency oversight rose, from both advertisers and broadcasters, many advertising agencies established radio departments.

Yet, in the early commercial broadcasting industry, neither the business model nor the lines of authority were clearly established. Advertising agencies, sponsors, and broadcasters debated who should control programming, advertising standards, and radio revenues. In Chapter 4, "'Who Owns the Time?': Advertising Agencies and Networks Vie for Control in the 1930s," I draw upon the archival record, specifically the NBC Records, to identify the battles for control between national networks and advertising agencies. Networks and agencies debated acceptable standards of commercialism and programming, how those standards would be determined and policed, the importance of live broadcasts, and the role of network programming departments.

Agencies differed among one another as to how to sell audiences by radio. Chapter 5, "The 1930s' Turn to the Hard Sell: Blackett-Sample-Hummert's Soap Opera Factory," begins with a look at why the economic crisis of the Great Depression stimulated advertisers' interest in "hard sell" advertising. Hard sell advertising uses repetitious hectoring and direct, rational appeals, consisting of product attributes and "reasons why" to buy, often presenting the product as solving a problem. An example of hard sell advertising is a 1935 Campbell's tomato soup advertisement that claims the soup has a "distinctive flavor universally acclaimed," an "enchanting bright red color," and a "taste that sets the tongue a-tingling!" If that does not convince, the ad suggests that "children should get the invigorating benefits of wholesome soup, for its nourishing food and its aid to digestion." If the reader is still in doubt, the ad copy includes more "reasons why" to buy: "Campbell's soups are made as in your own home kitchen, except that they are double strength"; after adding water, "you obtain twice as much full-flavored soup at no extra cost."[34] In a case study of the hard sell, I focus on Blackett-Sample-Hummert, an agency that specialized in daytime radio programs, especially soap operas, aimed at housewives. I show how many of the elements of Hummert soap operas, known for portentous seriousness, repetitiousness, drawn-out narratives, and clear enunciation, were deliberate choices made in alignment with hard sell advertising strategies. Frank and Anne Hummert structured radio soap operas as they would advertisements; their advertising strategies directly shaped their programming strategies.

"Soft sell" agencies, on the other hand, believed in the efficacy of the indirect appeal, couched in the audience-friendly context of humorous entertainment. Soft sell advertising often emphasizes emotional appeals, such as the need to be loved, as in the Woodbury soap campaign "The Skin You Love to Touch," in which a woman is depicted as enjoying the loving embrace of her husband because she uses Woodbury soap. While hard sell proponents believed humor undermines the selling message, soft sell practitioners argued that humor helps disarm consumers and makes them more receptive. In Chapter 6, "The Ballet and Ballyhoo of Radio Showmanship: Young & Rubicam's Soft Sell," I analyze the advertising industry debates over the use of entertainment and "showmanship" as a selling tool on radio before turning to the case study of Young & Rubicam, probably the most prominent of the soft sell agencies. Y&R's involvement in top radio comedy shows, featuring stars such as Jack Benny, Fred Allen, Eddie Cantor, and Burns & Allen, reflected its commitment to soft sell advertising strategies.

In Chapter 7, "Two Agencies: Batten Barton Durstine & Osborn, Crafters of the Corporate Image, and Benton & Bowles, Radio Renegades," I analyze two other important radio advertising agencies. BBDO approached radio as an ideal medium for building a corporate image, overseeing programs for large advertisers concerned not with product sales but with improving consumers' views of them as good corporate citizens. As a case study, I use the Du Pont archives to discuss BBDO's oversight of Du Pont's *Cavalcade of America.* In contrast, Benton & Bowles, though serving large companies such as General Foods, approached radio as an opportunity for innovating advertising by breaking rules and challenging advertising industry conventions.

By the time radio was established as a central entertainment medium in the late 1930s, star-driven entertainment forced Madison Avenue (as the advertising industry was known) to set up outposts in Hollywood, the better to supply radio with stars. In Chapter 8, "Madison Avenue in Hollywood: J. Walter Thompson and *Kraft Music Hall,*" I trace the intra-industry tensions between "Hollywoodites" and the colonizing admen from New York. Members of the film industry believed advertising agencies knew little about entertainment; members of the advertising industry believed the film industry understood little about how to appeal to audiences in the family stronghold of the home environment. I draw on the extensive archival records of the J. Walter

Thompson (JWT) agency, which had a major Hollywood branch office, and construct a case study of how JWT produced the Hollywood-based program *Kraft Music Hall*, featuring Bing Crosby, that was based on their advertising strategy to associate celebrities with products.

World War II at first threatened to dismantle the commercial entertainment radio industry, but the federal government ultimately decided to employ the existing radio industry in propaganda efforts on the home front. In Chapter 9, "Advertising and Commercial Radio during World War II, 1942–45," I look at how the advertising industry and then the commercial radio industry responded to the war and participated in the war economy. As a case study, I draw upon the papers of William B. Lewis, an advertising and broadcasting executive who oversaw the coordination of radio propaganda at the federal Office of War Information. Instead of separating war propaganda from entertainment, at the risk of losing the attention of millions of Americans wearied by didactic propaganda, Lewis asked agencies and sponsors to choose how to integrate propaganda messages into entertainment programs, thereby reaching the listeners willing to hear their favorite stars explain why, for example, they should plant their own food in victory gardens. As Bing Crosby urged listeners:

This is the old *Kraft Music Hall*, friends, battle station bound to every spot on the globe; where men are digging for victory in Tunisia, and in the Solomons they're digging foxholes, and from the skies above Germany they're digging up Berlin streets. The least we can do is dig a little too. We've got to dig for war bonds and we've got to be doing a little digging for that victory garden.[35]

After the war, however, listeners, reformers, and even members of the advertising industry criticized commercial radio for its very commercialism. Chapter 10, "On a Treadmill to Oblivion: The Peak and Sudden Decline of Network Radio," examines the "revolt against radio," the spread of the critique of sponsor control of programming, and advertising industry anxieties over the arrival of television. The transition to television in the late 1940s and early 1950s was a tremendously complex process that is beyond the scope of this book, so I focus on Sylvester "Pat" Weaver as a case study of how one adman helped shape the transition.[36] While president of NBC-TV, Weaver, a former Young & Rubicam executive, favored a system whereby networks, not sponsors, would control television programs. Weaver's "magazine plan" offered sponsors not thirty or sixty minutes of airtime to use as they liked but one-minute time slots within NBC programs, which, like ads in a magazine, were independent of the content amid which they appeared. This system soon changed the industry. The resulting shift to network programming control led to the eventual exit of advertising agencies from program production. Advertising agencies gradually built a more profitable business buying interstitial minutes of airtime for advertisers and producing television commercials.

That advertising agencies surrendered direct control of programming during the network television era, roughly the late 1950s through the 1970s, does not negate their seminal contributions to commercial broadcasting. Advertising agencies helped build radio as a popular commercial entertainment medium by producing programming designed to appeal to wide audiences, and they were the key developers of program forms such as soap operas. Advertising agencies developed audience-responsive strategies for entertainment and advertising. Advertising executives, some of whom became top broadcasting executives, took lessons from their work mediating between sponsors and broadcasters to help reformulate the structure of the broadcasting industry away from advertiser program control and toward the more flexible and effective commercialism of network television.

Mary Livingstone: "Jack, who're you calling?"

Jack Benny: "Batten Barton Durstine & Osborn."

Mary Livingstone: "Sounds like a trunk falling down stairs."

This joke, from the same *Jack Benny* episode quoted above, has survived its origins and has entered the lore of BBDO's history.[37] Mary Livingstone, a tart-tongued foil to Jack Benny, sounds as if she has dismissed one of the most important advertising agencies as a series of crashes, and by extension, a crashing bore. But, as in all humor that embraces contradiction, her joke highlights how important BBDO actually was. In the subsequent chapters, I tell a hitherto little-known story of American radio and advertising, one that repositions the advertising industry from the margins into the center of one of the most significant popular culture forms of the twentieth century. Not only do I expect my readers to rethink how and why twentieth-century broadcasting developed the way it did, I also hope they will apply these historical perspectives to understanding the changes affecting media industries in the twenty-first century, as program providers revive program financing forms such as sponsorship and advertisers and their agencies once again reformulate their theories and strategies of reaching and motivating audiences.

1

Dramatizing a Bar of Soap
The Advertising Industry before Broadcasting

What is the significance of advertising, and why did it develop the way it did? Advertising industry critics often assume its role is to produce myths that might perpetuate power structures or to brainwash consumers into pursuing false desires.[1] When the advertising industry aims to align cultural artifacts with commercial goals, when it seeks congruence between cultural salience and profit making, it most definitely does express the economic power of its clients, the advertisers.[2] However, the impact of advertising messages, usually the focus of academic "effects" research, cannot be substantiated any more than the impact of other cultural discourses.[3] Advertising boosters and critics, ironically, share the same unproven assumption: The former may claim that it produces higher sales, the latter that it produces false desires, but both impute to it enormous power, the latter generally trusting the self-promoting claims of the former on this point. In fact, both the worst fears of the critics (that advertising corrupts and undermines authenticity and truth) and the fondest hopes of its practitioners (that advertising actually influences and shapes behavior) seem equally dubious if we examine them amid the conflicts and contingencies of actual practices and effects.[4]

Instead of attributing magical powers to advertising, I propose we consider it as it is: not a single, unitary force, but a diverse set of institutions and practices, complex and contradictory, pulled this way and that by tensions, competing world views, and internal doubts about its use and effectiveness. We can learn much more about advertising as a social, cultural, and economic force if we study not its unknowable effects but its specific causes in the industry that produces it, an industry torn by internal debates and buffeted by changing practices, purposes, and goals. Through such study we may not only historicize advertising but also humanize it.

In order to better understand the role of the advertising industry in the development of broadcasting, we first need to know something about the advertising industry before radio arrived, about the formation of agencies and professional standards, the debates over selling strategies, and the underlying concerns of its practitioners. These inform many of the debates and concerns of admen in radio.

The Advertising Industry before Broadcasting

When did advertising begin? In his 1929 history of advertising, adman Frank Presbrey makes a claim for cave painting as its first recorded appearance, thereby expressing a faith, typical among his class, in its timeless presence and universal human relevance.[5] National advertising, however, did not arise until the nineteenth century, when mass production and consumption were made possible by the increased use of flow production (assembly lines), the improvement of transportation technologies (railroads), the branding of standardized goods to facilitate national distribution, and the development of new retail outlets, including department stores.[6] All this required increasingly specialized labor, including that of the new advertising agencies, which brokered newspaper space to advertisers beginning in the 1850s and 1860s. Agents bought advertising space from newspaper publishers at the lowest possible price and sold it to advertisers at the highest, making their profit in the resulting spread. The increase of nationally distributed branded goods and the rise of mass market magazines soon led to changes in the space-brokering business.[7] Agents such as George Rowell, J. Walter Thompson, and Francis W. Ayer introduced innovations such as compiling circulation figures in order to compare space rates, designing "open contracts" to ensure the agent represented the advertiser instead of the publisher, writing copy for advertisements, and researching a market.

By the 1870s, the space-brokering system was superseded by a commission system of compensation, in which newspaper and magazine publishers paid agents 15 percent of the value of the space sold. The commission system is at the root of two major characteristics of the advertising industry. The first is its organization into agencies operating as entities independent of both publishers and advertisers. The businesses buying the advertising space might have sought to analyze and purchase advertising space in-house—and in fact many companies developed internal marketing departments. However, the majority of such businesses found that independent advertising agents provided more flexibility and expertise in media pricing and placement than they could develop in an internal department.[8] In other words, advertising agencies evolved in part to mediate between the sellers of advertising space—that is, the publishers of newspapers and magazines —and the businesses that bought it.[9] Each benefited from the independence of the agencies: the sellers from the agencies' shared desire to sell space for the highest price possible and their contacts with buyers, the buyers from the preferential pricing offered by the agents with the most media access.

This led to the second important characteristic of the industry, its dependence on a commission system. Consider a typical transaction. The agency would contract for advertising space in a publication at a negotiated price reflecting "circulation" (or number of readers), and perhaps a discount for bulk space buying. The agency would bill its "client," the company seeking to advertise, for the cost of the space. When the client reimbursed the agency for the space, the agency would forward all but 15 percent of these "billings" to the publication; the agency would deduct 15 percent as the commission it earned from the publication for selling the space. Officially, then, publishers paid the agencies, not advertisers; but in actuality the agencies paid themselves by deducting their commissions from the advertisers' payments, most of which went to the publishers. To attract clients, agencies developed various services, such as market research, copywriting, layout, and art direction, but "billed" advertisers only for the media placement, thus avoiding the problems of setting fees for smaller services. Some advertisers suspected that the commission system provided too much incentive for agencies to buy unnecessary space, but clients also liked having the extra services agencies provided.[10] Agencies pointed out that the commission system benefited all parties—buyer, seller, and agent; by 1917, the agencies and the commission system dominated media buying.[11]

Despite the steady growth and increasing professionalism of the advertising business, admen were shadowed by images of earlier salesmen: the itinerant peddler, the drummer, the traveling salesman, the circus man, and the medicine tent show promoter—shady characters whose manipulative strategies succeeded in part because they were strangers passing through town.[12] The "medicine shows" were the common marketing device for nostrums, such as Lydia Pinkham's Herb Medicine, that promised cures for all manner of ailments. Traveling from town to town, they would attract audiences with dancers, musicians, and stunts, then deliver a sales pitch. Known as "patent medicines" because makers kept the ingredients secret, they were in fact not patented, nor always safe. Patent medicine makers were early and enthusiastic advertisers in print media; many early advertising agencies owed their success to patent medicine clients. However, they were thus entangled in their clients' disreputable practices—overcharging for cheap ingredients, promising unattainable cures, and including dangerous or addictive substances, such as radium, laudanum, alcohol, or cocaine. By the turn of the twentieth century, muckraking reports on patent medicine practices created political pressure for food and drug regulation, such as the federal Pure Food and Drug Act of 1906, which required product labeling. Although patent medicines declined over the next several decades, the advertising industry remained strongly associated with fraudulent tactics.[13]

To raise professional standards, as well as to deflect increased government regulation, members of the advertising industry founded trade organizations, promulgated industry standards, established clearinghouses of information, and supported the war effort.[14] The Associated Advertising Clubs of America (formed in 1905) and the American Association of Advertising Agencies (formed in 1917) sought to improve the public image of advertising and standardize practices by establishing codes of conduct. The Truth-in-Advertising movement emphasized the importance of credibility to the continued viability of advertising.[15] Hoping to eliminate distrust and fraud, publishers, advertisers, and their agents collaborated in the creation in 1914 of the Audit Bureau of Circulations (ABC), an organization that collected circulation data on publications. Because advertising space rates were set in part by circulation, or number of readers, ABC built reliability into the market by pooling this information in an organization overseen by buyers, sellers, and agents. Before the ABC, agencies held a virtual monopoly on circulation information; giving up that monopoly was a small price to pay for becoming more credible marketing advisors for advertisers. The advertising industry also improved its status during World War I by contributing bond drive slogans (such as Frank Hummert's famous slogan "Bonds Not Bondage") and participating in propaganda efforts under the aegis of the federal information agency known as the Creel Committee.[16]

As the advertising industry expanded and professionalized in the 1920s, its boosters sought to align it with educational and even religious ideals, and many admen began to adopt the language, goals, ethics, and professionalism of the progressive businessmen of the era.[17] "Business must aim to *serve*, instead of to *sell*," wrote Kenneth Goode in his 1929 how-to advertising book.[18] Alluding to progressive ideals of business practice, in 1926 President Calvin Coolidge claimed that advertising was "inspiring and ennobling the commercial world" and was part of the "greater work of the regeneration and redemption of mankind."[19] Coolidge suggested that advertising could help civilize capitalism because it "ministers to the spiritual side of trade."[20] One of the best-known proponents of progressivism in advertising was Bruce Barton, of the advertising agency Batten Barton Durstine & Osborn. Barton, a minister's son, published in 1924 the best-selling book *The Man Nobody Knows*, which presented the teachings of Jesus Christ as lessons for modern progressive businessmen. Barton claimed that business, and by extension advertising, should emphasize the ideals of service and sincerity, ideals that Barton believed Jesus Christ exemplified. Barton urged businessmen to apply biblical aphorisms to the practices of modern business. Although some accused Barton of reducing religion to sales slogans, his intention was to elevate and sanctify contemporary business methods, including advertising.[21]

Despite the efforts of boosters such as Barton, advertising in the 1920s still suffered a poor reputation. William Benton, a founder of Benton & Bowles, described it thus at the moment of his entry into the field: "At this time advertising was not looked upon as a good, sound, solid business by the business community of America. On the contrary, it looked a bit like a back alley business, a sort of shady business."[22] Consequently, in the spirit of professionalism that had transformed "real estate men" into "Realtors" and "undertakers" into "morticians," some advertising men sought to be called "attorneys" and the like.[23] Terms such as "consumption engineers" and "psychological engineers" echoed the scientism then fashionable in the business world, but they also implied suspiciously manipulative powers. Other suggested terms, such as "ambassadors of the consumer" and "liaison officers," also failed, perhaps because they sounded too high-minded.[24]

Members of the advertising industry, unable to elevate their professional status to that of engineer or attorney, more often went by the term "advertising man" or, in a breezily modern contraction, "adman." Although some viewed it as a vulgar term, many embraced it, undermining its pejorative power. The term "adman" reflected the demographic actualities of the industry and connoted the sense of fraternity within it. Most advertising agents of the 1920s and 1930s were white Anglo-Saxon Protestant urban males from upper-middle-class families. The hiring practices of many firms were discriminatory, reflecting the belief that only such men could have successful and personable relations with their clients, the white Anglo-Saxon Protestant urban males from upper-middle-class families who ran American businesses.[25] However, as the targets of most advertising were women, women were often welcomed into agencies as copywriters to provide "the women's point of view."[26] The J. Walter Thompson agency established a separate women's copywriting department that operated under the aegis of Helen Lansdowne Resor, the copywriter who was married to the agency's president, Stanley Resor. Helen Resor, while wielding great influence in the agency, never took the title of vice president that would have reflected her role.[27] Anne Hummert, married to Frank Hummert of Blackett-Sample-Hummert, wielded significant influence, yet she was also an exception in the male-dominated industry. Despite these openings for women copywriters, few women were able to penetrate the managerial ranks of the advertising industry.

Advertising Strategies: The Hard Sell versus the Soft Sell

As personal face-to-face salesmanship was gradually displaced in importance by manufacturers' reliance on impersonal, mass-mediated advertisement of nationally distributed branded goods, admen sought to extend the personal approach of the salesman into the impersonal medium of print.[28] Consequently, the advertising industry developed advertising strategies that emphasized sincerity and credibility. Positioning themselves rhetorically as "side by side" with the consumer, anonymous copywriters confidentially advised their unknown readers how to navigate the treacherous waters of modern living.[29] But did consumers believe these claims, in the wake of the fraudulent practices of the patent medicine trade? While tempted to stretch the truth in product claims, some admen believed in avoiding outright falsehoods, not on moral or legal but on practical grounds, because the credibility resulting from honesty would in the long run be a more successful goal.[30] Urged one advertising man to his peers, "[I]f we want to be credible, we would better be sincere."[31] The well-known advertising theorist Earnest Elmo Calkins argued that sincerity and honesty "have a definite dollars and cents value in business. . . . They build up that one commodity on which we all depend: belief and confidence."[32] That admen were debating the role of honesty and sincerity in advertising indicates how little such qualities had been deemed necessary up to this point. However, these proposals to at least *appear* sincere also reflected a growing unease with the outright deceptions of the patent medicine era. To develop credible and sincere advertising techniques, admen would have to develop theories of appeal.

Two schools of thought influenced advertising strategies during the first half of the twentieth century: the hard sell and the soft sell.[33] Each was rooted in basic assumptions about consumers—their cognitive abilities, their motivations, their malleability. The hard sell evolved in part because it seemed a means of reaching customers in the manner of face-to-face salesmen. In order to convince businesses that the impersonal medium of print could be just as effective as a live salesman, an adman named John E. Kennedy promulgated the concept that advertising is "salesmanship in print."[34] Kennedy inspired both Albert Lasker, who became the influential head of the Chicago-based Lord & Thomas agency, and Claude Hopkins, whose writings on advertising strategy, *Scientific Advertising* (1923) and *My Life in Advertising* (1927), are still widely consulted. Lasker and Hopkins, like other hard sell practitioners, assumed their audiences had limited intelligence and could not grasp complex ideas, an assumption apparently supported by U.S. military testing of inductees' "intelligence quotient" during World War I.[35] Hopkins dismissed new-fangled ideas from growing professions like psychology that could complicate his ideas about his audiences. According to Hopkins, "Human nature is perpetual. In most respects it is the same today as in the time of Caesar. So the principles of psychology are fixed and enduring."[36]

Lasker and Hopkins became chief proponents of what they called "reason-why" advertising. An ad should provide various "reasons why" to buy the product; the product, rather than the user of the product, should be the focus of the ad. Like the face-to-face salesman who, when one reason-why fails to clinch the sale, tries another reason, and yet another, reason-why copywriters would structure the advertisement to present a problem, such as dingy laundry, bad breath, or sleeplessness, solved by the product. For example, a 1926 Ruthrauff & Ryan ad for the laundry soap Rinso (see Figure 1-1), headlined "Who else wants a *whiter* wash—*with no hard work*?," lists multiple "reasons why" housewives should choose it to solve their washday problems: "Dirt floats off—stains go"; "No laundry soap is easier on clothes or on hands than Rinso"; "there's no hard rubbing against a board"; "Recommended by 23 leading washing machine makers for safety, and for a whiter, cleaner wash"; "Safe for clothes, easy on hands"; "Contains no acids, harsh chemicals or bleaches"; "In half the time, without a bit of hard rubbing, the wash is on the line—*whiter than ever!*"[37] If one of those

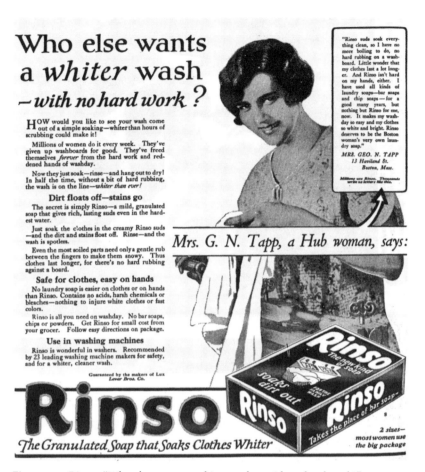

Figure 1-1. Rinso: "Who else wants a *whiter* wash—*with no hard work?*" (Reproduced in Julian Lewis Watkins, *The 100 Greatest Advertisements* [New York: Dover, 1959], 80.)

reasons was insufficiently convincing, another one might be, or perhaps all together the multiple reasons would overwhelm the consumer's resistance.

The "reasons why" were to be clearly listed and repeated in case the reader misunderstood the first time. Repetition was important; a copywriter could not risk assuming a reader's easy comprehension. Repetition might also reassure a client that his adman was making every effort to push the product. An advertisement placed by a reason-why proponent in the trade magazine *Printers' Ink* explains the strat-egy thus: "True 'Reason-Why' Copy is Logic, plus persuasion, plus con-viction, all woven into a certain simplicity of thought—pre-digested for the average mind, so that it is easier to *understand* than to *misun-derstand it.*"[38] The "logic" refers to the rational appeals of the advertise-ment, which ask the consumer to rationally consider the benefits of a whiter wash, softer hands, and an easier washday. "Persuasion" and "conviction" reflect the sincerity of the copywriter's effort. "Simplicity of thought" refers to the belief that explicitly challenging readers' abil-ity to comprehend would risk losing the sale. The best strategy was to use the most direct, obvious, and clear language, "pre-digested for the average mind," to avoid any misunderstanding by the cognitively chal-lenged consumer.

The hard sell's emphasis on rational appeals—using reason and facts to persuade—might appeal to the many critics who today decry advertising's deviousness.[39] However, hard sell practitioners like Hop-kins were infamous for manipulating "facts." Hopkins realized that statements which resembled facts, especially if those statements in-cluded unverifiable figures and scientific-sounding claims, could per-suade without being actual facts. For example, Hopkins's ad copy describes Puffed Wheat cereal as "scientific foods," "invented by Prof. A. P. Anderson—a famous dietician," with "the grains puffed to 8 times normal size." Moreover, "They are the only grain foods so pre-pared that every food cell is exploded. Digestion is made easy and complete, so that every atom feeds." This miracle is effectuated by shooting the wheat from guns: "A hundred million steam explosions occur in every kernel."[40] How could Hopkins know exactly how much larger a puffed wheat kernel was than a normal kernel—did he mea-sure it? How could he or anyone count these "steam explosions" in a kernel of puffed wheat so as to prove or disprove such a claim? How could he know that every "atom feeds"? And on what basis rested his claim that exploded "food cell[s]" provide better nutrition? Hopkins was careful to create "facts" out of the unverifiable. He also employed the *incomplete* fact. In a campaign for Schlitz beer in which Hopkins trumpets the actual fact that the Schlitz brewery washed its bottles with "live steam," an industry term for pressurized steam, Hopkins implies that Schlitz bottles were more hygienic than other bottles. But he omits the fact that every other brewery also washed its bottles with live steam.[41]

This reliance on the partially true, the borderline deceptive, and the unverifiable but fact-like, scientific-sounding claim, and the attendant exaggeration and hyperbole reflects the legacy of the patent medicine trade, but it may also reflect a continuing belief that consumers had to be manipulated for their own good. Consumers could not be trusted to understand on their own, hence repetition, exaggeration, and excessive facticity were mainstays of an advertising strategy that was presumably based on rational appeals. Advertising critics called this type of advertising "ballyhoo" and "puffery." Admen seeking higher professional standards worried that ballyhoo increased the risk of greater government regulation and would undermine the credibility of all advertising. Hard sell proponents dismissed this last point by citing sales results—the only results that mattered to their clients.

While hard sell strategies focused on the product, soft sell strategies focused on the user and the user's feelings. Copywriter Theodore MacManus was one of the best-known early proponents of the soft sell, relying on the indirect means of suggestion, association, and atmosphere. In his 1915 campaign for General Motors' Cadillac, MacManus eschews product description or "reasons why." In a full-page ad in the *Saturday Evening Post* headlined "The Penalty of Leadership," MacManus describes how those who produce great art are often criticized or misunderstood before they are accepted and celebrated.

Long, long after a great work or a good work has been done, those who are disappointed or envious continue to cry out that it cannot be done. . . . Failing to equal or to excel, the follower seeks to depreciate and to destroy—but only confirms once more the superiority of that which he tries to supplant. . . . That which is great makes itself known, no matter how loud the clamor of denial. That which deserves to live, lives.[42]

Without ever mentioning the automobile or its features, MacManus implies that Cadillac belongs to an august group of misunderstood geniuses, including the painter Whistler, the steamboat inventor Fulton, and the composer Wagner, all subjected to ridicule before being acknowledged as masters. The "penalty of leadership" is to suffer attacks before being recognized for achievements. MacManus thus disposes of any Cadillac critics as the "envious few" who deprecate its superior quality. Those who understand the Cadillac's quality, by contrast, take on almost heroic qualities because they are just and brave enough to acknowledge the "great" who live on "no matter how loud the clamor of denial." MacManus cleverly avoids specific product claims, allowing the reader to anthropomorphize the product with admirable traits such as bravery and strength. This strategy of association would become an important technique in soft sell advertising.

MacManus criticized reason-why theorists such as Hopkins for "a clever and semi-scientific application of the thesis that all men are fools." MacManus claimed to hold "the mass-mind in somewhat higher esteem" and to make "appeals of a substantial and more or less virtuous character."[43] Soft sell proponents like MacManus believed that consumers are rarely influenced by direct admonition. Hard-hitting direct advertising threatened to alienate them, while the indirect approach, using association and user-centered appeals, might lower their resistance. Appealing to consumers by associating a product with feelings or ideas rather than with "reasons why" may have seemed vague to the hard sell proponents, but MacManus designed his advertising not so much to produce immediate sales as to develop a good image for an advertiser's company, which might then build a relationship with consumers over time. MacManus sought to make a reader have positive feelings about an advertised product. As the magazine publisher Cyrus Curtis describes the effect, "It's the atmosphere in these [advertisements] that sells . . . the quality that gives prestige, the little imaginative sure touches that bring the thing before you."[44] By focusing on "atmosphere" and building a sense of "prestige," MacManus trusted readers to understand the implications and draw their own conclusions.

While reason-why theorists made scientistic claims about the efficacy of their advertising, MacManus believed consumers' responses were too variable to be reliably predicted by some objective scientific method. His followers disdained the copy testing and research many hard sell proponents engaged in to "prove" their advertising's effectiveness and develop new campaigns. Soft sell proponents, avoiding behaviorist theories of consumer response, instead relied on their own imagination and intuition for generating advertising ideas. For Mac-Manus and his followers, such as Raymond Rubicam, founder of Young & Rubicam, advertising was an art, not a science. Consequently, soft sell print advertising evolved to emphasize the images over the words. Rather than craft a dozen "reasons why" to fill multiple paragraphs of text, soft sell proponents preferred the eye-catching visual. While text-based advertising relied on rational appeals that the product would solve a putative problem, soft sell advertising's emphasis on the visual association opened the door to a wider variety of appeals: appeals that depended on feelings, such as a sense of belonging or desire for a mate, or associations, such as with tradition or wealth, none of which are inherent in the product or the result of product use. The soft sell focused on the user, on how the user thought of herself, how the user felt or might want to feel, rather than on the product and its attributes.

Emotional appeals often centered on the need for love. A 1928 Woodbury Facial Soap ad, headlined "A Skin you love to touch," shows an illustration of a handsome, wealthy couple in an embrace (see Figure 1-2).[45] The woman, dressed in a frock cut low enough to expose her shoulders, gazes directly at the reader, her lowered eyelids indicating pleasure and satisfaction. The man, presumably her husband, dressed in white tie, has wrapped his right arm possessively around her shoulders and is holding her right hand with his left. His face, in profile, nuzzles hers; the intimacy of the gesture delicately implies the pleasure of further skin-on-skin contact. Associating soap with wealth and beauty, the ad also implies that the true desire of soap buyers is emotional intimacy and love, not just clean skin. All soaps clean skin, with more or less the same effectiveness, so why choose one over the other? By shifting the consumer's attention away from product attributes, so relentlessly enumerated in the reason-why hard sell strategy, and refocusing attention on the consumer's deepest desires, emotional appeals

Figure 1-2. Woodbury's Facial Soap: "A Skin you love to touch." (Reproduced in Robert Atwan, Donald McQuade, and John W. Wright, *Edsels, Luckies, and Frigidaires: Advertising the American Way* [New York: Dell, 1979], 337.)

could succeed in managing that attention in ways that the hard sell could not.

In their effort to attract attention and disarm consumer resistance, soft sell proponents often depended on humor. A 1920s advertisement for Kelly-Springfield tires is dominated by a large illustration of two men getting into an automobile late at night (see Figure 1-3). We can see the light on their faces, and the view of the rear of the automobile shows clearly the brand of tire mounted as a spare: "Kelly Springfield Balloon." At the very bottom of the illustration, we read this dialogue:

"Well, Bob, it's five minutes past two. What's the story going to be?"

"Oh, I'll tell her we had a blowout."

"That would never get past my wife. She knows I use Kelly-Springfield."[46]

Rather than list product attributes, the ad sets up a visual of a situation, easily understood as two husbands out too late on the town faced with the problem of how to explain themselves to their wives. We learn that one man's wife "knows" that Kelly-Springfield tires are too reliable for them to claim they had a "blowout." Thus, unlike the direct address of a hard sell ad, this soft sell ad implies indirectly that everyone "knows" the quality of Kelly-Springfield. A product claim is communicated through the humorous situation rather than through a list of "reasons why." The humor may amuse the reader, who may recall the positive feeling when shopping for tires.

Humor could bring pleasure to the reader, creating positive associations with the product; however, humor is difficult to measure and difficult to control: Could it backfire and reflect badly on the product? As Calkins warned in 1915, "Humor is a very good servant but a bad master."[47] Hard sell proponents feared that humor undermined the seriousness of advertising and deflected consumers from the real purpose of the ad: to sell, not to entertain. Soft sell strategies such as humor or elegant visual design might please consumers, but would they buy? Hard sell proponent Lasker dismissed humor as the "Circus ideas" of an "unenlightened age." He also dismissed the soft sell proponents' strenuous attention to visual aesthetics: "Vanities and furbelows

"Well, Bob, it's five minutes past two. What's the story going to be?"
"Oh, I'll tell her we had a blowout."
"That would never get past MY wife. She knows I use Kelly-Springfield."

Figure 1-3. Kelly-Springfield Tires. (Reproduced in Watkins, *100 Greatest Advertisements*, 24.)

have no place in salesmanship to the millions."[48] For Lasker and other hard sell proponents, the success of an advertisement is measured by increased sales, not by increased readers' attention, and humor or attractive illustrations risked deflecting attention from the product.

Eventually, Lasker and his followers would lose these arguments; by the end of the twentieth century, most advertising depended on soft sell strategies emphasizing images, emotional appeals, associations, and humor. But during the radio era, debates over the efficacy of these two competing approaches helped shape radio advertising and programming. Hard sell advertising strongly shaped much radio programming, especially soap operas, as detailed in Chapter 5. Likewise, many of the criticisms leveled against commercial radio in its first decades—repetitiveness, obviousness, lack of subtlety—were precisely the criticisms that soft sell proponents made about hard sell advertising.

The Culture of the Advertising Industry

As these debates over the hard sell and soft sell indicate, the advertising industry reflects, incorporates, and comments on the culture of its society and time. Even a cursory analysis of advertising illuminates its deep involvement in multiple ways of talking about the world: medical, scientific, and sociological discourses on the one hand; artistic, literary, and religious ones on the other.[49] Advertising practice, then, evolves not in a vacuum but in dialogue with myriad other institutions and practices. And the industry itself is a diverse set of institutions, primarily privately held partnerships and professional organizations, rife with conflicting aims and strategies that reflect internecine power struggles, anxiety over efficacy, and differing views on the relative importance of commercial and cultural goals.[50] Members of the advertising industry also debated advertising's cultural salience, the risks of innovation, the problem of instrumentality, the burdens of anonymity, and the need for "two-faced-ness" in meeting the conflicting needs of clients and audiences. A close analysis of advertising institutions and debates explains a large part of why radio and advertising, separate but intertwined media industries, evolved the way they did.

Admen's success depends on their work's perceived salience to existing cultural discourses. They must "be sensitive to the latent correspondences in the cultural order," the anthropologist Marshall Sahlins writes, "whose conjunction in a product-symbol may spell mercantile success."[51] Admen must aim to innovate, but at a carefully calibrated pace. Advertising relies on existing aesthetic conventions in order to be recognizable and easily understood. But in order to attract favorable attention, it must also display a degree of innovation or originality. If too original or unusual, it may be incomprehensible to its audience; if too conventional, it may fail to attract attention. Advertising photographers have used the term "original standard picture" to describe the ideal goal of their work.[52] Such a picture is fully recognizable within operating aesthetic conventions and yet involves enough innovation to elevate it into originality. Thus, as the media historian Eileen Meehan points out, the economic structure of media industries must allow for and encourage "bursts of innovation and creativity just as surely as it mandates duplication and imitation."[53] Culture industries like advertising cannot afford simply to reproduce the past; they must continually innovate, yet the innovation cannot be too radical or it will not find a market.

Despite the pressure to innovate, advertising workers lack full recognition as authors of their creative work. Many display an acute awareness that their profession's instrumentalist aims preclude them from engaging in the individualistic form of expression so valued in the bourgeois and romantic ideologies of art.[54] Nonetheless, many in the advertising industry subscribe to those ideologies, claiming their work to be as culturally and artistically significant as that of those normally designated "artists."[55] One barrier to fully claiming such authorship is the fact that the advertising creators' creativity, innovation, and showmanship are not publicly credited. Despite one bold proposal in the 1920s that copywriters sign their copy, print advertisements were not labeled as written by either a copywriter or an agency.[56] Advertising industry ethics require that the makers of advertising subordinate their individual creative contributions to the economic imperatives of their clients, the advertisers. Claims of authorship by admen might shift attention away from the advertised product and thereby undermine the effect of the advertising message. As the well-known J. Walter Thompson executive James Webb Young reminisces: "As an Advertising Man you may conceivably produce a piece of deathless prose—but your name will never appear on it. You may initiate an advertising campaign that eventually brings about a minor revolution in social habits, but there will be no mention of it in your obituary."[57] During the radio era, when advertising agencies produced many prime time programs, a 1933 NBC policy specifically banned on-air credits of advertising agencies as "contrary to advertising industry ethics" and a potential annoyance to listeners.[58] Thus, the J. Walter Thompson agency intentionally presented host Rudy Vallee as the "author" of *The Fleischmann's Yeast Hour* despite the fact that the agency wrote the program and booked the guests.[59] Advertising ethics and network policy intentionally obscured the deeply intertwined relationships between advertising agency producers and performers of radio programs. Thus, unlike the film industry, in which directors were later labeled as authors despite similar industrial production practices, the authors of most radio programs were never publicly acknowledged as such.

While admen of the radio era were perhaps more resigned to the anonymity of their work than today's "creatives," as copywriters and art directors are now called, many of them nonetheless chafed under the yoke of subservience to their clients, the advertisers. Advertising agents, hired for their expertise, sometimes complained of being undermined by the meddling and arbitrary demands of their clients. Given their clients' power to replace them on any whim, agencies had little incentive to insist in the face of an uncomprehending or dismissive client. This form of impotence deeply disturbed some radio admen. The adman author of the bestselling 1947 novel *The Hucksters* lays the blame for poor radio programming at the feet of the obnoxious sponsor, modeled on American Tobacco's chief George Washington Hill, known for humiliating his underlings. Although the author wreaked revenge in the form of a thinly disguised roman à clef, opportunities to even the playing field with clients were few.

The obsequiousness necessary for maintaining good client relations encouraged the perception that admen lacked honesty. Advertising agents were accused of being "two-faced": on the one hand, eager to convince the client that their advertising would direct consumers to buy, while on the other hand reassuring consumers that their work merely reflected existing consumer desires and could not, of course, manipulate their minds. While admen bowed and scraped to their clients, only occasionally insisting on their superior expertise, they commonly saw their audiences—the readers, consumers, listeners—as dim-witted and malleable.[60] Because the industry accepted the flawed IQ testing of the Army in World War I, which concluded that the intelligence of most Americans was low, many advertising makers offset their discomfort about subservience to clients by feeling intellectually superior to their audiences. However, at least in appearance, admen had to mediate between advertisers and consumers, appealing to both. They assured advertisers they were expert at manipulating the weak public mind, while to audiences they likewise insisted they were only reflecting back the audiences' truest needs and desires.[61] And yet they often resented their clients and despised their audiences. These competing claims undermined their fervent claims of integrity and objectivity.

The advertising industry structured itself—forming agencies and a system of compensation by commission—to mediate among print media publishers and advertisers. By establishing itself as a key mediator, the advertising industry would, in time, also shape the development of emerging media, such as radio, and affect the fortunes of its clients, the advertisers. Advertising makers in the early decades of the twentieth century struggled with how to establish professional standards, develop effective advertising strategies, claim authorship, and conceptualize their audiences. These concerns would shape their role in the new medium of radio in the 1920s and 1930s. Most important, the debate between hard sell advertising proponents and soft sell practitioners would strongly shape radio advertising and programming. The many contemporary criticisms of radio—that it was strident, loud, repetitive, and dumbed-down—may actually have been a form of resistance to the predominance of hard sell strategies on radio.

2

The Fourth Dimension of Advertising
The Development of Commercial Broadcasting in the 1920s

According to adman Charles Hull Wolffe, advertising has always been available "on the air": "In the haze of prehistory, a savage beat out tom-tom signals along a jungle-lined river and caused the magic of sound to rouse a distant audience of tribesmen."[1] Commercial radio, implied Wolff, was rooted in human history and behavior. And in the United States, radio carried promotional messages almost from the outset: For example, a broadcast sold radio equipment over the air in 1915.[2] As early as 1922, one observer noted, "Concerts are seasoned here and there with a dash of advertising paprika."[3] However, the commercialization of radio was not an unavoidable outcome, the irresistible result of our need to rouse our tribesmen with tom-tom signals. Broadcasting in some other countries, such as the United Kingdom, developed as tax-funded, government-controlled communication systems with far different goals.[4] The American system, commercially controlled and funded, developed because of specific political decisions and particular economic incentives, a few of which I touch on here. Although some in the United States proposed that radio programming be funded with taxes or license fees paid by set owners, advertising, particularly indirect advertising, seemed a simpler and less politically fraught way to pay for programming.[5] Once it was established that broadcasting would be supported by advertising rather than taxes, the radio networks, in search of backers, turned to members of the advertising industry to advertise radio advertising to advertisers.

The Origins of Broadcast Commercialism

Initially the business of radio was not advertising but the manufacturing and sale of radio equipment. As radio use increased after World War I, spread in part by radio-trained war veterans, commercial and noncommercial interests struggled over who was to have access to the airwaves. Commercial interests blamed amateur "hams" for airwave congestion;[6] and in 1922, ignoring the broad use of radio by amateurs, schools, and churches, the federal government defined broadcast stations as commercial entities and assigned them to the purview of the Department of Commerce. Secretary of Commerce Herbert Hoover set priorities by assigning the best and strongest frequencies to stations with commercial interests. The rationale was that commercial entities would be more responsible and accountable to the public than individual amateurs or those with a particular political viewpoint the government did not want to be perceived as supporting. Broadcasting was thus constructed as a "promotional medium" for the likes of retailers, newspapers, and manufacturers, who invested in stations to promote themselves.[7] Investment in radio technology was nonetheless risky in the early years, and turnover of station ownership was high. Businesses often found radio's public relations function too expensive to maintain, at tens of thousands of dollars a year, and some began to wonder how else the medium might be used commercially.[8]

An important step in commercializing broadcasting was the development of "toll broadcasting" in 1921 by the largest telephone company, American Telephone & Telegraph. AT&T held radio patents, but because none of them concerned the manufacturing of radio sets, it was forced to look for other sources of revenue to profit from radio. So it decided to try selling radio facilities for public use, like telephone booths of the air. And like a telephone call, AT&T imagined, the cost of the broadcast should be borne by the originator.[9] Because only a limited number of broadcast licenses were available, according to former AT&T employee Mark Woods, "the Telephone Company decided they would have one central station which they would lease to advertisers and others for sales with certain restrictions, rules and regulations."[10] That station was WEAF, based in Manhattan. AT&T's strategy, then, was to centralize and regulate the commercial messages that had already been going out on the air from various locally owned stations, often for free.

"Toll broadcasting" was conceived initially as a way to send out a message. The sales staff at WEAF sought clients who would pay $50 or so to speak about their business for fifteen minutes. Most famously, the Queensboro Corporation promoted its new cooperative apartments in the uncongested New York borough of Queens in August 1922: "The cry of the heart is for more living room, more chance to unfold, more opportunity to get near to Mother Earth, to play, to romp, to plant and to dig."[11] William H. Rankin, a prominent New York advertising agency, was one of the first businesses to try a "selling talk," in late 1922.[12] However, by 1923 it was clear to AT&T management that potential customers were shying away from WEAF, put off by the strict rules AT&T had imposed limiting what could be said on the air. Because it viewed toll broadcasting as a type of public service, AT&T had prohibited "direct advertising"—that is, specific product and price information.[13] WEAF policy stated that the advertising message had to be "confined" to the mention of the advertiser's name and product. Sensibly enough, many advertisers believed such "indirect advertising" would do little to increase sales.[14] AT&T recruited George McClelland, then an officer of the Association of National Advertisers, to promote broadcasting to advertisers; still it had trouble selling airtime except for times advertisers thought most promising, such as Thursday, Friday, and Saturday evenings.[15]

According to radio promoter Edgar Felix, WEAF time salesman H. Clinton Smith convinced AT&T executives to expand radio advertising beyond selling talks: He proposed that advertisers be persuaded to sponsor entertainment instead.[16] Smith, a master salesman known as "Father Smith," undoubtedly noticed that musical and dramatic programs had attracted listeners on other stations.[17] It was no violation of WEAF's indirect advertising policy for program sponsors to promote themselves through the program title, followed by a brief message: "Let those Gold Dust Twins into your hearts and homes tonight, and you'll never regret it, for they do brighten the dull spots."[18] Although WEAF did not invent the concept of program sponsorship—entertainment had been provided at other stations owned by commercial interests—its superior wattage allowed it to broadcast some of the best-known early sponsored programs, including *The Eveready Hour, A & P Gypsies,* and *The Goodrich Silver-Masked Tenor,* all on the air by 1923 and each produced by an advertising agency.[19] AT&T's competitor Radio Corporation of America (RCA) likewise broadcast sponsored programs, such as *Wanamaker Organ Recital,* on its New York stations WJZ and WJY. These early sponsored programs, like most of what was on radio at the time, featured predominantly music, the program type that had attracted the earliest audiences to radio in 1919 and 1920 when Dr. Frank Conrad experimented with broadcasting music recordings from his garage in Pittsburgh.

Once they perceived an audience demand for music, and with it an opportunity to advertise as its sponsors, advertisers were eager to reach beyond the range of a local broadcast signal; they were ready to use a network. And so commercially sponsored and regularly scheduled programs such as *The Eveready Hour* were transmitted over distance by telephone landlines to multiple stations and produced in broadcast station facilities by advertising agencies hired by an advertiser. By 1923, the elemental foundation of commercial broadcasting had been laid.[20]

Philadelphia-based advertising agency N. W. Ayer & Son helped produce *The Eveready Hour,* one of the first variety programs, on which various musical and comedic artists performed every week, some returning, some appearing only once. By presenting a variety of artists, the sponsor, radio battery manufacturer National Carbon Company, could appeal to a wide audience. N. W. Ayer in 1923 formed what may have been the first advertising agency radio department. It was also involved in radio through one of its most important clients, the "American Company," as AT&T was known. N. W. Ayer, a specialist in this kind of work, had been producing "institutional" print advertising for AT&T, designed to promote its corporate image. For example, in a 1913 print advertisement headlined "The Spirit of Service," AT&T's commitment to keep telephone service operational even "when trains are stalled and roads are blocked" is depicted by the image of a telephone lineman in a snowstorm, waging "his lonely fight to keep the wire highways open."[21] Because of AT&T's own policy of avoiding direct selling on radio, N. W.

Ayer initially relegated radio to its public relations department as a "tool for large corporations to make friends" rather than as a selling medium.[22] Many in the advertising field similarly believed that radio's primary commercial role would be to establish a corporation's identity, trademark, and public image—all institutional advertising goals.[23]

Thus AT&T sought to channel the commercialism inevitable in a profit-based broadcast system into the acceptable form of "public relations," and WEAF broadcast primarily institutional or "good will" advertising until 1925. Thereafter, however, product mentions and selling messages were permitted more and more often, especially for favored clients, such as early radio sponsor Cities Service.[24] This loosening of the rules was in part a response to WEAF's competitors: other local broadcast stations that imposed fewer restrictions on advertisers.[25] These changes upset some of the top executives at AT&T. Then-president Walter Gifford soon concluded that AT&T's involvement in advertising and entertainment threatened to "adversely affect" its public image.[26] Having finally established itself as the monopoly provider of a necessary public communications service, telephony, AT&T sought to avoid any association with the morally dubious business of entertainment. As a result of this internal conflict, as well as pressure from antitrust investigations which questioned AT&T's claim that it alone among radio patent holders was permitted to profit from "toll broadcasting," AT&T sold WEAF to RCA in 1925 and withdrew from the radio business, retaining its control over the long lines that connected stations. By leasing access to these lines to stations, linked into networks, for the simultaneous distribution of programs, AT&T would profit from radio without having to sully its public image by directly handling the vaudeville-originated programs increasingly demanded by audiences.

Yet indirect advertising persisted in the industry, at least as an ideal. Despite the 1922–25 Radio Conferences' endorsement of advertising as the best source of funding for broadcasting, from 1924 to 1927 government officials and Congress frequently debated how and if advertising on the air should be regulated.[27] Secretary Hoover reflected the concern of many in broadcasting when he pointed out in 1924 that unlike a reader of magazines and newspapers, a radio listener would have no option to skip the advertisement; the potential for offending listeners with "direct advertising" could be the "quickest way to kill broadcasting."[28] His disapproval of direct advertising was not inconsistent with his support for commercial broadcasting.[29] Like many others, Hoover viewed indirect or "good will" advertising as more appropriate for radio, which ideally would become a medium of cultural uplift. If radio were to supply educational and highbrow programming unsullied by direct advertising, the political pressure for federal oversight of the industry would diminish. Thus, the Fourth Radio Conference of 1925 resolved that "public opinion" would supply the necessary curbs on offensive material and that commercial announcements would function primarily to create "good will" because they would be explicitly designed to avoid "ill will"; thus there was no need for government "censorship."[30]

This endorsement of indirect advertising was coupled with calls for increased self-regulation through industry trade associations such as the National Association of Broadcasters. Like the Truth-in-Advertising movement of the first decade of the 1900s, the promulgation of codes of ethics by the targeted industry itself prevented the formulation of new regulations designed by anyone who did not have a financial stake in the industry. Consequently, despite congressional debates over advertising, the federal Radio Act of 1927 required only that sponsored programs be announced as such. Furthermore, a new Federal Radio Commission responded to complaints that federal facilities (the airwaves) were used to the advantage of certain commercial interests over others and ought to be fairly allocated, claiming it was "unwise" to "make universal rules about advertising."[31] Thus, while broadcasters invoked First Amendment principles to deflect government control over content and to justify the use of public airwaves for commercial messages, self-regulation, in the form of avoidance of direct advertising, helped facilitate commercial broadcasting's political acceptance.[32]

Networking, or the Radio Web

The importance of building viable radio networks by connecting stations with AT&T's telephone lines became clear during AT&T's WEAF experiment. The impetus for these efforts, which began between 1923 and 1926, came, at least according to the agency's later claims, from N. W. Ayer, which demanded linked stations for its radio clients.[33] Obviously AT&T, which owned the lines, also benefited, as did its agency, N. W. Ayer.[34] Linked stations could share programming, thus splitting its costs among them. Also, performers at one broadcast station could reach listeners of a different broadcast station and so spare themselves the trouble of packing up and taking the show on the road. The economies of scale presented strong incentives to individual stations to join networks.[35]

Furthermore, national advertisers, put off by the amateur production values that dominated local broadcasting as well as the limitations of local markets, demanded "a wider circle of listeners" for their sponsored programs than local broadcast signals could provide.[36] Networking allowed them to penetrate multiple markets on a scale hitherto unseen in the print media, even national magazines like the *Saturday Evening Post*. National advertisers, who would not have bothered with local markets, were thus lured into radio sponsorship.[37] Likewise, major advertising agencies, having previously helped establish magazines as a national advertising medium, were also interested in developing a market for national or networked radio, a potentially more lucrative business than local or "spot" broadcast advertising.[38] National advertisers, aiming at large markets, were likely to invest far more than local advertisers in high-cost and high-quality programming that could sustain radio. Advertisers like Procter & Gamble, General Motors, and Kraft sought to develop mass markets for their products and were willing to invest heavily for such a purpose. As the radio analyst Herman Hettinger noted in 1933, "[I]t was the large national advertiser who could benefit most from this new medium of mass communication." Moreover, it was this type of advertiser "who financially was best equipped to make the large expenditures required" for high-quality programming.[39]

Considering the interests of these larger advertisers caused a basic shift among radio interests in how to build a business model for broadcasting. Instead of set sales, the first business model, which depended on selling as many sets as possible, or local advertising, the model for many local stations, the national advertising business model required gathering large audiences around broadcasts. Centralizing audience attention through networking could build large audiences more effi-ciently.[40] This also required reducing the number of broadcasters; lim-iting station licensing helped consolidate the field. The move toward networking was, as the historians Susan Smulyan, Clifford Doerksen, and Alexander Russo document, far more conflicted than not.[41] For to build dominant national networks, the radio interests such as AT&T and RCA had to also quash or marginalize the elements of the radio industry which challenged their assumptions that radio should be a genteel medium unsullied by direct advertising and lowbrow cultural forms.

The most important early network of stations was the National Broadcasting Company (NBC), created in 1926 by a consortium of radio patent holders, including RCA, General Electric, and Westing-house. WEAF, formerly owned by AT&T and soon to be renamed WNBC, was merged with RCA's WJZ. Although others had already created loose "chains" of stations, the formation of NBC was significant in that its powerful corporate backing inspired the confidence of na-tional advertisers.[42] NBC sought to add other stations to its "web." Local stations that agreed to affiliate with NBC paid it fees for receiving programming over AT&T lines and were identified on air as NBC affil-iates. NBC developed two networks: the "Red" network, which in-cluded its powerful stations in New York City, and the smaller and weaker "Blue" network. The leaders of NBC, David Sarnoff at RCA and Owen Young at GE, considered its purpose the promotion of such progressive business ideals as public service and cultural uplift, bring-ing high culture to those otherwise unexposed, and to counter the wor-risome influence of entrepreneur-owned stations that persisted in broadcasting "lowbrow" forms of popular music such as "hot jazz."[43] More practically, they regarded programming as a loss leader to stimu-late set sales for RCA, the largest radio set manufacturer. Audience desire for programming would drive sales of RCA hardware, the profits from which would partly offset the cost of programming. Sarnoff pre-ferred to describe the business model in public service terms: Program-ming would be circulated for free like books from a lending library.[44] This raised the question of who would finance that programming. NBC hoped advertisers would take over most of the costs but did not want its high-minded service tainted with direct advertising. Before 1930 the official policy at NBC was that radio was a "good will medium" and "not a selling medium"; advertisers were governed by rules forbidding pricing, the use of superlatives, and sample offers.[45] This rigidity, inherited from AT&T, would generate internal conflicts at NBC and damage its relationships with major advertisers until, eventually, Sarnoff acknowledged advertising as a "reputable practice" that would preserve "free" broadcasting.[46]

NBC's chief rival, the Columbia Broadcasting System (CBS), founded in 1927, reshaped the commercial broadcasting business model. Originally formed by a music recording company concerned that radio's distribution of free music would destroy the recording business, it was bought in 1927 by William Paley, the son of a cigar advertiser, who noticed that when the Paleys advertised La Palina cigars on the radio, their sales rose dramatically. Paley entered broadcast networking not to provide a high-minded public service but to sell things.[47] As one observer noted, CBS was "free to make money" from advertising.[48] However, while NBC enjoyed cross-subsidization from its parent company, RCA, CBS had no parent company to protect it or provide it with capital in lean times. It had to pursue advertisers and aggressively bring in affiliates in order to survive.

CBS, under Paley, adjusted the basic relationship between network and affiliated stations. Initially, affiliates had the option not to carry the network's programs and, because they were required to pay to carry the network's "sustaining" (unsponsored) programs, an incentive to choose this option. This system, however, undercut the very goal of networking, which was to reach the largest audience possible. How could a network guarantee a national audience to an advertiser if local station affiliates made their own programming decisions? It was tantamount to a magazine distributor's simply refusing to distribute a national magazine in a particular city, thereby undercutting the national distribution of advertising. To solve this problem, CBS offered network sustaining programs to affiliates for free in return for affiliates' guaranteeing "clearance" (or carriage) of all network programs during the network "option" times. And CBS offered to pay affiliates "compensation" for carrying network-sponsored programs.[49] CBS thus gained control over hours of airtime and affiliates gained free top-quality programming plus a new revenue stream. The affiliates' guaranteed "clearance" of sponsored programs then attracted to CBS national advertisers interested in reaching the largest audiences possible and therefore willing to pay higher prices for network airtime. High-quality network programming also attracted larger local audiences to the affiliates, which in turn could negotiate increased prices for airtime in locally programmed time slots. Once it became clear that CBS was gaining new affiliates and attracting advertisers with this compensation structure, NBC was forced to follow suit and began paying its affiliates as well.

Thus, by the late 1920s, the linkage of stations into networks that could efficiently share programming and connect advertisers with national audiences provided the infrastructure for radio's emergence as a national medium of American popular culture. Amid a booming economy, urbanization, modernization, and a growing consumerism that was reshaping daily life, radio quickly found a place in American homes that were simultaneously adopting other technologies, such as refrigerators, washing machines, and private automobiles.[50] The radio "fad" of the mid-1920s, based on the novelty of the talking box, gave way to high-quality national programming, and from a technological novelty radio became a cultural necessity. Listeners all over the country could hear stars from vaudeville and Broadway as well as music live from New York, instantaneously connecting them with the centers of culture and apparently with one another. What the radio historian Alexander Russo calls the "radiophonic"—the multi-tiered structure of local and national broadcasters, technologies, and economic relationships—began to evolve rapidly.[51] Radio set ownership increased steadily through the 1920s, from 400,000 in 1923 to 1.25 million in 1924 when the "fad" first exploded, to 4.5 million in 1926, when NBC was established, to 13.75 million in 1930.[52]

The Networks Woo Advertisers and Their Advertising Agencies

The establishment of national networks was the keystone of the development of commercial broadcasting, but broadcasters still faced the challenge of convincing advertisers to use this new medium. The advertising industry was essential in helping convince advertisers to use radio, and, in the process, it helped shape the new medium for commercial purposes. Agencies were pushed into radio in part by pressure from broadcasters, who needed their expertise to build advertiser interest in radio, and from advertisers, who sought entry into this potentially powerful new advertising medium through trusted advisors. Admen were at first reluctant and then increasingly enthusiastic about radio. On the one hand, they worried it would undermine their existing business relationships; on the other hand, they were uniquely positioned to exploit the new medium.

First, as broadcasters had to acknowledge from the outset, advertising agencies already had relationships with advertisers: the potential radio sponsors.[53] They controlled their clients' media buying, and so broadcasters could enlist a sponsor only through its agency. An agency functioned as "an intimate advisor" to its client, bringing an "inside angle" to an advertiser's marketing problem.[54] An agency could convince an advertiser either to try radio or to avoid it. To be sure, there were a few cases in which an agency was so opposed to radio that its clients simply circumvented it.[55] As the president of the Clicquot Club beverage company declared in 1923, "My advertising agency doesn't believe much in radio, so we'll go ahead without consulting it."[56] The company's program, *The Clicquot Club Eskimos*, featuring a band of banjo players dressed in furry Eskimo outfits and named after the fictional Eskimo boy who served as the brand trademark, was one of the first to be networked among multiple stations. But for the most part, the key to convincing an advertiser to allocate some of its advertising budget to radio was in the hands of the advertiser's agency.

Second, admen trained in the persuasive arts could use those same arts to overcome advertiser resistance to the new medium. The networks' sales departments promoted radio's advertising efficacy; however, their need to sell time affected their credibility. Advertising agencies, on the other hand, could claim to be marketing experts, analyzing the advertiser's needs and recommending broadcast media with the same objectivity as they had print media. And as marketing advisors to a diverse array of advertisers, admen were far better positioned to evaluate the marketing needs of their clients than the radio industry.

Third, ad agencies offered advertisers expertise with markets and methods of appeal. Their experience in print media, in such matters as the timing, aesthetic appeal, and context of a commercial message, made them better qualified than either networks or independent program producers to evaluate entertainment vehicles as appropriate contexts for an advertiser's message. And, with their experienced sense of business needs, they were better able than networks to mediate between entertainers and sponsors.[57] Advertising agencies could speak both the "trade language" of industry and the "personal language" of audiences; representing advertisers, they could function as an "interpreter of sales ideas."[58]

Fourth, although they provided copywriting and art for advertising, advertising agencies' primary revenue source was media placement. Agencies offered advertisers special rates with publishers based on volume and circulation; as time passed, agency media buyers would become expert at time-buying strategies as well, learning to fight on behalf of their clients for the best deals. Some agencies, such as J. Walter Thompson, developed multiple broadcasting accounts at networks and were then able to wield a great deal of leverage in negotiations with networks over scheduling and rates.

Finally, ad agencies could promote their clients' advertising primary interest—the sale of products. The broadcasters and networks might try to enforce their own standards for advertising and programs, occasionally in opposition to advertisers and their agencies. Independent program producers, hailing mainly from the show business worlds of theater and vaudeville, might try to advance entertainment values over advertising goals, as might the musical and theatrical performers enlisted for sponsored programs. And advertisers, especially if new to the medium, might not know how to use entertainment as a selling tool. But admen, with their marketing experience and unwavering concern with product sales, were well equipped to negotiate with broadcasters, talent, and program producers on behalf of the advertisers who were paying the bills. As one claimed in 1929, the adman "is an impresario because he is an expert on popular taste and how to cater to it, to educate it and improve it. It is logical to think that he is destined to be an important factor in radio."[59]

The networks pursued two strategies to entice the agencies into supporting advertiser use of radio. First, during the WEAF experiment and then more formally at NBC during the presidency of Merlin Aylesworth, broadcasters offered a 15 percent commission to agencies on the airtime sold to their clients, whether or not the agencies had any involvement in the broadcast.[60] Second, the networks hired advertising men to promote radio, recognizing that only through personnel familiar with advertisers and agencies could they address the industry's concerns and counter the arguments of the established print media and conservative corporate leaders. In 1926 the NBC board of directors hired Frank A. Arnold, the well-known advertising account executive and director of the Frank Seaman advertising agency, as NBC's "Ambassador at Large to the American Business World."[61] A year later they hired British adman E. P. H. James to provide promotional support. At CBS, initially William Paley himself solicited accounts. By 1930, the network hired former adman and Lennen & Mitchell executive Paul Kesten to furnish promotional campaigns, thereby dramatically improving CBS's relations with advertisers.

Rather than sell advertisers specific programs to sponsor, Arnold was directed to tell the "wonderful story" of the "modern miracle" of radio to constituencies involved in advertising, including advertisers, advertising agencies, and advertising media.[62] He had had a long career in retail merchandising, publishing (*Dry Goods Chronicle, Suburban Life*), and advertising before he joined NBC and was able to capitalize on his personal relationships with agency leaders. Touring the country, he addressed trade groups and visited the "head man" of local advertising organizations in order to encourage them to convince their clients to try radio.[63] According to his colleague E. P. H. "Jimmy" James, the fact that Arnold was "an oldish man" who "embraced the brand new medium of radio made it a little more respectable than if he hadn't."[64] His age and experience lent an imprimatur to the new medium, considered by many to be "a young man's fancy."[65] Likewise, Mark Woods, a WEAF veteran and later president of NBC Blue and founder of his own advertising agency, Woods and Warwick, claimed that Arnold's embrace of radio "lent a certain amount of stability to the broadcast business among agency men, which it didn't previously have."[66]

In order to position radio as an effective advertising tool, Arnold considered and discarded several terms referring to what NBC offered advertisers. He rejected the term "broadcasting," because that could include noncommercial radio. He rejected "radio advertising" because it suggested that NBC was advertising radio sets. Instead he invented the phrase "broadcast advertising," and that became NBC's official name for the medium (see Figure 2-1).[67] Because NBC had no promotion department initially, Arnold himself wrote and commissioned a number of pamphlets he titled "Little Books on Broadcasting," which he distributed to advertisers and their agencies.[68] Titles included "What Broadcasting Means to Business," by NBC president Merlin Aylesworth; "Broadcasting and the National Advertiser"; "The Technique of Broadcast Advertising"; "The Advertising Agency and the Broadcasting Medium"; and "Popular Reactions to Radio Broadcasting."

Suggesting that broadcast advertising would supplement rather than supplant print advertising, Arnold designated radio the "fourth dimension of advertising." Newspapers, the first dimension, are "the bulwark of our civilization." Magazines, the second, contribute to "the literary culture of the people." Outdoor advertising, the third, includes billboards and display advertising. And broadcasting, the fourth dimension, adds "height" to advertising because it extends "100 miles up to the roof of the sky."[69] With this construct, Arnold positioned radio as a partner to and extension of existing media, as well as an otherworldly addition to advertising means.

James, NBC's other promoter of radio to advertisers and their agencies, was a British advertising man recruited by the Lord & Thomas agency for their client RCA, NBC's parent.[70] James worked to help potential advertisers create a "copy slant" for their broadcast advertising. He grouped broadcast advertising into five categories, each associated with a particular type of radio entertainment. *The Ipana Troubadours* exemplified "institutional" broadcast advertising; Bristol-Myers sponsored the music program to promote Ipana toothpaste and never announced the name of the orchestra leader, Sam Lanin, well known in his own right, in case doing so would inadvertently promote Lanin rather than Ipana. *The Schickerling Crystal Gazers*, a music program sponsored by a radio tube manufacturer, was, according to James, an

BROADCAST
ADVERTISING

NATIONAL BROADCASTING COMPANY, INC.,
NEW YORK
1927

Figure 2-1. NBC: *Broadcast Advertising.* (Courtesy of the Library of American Broadcasting.)

example of "fantastic" broadcast advertising, possibly because of its reference to fortune telling. The *Gold Dust Twins* program was an example of "personification" because it featured two performers, Goldy and Dusty, based on the brand's trademark image of two young African Americans, who incorporated Gold Dust cleaning powder into their act. According to James, *Atwater Kent Radio Artists*, sponsored by the radio manufacturer, was an example of "feature" broadcast advertising presumably because it featured well-known performers. A program sponsored by the film company First National Pictures was an example of the "dramatic" advertising strategy.[71] Having defined the categories, James recommended that advertisers associate themselves with compatible entertainment vehicles. Thus, the Clicquot Club ginger ale company should provide entertainment that was "effervescent," like ginger ale.[72]

As these program names indicate, Arnold and James were primarily concerned with promoting radio as a "good will" medium. Prices, product claims, and even the naming of specific products were to be avoided. These programs' link to their sponsors was made most clear by their titles. They featured little, if any, direct advertising; instead, after an introduction that included a short description of the sponsoring product, the program would commence. As James recalls, NBC policy was that the "announcer is an invited guest in the home of the listener," and so radio could not be "a selling medium."[73] Good will, argued Arnold, is "the greatest single element in business today," and broadcast advertising should thus avoid creating offense and instead "bring about a feeling of gratitude and pleasant obligation" on the part of the listener.[74] The programs, then, did not promote the performing musicians, singers, and actors but the sponsor only, who hoped that listeners who enjoyed the performances would buy the product out of a sense of gratitude.

Unlike NBC, which initially emphasized public service over commercial aims, CBS lacked the cross-subsidization of a corporate parent or the financial muscle of a manufacturing division and thus from the outset staked its success on its ability to please advertisers. Before Paley took over the network, he solicited the opinions of top advertising men on the future of radio and then moved CBS headquarters from Times Square to Madison Avenue for better proximity to the advertising industry.[75] According to its promotional literature, CBS employees charged with handling advertisers were proudly regarded as "first of all advertising men."[76] The sales staff at CBS by 1932 had "an intimate knowledge of agency practice" and usually "had long experience selling 'space.'"[77] In a CBS promotional brochure published in 1929 and aimed at advertising executives, broadcasting is presented as a "subtle" form of advertising that "creates a subconscious obligation in the mind of the listener" to buy sponsors' products out of gratitude for the sponsored programs. Listing the ways in which radio works for the advertiser, the writers of the pamphlet claim that broadcasting is "emotional," because musical programs affect "mind, heart and soul." By "owning a certain hour on the air each week," the advertiser gains a "right-of-way through the ether, permitting him to permeate practically every square inch of the width and breadth of the land with his name and sales story."[78] In case readers remain unconvinced of these powers, another pamphlet explains that only radio can solve the publicity problems created by mergers, consolidations, and interlocking directorates, because it is the only medium "that will reach everyone—everywhere!" (see Figure 2-2).[79]

Paul Kesten, at CBS, viewed his task as director of sales promotion as "advertising advertising—to *advertisers*."[80] Before Kesten joined CBS in 1930, he had a career in retail and advertising, working for Gimbel's department store and the Lennen & Mitchell advertising agency, where his CBS colleagues William Klauber and Hugh Boice had also worked.[81] Initially he filled his pamphlets with general arguments in favor of radio, but he soon switched tactics. Radio, according to Kesten, had been seen as "ephemeral, fantastic. It was drama, mystery, music. It lacked a background of facts. It had never been placed in a frame of statistics and hung upon a wall of evidence, along with other advertising media."[82] So he went about collecting and publishing radio facts in his pamphlets, such as the number of radio sets in use ("The Flood Hits the Valley"), and radios in households defined by income ("Has Radio Sold the Goods?").

Kesten also worked to provide statistical data about listenership at a time when there was little available. In 1930 the Association of National Advertisers sponsored the "Crossley" ratings, which ascertained

Figure 2-2. CBS: *Broadcast Advertising—The Sales Voice of America.* (Courtesy of the Library of American Broadcasting.)

listenership through telephone surveys. Because the Crossleys indicated that NBC stations had larger audiences than CBS stations, Kesten sought to undermine them. His own surveys, conducted by postcards asking what radio stations the respondent listened to, favored CBS.[83]

Throughout his tenure at CBS, Kesten emphasized the use of numerical data and statistics, and his protégés, such as Frank Stanton, further developed the strategy. Although the data Kesten massaged tended to promote CBS specifically, he also claimed his research supported the value of broadcast advertising in general.[84] This professed lack of self-interest was not only a canny sales pitch to doubting advertisers but also an acknowledgment that the medium itself had to be sold before CBS's success could be assured.

In breaking down sales resistance to broadcast advertising, radio promoters routinely emphasized certain virtues: Radio "appeals to the ear,"[85] radio is a personal medium, and radio penetrates the domestic space of the home. The "ear," as opposed to the eye, can be considered "a most receptive channel for appeals to reason or emotion."[86] Whether advertisers preferred rational or emotional appeals, they were safe with radio because, unlike print, the human voice could convey nuances of meaning or express feeling and intimacy. As the radio promoter and academic Herman Hettinger claimed, "[T]he human voice still remains the most potent instrument of emotional expression."[87] Having struggled to communicate sincerity in print copy, some admen embraced the radio voice as a better means to this end. This voice, whether authoritative or coaxing, knowledgeable or questioning, brought a human presence to the advertising message that print could not. Vocal impersonations of the friendly local grocer, or the neighbor lady down the street, were likely to engage the listeners' trust. The radio columnist Edgar Felix announced in 1928 in *Advertising & Selling* that "[r]adio oracles are winning confidence not only by real radio personality, but by conscientious service."[88] At CBS, Kesten claimed even greater powers for the radio voice: Listeners, he wrote in one of his pamphlets, do as they are told. Alone among advertising media, radio "presents the *living* voice of authority," which gives it the "supple power to move people and mold them, to enlist them and command them."[89] Radio voices were not domineering, according to Kesten, but simply authoritative, like those of a parent or teacher.

Radio's dependence on the human voice thus offered opportunities to personalize advertising messages, to build the confidence of listeners, and to develop more humanized images of advertisers.[90] By cultivating personalities that spoke directly to "you" the listener, radio could moderate the potentially alienating effects of fast, novel, mass-oriented technologies. Radio could reach millions simultaneously but was experienced by listeners individually, in the intimacy of their homes. Radio also promised to strengthen the seller–purchaser relationships undermined by national distribution systems. Felix claimed that radio "humanizes an impersonal business," in part because "personality is still a necessary qualification of salesmanship" in an era of national brands rather than local goods.[91] As an NBC salesman wrote to an ad agency in 1928, broadcasting "promotes a pseudo-friendship . . . between the listeners and certain performers whom they have come to associate with a product or company. The listener feels an increased interest and attachment instilled by a phantasmagoric contact between them and him."[92] Far from alienating the listener, the new technology might instead provide a nurturing, if ghostly, companionship. Hearing the voice as directed to herself alone, a listener might interpret the message sent to thousands as the personal message of a confidante. The attribution of magical powers to radio reflected its status as a "new" medium, and perhaps the hyperbole also suggests a continued resistance to radio among skeptics.[93]

Radio also provided advertisers an entrée into private domestic space. Fearing that potential customers brace themselves to resist the advertising they are exposed to at work and on the street, some advertisers hoped that at home in front of the radio, potential customers would be "at leisure and their minds receptive."[94] Unlike the door-to-door salesman, whose efforts to get in the door might be resented, the radio program was "invited" to speak directly to people as they relaxed in privacy. A relaxed audience was potentially a more receptive one. As Arnold argued, "Here you have the advertiser's ideal—the family group in its moments of relaxation awaiting your message. Nothing equal to this has ever been dreamed of by the advertising man."[95] Likewise, James pointed out to potential advertisers that "[a] broadcast advertisement is intimate, confidential. It is permitted to take part in the family life. It enjoys the confidence of the family circle."[96] Noting that people behave differently when alone or in a group or with family, NBC president Aylesworth argued, "It is the 'member-of-the-family'

self to which broadcast advertising most often appeals."[97] Some advertisers thus viewed this access to the family circle as an opportunity; a
manager at Kraft believed that "[i]t is indeed a rare privilege for the
advertiser to enter the American home . . . without even a knock on
the door. . . . In radio we have an invisible power."[98]

If references to radio's potential "invisible power" did not convince,
promoters were quick to point out more practical applications. Radio
could be a "supplementary" advertising medium, part of an overall
marketing plan, creating "tie-ins" with other promotional efforts.[99]
James recalls that as an advertising man with print experience he
worked to encourage advertisers to *add* radio advertising to marketing
plans rather than drop print advertising in favor of radio. He would
point out that "a chorus is more effective than a solo."[100] Broadcast
advertising promoters were anxious not to alienate the print media,
and so consistently urged advertisers to consider broadcasting as one
more instrument to use in concert with already proven media.[101]

Perhaps most important, however, was promoters' awareness of
the unique quality of radio not shared with other media: Radio could
address "vast audiences simultaneously" because broadcasting "perme-
ates everything, everywhere."[102] No print medium enjoyed the advantages of network radio, which would eventually reach nearly every
home. Most print media were either local, like newspapers, or limited
by interest group, like magazines. To be sure, some national magazines, such as the *Saturday Evening Post*, were vastly popular; nonetheless, even they could never garner as large an audience (including the
illiterate) as did radio. Radio promised to revolutionize communication
by compressing time and space and so becoming the first truly national mass medium. To advertisers concerned about the fragmenting
of their messages among various print media, radio could be sold as
having the potential to create a unified message with a national impact.

The true origins of commercial broadcasting lie not in the advertising
industry but in a number of political decisions and economic incentives that developed throughout the 1920s: the decision to pay for
broadcasting with advertising rather than taxes, the decision to regulate it weakly or not at all, the incentives among radio patent holders

competing for revenues, and the potential profitability of linking chains of stations into national networks. While admen were well positioned to become mediators in broadcasting, both advertisers and their agencies had to be "sold" on using radio for advertising. Hiring members of the advertising industry to reach out to the advertising and business worlds, the two largest networks, NBC and CBS, cannily developed appeals to promote the new commercial medium effectively. By 1933, advertisers in the food, drug, and personal products industries, along with the tobacco companies, had become "the backbone of American broadcast advertising."[103]

3

They Sway Millions as If by Some Magic Wand
The Advertising Industry
Enters Radio in the Late 1920s

In the 1920s unending economic growth seemed possible, and the advertising industry appeared to be its motor; would radio technology help fuel further growth? By the end of the decade, advertising industry revenues reached a record $3.4 billion.[1] In claiming much credit for stimulating the booming economy, the advertising industry was perhaps a bit overconfident of its power over consumers. But in confronting the prospect of broadcast advertising, it expressed misgivings along with such confidence. While boosters promoted broadcasting as a better way to express business ideals and personalize selling than the voiceless medium of print, others dismissed it as a fad. To some admen, radio advertising remained mysterious; as *Fortune* magazine later pointed out, radio was a business of "sell[ing] time, an invisible commodity, to fictitious beings called corporations for the purpose of influencing an audience that no one can see."[2] Advocates of both the hard and soft sell expressed resistance, some citing radio advertising's ephemeral nature, others the risk of offending audiences. Nonetheless, advertising agencies began, in the late 1920s and early 1930s, to create internal radio departments for handling the new medium. Having entered radio, advertising agencies were forced to consider which print strategies could be translated to radio—and which could not.

Resistance to Radio: "Acute Inflammatory Radioitis"

Initially many admen resisted the new medium. NBC promoter E. P. H. James recalls that most agencies in the 1920s were "quite indifferent to radio."[3] The conservative trade journal *Printers' Ink,* in an editorial against radio advertising in 1922, complained that "[t]he family circle is not a public place, and advertising has no business intruding there unless it is invited."[4] Unlike print, consumed by a reader in silence, radio could be heard by anyone in range. The entire family would have to listen, and the young might be exposed to sexual innuendo, jazz, or other inappropriate material. But even if the program were "high-class entertainment," *Printers' Ink* further editorialized in 1923, listeners who have been "wheedled into listening to a selfish message will naturally be offended," because a high cultural experience will have been debased by advertising.

However, *Printers' Ink* revealed what was probably its chief motive in attacking radio when it warned that newspapers would stop publicizing radio programs "if the broadcasters are themselves going to enter into advertising competition with the newspapers."[5] Thus, concern over straining relations with their primary business collaborators, the print publishers, motivated some admen to protect their interests in the print media by openly criticizing radio. Furthermore, most of the advertising pages in *Printers' Ink* were sold to newspaper publishers, and thus the trade magazine sought to cater to its own largest advertisers.[6] Newspaper publishers alternately tried to quash or take over radio: In the press–radio "wars" of the early 1930s, the major print wire services, such as the Associated Press, refused to allow radio stations to subscribe to their news services. The penetration of radio into the news market, claimed the head of one newspaper trade association, "is seriously depreciating the value of the newspaper's chief asset in the minds of listeners." As late as 1933, some newspapers still refused to carry any radio program listings, arguing that listings were advertising, not news, and therefore should be paid for as such.[7]

But advertising agencies had other concerns about radio aside from their desire to maintain good relations with print publishers; they had also to consider the reputation of their profession. The historian Roland Marchand usefully divides the admen who sought to advance professionalism in advertising into two general groups, the "real pros" and those who viewed advertising as "uplift." Real pros believed advertising was only as good as the sales figures it generated. Seeking to shake its association with medicine show–style entertainment and bring it into the mainstream of conventional business practice, real pros represented advertising as both a business and a science; they favored quantifiable results and emphasized hard sell strategies, such as "reasons why" to buy a product, over soft sell strategies, such as the use of associations and emotions. Admen such as Albert Lasker and Claude Hopkins of the Chicago agency Lord & Thomas subscribed to many "real pro" beliefs. The "uplift" model of advertising, on the other hand, promulgated most famously by Bruce Barton of Batten Barton Durstine & Osborn, represented advertising as a form of education and a kind of public service and sought to associate it with high forms of culture. Many who believed in the uplift model looked to education, especially the formation of advertising curricula in higher education, as a route to respectability and professionalism.[8]

Radio presented problems for both factions. To begin with, in the early to mid-1920s radio appeared to be a passing fad, a pastime for amateurs and engineers.[9] Both real pros and uplifters feared that associating their clients with a fad of limited appeal could detract from the seriousness of their business. Furthermore, before standards improved with the establishment of the networks, uplifters wished to avoid juxtaposing commercial messages with local programs of variable quality, many of which relied on unpaid and amateur performers. The inconsistency of program quality and the outrageousness of fraudulent advertisers such as John Brinkley, who promoted goat glands as a cure for impotence until his station license was revoked, tainted radio as vulgar, especially for uplifters. Consequently, beginning with NBC's announcement in 1926 that it would improve programming,[10] the networks continually stressed their ability to elevate the quality of programming precisely in order to attract advertisers and agencies concerned with potentially damaging associations.

Real pros dismissed radio for its ephemeral nature: No one knew how many listeners received a broadcast commercial message; it left no mark or solid evidence of its existence.[11] The historian Alexander Russo notes that this was the central problem of broadcasting, generating anxiety for both broadcasters and advertisers.[12] Unlike print media circulation, for which the advertising and publishing industries had established "audited" figures overseen by the Audit Bureau of Circulations, radio's reach or penetration could not be measured.[13] Unlike film and theater, radio provided "no box office receipts, nor rising or falling subscriptions to measure the public's approval or indifference," as one agency pointed out.[14] Some argued that this lack of hard data did not mean radio advertising was ineffective; they compared radio to billboards or transit advertising, for which there were likewise no circulation measurements.[15] Some sought to measure listenership through fan mail and instigated promotions, contests, and giveaways to stimulate such mail. A high volume of mail could be used to persuade a potential sponsor of the size of radio audiences. John Sample, of the agency Blackett-Sample-Hummert, described the results of one premium offer made on the *Ma Perkins* radio program:

Then we offered a package of zinnia seeds for a dime. We drew about 1,000,000 dimes. The letters covered the floor of an office. . . . I took Mr. Deupree and some other top [Procter & Gamble] people and I went in there and we walked around on top of all those letters. That's the first time P&G executives had demonstrated to them the power of this relatively new advertising medium.[16]

Detractors, however, dismissed such mail because fans usually gushed about the program rather than the product sponsoring it. Most letters requesting offered premiums expressed no gratitude toward the sponsor such as might manifest itself in the purchase of the sponsor's product.[17] Real pros, then, distrusted this measure of radio circulation. As the radio director of J. Walter Thompson (JWT) admitted in a private staff meeting, mail volume was no true indication of a program's selling effectiveness.[18] By 1930, the Association of National Advertisers established the first "circulation" figures for radio broadcasts.[19] But though networks' circulation claims thus gradually grew more credible, many admen worried that radio provided "wasted coverage" because networks broadcast to markets in which their clients did not sell, thus incurring increased expense without increased sales.[20]

Some admen, including real pros, doubted the usefulness of "good will" advertising, arguing that good will advertising was simply not worth the expense of program production for most advertisers. Good will advertising would be useful only to advertisers more concerned with national corporate image than with product sales. Many admen therefore viewed advertisers' interest in radio as simply a case of "acute inflammatory radioitis," or the desire of corporate leaders to scratch the "publicity itch"—to seek glory, not sales.[21] Furthermore, the model of radio as a good will medium had obvious limits. As one dissenter at JWT pointed out, if two competitors each provided sponsored programs, such as Clicquot Club and Canada Dry for similar products, then which ginger ale company would reap good will from listeners? Would all that good will cancel itself out?[22]

Many of the uplifters, on the other hand, extolled radio as a good will medium. Many in the professional middle classes regarded radio as a vehicle of cultural uplift for the masses through educational and high cultural programming.[23] Corporations applying enlightened self-interest would, they felt, sponsor opera, theater, and educational talks aimed at raising the level of cultural discourse.[24] Many admen regarded radio as a kind of home theater, to be quietly appreciated with all the dignity and gravitas that accompanied the attending of opera. Direct advertising of packaged goods and the like could only jar and offend audiences with such expectations. The fear that direct advertising would undercut the medium's effectiveness lay behind the consistent emphasis on indirect selling within agencies throughout the 1920s. Radio, according to *Advertising & Selling* radio editor Edgar Felix, should be recognized as "a medium for winning good will and as a method of establishing a pleasant association with a trade or firm name."[25] Admen who believed this often reflected the views of their clients. For example, in an exchange with the B. F. Goodrich Company in 1925, the advertising manager of the Kolynos Co., later a significant radio advertiser, was asked the value of radio advertising. He responded, "We feel that direct advertising through the radio would be more likely to antagonize rather than produce sales, and that anything that is done should be put in the form of entertainment."[26] The Goodrich advertising manager concurred, concluding that the "value of this advertising is in the indirect effect it has on its listeners."[27] By 1929,

an industry-sponsored survey indicated that just over half of radio listeners were "annoyed" by radio advertising.[28] Thus, as late as 1930,
many in broadcasting and advertising remained certain that direct selling on radio would offend listeners.[29]

The debate over the viability of direct advertising on radio repeated to some extent a similar debate over whether radio should be
"selling its editorial pages."[30] Following the print model, some admen
argued that editorial and advertising functions on radio should be
kept distinct, that advertisers should not be providing the editorial
material—that is, the programs. In 1926 the advertising manager for
General Electric, while enthusiastic about radio advertising, assumed
that "[b]roadcasting will probably not be employed in direct selling
until some plan is provided by which such advertising can be definitely segregated from all other programs."[31] An anonymous but
"prominent" adman argued in the trade press that the conflation of
editorial and advertising on radio by way of sponsored programs
would eventually undermine the advertising effectiveness of the medium.[32] In 1928, a staff member at JWT argued that because "All radio
'space' is *editorial space*" and because advertising space cannot be
"skipped or delayed until time suits its reading," advertisers risk earn-
ing "ill will" from listeners if the advertising is not "universally pleasing."[33] In print media, the publisher has the responsibility to attract
readers with editorial material; advertisers buy the attention of those
readers only by purchasing space adjacent to editorial material. Some
admen argued that broadcasters should likewise provide content instead of "scattering the responsibility" for it among advertisers and
their agencies.[34] They suggested that, to guarantee the medium's viability, the networks should take control over programming, leaving
only brief periods, at intervals of a half hour or so, to the agencies
and their advertisements.[35]

Radio advertising's detractors had other concerns about the value
of the airwaves. By defining advertising as "salesmanship in print,"
admen sought to associate selling not with the patent-medicine trade
but with the sober, calculated, and literate venue of print. Radio
brought this association into question. As one adman claimed, "The
longstanding definition of advertising, 'Salesmanship in print,' passed

into the discard when radio made its debut."[36] Radio "is oral salesman-ship instead of salesmanship in print."[37] The reliance on oral selling strategies raised uncomfortable associations with the carnival barker and the medicine show. Some admen cheerfully admitted that radio selling was not unlike the traveling medicine shows, in which the ven-dor would put on a show out of his wagon to attract crowds for sales of patent medicine. Robert Colwell of JWT conceded, "Get the crowd around, and then sell your wares. Good radio is just as simple as that."[38] More often, however, radio critics of the 1930s would use the medicine show analogy to criticize commercial broadcasting.[39]

Another objection, one that would affect debates over the role of the advertising industry in broadcasting well into the 1950s, was whether advertising men should be involved in entertainment. If ad-vertising were to become a respected business enterprise, then involvement in show business would seriously undermine admen's insistence that they were professionals, or "consumption engineers," in Calkins's phrase. The entire discourse of progressive business prac-tice was predicated on the application of scientific principles to shape predictable outcomes. Many admen seeking the imprimatur of busi-ness professionalism viewed show business as an unpredictable and risky enterprise, operating in a marginal and disreputable social sphere populated by hustlers and subject to the disruptive sexuality of fallen women. As George Faulkner of JWT explained, "[T]he word showman carries an undignified, cheap connotation. It has a vaguely Semitic, Barnumish, Broadway air to it."[40] How could respectable men of business enter show business and guarantee results for their adver-tising clients? Too many factors were difficult to control: the tempers of talent, the whims of popular taste, the risks of offending audiences, and other imponderables. The tension between the strategies of ratio-nal appeals and the strategies of the carnivalesque would shape the intra-industry debates throughout the history of advertising agency involvement in programming.

Advertising Agencies Found Radio Departments

Former WEAF staffer Mark Woods credits the William H. Rankin agency with being one of the first major agencies to "back this new medium."[41] Rankin's broadcast of actress Marion Davies promoting cosmetic company Mineralava on WEAF in 1922 was probably the first agency-produced sponsored program.[42] Pointing out that agencies had already experienced a change of function, from space brokers into marketing specialists, Edgar Felix urged agencies to consider radio as just one more function to add to an ever-increasing roster of services to provide clients.[43] However, many agencies signaled their reluctance to engage too deeply with radio by keeping their newly formed radio departments somewhat apart from other departments; and despite their increasing importance over the next two decades, many radio departments remained marginal. Many heads of agencies, such as Raymond Rubicam of Young & Rubicam, continued long into the radio era to view radio as "a necessary evil."[44] According to one observer, agencies "resented the new form."[45]

Nonetheless, agencies began to expand into radio and counter the competition for clients who needed programming. Agencies competed with "radio service bureaus," which were independent program producers. JWT radio executive Robert Simon dismissed these competitors as just "concert managers or broken-down actors or anybody who thought he could sell an idea."[46] The independent bureaus, as well as stations, "do not have many seasoned advertising men" to help advertisers.[47] Advertising agencies' competitive advantage was that they could put the advertiser's marketing needs foremost and apply their selling expertise. According to Roy Durstine, one of the founders of BBDO, "The showman isn't an advertising man," and thus advertisers needed agencies to protect them from these dubious show business figures.[48] Felix urged agencies to learn the broadcasting and entertainment businesses, not necessarily to become full-time "showmen" but to have a "most wholesome and constructive influence" on the broadcasting industry, as well as to intervene to save clients from the "self-appointed unauthorized middlemen" who sought to profit from clients' inexperience in show business.[49] The other major competitors to the agencies were the network programming departments. While network programming departments built programs and then looked for an advertiser to buy them, the advertising agencies' competitive advantage was that they began with the advertiser's needs and then located or developed programs to fit those needs.

As a rule, agencies did not have expertise in show business any more than the showmen had expertise in advertising. Ralph Hower, in his 1939 in-house history of the N. W. Ayer agency, notes that radio was "no special boon" to agencies because it "forced them into the entertainment business, a field in which they had no experience."[50] JWT's Colwell argued, however, that admen in radio therefore worked harder than showmen. The "average Broadway writer," for example, "takes his assignment with the attitude that he can dash it off with one hand." Admen were not only more modest about their expertise, they took the job more seriously.[51] Mark Woods later suggested that the involvement of agencies in radio helped promote programming innovation in the late 1920s because agencies convinced advertisers to spend more on programming—budgeting for star talent and the like—in order to attract larger audiences. Furthermore, Woods pointed out that, unlike other producers perhaps, the agencies were motivated to distinguish their clients' programs from other programs so as to establish their unique radio presence, thereby spurring more program "diversification."[52] With more hyperbole, the manager of the Erwin Wasey radio department suggested that advertising agencies were also "contributing to the daily contentment and culture of millions."[53]

Whether or not agencies believed they belonged in radio, they felt pressure from their clients to get into radio. In the privacy of a staff meeting, a JWT staffer asserted that advertisers wanted to be involved with radio because it was the "more or less suppressed desire of every capitalist to become involved in show business" without "the suggestion of something naughty that goes with the backing of a show on Broadway."[54] Chester Bowles, founder of Benton & Bowles, claimed that once agencies realized that "radio was no passing phenomenon" and that "they would have to take a more and more active part in the building of radio programs," agencies began to recruit personnel who might bring them show business expertise.[55] Thus, many agencies that had been go-betweens for sponsors and broadcasters eventually began producing programs for sponsors directly. By 1929, according to one

count, 33 percent of one network's programs were produced by advertising agencies, 28 percent by the network itself, 20 percent by sponsors, and 19 percent by independent program packagers, or radio
bureaus.[56] Network radio advertising revenues jumped from $3.9 mil-
lion in 1927 to $19.2 million in 1929.[57]

As advertising agencies began to respond to clients' interest in
radio, many newly created agency radio departments included at least
one man with network or broadcast experience who could explain the
ins and outs of the broadcasting "game." According to Mark Woods,
NBC began loaning out some of its personnel to help agencies set up
radio departments; agencies also began to recruit network personnel,
offering them higher salaries, so NBC "lost a number of men to the
advertising agencies."[58] Advertising agencies also recruited from CBS;
for example, Ralph Wentworth and Norman Brokenshire left CBS in
1929 to join radio departments in agencies.[59] Many of the network
men recruited by the agencies were time salesmen who knew how to
sell broadcasting generally. These men were often joined at the agencies by someone who could specialize in program building, and by a
"statistician" who could present data to clients on radio's effectiveness.
The salesman would sell the idea of radio to clients, the program man
would present program ideas, and the statistician would supply circulation (or listenership) data.[60]

N. W. Ayer, a well-established agency based in Philadelphia, became involved in radio as early as 1922 while serving its client AT&T,
and by 1923 it was also helping produce *The Eveready Hour* for its
client National Carbon Co. *The Eveready Hour* was probably the first
sponsored program distributed to multiple stations simultaneously; a
variety show, it featured the announcer Graham MacNamee and performers such as Will Rogers and Art Gillham, the "Whispering Pianist." N. W. Ayer, which had already claimed to have founded the first
agency copy department, the first agency art department, and the first
agency publicity department, now also claimed to have founded the
first agency radio department.[61] N. W. Ayer leader H. A. Batten claimed
for his agency nearly every innovation that occurred in early radio
programming, including the first "drama-type program designed for
broadcasting" in 1924, the first adaptation of a full-length novel in

1926, the first variety show in 1926, and the first "informal commercials" with Jack Benny in 1932.[62] Whatever the truth of these claims, they served to promote N. W. Ayer to potential clients, positioning the agency at the cutting edge of advertising practice.

National Carbon Co.'s incentive for sponsoring radio programming is obvious in a 1927 print advertisement (see Figure 3-1).[63] As manufacturer of Eveready radio batteries, National Carbon hoped to stimulate radio set and battery sales. Under the headline "Perfecting the gift of radio" and an illustration of a family enjoying gifts beside a Christmas tree, the text explains that "When you give the great gift of a radio set, remember that you are giving not merely a handsome, intricate and sensitive instrument, but you are also giving radio reception, radio enjoyment, radio itself." N. W. Ayer's ad copy thus emphasizes not just the technical quality of the product—radio batteries—but also the "enjoyment" of radio entertainment, the actual interest of radio listeners. Acknowledging that buyers seek radios that reliably provide entertainment, the text further explains that Eveready batteries are so dependable that they will provide "hours, days, weeks and months of use, of solid enjoyment of radio at its best." Integrated into the ad is a reminder: "Tuesday night is Eveready Hour Night," including a list of every radio station carrying the program. Along with the tag line "Radio is better with Battery Power," the ad concludes with the urgent reminder that "The air is full of things you shouldn't miss."

Although its client AT&T was the impetus for N. W. Ayer's initial involvement in radio, the agency culture at N. W. Ayer was not well suited for radio.[64] At least one agency leader, Wilfred Fry, disliked radio advertising.[65] The radio department was never well integrated into the rest of the agency and was dismissively called the "wireless department" by some.[66] N. W. Ayer's longtime relations with print media such as the *Saturday Evening Post* predisposed its leaders to consider radio as an adjunct. Even at the peak of radio revenues, in the late 1930s and early 1940s, N. W. Ayer leaders believed radio should be used only moderately and in tandem with other media.[67] N. W. Ayer therefore did not pursue radio accounts, and other agencies quickly took the lead, especially after the Philadelphia-based agency moved its broadcasting department from New York back to Philadelphia. New

The Literary Digest for December 17, 1927

Perfecting
the gift of radio

Everady's greatest provider of Battery Power—the Eveready Layerbilt "B" Battery No. 486.

Radio is better

WHEN you give the great gift of a radio set, remember that you are giving not merely a handsome, intricate and sensitive instrument, but you are also giving radio reception, radio enjoyment, radio itself. So give a receiver that can use the best source of radio power—batteries, for batteries perfect the performance of a radio receiver. The power they provide is pure D. C., Direct Current, which is entirely silent. Battery Power will insure the enjoyment of the listener, for battery-run sets produce exactly the tone their designers built into them.

All Eveready "B" Batteries will give you the vital qualities of Battery Power. Behind Eveready Radio Batteries are 33 years of dry battery making, of pioneering, invention,

with Battery Power

discovery, continual leadership. Buy Eveready Radio Batteries and ahead of you are hours, days, weeks and months of use, of solid enjoyment of radio at its best.

For modern receivers, choose the Eveready Layerbilt "B" Battery No. 486, built according to a radically new design that gives it ample and even excess capacity to meet the demands of powerful sets. This battery is the longest lasting of all Evereadys. Its unique, patented construction packs the maximum possible quantity of active materials within a given space, and also

makes those materials more efficient producers of current.

NATIONAL CARBON CO., INC.
New York [UCC] San Francisco
Unit of Union Carbide and Carbon Corporation

Tuesday night is Eveready Hour Night—
9 P. M., Eastern Standard Time

WEAF–*New York*	WOC–*Davenport*
WJAR–*Providence*	WCCO {*Minneapolis* / *St. Paul*}
WEEI–*Boston*	
WFI–*Philadelphia*	WDAF–*Kansas City*
WGR–*Buffalo*	KSD–*St. Louis*
WCAE–*Pittsburgh*	WRC–*Washington*
WSAI–*Cincinnati*	WGY–*Schenectady*
WTAM–*Cleveland*	WHAS–*Louisville*
WWJ–*Detroit*	WSB–*Atlanta*
WGN–*Chicago*	WSM–*Nashville*
	WMC–*Memphis*

Pacific Coast Stations—
9 P. M., Pacific Standard Time

KPO–KGO–*San Francisco*	KFI–*Los Angeles*
KFOA–KOMO–*Seattle*	KGW–*Portland*

EVEREADY
Radio Batteries

The air is full of things you shouldn't miss

Figure 3-1. Eveready: "Perfecting the gift of radio." (*The Literary Digest,* 17 December 1927, n.p.)

York had developed as the center for most radio production, and when given the choice of going "ninety miles to Philadelphia as opposed to going across the street to a New York agency," most broadcast advertisers found other agencies.[68] By 1932, in the estimation of competitor JWT's Robert Simon, N. W. Ayer's radio star had fallen. Its good reputation from producing *The Eveready Hour* had dissipated: "Since then, nothing important has emanated from the Ayer offices."[69]

The main competitor to the claim for first agency radio department was Batten Barton Durstine & Osborn. The Batten agency, before it merged with Barton Durstine & Osborn (BDO) in 1928, had hired George Podeyn (formerly of WEAF) to run its radio department, and BDO had hired Arthur Pryor Jr., the son of a bandleader, for his putative skills in the music industry.[70] As early as 1925, BDO oversaw, but did not produce, radio manufacturer Atwater Kent's presentations of the Metropolitan Opera.[71] BBDO hedged its claim by saying it had established the "first complete radio department" in about 1926.[72] Among BBDO's hires after the merger in 1928 were an NBC executive, Herbert Foster, and a former WEAF programmer, Annette Bushman.[73] Radio's chief supporter at BBDO was Roy Durstine, a vocal proponent of agency involvement in the medium. Although one of its most important programs, the Atwater Kent program, was not produced by the agency, Durstine was convinced by client interest in radio that agencies should take a stronger role in programming.[74] In 1928, BBDO oversaw five programs in addition to the Atwater Kent program: *General Motors Family Party, Soconyland Sketches, National Home Hour, Happy Wonder Bakers*, and *The Armstrong Quakers*, all but the last broadcast on WEAF.[75] BBDO's radio department soon became a general selling point for the agency; having a radio department indicated a facility for forward thinking, modern technical know-how, and serious commitment to the cultural uplift of the masses. In a 1930 advertisement to the trade, BBDO boasted of a radio staff of twenty-three, "which is becoming as familiar with this new art as it is with any of the older forms of advertising."[76] BBDO also noted that, with three exceptions, "the creative work of writing, rehearsing and directing . . . is all ours."[77] By 1933, the trade magazine *Variety* described BBDO as "innovators of the big name and money star" programs for their institutional advertising clients, General Electric, General Motors, and Atwater Kent.[78]

Lord & Thomas, the large Chicago-based agency led by Albert Lasker, became involved in radio on behalf of one of its clients, RCA, parent company of NBC. However, because of its relationship with the network, Lord & Thomas left program production to NBC.[79] Lord & Thomas's most significant action in early radio was to pick up what would become the *Amos 'n' Andy* show, then locally syndicated out of Chicago, and put it on the NBC network in August 1929. The spectacular rise in sales for *Amos 'n' Andy*'s first sponsor, Pepsodent, helped establish national network programs as significant advertising vehicles.[80] *Amos 'n' Andy*, firmly based in minstrel traditions, featured white actors performing in aural blackface as versions of the minstrel characters Jim Crow and Zip Coon. Its explosive popularity single-handedly raised audience awareness of radio networks.[81] Although it was closer in format to today's situation comedies than soap operas, open-ended storylines about Amos and Andy's migration north, their efforts to run a business, and their romantic entanglements continued over weeks and months, keeping listeners returning for the latest developments. Reputedly, movie theaters piped in the weekly broadcast in order to retain their audiences. Although the two performers wrote the program, L&T supplied the brief advertising announcements—one minute at the opening and a short announcement at the end. Announcer Bill Hay read this 1932 commercial after the opening theme song—note how it reflects the hard sell tenets of L&T's Lasker:

As we have told you repeatedly, Pepsodent Tooth Paste today contains a new and different cleansing and polishing material. We want to emphasize the fact that this cleansing and polishing material used in Pepsodent Tooth Paste is contained in no other tooth paste. That is very important. It is important to us, because Pepsodent laboratories spent eleven years in developing this remarkable material. It is important to the public, because no other cleansing and polishing material removes film from teeth as effectively as does this new discovery. What's more, this new material is twice as soft as that commonly used in tooth pastes. Therefore, it gives greater safety, greater protection to lovely teeth. Use Pepsodent Tooth Paste twice a day—See your dentist at least twice a year.[82]

The earmarks of reason-why advertising appear in the repetition of key points ("cleansing and polishing"), the claim of scientific progress ("Pepsodent laboratories"), use of superlatives ("new and different," "new discovery," "greater safety"), and multiple "reasons why" to buy the product.

By 1933, *Variety*'s assessment was that L&T's admen were "specialists in human-interest script serials," which also included *Clara, Lu 'n' Em* (1931–36) and *The Goldbergs* (1929–46).[83] The former, one of the very first radio serials and sponsored by Colgate-Palmolive, sold Super Suds dishwashing soap while the three title characters chatted and gossiped. *The Goldbergs*, like *Amos 'n' Andy*, was an ethnic humor situation comedy, in this case about a Jewish family in the Bronx, with continuing storylines written by their chief performers. Each program traced the struggles of immigrants (foreign and domestic) sympathetically, but through the strategy of illustrating their characters' "cultural incompetence" with accents, dialect, cultural confusion, and "fish out of water" situations, perhaps flattering the potential user of Super Suds or Pepsodent for a superior level of general know-how that might be applied to the choice of "scientifically proven" domestic products.[84]

By 1928, a number of other New York agencies had begun radio departments, including Lennen & Mitchell, Thomas & Logan, Young & Rubicam, Frank Seaman, Erwin Wasey, and Calkins & Holden.[85] Lennen & Mitchell's early programs featured stars such as Paul Whiteman and Fred Waring, well-known bandleaders.[86] Initially, Erwin Wasey's department operated almost independently of the rest of the agency. However, once the radio department was better integrated, according to JWT's Simon, "What followed was a regime that probably holds all records for literal-mindedness. It obeyed all rules, including imaginary ones. If a music program had been approved by a client, no deviation could be made under any circumstances. . . . The agency allowed itself no latitude, no discretion." Simon's evaluation of the Erwin Wasey radio department by 1932 was that, though headed by "a bit of an aesthete," it still suffered from too much "adherence to routine" and "very little creative talent."[87] However self-serving Simon's critique of a competitor, his summary points up an important dilemma in early radio departments: to hew closely to client demands, or to develop independent expertise?

H. K. McCann, soon to become McCann-Erickson, would found a radio department, as would Campbell Ewald. In 1930, McCann's director of radio, Ruth Cornwall, asserted that radio should be regarded "as a supplementary medium" to print. The direct sales pitch should be made in print; on radio, only the advertiser's name and product should be mentioned.[88] One of McCann's first programs was for Chesebrough Manufacturing Co.'s Vaseline. In a series of sketches about small-town life, with a "simple, homely and old fashioned" atmosphere, characters integrated Vaseline into their conversations, introducing its various uses.[89] By 1933, McCann-Erickson oversaw programs for Standard Oil featuring the Marx Brothers and music stars.[90]

Young & Rubicam (Y&R), founded by defectors from N. W. Ayer, started its department in 1928 in order to sell a daytime radio program for women called *Radio Household Institute*.[91] The program consisted mostly of advice, tips, and recipes, many of which involved the sponsors' household products. This early instructional format would soon be jettisoned in favor of more entertaining formats for housewives, specifically serials. By the mid-1930s, Y&R had developed a major radio department, led by Hubbell Robinson, who would later run programming at CBS Television. Despite founder Raymond Rubicam's distaste for radio advertising, the radio department was an important innovator, developing a staff that wrote all of its programs and in which there was "a constant striving for novelty."[92] Y&R understood early the value of innovation and novelty for attracting audiences and developed its radio department to exploit that understanding.

J. Walter Thompson recruited former WEAF staffer William Ensign to help start its radio department in 1927. Gerard Chatfield and Roosevelt Clark also joined JWT from NBC in 1928.[93] Ensign, who came to JWT as a radio man, not an adman, had to build interest in radio not only among JWT's clients but among agency personnel as well. He wrote articles for the in-house news organ to promote radio use and in a staff meeting confessed that JWT's relative slowness to expand into radio might be his fault: "I probably have not been as aggressive as I should have been in trying to sell you gentlemen on the medium."[94] Ensign felt his closeness to radio, after his experience producing *Roxy and His Gang* at WEAF, might have blinded him to how others perceived it. *Roxy and His Gang* had been an extremely successful musical variety show featuring Samuel Rothafel, the entertainment impresario; its success informed his enthusiasm for radio, which clashed with the skepticism of other JWT departments, which viewed it as new competition for billing dollars. In 1928, explaining that radio was in all their interests, Ensign remarked, "It's not billings alone but the fact that I feel that some J.W.T. clients are missing a good thing in not being on the air."[95] JWT leader Stanley Resor then exhorted his staff to cooperate with Ensign and help him with client contacts. At this time, JWT had only one client on the air, Maxwell House coffee, but within a few years, it became one of the largest radio agencies. By early 1930, radio head John Reber reported that JWT oversaw thirty-one programs a week that were "successful from a business point of view."[96] JWT claimed 14 percent of the commercial radio "business" in 1932; by 1933, NBC recognized JWT as its "largest revenue producing agency."[97] By 1933, *Variety*'s analysis of agencies placed JWT near the top as "the flashy lads of the air" and "a staunch proponent of the use of stage and screen names and one of the most successful air merchandisers in the business."[98]

As advertising agencies became more involved with radio, their radio departments evolved. At first these departments were loosely structured and staffed, but gradually, as radio revenues increased, they expanded and professionalized. In a few years, more potential employees had had radio experience, and so the labor pool widened and deepened. An adman named M. Lewis Goodkind described this process as occurring in three phases.[99] First was the "delegated authority" stage, when agencies gradually took over more and more radio production tasks and, to run their radio departments, hurriedly hired anyone who claimed to know something about the medium, such as "the sponsor's nephew." During this phase, according to JWT's Simon, the radio department was often a "one-man" operation, run by announcers or "broken-down actors" or agency "relatives who had to have jobs, or for

venerable employees who had never been good at anything."[100] The
second phase was the "performer's vogue," when agencies looked to
musicians and theatrical directors for guidance in running radio departments. The third and final phase was when an agency at last developed a fully professional radio staff. In the case of JWT, one of the
first radio department heads was a musician named Henry Joslyn, who
took over the radio department in 1929. When radio billings began to
expand rapidly, Joslyn was replaced by former "new business" manager Reber, an account executive charged with finding new clients for
JWT. His ability to "sell" (or sign) new clients won him the position of
radio department head over competitors Joslyn and Aminta Cassares,
who managed the women's division.[101] His appointment signaled the
new importance of the radio department within the agency. Joslyn,
the musician, and Cassares, the women's specialist, despite experience
apparently relevant to radio programming, lost the contest to an executive who was able to prove he could deal with clients effectively. Reber
went on to build one of the largest and most stable agency radio
departments.

The advertising agencies that first entered radio usually fit one of
two categories: the well established and the upstart. The former, such
as BBDO, JWT, or N. W. Ayer, developed radio departments as an
extra service in order to retain already existing clients. However, these
agencies were also staffed with many conservative executives who did
not necessarily trust radio advertising. While the establishment connections of these agencies helped bring more conventional advertisers
into the untested medium, their underlying bias toward print media
may have undermined their ability to innovate in the aural medium of
radio. The latter, the upstart agency, such as Benton & Bowles, founded
in 1929, turned to radio as a way of getting started in business and to
attract clients away from agencies unwilling to manage their clients'
radio needs. Benton & Bowles, unfettered by convention, changed
radio practices in key ways. Another major radio agency, Blackett-
Sample-Hummert, founded in 1927, focused most of its efforts on
radio advertising, becoming one the single largest buyers of airtime
during the 1930s. Whether an agency moved into radio for defensive

or offensive competitive purposes, by the mid-1930s radio was acknowledged as a powerful advertising medium.

Translating Print Strategies to Radio: "They Sway Millions as If by Some Magic Wand"

As radio advertisers moved away from indirect advertising approaches, such as naming the program after the product, and toward direct advertising approaches that included product information, admen accustomed to print media struggled to adapt. Many print strategies were obviously inapplicable; there were no visual illustrations or typefaces in radio. Nonetheless, print-trained admen sought to translate what they could into the new medium. In a 1930 staff meeting, JWT staffer George Faulkner listed the challenges of radio: "1. Lack of visual aids. 2. Fleeting impression. 3. The human voice in place of type as medium. 4. Censorship barriers. 5. Need for showmanship."[102] The first issue, the lack of visual aids, stymied admen who distrusted a nonvisual approach to selling; one BBDO staffer worried that "the ear as a sense organ has never been educated as the eye has been."[103] JWT radio department head Reber argued, in contrast, that communication was in the first instance an oral experience and thus radio, by "speak[ing] to a lot of people at once," was "getting back to the first principle" of communication.[104] Unable to rely on well-known visual strategies, admen had to invent new aural strategies, such as sound effects, that would "educate the ear" to receive advertising messages.

The second problem, radio's "fleeting impression," was a result of its evanescence. Once the message was out on the air, it could not be recaptured, measured, repeated, or reviewed by listeners. Magazine readers were able to reread an advertisement, but a radio listener had no means of rehearing one. What if audiences did not listen closely enough, or grasp the meaning well enough? Rather than compare radio to print, consider it analogous to billboards, advised JWT staffer Colwell, and effective even though passing viewers may catch only a glimpse, an impression, and may not see the entire message. Colwell advised radio copywriters to keep the advertising copy simple and "avoid quick transitions, complex ideas, or concepts which the listener cannot grasp as the words fly by."[105] Keeping copy short and simple was also necessary because of the limitations of audience attention. Young & Rubicam radio department head Robinson underlined this principle when he explained that "the public's memory is conspicuous chiefly for its brevity, its loyalty chiefly conspicuous for its ability to waver."[106] Admen could not rely on audiences to focus or remember; they would have to catch an audience's attention and make the message memorable.

As to the third issue, the use of the human voice as a medium rather than typeface or type size, some admen extolled the advantages of voice over print. Referring to the admen who wrote radio scripts that incorporated both program and advertising copy, adman George W. Smith claimed, "Continuity writers have transformed the *divinity* of the printed word into the still more divine eloquence of the spoken word. They tug at heart strings; they inspire appetites; they change deep-rooted habits. . . . In so doing, they sway millions as if by some magic wand."[107] Other admen did not share Smith's confidence in the power of speech to sway millions. BBDO staffer J. T. W. Martin argued that print was intrinsically more credible: "The very fact that advertising copy is printed lends it a sincere appearance. Any size or style of type seems to stamp a statement as truth."[108] Advertising copy that seemed "sincere" in print, Martin argued, had a different effect when spoken on the air: "It is astonishing how exaggerated and ridiculous an extravagant claim for a product sounds over the air."[109] While claiming that the differences between radio and print advertising had been overblown, another adman acknowledged, "It is, of course, easier to commit the sin of blatancy over the air than in print."[110] How could admen avoid the pitfalls of applying print strategies to radio? Hill Blackett, of Blackett-Sample-Hummert, argued, "There are two entirely different techniques" for copywriting. "One is the technique of the spoken word, and the other the technique of the printed word. . . . [I]n the early days of radio, the commercials sounded like somebody getting up and reading a piece of advertising."[111] Continuity writers, those writing scripts that incorporated both advertising and program text, must, according to one adman, avoid "unnatural or 'advertisy' dialog" that would undercut the seamless integration of program and advertisement.[112]

The program's announcer translated the printed word into the spoken. Announcers mediated between the program and the advertising: When introducing the program and the players, they usually spoke the text of the advertisement as well, in effect representing the sponsor. After a short musical introduction, a 1930 broadcast of *The Coca-Cola Top Notchers* is introduced thus: "Good evening, ladies and gentlemen of the radio audience. This is Graham MacNamee speaking. We bring you a period of delightful entertainment sponsored by Coca-Cola, the pure drink of natural flavors, served nine million times a day."[113] Victor Ratner, from the Lennen & Mitchell agency, characterized announcers as "the 'type-faces' of radio," and as in print, their proper use was essential: "the right announcer adds a dynamic quality to any copy he is given to deliver. He can step-up advertising 'voltage' as much as a poor announcer can step it down."[114] Some announcers were stars in their own right, announced by another, no-name announcer, as in an episode of *The Chase & Sanborn Hour* in which the first announcer introduced the program title "and your host, Don Ameche!"—who then introduced the stars and the sponsor.[115] In a 1930 staff meeting, JWT staffer Colwell described the different styles of well-known announcers: "Graham MacNamee races along, Alwyn Bach is very slow and dignified, Alois Havrilla is about half way between."[116] Some announcers were prized for their skills at delivering the advertisement and setting up the comedy talent, such as Don Wilson for Jack Benny, Bill Goodwin for George Burns and Gracie Allen, and Bill Baldwin for Edgar Bergen and Charlie McCarthy. The continuity writers needed to take their announcer's style into account. As Colwell explained, "A good continuity man will 'write to his announcer.' Like an actor in a play, an announcer suffers when he is given a part that is out of character. Listeners realize . . . when an announcer is saying something that does not sound sincere and spontaneous."[117] Ernest S. Green provided advice to copywriters in a *Printers' Ink Monthly* article titled "What 'Typeface' for Your Radio Commercials?" (see Figure 3-2).[118] The illustration depicts announcers labeled variously "corny" or "smooth" or

WHAT "TYPE FACE" for Your Radio Commercials?

by ERNEST S. GREEN

Figure 3-2. "What 'Type Face' for Your Radio Commercials?" (Ernest S. Green, "What 'Typeface' for Your Radio Commercials?" *Printers' Ink Monthly*, May 1938, 18–19.)

"punchy" or "factual" and then dressed to reflect that style: The "corny" announcer wears a farmer's hat, the "punchy" announcer wears boxing gloves. To emphasize the importance of announcement style consistency, a list of questions set in different fonts further illustrates the issue: "Am I being *smooth* in a Corny Commercial?" and so on.

Agencies worried about their reliance on announcers to mediate between the advertising and the audience. JWT's Colwell warned his coworkers that one could never be sure if an announcer would "say it in the right way." Consequently, JWT exercised close control over announcers. According to Colwell, "To insure this we have generally a production man at all of our programs to be certain that the announcer gives the words the exact shade of meaning that they should have."[119] Fears that listeners would be alienated by the apparent insincerity or wooden delivery of an announcer prompted another adman to urge agencies to use announcers whose "words must be felt as well as spoken."[120] Credibility and sincerity depended on announcers' emoting rather than reciting. An announcer who was too glib and smooth could undercut an advertisement's effectiveness. For this reason, the JWT Radio Department would also, on occasion, use a radio performer who was not an announcer to present the advertising message: He or she would provide a "fresh voice, a voice which may not be quite so much on its guard and more sincere, frank and open than [that of] the ordinary 'announcer.'"[121] Authenticity and credibility, then, occasionally required the employment of the not-announcer, whose sincerity would be less questionable.

The push to enter radio in the late 1920s came not from within the advertising industry but from without, especially from clients who wanted to sponsor programs and were frustrated with other program producers. Advertising industry resistance to radio arose primarily from its dependence on print publishers, who feared the competition of a new medium, in addition to concerns that the industry's hard-fought path to professional respectability could be undermined by associations with show business and the memories of patent medicine "medicine shows." Advertising agencies, facing competition for clients from other program producers, soon moved into radio with varying levels of enthusiasm and commitment. Well-established agencies founded radio departments to complete the range of services it could offer clients. Upstart agencies specialized in radio to gain the competitive edge over the more conservative agencies. Once in radio, agencies were responsible for overseeing programming and integrating it with advertising strategies. Translating their print strategies into an aural medium proved challenging because radio's ephemeral nature, lack of visuals, and reliance on human voices limited admen's options. Analogizing the human voice as a "typeface," admen began to explore alternative strategies for engaging audiences. By the beginning of the 1930s, the significance of radio to the advertising industry had become clear. As a JWT staffer explained, "Rarely—if ever—can a single printed advertisement result in doubling returns. . . . In radio, however, this is a rather common experience, and one which we who are immersed in radio day and night are only beginning to understand."[122]

4

"Who Owns the Time?"
Advertising Agencies and Networks Vie for Control in the 1930s

Commercial radio developed in the 1920s amid a booming economy and progressive ideals. However, only a few years after the establishment of national networks, the Crash of 1929 and the ensuing economic crisis of the Great Depression severely challenged the young broadcasting industry. At the moment when radio was poised to complete its transition from a local to a truly national medium, capital markets dried up, consumption dropped, and unemployment soared. And yet, radio grew anyway. Despite the overall drop in consumer spending, the number of radio sets "in use" climbed from 9 million in 1929 to more than 16 million in 1932.[1] Meanwhile, advertising expenditures overall plummeted from about $3.4 billion in 1929 to $2.3 billion in 1931.[2] Newspaper advertising expenditures dropped from $260 million in 1929 to $160 million in 1932.[3] However, national advertisers on network radio increased their spending from $18 million in 1929 to $39 million in 1932. Despite a dip in radio advertising expenditures between 1933 and 1935,[4] by 1937 total annual advertising expenditures on radio (local and national) had climbed to $165 million, matching annual advertising expenditures on magazines.[5] The economic exigencies of the Depression put pressure on the advertising industry, acutely in need of new revenues, to become more involved in radio, the only medium that was growing rather than shrinking.

Pressure to move more forcefully into radio came from three directions: from within the advertising industry, from advertisers, and from broadcasters. Faced with competition from within the industry, agencies offered radio services in order either to build a client list or to retain one. By 1931, the competition among agencies for radio business had grown: As many as 105 agencies handled radio network advertising.[6] Advertisers, a second source of pressure, were increasingly willing, in the face of rapidly dropping consumption levels, to take risks on new strategies, including radio.[7] To satisfy such clients, agencies developed market research techniques, such as surveys, to identify and confirm effective strategies.[8] A third source of pressure were the broadcasters, who were strapped for cash and looking for somebody to pay for programming, because listeners could not be made to pay for it directly.

In the broadcast business model that developed to relieve broadcasters of the burden of program financing, an advertiser, known as the "sponsor," bought a block of time from a broadcaster and then filled it with whatever programs it chose. An advertiser controlled the time it rented, which was called the "time franchise," and could change the programming at will. This model is usually called single sponsorship, because a single advertiser bought a time period and promoted a single product through a program produced and paid for entirely by that advertiser. Advertisers sometimes bought preexisting programs, such as "sustaining" programs—programs sustained at a cost to the broadcaster until they could be sold to an advertiser. Implicit in the term "sustaining" was the broadcaster's expectation to shift program financing and producing to others. By the mid-1930s the networks' focus was not on developing their own programs but on shifting the programming burden to advertisers and their agencies.

If advertisers and their agencies financed and controlled program choices, what was the role of the networks? NBC executive Donald Shaw noted that the key question in the growing conflicts among advertisers, agencies, and networks was "who owns the time and who has a better right to say what is to be done with it?"[9] Agencies, which increasingly oversaw the production of their clients' programs on national networks, had varying relations with broadcasters, ranging from close collaboration to insistent autonomy. The surviving correspondence between agencies and NBC shows how the institutional frameworks for agency involvement in radio evolved during the 1930s. The networks, once they ceded most program control to the advertisers, were nonetheless responsible, via their affiliates, to federal regulators and to the listening public for the quality of their programming. Their efforts to set standards, rules, and limitations on advertisers and their proxies, the agencies, stemmed from a desire, if not to serve the public interest, at least to avoid increased regulatory oversight. The advertisers, having financed, produced, and scheduled the programming, were sure their property rights over programs and time slots should trump the networks' claims for control, and their advertising agencies battled the networks hard in their clients' interests. The conflicts were inherent in the sponsorship business model, problems that would contribute to the formation of a different business model for television, one based on direct network control of programming.

NBC and CBS: Different Attitudes toward Commercialism and Advertising

NBC inherited, via its absorption of AT&T stations, AT&T's "toll broadcasting," a common carrier model in which the broadcaster was the transmitter but not the producer of programming. As part of the AT&T legacy, NBC adhered to a public utility ideal of broadcasting, whereby it provided a public service to all program producers without discrimination. Just as AT&T did not control the content of voice calls, NBC assumed it would not fully control the content of radio programming, except, of course, insofar as the public interest could be affected. The serving of the public interest, formalized in the federal Radio Act of 1927, provided the only justification for NBC's control over programming. From the outset, NBC-produced programs were designed to be sold eventually to advertisers, thus relieving the network of continuing programming costs.[10] RCA, NBC's corporate parent, expected NBC's programming to stimulate the sales of RCA radio sets. Batten Barton Durstine & Osborn (BBDO) executive Howard Angus explained in 1931 that NBC and its parent, RCA, were in "the business of manufacturing electrical gadgets—not entertainment." Because they could not directly recoup programming fees from listeners, according to Angus, "they naturally looked for somebody else to furnish the entertainment necessary if they were to sell radio stations and sets."[11]

NBC's main competitor, CBS, had very different assumptions and goals.[12] CBS was an advertising medium, not a public utility. William Paley, an advertiser himself, located CBS in the heart of the advertising business on Madison Avenue.[13] His development of network compensation for affiliates to carry CBS programming was designed to guarantee audiences for advertisers. In contrast to NBC's high-mindedness, Paley's attempt to raise capital for CBS through an alliance with the Hollywood studio Paramount reflected his view that CBS was in the entertainment business. As a J. Walter Thompson advertising executive explained,

In general their policies reflect the policies of their owners. NBC is a General Electric products [sic]:—conservative, oozes prestige—fixed in its ways and exercises the strictest censorship in the field. . . . Columbia is owned by Paramount-Publix—more liberal—flexible in its set-up—caters a bit more to the advertiser—more progressive in everything but technical development— where NBC and General Electric have them licked.[14]

Despite NBC's technical advantages and its ownership of a greater number of high-power stations, its underlying assumption that programming was a loss leader for radio hardware sales undercut its competitiveness with advertisers. CBS, on the other hand, made advertisers and their needs the main part of its business.[15]

CBS pursued a number of strategies to attract these advertisers. It offered discounts to preferred buyers; it pioneered many audience measurement techniques under the supervision of former adman Paul Kesten and his protégé Frank Stanton. Its research department generated data suggesting the growth and impact of radio in general, not just CBS; this helped agencies convince advertisers to use radio. As Stanton recalled, "We got business that way, not because of our facilities but because we helped the agencies get the business."[16] In 1936 Roy Durstine of BBDO wrote David Sarnoff at NBC directly about why his agency preferred to use CBS: CBS offered better time slots, provided faster clearance of programs because of its better affiliate relations, and supported agency control of programs. Durstine concluded, "[S]omehow we always found Columbia a little easier to deal with than

NBC." He attributed this to rapid growth at NBC and its confusion over its mission and structure.[17]

To advertising agencies NBC appeared indifferent to its clients' interests. The head of the Frank Presbrey agency informed the NBC Sales Department that, in his view, "advertisers failed to receive the cooperation from NBC that they did from CBS, and that something should be done about it if NBC expected to hold its clients."[18] Within NBC itself, members of the Sales Department tried to convince NBC leadership that advertisers were NBC's main customers and those advertisers' interests had to become paramount.[19] Still exasperated as late as 1945 by internal resistance to this view, Sales Department executive Roy Witmer pointed out that many departments at NBC still held the attitude that "a customer"—that is, an advertiser—"was supposed to be a necessary evil" rather than the reason for NBC's existence.[20] However, for NBC's parent, RCA, the customer was not the advertiser but the radio set buyer.[21]

Another issue that frustrated advertisers and their agencies was the difference between NBC and CBS regarding the promotion of programs. According to NBC's promotion director, the Sales Department was not allowed to use broadcast time to promote programs: "We could not use our own medium to get people to tune in."[22] NBC executives worried that if they helped promote one program for one advertiser, other advertisers would complain of special treatment, and the network's guiding principle was nondiscrimination among clients. NBC executives also assumed that spending money on print advertising for programs would cut into the network's margins too deeply.[23] But agencies complained about this false economy. The agency Benton & Bowles accused NBC in 1933 of having "fallen down on publicity and propaganda" compared with CBS.[24] B&B cited CBS's publicity expenditures of $25,000 a year for a B&B program in order to pressure NBC into providing similar publicity for an NBC-carried B&B program. The NBC Sales Department disapproved of this extra service; it feared that if print editors became "swamped" by radio promotion requests, they would refuse to carry program promotion at all.[25]

Thus, fears of offending constituencies, whether they were regulators, audiences, print media, or competing advertisers, kept NBC from fully exploiting its own resources to expand audiences, and so CBS gained on it throughout the 1930s. In 1932, CBS sold $12.6 million in airtime to advertisers, NBC $26.5 million, more than twice as much. By 1937, CBS had more than doubled its sales to $28.7 million, while NBC's sales had grown only by half, to $38.6 million.[26]

Network and Agency Turf Wars

Networks and agencies engaged in a number of turf wars. Who had priority with the sponsor? Who had editorial control? How did editorial control affect the paying of commissions? How was audience size measured and how would audience size affect the price of airtime? Who decided which time slot went to which advertiser, and for what reason? As to the first issue, access to networks' and agencies' mutual client, the advertiser, a 1933 NBC pamphlet instructed its employees that "Cooperation with agencies [is] essential to the welfare of broadcast advertising," but the network nonetheless refused such cooperation at times. For example, as a matter of policy, NBC refused to allow offsite broadcasts from agency facilities.[27] More informally, NBC staffers resented and sometimes tried to circumvent the agencies' control over their access to advertisers. NBC sales executive Roy Witmer complained about BBDO's "insistence upon standing between us and our clients."[28] Another staffer complained that agency executives leveraged their control by withholding information from NBC: "[B]y continually remaining incommunicado, they are enhancing their own importance."[29] Sometimes NBC staffers threatened to sidestep the agencies and go directly to sponsors if "we cannot get reasonable cooperation" from the agencies.[30] The agencies, on the other hand, understood that a great part of their leverage in negotiating with the networks over such issues as scheduling, time rates, and program content depended on their exclusive control over access to sponsors. Young & Rubicam vice president Chester LaRoche wrote to Witmer reminding him of the importance of maintaining the proper lines of communication. Pointing out that "We understand your salesmen have been contacting our clients without working through and with our Radio Department,"

LaRoche warned NBC, "You can expect on our part the same cooperation that we know we are going to get from you."[31]

Despite the NBC salesmen's chafing at this dependency, they knew
that the agencies could easily switch networks and so NBC could not
afford to alienate them.[32] One case, involving the advertiser Chevrolet,
illustrates the uncomfortable position into which network salesmen
were forced by this system. The president of Chevrolet, a Mr. Coyle,
lost a time slot on NBC when negotiations over time purchase stalled.
He therefore moved his account to CBS, complaining in a letter to NBC
that the network's salesmen had been lax in pursuing his account
when they failed to contact him directly during these negotiations.
When Coyle's letter arrived at NBC, a salesman involved in the case
thus defended himself to NBC executive Edgar Kobak: "I believe you
realize what would have happened had I gone direct [sic] to Mr. Coyle
over the heads of the Agency, the Advertising Manager and the Sales
Manager."[33] Circumventing the agency would have endangered future
relations with not only that advertiser but all advertisers controlled by
that agency.

Another turf war concerned editorial control. In 1933 eighty agencies bought airtime from NBC. Of these, according to one NBC staffer,
"More than half build their programs with practically no deference to
the NBC."[34] By 1934 one NBC staffer would complain that it was not
always clear that NBC knew "what goes on in its own building."[35]
While both NBC and CBS had programming departments, CBS actively
supported agency control of programming. Although NBC's Program
Department, headed by the renowned theater producer John Royal,
produced "sustaining" programs for potential sale to advertisers,[36] Royal's efforts were often undermined by competition from agencies,
which had a much better sense of what would appeal to advertisers.

In radio, there were no publishers: Advertisers and their agencies
bought media time *and* provided media editorial content—that is, programming. On the whole, agency production of programming appeared to suit everyone concerned: The networks had programming
without expense, the advertisers had trusted delegates to handle their
radio needs, and the agencies had a reliable source of revenue from

clients they might thus retain. However, the shift of editorial responsibility to the agencies was a marked departure from the traditional media advertising business model. As BBDO executive Howard Angus pointed out, by handing over responsibility for programming to the advertisers and their agencies, "the radio companies actually said to the advertisers: 'Here is a nice chair marked "Editor" and another nice chair marked "Circulation Manager." Would you kindly sit in both and do their jobs as well as your own?'"[37] Rather than buy interstitial pages adjacent to editorial content, as in a magazine or newspaper, advertisers were required to fill radio time with editorial content (as the "Editor") as well as attract audiences (as the "Circulation Manager").

This departure from tradition led to two crucial issues: whether or not the agencies, as proxies for the advertisers, would have control over content—act as their own editors, in other words—and, even more important, how they would be compensated for it. The two issues were related: By establishing editorial control, agencies could more clearly justify their commissions. Agencies approached these issues in various ways. To cover the costs of programming (and make a profit on it), some agencies charged the advertiser a commission on fees paid to "talent"; others charged flat fees for producing programs. The major radio agencies, including JWT, B&B, and Y&R, insisted on tight control, refusing to subcontract out programming to the networks or independent producers. Other agencies used the networks' programming departments or collaborated with other program producers. Lord & Thomas (L&T), the leading agency to disavow program control, preferred to function as an overseer of network-produced programs and therefore charged no commission on talent fees. Not coincidentally, L&T had close ties to NBC management through its client RCA. A JWT staffer noted that, although L&T's arrangement that NBC handle programming might have been useful from an "administrative point-of-view," its disengagement from program control "eliminates automatically a large revenue, at the same time making the agency responsible for work over which it has no final control."[38] Some agencies with no radio departments and no means of producing programming were reluctant to enter the radio business at all because, as an NBC pamphlet written for time salesmen explained, "an agency may fear that if a major part of the appropriation is diverted into radio programs which the agency does not prepare, the agency commission may become the subject of argument and the agency's hold on the account may be weakened."[39]

Because agency commissions were based on time sales, a third turf war concerned how to set the price of time. In publishing, the price of page space was valued by circulation—that is, the number of issues published and sold. An ostensibly independent bureau disseminated circulation figures relied upon by both buyers and sellers of space. Measurements of the value of radio time were, in contrast, relatively primitive in the 1930s, drawn from a variety of sources, including radio set sales, listener mail, telephone surveys, and signal reach. Networks set time prices based on educated guesses of listenership: They priced evening hours at double the rate of daytime hours on the assumption that evening audiences were larger. Unlike print media, where print runs could provide some kind of evidence of circulation, radio's ephemeral nature allowed no such post-broadcast verification strategy; radio "circulation," wrote advertising analyst Warren Dygert, "is a very elastic affair."[40] The agency Kenyon & Eckhardt once refused to pay NBC for time without "proof of performance" that the program reached the intended audience, arguing that such proof is normal for other media and that "There seems no justification for making an exception in the case of radio."[41] Moreover, even if "circulation" could be ascertained, there was no proof that a large audience guaranteed sales increases. Even C. E. Hooper, whose Hooper Ratings were an early audience measurement tool, acknowledged that "there is no clear-cut relationship between listening audience size and sales."[42]

There was another important difference between print and radio "circulation." In print media the publishers provided the editorial content; on radio, advertisers had to provide it themselves. Thus, as CBS executive Howard Meighan explained, "While a Chase and Sanborn Tea ad in the *Bulletin* would have little, if any, effect on the paper's circulation, a Chase and Sanborn Tea program on a radio station would have a substantial effect on the station's circulation," or listenership.[43] The onus, then, was on the advertiser to produce its own circulation or listenership. As the General Foods executive Ralph Starr Butler explained, "There is no circulation guarantee on the air; the advertiser must guarantee it for himself."[44] Paradoxically, however, when advertisers succeeded in drawing larger audiences, they were then subject to airtime rate increases. In a sharply worded letter to the president of NBC, the head of the Compton agency complained about NBC's rate hikes:

[Programs] are the product of the advertiser and his agent, and not the product of the networks. To attempt to justify a unilateral increase in rates on the score that more people are listening longer hours to radio programs as a whole, in effect, is to say, "The more capable you, my customer, are, the more I will charge you for my facilities."[45]

The agency's outrage over rate increases pointed to a key weakness in the sponsorship business model. As long as advertisers fully financed and controlled the programming, the network would always be vulnerable to the charge that its rate hikes were based on advertiser efforts, not network efforts. Not until the television era, when networks gained ownership stakes in programming and sold the interstitial minutes between programs as magazine publishers sold pages for advertisements, could networks justify increased prices for time by pointing to increased circulation, or viewership.

Advertisers and their agencies often disputed the price of time with the networks. The networks occasionally offered rate discounts to favored or large time buyers. This incensed Arthur Sinsheimer, radio director at the Peck agency, who complained to NBC president Merlin Aylesworth about competing agencies' enjoying "preferential rates."[46] Despite NBC's assertion that it followed its rate card and favored no agency over another, NBC did in fact extend preferences. In one case, NBC had been charging preferential prices to Procter & Gamble for years because it was one of the first advertisers to buy a large amount of daytime hours. In 1938 NBC executive C. E. Rynd tried to calculate the costs and benefits of discontinuing the P&G discounts because, he argued, once network overhead was accounted for, NBC may have been broadcasting the P&G serials at a net loss. Addressing the problem of alienating an advertiser, the primary deterrent NBC faced when trying to renegotiate these arrangements, Rynd made the following argument:

There is no doubt that P&G helped us build daytime business; however four years at cut rate prices certainly should be sufficient repayment. I see no need to fear that P&G will withdraw all of its business from NBC because it will be impossible for them to find suitable time on any other network, and certainly the additional profit to us of over half a million dollars a year should be reason enough for us to overlook the possible strained relationship that might result temporarily.[47]

Rynd's proposal reflects the fact that by the late 1930s the demand for time exceeded the supply.

The fourth turf war concerned scheduling and the allocation of time slots. The two major networks approached the problem very differently. CBS offered prime time slots and discounts to attract advertisers to its network. NBC tried to treat all customers alike, as if it were a nondiscriminating public utility, and so as a policy did not provide special deals to advertisers. NBC's policy of equal treatment prevented it from effectively adjudicating disputes with advertisers over time slots and issues of station carriage; CBS, in contrast, gave prompt attention to advertisers with clearance and scheduling problems, aiming to satisfy any dissatisfied customers.[48] NBC and CBS also differed in how they sold time slots. NBC's policy was to sell a time slot to the first advertiser who wanted it, and then allow that advertiser to keep the time slot as long as it liked. The advertiser controlled and programmed its "time franchise." NBC kept a waiting list ("abeyance") in case a time slot opened up and then methodically offered the time slot to the next advertiser on the list. This policy catered to incumbent advertisers and prevented other advertisers newer to radio from gaining access to prime time. CBS kept no elaborate waiting lists; instead it sold time slots to the highest bidder, allowing newer advertisers to use radio.

Although CBS preferred higher-paying advertisers to advertisers with seniority, neither CBS or NBC could control the schedule effectively because advertisers and their agencies selected the programs. An agency would develop a program geared to its client's advertising needs but without regard to the genre of program scheduled before or after it, or to which audiences might already be tuned in. So incompatible programs would be juxtaposed: A large portion of an audience tuned in to a comedy program sponsored by one advertiser at 8:00 P.M. might abruptly tune out the network when a historical drama came on at 9:00 P.M. Network time sales policies prevented networks (or advertisers) from building audience flow, or the movement of audience attention from one program to the next. Print media space pricing, on the other hand, depended on adjacencies and contexts. Advertisers sought editorial content that would provide an appropriate context for their advertising and attract the consumers appropriate for their products. In broadcasting, as the advertising analyst Herman Hettinger pointed out, the advertiser "has little or no control" of what preceded or followed its program.[49] Although some advertisers sought better adjacency policies, as long as advertisers controlled their individual time slots, network management of the schedule was limited. The need to build audience flow and to shape a program schedule eventually would motivate the networks to assert programming control in the television era.

Until then, however, the networks adjudicated scheduling conflicts not according to program and audience flow but according to the market power of the advertiser. For example, when Palmolive wanted to move to an earlier time slot and threatened to take its $4 million per year's worth of business to CBS if NBC did not offer it one, NBC sales staff negotiated with other advertisers to give up a time slot for Palmolive, only to have one renege on such a promise. After threats of legal action, NBC finally settled with Palmolive in exchange for a merchandising subsidy.[50] In other cases, when NBC pre-empted some advertisers for holiday programming or sports events, those advertisers would threaten to move to CBS, and NBC would offer "make-goods," or free time to make up for the time pre-empted. NBC insisted to the advertisers that its commitment to public interest required that it pre-empt some advertiser time, yet without full control over the schedule NBC had to placate its advertisers however it could.[51]

Some NBC executives, including Edgar Kobak, tried to address advertisers' dissatisfaction with the lack of "availabilities." Kobak handled a number of advertiser issues while he worked at NBC, and when he left NBC to join the advertising agency Lord & Thomas, he wrote his former NBC colleagues about how they could improve the network's relations with advertisers. Kobak advised NBC sales director Witmer to build up the smaller NBC network, known as NBC Blue, for sponsorship. This network, in contrast to the more commercial NBC Red network with its popular advertiser-sponsored programs, was supposed to provide more public service–oriented and culturally uplifting programs. Its purpose was to demonstrate to regulators and radio critics that NBC did provide cultural and educational programming despite the increasing commercialism of the Red network. At the time of Kobak's memo, many prime time slots on the Blue network were not controlled by advertisers, so he urged his former colleagues at NBC to release some of those slots to advertisers in order to win their loyalty back from CBS.[52]

Program Control: Live Broadcasting and NBC's Continuity Acceptance Department

Networks exerted what control they had over programming mainly by requiring live broadcasts as a means of maintaining discipline over affiliates and guarding monopoly control over New York–based entertainment.[53] Affiliate use of program "transcriptions" (a special type of phonograph record) might allow greater independence from network control, because stations would be free to buy and sell recorded programs outside the networks' centralized control structure. A 1937 NBC memo regarding agency Blackett-Sample-Hummert's request to record programs revealed another reason NBC resisted recordings:

If an advertising agency enters the business of recording they become, insofar as the recording business is concerned, a competitor of NBC and should not, in my opinion, be encouraged in this competition any more than any other competitor.[54]

The networks masked their agenda by justifying this policy with the rhetoric of personalization. A handbook for NBC time salesmen spells out various reasons live programming serves the advertiser's interest:

Show that live programs alone offer the great advantage of establishing personal contact between the advertiser and the public. Stress the advantage of a uniform hour, which builds up its regular audience of loyal listeners. Point out that the network advertiser can keep his programs up-to-the-minute, every week, instead of having to rely on something recorded weeks before.[55]

However, live broadcasts did not necessarily serve advertisers' actual interests. They did not allow for the correction of errors or the prevention of inappropriate ad-libbing, they made it difficult to achieve particular sound effects, and they prevented the re-use of the performance at a different date or place. Arthur Pryor Jr., radio director at BBDO, complained to NBC that its policy of prohibiting recorded sound of any kind was a "handicap" in its competition with CBS. Most local stations, Pryor pointed out, broadcast transcribed (pre-recorded) programs regularly.[56] Yet, though it occasionally bent the no-recording rule, for the most part NBC enforced it as a means of maintaining distribution and content control.

The federal government, through the Federal Communications Commission, could not regulate broadcast content per se without intrusion on First Amendment rights; however, the Communications Act of 1934 required broadcasters to operate in the public interest, convenience, or necessity (PICON). Stations that broadcast programming in violation of the PICON standards risked license revocation by the FCC (though this rarely occurred). The FCC licensed stations, not networks; networks were indirectly regulated through their local station affiliates. Affiliates were supposed to be sensitive to local audiences; audience complaints could trigger an FCC license review. Affiliates could threaten to leave a network if network programming offended audiences and put their licenses at risk. Thus, networks had to manage program standards in order to maintain good relations with affiliates, through which they gained access to local audiences. However, the networks' revenues came from the advertisers, not the affiliates (who were paid by the network). When networks attempted to limit or control advertiser-produced material, they risked offending and possibly losing the source of their revenues, the advertisers. [57] While the live broadcast policy may have helped networks enforce their control over affiliates and scheduling, it simultaneously undermined their control over what actually went out on the air: They had no way to take back or edit a broadcast once it was transmitted.

NBC's method for ensuring appropriate broadcasts was to review scripts at the Continuity Acceptance Department, headed by Janet Mac-Rorie, and to delete from the scripts any potentially offensive references or double entendres in advance of the broadcast. ("Continuity" was the industry term for scripts.) Sometimes entertainers and agencies failed to provide a script soon enough before broadcast. Comedian Fred Allen, for example, wrote his scripts on Sunday night, submitted them to NBC on Monday morning, and wanted them approved by 1:00 P.M. for rehearsal. When Continuity Acceptance requested more time to review the scripts, "this always brings profanity from Allen, protests from the client and a tirade from the agency," according to NBC executive I. E. Showerman. Showerman explained that Allen's sponsor Bristol-Myers was an "old client of ours" that was spending "over a million dollars annually with us," and so, demonstrating a clear awareness of NBC's financial interests, suggested MacRorie drop the request.[58] Even when Continuity Acceptance had enough time to review a script, it lacked control, of course, over the manner of its performance. It failed, for example, to prevent Mae West, in a skit about Adam and Eve on a 1937 episode of *The Chase & Sanborn Hour,* from performing her approved script so lasciviously as to outrage some pure-minded listeners. Nonetheless, the Continuity Acceptance Department served its function of proving to regulators that NBC was indeed working to maintain standards and thereby helped the network avoid increased regulatory oversight.[59]

Advertising executives often complained about Continuity Acceptance. A Y&R executive claimed that, whereas CBS worked in tandem with agencies, NBC attempted to impose unrealistic standards:

CBS . . . assumes that the agency, as much as the network, has no desire to give offense to anyone and thereby injure its client. Their suggestions are always very reasonable and they show an understanding of the problems of the program. . . . NBC, however, as represented by Miss MacRorie's office, functions in the capacity of teachers of wayward children—their attitude being that if they were to relax their vigilance for a second, the agency would exercise no judgment whatsoever.[60]

Nonetheless, many agencies—no matter how vociferously they fought to have their programs and advertisements aired as they wished—expected, and wanted, the networks to take on the role of adjudicator of standards. BBDO radio director Arthur Pryor Jr. gave a speech to the National Association of Broadcasters in 1937, asserting:

The advertiser is not responsible for improving, or even maintaining[,] the quality of your medium. It's up to the broadcasters entirely. And when an advertiser wants to broadcast something that's stupid or in bad taste, you have got to be the one that says: "No."[61]

Admen were generally aware that the overcommercialization of radio could endanger the effectiveness of broadcast advertising and so looked to the networks to preserve acceptable standards much as a magazine publisher would. Robert Colwell at JWT noted in 1930 that network censorship maintained standards of good taste that could only benefit the agency: "All in all we feel that it is a good thing that everybody can't say everything they want to over the air." Considering that the audience included women and children, Colwell continued, "the fact that you are in excellent company on the radio"—that is, the fact that the networks refused to air programs not in "good taste"—and "the fact that the censorship *is* rather strict—[we feel] that these are real assets."[62] Network censorship policies created an environment for the agency's programming and advertising that reduced the risk one advertiser would be adversely affected by another's lack of "good taste."

These debates over censorship illustrate the basic conflict between networks and agencies over programming control. Sponsors, having paid for the time, believed they ought to control the content. The networks, although they had shifted a great deal of the programming responsibility to advertisers, had to answer to audiences and regulators for any programs that offended and so had to impose standards. Having worked for both a network and an agency, Donald Shaw pointed out that the networks were especially vulnerable if "there be one slip of the tongue or dip of the dipthong," and so they had to apply policies that they "hate . . . as much [as] or more than agencies and sponsors do."[63] Shaw suggested relieving the networks of responsibility for policing broadcast content by the appointment of a radio "czar," the equivalent of a Joe Breen of Hollywood's "Hays Office" (otherwise known as the Production Code Administration), who was hired by the film studios to set standards voluntarily followed by all members of the film industry trade organization.[64] A radio czar could regularize policies and standards among networks, agencies, and advertisers. Although never realized, Shaw's proposal reflected the fact that advertisers and their agencies, as well as networks, were frustrated with the lack of clear guidelines. Like the networks, the agencies depended on advertisers for their business and had to deal with their advertisers' demands. Understandably, agency executives preferred that the networks police standards, thus absolving them of any need to contradict their clients.

Who Sets Advertising Standards?

In 1936 NBC ran an ad in the advertising trade magazine *Printers' Ink* addressed to advertisers and their agencies, rather than to listeners, headlined "How NBC Saves Millions of Americans from Red Radio Ears" (see Figure 4-1). Under an illustration of a social gathering in which a gentleman is clearly embarrassing the ladies, NBC explains that the danger of a "naughty number in the wrong company" can happen not just at the "whist club" but also on radio.

That the blight of the misplaced bon mot is apt to cause Red Radio Ears in not *one* American home, but in *millions*. That certain subjects which bloom

HOW NBC SAVES MILLIONS OF AMERICANS FROM RED RADIO EARS

"Oh, I wouldn't tell *that* one, dear"

REMEMBER that prickling sensation which presages the narration of a naughty number—in the wrong company? A number which would strew them in the straw in the livery stable, perhaps, but which would put the chill of death on the Saturday Evening Whist Club? Of course you do.

And your almost audible relief when the raconteur's wife sensed the situation and sweetly Signed Him Off! "There," you said, as your ears cooled, "*is a woman!*"

Multiply this danger by Millions

Perhaps you have never paused to reflect that the same danger is constantly present with radio. That the blight of the misplaced bon mot is apt to cause Red Radio Ears in not *one* American home, but in *millions*. That certain subjects which bloom beautifully and naturally on the shelves of the nation's pharmacies wither and die when introduced as dinner topics.

Here at NBC, we make it *our* job to fend off Red Radio Ears. We keep the family circle soothed and entertained.

Not with any idea of setting ourselves up as a Board of Advertising Morals, but with the conviction that common sense and good taste are ageless. Our Audience Mail Department confirms us—daily. You'd be surprised to learn how evenly the national common sense and good taste are buttered across the country.

Portland dittoes Park Avenue

The word that puts the delicately attuned ears of Park Avenue into the red also tints the ears of Portland, Ore. The exaggerated claim that draws a Bronx cheer north of the Polo Grounds will draw its counterpart—like an echo—in the suburbs of San Diego. The derogatory reference ("Dirty dig," to you boys in the back room) is as swiftly resented in Seattle as in Savannah.

"We're both playing ball for the same team—the advertiser"

NBC is greatly heartened by the cooperation of clients and their advertising agencies. Much remains to be done, but we are on the right track. So far as we are concerned, Red Radio Ears will yet be but a memory—one with red flannel underwear!

NATIONAL BROADCASTING CO., Inc.

AN RCA SERVICE • NEW YORK • CHICAGO • WASHINGTON • SAN FRANCISCO

Figure 4-1. NBC: "How NBC saves millions of Americans from Red Radio Ears." (*Printers' Ink Monthly*, March 1936, 65.)

beautifully and naturally on the shelves of the nation's pharmacies wither and die when introduced as dinner topics. Here at NBC we make it *our* job to fend off Red Radio Ears. We keep the family circle soothed and entertained. Not with any idea of setting ourselves up as a Board of Advertising Morals, but with the conviction that common sense and good taste are ageless.[65]

NBC positions itself here as the guardian of the "family circle" but is careful not to claim itself as the only adjudicator of "good taste." Rather plaintively, NBC explains it is not a "Board of Advertising Morals" yet scolds advertisers for perhaps not understanding that "the word that puts delicately attuned ears of Park Avenue into the red also tints the ears of Portland, Ore." Having made the point about NBC's national reach and the sensitivities of the imagined audience, NBC gestures toward the partnerships it has with its customers, the sponsors: "NBC is greatly heartened by the cooperation of clients and their advertising agencies. Much remains to be done, but we are on the right track." This diplomatic approach, coupled with the commitment to radio as cultural uplift, soon proved unequal to advertisers' shift to the hard sell once the Depression was fully underway.

In 1932, during the worst of the economic crisis, broadcasters were faced with a resolution by the U.S. Senate, driven by complaints about hard sell direct advertising, that radio advertising be limited to program sponsorship (or indirect advertising). The advertising industry, led by the American Association of Advertising Agencies, mounted a vociferous defense of direct advertising on radio. Ad agencies wrote the Federal Radio Commission (the precursor to the Federal Communications Commission) warning that "at least 75 percent of the radio programs will disappear from the air" if program sponsors were prevented from advertising.[66] H. K. McCann, founder of the ad agency McCann-Erickson, argued, "We know of no radio program which contains as great a proportion of advertising to entertainment as any one of the leading newspapers or magazines in this country. Yet we hear no agitation to eliminate the advertising in these publications."[67] The Senate resolution failed. In September 1932, both CBS and NBC announced a new policy allowing "price mentions" for the first time: Advertisers would be allowed to mention a product's price up to two times in a fifteen-minute program or three times in a thirty-minute program. As the trade journal *Printers' Ink* reported, this new policy was in part a response to the Senate resolution. The networks decided to expand advertising because to restrict it further "would drive advertisers from program sponsorship," destroying the advertising revenue business model.[68]

Meanwhile, the networks, especially NBC, promulgated a number of rules and limits on broadcast advertising designed to maintain a sense of decorum and prevent conflicts among sponsors. NBC advertisers were initially discouraged from using superlatives or the word "free" under the assumption that these common advertising strategies would "cheapen" the network.[69] Competitive copy was also disallowed: Advertisers were not supposed to name competing products and disparage them; but the rule was hard to enforce fairly. JWT, representing Chase & Sanborn coffee, invoked this rule to NBC against its competitor Maxwell House, complaining that Maxwell House copy disparaged coffee products packaged in paper bags, as was Chase & Sanborn coffee, in order to promote its coffee packaged in cans. NBC salesman George Frey, however, pointed out that JWT was guilty of infringing the same rule, having aired advertisements claiming that Chase & Sanborn was "a blend of choice costly coffees, not cheap coffee in a costly can."[70] In another instance, Chester Bowles visited NBC, ostensibly hoping to improve B&B's rocky relationship with the network and "anxious to eliminate the arrogant and arbitrary attitude of his employees" toward NBC, but actually to challenge NBC to justify its application of its policies. According to a report to program department head John Royal, Bowles claimed that B&B had never refused to accept in full a policy of NBC once it was sure that the policy was being applied to all comers, but he added that in fairness to his clients, as long as competitive products were allowed to use certain phrases, he could not help but fight for the inclusion of such phrases in his clients' copy.[71] The networks' advertising rules, then, were simultaneously resisted and exploited by advertisers and agencies, who hoped to advance themselves and to maneuver against their competitors through the mediation of the network continuity approval process. The rules provided advertisers and their agents an opportunity to exploit advantages against their competitors, with the networks' participation.

Many of the struggles over advertising standards concerned products of a personal or medicinal nature: laxatives, tonics, yeast, and deodorants. By 1934, CBS and NBC had twenty-eight "medicinal accounts" between them. In answer to criticism that advertising of such products was offensive, the networks attempted to reduce the number of tonic and laxative advertisers.[72] Laxative advertisers canceled some accounts in protest, and one adman argued that laxative advertising was not objectionable in itself: "To cure vulgarity, ban vulgarity, not laxative advertising."[73] However, prominent admen such as Roy Durstine of BBDO supported the reduction of laxative advertising and furthermore recommended that networks exercise even more editorial control by giving "preference in desirable time to those who keep their commercials brief, interesting, nonrepetitive. (A little more spine in the net[work]s and agencies would accomplish this.)"[74] Durstine's point reflected the ongoing concern that excessive commercialism could alienate audiences. Durstine, like many in the industry, believed that the networks should exercise more editorial control to maintain radio's effectiveness.

Janet MacRorie, head of the Continuity Acceptance Department, concurred that the network had allowed too many "medical and nostrum accounts" on the air, and that the "constant bickering" over Continuity Acceptance's efforts to "keep such advertising within the bounds of truth and common sense" was endless as long as there was "no policy on which to challenge the statement made."[75] In 1935, MacRorie undertook an analysis of seven years' worth of Fleischmann's Yeast commercial copy promoting yeast for its supposed medicinal properties as a remedy for headache, fatigue, acne, and constipation. The account, overseen by JWT in both print and radio, increasingly relied on hard sell advertising strategies, such as "expert" testimonials and fear-mongering hyperbole. A typical print ad headline, quoting a mysterious "Dr. Antoine of Paris," announces, "I have treated thousands of cases of Constipation" (see Figure 4-2).[76] MacRorie charted the rise, fall, and rise of acceptable copy from the Fleischmann's account beginning in 1929, when the copy "contained very few exaggerated, unfounded

"I have treated thousands of cases of CONSTIPATION—"

declares Dr. Antoine of Paris

*"The best way
to correct this evil,"*
he states, *"is
to eat fresh yeast."*
Try it now!

DR. ANTOINE is the physician to a European king. He is a specialist on the stomach and intestines. He is one of the most famous diagnosticians in France. *He states:—*

"I have treated thousands of cases of intestinal and stomach disorders. The majority were directly traceable to constipation.

"Unfortunately, the first act of the patient who is constipated is usually to take a laxative. But this helps only temporarily. Next time he needs a still stronger dose.

"In my opinion, the most effective means of correcting constipation is the eating of fresh yeast."

Fleischmann's Yeast is a food. It has the remarkable power to stimulate and literally *strengthen* your intestines. At the same time, it attacks and softens the intestinal wastes so they can be easily cleared away.

In this way yeast brings about regular, *natural* evacuations. And as it gently rids your body of harmful poisons, your "pep" comes back. Headaches go. Breath sweetens. Ugly skin blemishes in most cases very quickly disappear.

And — don't forget — yeast is entirely harmless. It's not a drug in any sense. It's not a medicine. It's richer than any other food in the group of three health-building vitamins—B,G,D.

So add Fleischmann's Yeast to your diet now—just plain, or dissolved in water (about a third of a glass). Eat 3 cakes every day, before meals, or between meals and at bedtime.

You can get Fleischmann's Yeast at grocers, restaurants and soda fountains. For free booklet write Dept. Y-H-2 Standard Brands Inc., 691 Washington St., New York City.

*"Yes, the doctors are right in
what they say about yeast***"*

"I have a job that calls for one long smile," *writes Miss Ruth Clarey, of New York* (at left), "at the reception desk of a big company. But it's hard to be cheerful when you have a headache.

"I had let myself get run-down. Felt 'loggy.' I tried pills to correct my sluggishness, but results were only temporary.

"I took a friend's example—tried Fleischmann's Yeast. In 2 weeks—improvement. Sluggishness left. No more headaches. And back came the smile."

*IMPORTANT

Fleischmann's Yeast for health comes only in the foil-wrapped cake with the yellow label. It's yeast in its fresh, effective form—the kind doctors advise. Ask for it by name!

Figure 4-2. Fleischmann's Yeast: "'I have treated thousands of cases of CONSTIPATION—' declares Dr. Antoine of Paris." (Reproduced in Frank Rowsome Jr., *They Laughed When I Sat Down: An Informal History of Advertising in Words and Pictures* [New York: Bonanza Books, 1959], 171.)

or unpleasant statements." In 1930, MacRorie judged that "Claims [were] stronger and less pleasant in character"; in 1931, "alarmist material was often present. Testimony of doctors is frequently used, and often is unfairly treated to make it appear that they are advising Fleischmann's Yeast more strongly than they actually are." By 1932, at the worst of the economic crisis, the commercials were longer, and their "case histories . . . were tiresome and often unpleasant," filled with more testimony from such characters as "Dr. Georges Faroy of Paris" of the "French Army Bacteriological Laboratories." In 1933, Mac-Rorie found that yeast was advertised as a cure for "faulty elimination" on the testimony of more foreign doctors, who claimed, "When the intestines are sluggish, poisons develop and filter into the blood stream. The whole system is affected . . . the body feels tired; the head is heavy and often aches; . . . digestion becomes slow; and the nervous system is upset." In 1934 the commercials "grew steadily worse until November when a definite improvement could be noted." Before November, "boils, pimples, and similar terms were frequently used," as in: "The skin is an organ of elimination. It naturally breaks out when the system is overloaded with impurities. By ridding you of these poisons quicker, 'XR' Yeast clears your blood sooner. Pimples, boils, and other eruptions disappear in a shorter time." However, by 1935, when pressure had increased to clean up radio continuity copy, MacRorie found a "great decrease in the mentions of constipation, pimples, and similar unpleasant terms."[77]

Because these strategies had provoked the Senate resolution against direct advertising in 1932, NBC hoped the worst elements of the hard sell could be ameliorated through its Continuity Acceptance Department. By February 1936, the network released a report claiming that the department had "succeeded in avoiding 560 violations of NBC's policies," including 164 superlative claims, 88 cases of impropriety, 87 derogatory references to competitors, and 42 unfairly competitive advertisements.[78] MacRorie's quantitative analysis of these prevented violations of advertising standards appeared to prove that NBC was exercising some measure of editorial control. However, ad agencies routinely bypassed Continuity Acceptance by appealing to the Sales

Department or more highly placed NBC executives, who would over-rule MacRorie or negotiate a solution with the agencies. Her department's authority was limited by the immediate financial necessity of accommodating important advertisers.

The existence of the Continuity Acceptance Department, whatever its effectiveness, was useful to both the agencies and the network. For the network, it demonstrated that NBC took seriously Congress's demand that it act in the public interest and that it be responsive to its audience. MacRorie's quantitative accounting of suppressed offensive advertising documented its commitment to the public interest. For the agencies, on the other hand, the Continuity Acceptance Department provided a useful target should their scripts not be broadcast as written. Agencies could tell their clients they'd done their best but NBC had opposed their interests. Furthermore, the Continuity Acceptance Department's rules and standards also provided opportunities for agencies to attack their clients' competition, claiming the competing sponsor was violating a standard, thereby giving agencies another way to prove their worth to their clients.

––––––––––––––

During the 1930s, the networks provided advertisers access to mass audiences and the agencies provided the programming to attract those audiences. This system of interdependence served each; however, ensuing conflicts exposed the inherent flaws in this arrangement. Who was the publisher? The editor? Who should adjudicate disputes and set standards among users? Concerned that advertising excesses would endanger the viability of broadcast advertising, the agencies expected the networks to set and enforce standards, as publishers of magazines would. However, having been handed responsibility for programming, or editorial content, agencies resented network interference with their own programs and advertising.

Differences between the two major networks exacerbated the matter. NBC held on to the common carrier model it inherited from AT&T; its careful policies of waiting lists for time slots and equal treatment of advertising copy, designed to prevent discrimination among its program providers, served only to frustrate its customers and handicap the network in its competition with CBS. CBS, unhampered by ideals of public service and more flexibly attending to advertisers' needs, was still handicapped by the system of single sponsorship. Advertiser control over time slots prevented effective scheduling and the building of audience attention flow from one program to another. The economic exigencies of the Depression underlay the networks' embrace of the single sponsorship model. When the overall economic climate improved, the networks reconsidered. Admen, deeply involved in the conflicts generated by the single sponsorship model, would likewise reconsider its viability in the television age.

5

The 1930s' Turn to the Hard Sell
Blackett-Sample-Hummert's Soap Opera Factory

The impact of the October 1929 stock market crash was not immediately felt or understood by many in the advertising industry. "Business
itself is healthy," argued advertising columnist Kenneth Goode in November 1929.[1] The president of the American Association of Advertising Agencies asserted, "The main damage by the stock market
situation may be psychological and that condition is one which advertising is best able to correct."[2] If the economic crisis was a matter of
perception, according to this rationale, the advertising industry ought
to be able to help solve the crisis. Goode suggested that "While the
bankers are busy on finances, let advertising men volunteer to take
charge of public sentiment."[3] However, the advertising industry itself
soon suffered from the deepening crisis. The massive contraction in
production and consumption in the 1930s not only led to a drop in
advertising revenues but humiliatingly undermined its claim that it
had been partly responsible for the boom. As advertisers cut back on
advertising expenditures to preserve shrinking profit margins, agencies were forced into bankruptcy, consolidations, pay cuts, and layoffs.
The advertising industry was on the defensive during the Depression—not only from disillusioned clients but also from negative public
opinion that buoyed the consumers' movement during the 1930s.[4] To
combat the spiral down in consumption, many advertisers turned to
the hard sell. Top hard sell proponents, such as Frank Hummert, rose
to greater prominence as advertisers hoped that the repetitive, reason-
why, rational appeals of the hard sell would stimulate sales.

The hard sell strategy became particularly prominent on radio,
where Hummert's agency, Blackett-Sample-Hummert (B-S-H), dominated

daytime programming, especially serial dramas aimed at housewives. Hummert's thorough application of hard sell "reason-why" advertising strategies to serial dramas was an almost total integration of advertising theory with practice. While serials had appeared in nearly all media before radio (including books, films, newspapers, magazines, and comic strips), the radio serial, soon known as the "soap opera," was more than a narrative strategy; it was also an *advertising* strategy. An analysis of B-S-H's practices will illustrate their specific and deliberate application of advertising strategies to program texts. B-S-H's production practices, such as its "assembly line" scriptwriting process, strongly influenced subsequent broadcasting production processes. Although Hummert-produced soap operas ended during the early television era, their impact was such that when the prototypical radio era program comes to mind, it is likely to be a Hummert serial.

Advertising on the Defensive during the Depression

Admen faced challenges from two fronts: external critics who demanded reforms and increased federal regulation, and their clients, the advertisers, who questioned advertising's efficacy. On the first front, the level of public criticism was unprecedented in the 1930s. The advertising historian Ralph Hower noted in 1939 that the "public attitude toward advertising and private enterprise as a whole" had gone through a "profound change" at the advent of the Depression, when advertising "was an obvious field for attack."[5] Having appeared blind to the severity of the downturn, admen were, according to Hower, "subjected to public ridicule and to sharp attacks by reformers," forcing change and adjustment in "every phase of advertising."[6] Strategies had to be revamped, reconsidered, and reconfigured. Perhaps admen had overreached as "missionaries of modernity"; they seemed unable to explain the crisis and ill equipped to repair it. In a tell-all book, *Our Master's Voice* (1934), former adman James Rorty exposed the corruptions of the advertising industry as he had experienced them at BBDO. He mockingly described Madison Avenue as a place where appearances were maintained even as the foundation was cut from underneath it: The "priests of the temple of advertising go about the streets in snappy suits and tattered underwear."[7] The magazine *Ballyhoo* (1931–39), a forerunner of the satiric *Mad* magazine, consisted primarily of advertising parodies and proved so popular that it attracted advertisers.[8] Its success, as well as that of imitators, such as *Hullabaloo*, indicated a widening backlash against advertising.

Who was attacking the advertising industry? "The vocal critics," according to one adman, "are mainly: Women's Clubs, the Home Economics Associations, some Government Officials, Consumers Research and the College Campus."[9] If most admen viewed these groups as uninformed or irrelevant, perhaps because they were predominantly female or politically suspect, these "vocal critics" still wielded some political and cultural leverage as their complaints about the gap between the promise of advertising and the reality of product quality seemed increasingly accurate.[10] Consumers' Research, founded in 1931, built a large constituency publicizing defective products. One of its founders, F. J. Schlink, in 1933 published a bestselling expose, *100,000,000 Guinea Pigs*, that accused the industry of deceptive practices.[11] The advertising industry countered the consumers' movement in some imaginative ways. In a move designed to appeal to women listeners, the Philadelphia Club of Advertising Women put on a radio play to build the reputation of advertising with two characters, Aunty Antique, "a lovable, well meaning but skeptical homemaker," and Mary Modern, her "up-and-coming young niece in the advertising business":

Aunty Antique: "You must do all your shopping by the advertisements, then!"

Mary Modern: "Aunty, I do! And it makes dressing so much easier. Why I read all the advertising first to know what's in style!"[12]

Despite such attempts to counter anti-advertising sentiment, the consumer movement grew. By the end of the 1930s, the Consumers Union had a membership of 80,000. The obnoxiousness and potential deceptiveness of hard sell advertising was a handy justification for supporters of increased government regulation who showed their growing power when Congress passed amendments to the 1938 Wheeler-Lea Act, giving the Federal Trade Commission the power to halt unfair or deceptive advertising.[13] The Franklin D. Roosevelt administration pushed to increase the ability of the Food and Drug Administration to regulate advertising as well.

Assuming broadcasting ought to be used for more uplifting and educational purposes than entertainment and advertising, reformers sought to impose more regulation and roll back commercial control of the airwaves.[14] As one critic, complaining about the "yeast racket," put it: "The American system of broadcasting, as it exists today, is a direct development of the medicine tent-wagon that was so common on the American scene before the days of radio."[15] According to this critic, the tricks of the patent medicine trade had merely been updated to fit a new technology and thereby made even more intrusive. Radio critics pointed to the strident, repetitive, hectoring of hard sell techniques as particularly obnoxious. But of even more concern than annoying advertising was the fact that a public resource, the airwaves (actually the electromagnetic spectrum), had been taken over for commercial purposes. As the journalist John T. Flynn pointed out, because the advertiser "pays the piper he is in a position to call the tunes. Thus the freedom of the radio as an institution of public discussion and news . . . is threatened."[16]

On the second front, some admen had to revise earlier claims of the power of advertising. Bruce Barton, a founder of Batten Barton Durstine & Osborn (BBDO) and author of the bestseller *The Man Nobody Knows*, had argued in 1924 that as it was "human nature" to be forgetful, businesses had to diligently remind consumers through advertising what to buy.[17] By 1936, however, Barton explained that admen were not going to "tell the public what to think"; their job was to communicate to *advertisers* "what the public thinks, what it wants, how it feels, what are its hopes and aspirations and ideals."[18] Gone was the confidence that admen could shape consumers' wants in service of advertisers' needs. Rather than dictating down to the consumer, admen needed to work from the bottom up, to listen to consumers and translate consumers' wants into effective advertising strategies.

The increasing pressure on the advertising industry from both consumers and advertisers affected advertising strategies during the Depression. Radio advertising began to shift away from institutional, "good will," and indirect advertising and toward more direct selling.

While the goal of institutional advertising was to evoke positive feelings in a consumer toward a company, the goal of direct selling on radio was to increase product sales, but both were predicated on listener gratitude for the free program. Direct sellers hoped that listeners would buy the sponsors' products as a form of thanks. But listeners' sense of "gratitude" toward a sponsor depended on "sponsor identification"—that is, on the listeners' remembering which sponsor deserved gratitude. The measures for determining whether this sequence of events (listener gratitude, listener recall, and identification of sponsor) actually took place were crude and unreliable. The most common tool was to urge listeners to write in—for coupons, free samples, recipes, prize drawings, and so on. B-S-H executive John Sample's stunt of piling up listener mail in an office and inviting Procter & Gamble executives to walk on it was a dramatic way of demonstrating the existence of a loyal audience. However, mail volume proved listener interest in the program, not necessarily in the product. Many doubted the efficacy of listener gratitude for increasing sales. In 1932, Robert Colwell at J. Walter Thompson declared, "Most people are *not* grateful for radio programs."[19] Sponsors depending on listener gratitude alone, according to one adman, "have all been disillusioned."[20] Advertisers and their agencies would have to develop new strategies that would increase sales, not just listener interest.

This pressure to increase sales underlay the resurgence of the hard sell during the early Depression.[21] In 1931 BBDO executive Howard Angus pointed out, "Whether we like it or not broadcasting is now being used by practically every advertiser on the air for hard, direct selling. The depression did that."[22] The increasingly strident tone of a majority of advertising betrayed a degree of fear that the message was not getting through. Radio provided an opportunity to reach consumers with a louder voice than that of print, and so the hard sell, having been challenged by the soft sell in the 1920s, staged a strong comeback.

Blackett-Sample-Hummert Enters Radio

One of the best-known and most prolific radio advertising agencies was also well known for its reliance on the hard sell: Blackett-Sample-Hummert.[23] B-S-H formed in 1927 when John Glen Sample and his partner, Hill Blackett, lured Frank Hummert away from the Lord & Thomas agency. Sample and Blackett were able to recruit the famous reason-why copywriter Hummert by promising to move aggressively into the new medium of radio, which intrigued him. B-S-H produced a range of programs but concentrated on dramatic serials as particularly effective vehicles for their "reason-why" advertising strategies, including *Stella Dallas, Ma Perkins, Just Plain Bill,* and *The Romance of Helen Trent.*[24] Its client billings increased 167 percent from 1930 to 1934, and B-S-H thus became one of the few advertising agencies to flourish during the Depression, almost entirely because of its involvement in radio.[25] In 1937, B-S-H bought more airtime on the major radio networks than any other agency.[26]

Hummert had established a reputation as a successful reason-why copywriter at Lord & Thomas (L&T) under the tutelage of Albert Lasker, proponent of "salesmanship in print," and that of the hard sell theorist Earnest Elmo Calkins. Hummert's fame as a copywriter arose in part from his authorship of the World War I slogan "Bonds or Bondage," credited with increasing war bond sales.[27] At L&T, Hummert wrote advertisements that identified problems solved by products. "Troubled with Sleepless Nights?" asks a Hummert Ovaltine ad, "Accept, then, this Unique Test"; a Quaker Quick Macaroni ad offers "that New Food Invention which Banishes Burnt Macaroni"; and an ad for Neet hair remover reassures readers that, "If Arm or Leg Hair Worries You, Remove Now Without Bristly Re-Growth."[28] Blackett later recounted Hummert's key insights for selling soap and flour, products that suffered the disadvantage of appearing to be the same whatever the brand. For Gold Medal Flour, he came up with the idea of supplying "kitchen tested" recipes on the flour bag itself, recipes that were said to guarantee a cook's success. For Palmolive soap, Hummert threw out depictions of "slaves bringing palm oil out of Africa" and instead placed a headline, "Would Your Husband Marry You Again?," over "the picture of a little boy looking up at his mother and saying 'Gee Mother, I'll bet the Princess Looked Like You.'"[29] To distinguish a product indistinguishable without its branded packaging, Hummert appealed to the consumer's need to impress. After Hummert left L&T, B-S-H launched itself by touting Hummert's copywriting as the most successful ad copy "from a dollars and cents standpoint."[30] Account executive Sample pitched to new clients by saying, "Gentlemen, if you hire us I can deliver Frank Hummert's brain to you."[31]

B-S-H identified an opening in daytime radio that had hitherto been little used. In the first years of commercial radio, advertisers and networks thought daytime audiences too small to justify investment in programming. Housewives might be too busy and distracted to focus on a sponsor's message. Networks sold daytime airtime for half the price of evening airtime on the assumption that the audiences were worth that much less. However, daytime appealed to certain advertisers, particularly manufacturers of low-priced products such as soaps, cereals, and cosmetics who were seeking greater access to their target market, housewives. These low-margin products depended on high sales volume for profitability; high sales volume was best achieved with heavy advertising. In the early days of radio, some of these advertisers sponsored direct selling programs in the daytime, offering recipes, beauty tips, and household hints incorporating sponsors' products, such as *The Betty Crocker Cooking School of the Air.* By 1933 most of these instructional programs were in decline. The advertising theorist Herman Hettinger suggested that "American women are tiring of the repetition of these matters and are demanding more in the way of entertainment."[32]

The targeted daytime audience for soap and cereal advertisers was female, and Sample believed that hiring a woman would help B-S-H penetrate this market. Most advertising in general targeted women; as *Printers' Ink* put it, "The proper study of mankind is *man* . . . but the proper study of markets is *woman.*"[33] Hummert, opposed at first, was eventually convinced to hire a woman; as Sample later recounted, "We were selling a lot to women in those days and I knew that a writer with the women's [sic] touch would be a great asset."[34] Sample selected divorcée and journalist Anne Ashenhurst to be Hummert's assistant, assuming that any woman would have insight into housewives. In fact, as a working professional, Ashenhurst had no more experience as a housewife than Sample or Hummert; however, Ashenhurst's experience as a journalist, her attention to detail, and her devotion to improving sales for B-S-H's clients soon proved indispensable to its expanding radio production department. By the time she married Frank Hummert in 1935, Anne Ashenhurst Hummert was widely regarded as the organizing force in B-S-H's radio department, "translating" Hummert's ideas to subordinates, clients, and networks.[35] Although the Hummerts maintained a reputation for secrecy, their growing production partnership became well known.[36]

With Ashenhurst on board, B-S-H turned to the problem of creating programming that would attract housewife listeners. Hummert considered the serial format. Noting the popularity of film serials, serialized novels, comic strips, and "advice for the lovelorn" columns in the print media, Hummert thought that housewives would likewise respond to serials on radio. He later described his insight as a guess, not a carefully thought-out strategy: "Not a flash of so-called genius, but a shot in the dark."[37] While at L&T Hummert had already seen how effectively the serialized *Amos 'n' Andy* had attracted and retained audiences for Pepsodent during prime time. Hummert guessed that serials designed for housewives could provide an ideal vehicle for keeping them attentive to the soap or cereal advertiser's message. Open-ended serial narratives secured listeners' attention by providing them with narrative incentives to tune in next time. More entertaining than the recipe and housekeeping programs, which resembled present-day "infomercials," the open-ended serial form offered advertisers the possibility of exposing housewives to their advertising over and over again. Serials could provide a key element of the reason-why strategy: repetition.

One of the first clients sold on B-S-H's idea for daytime serials was the soap manufacturer Procter & Gamble (P&G), for whose Oxydol laundry soap B-S-H developed its serial *Ma Perkins*, the first of many such successful product–program pairings. By 1935, P&G was the leading national radio advertiser, spending more than $2 million a year for radio airtime and production costs alone.[38] Two other B-S-H clients, serial sponsors Sterling Drug and American Home Products, ranked sixth and seventh, respectively, in radio ad spending.[39] By 1940, P&G was sponsoring fourteen different soap operas advertising eight different products.[40] Although some referred to daytime serials as "washboard weepers," the term "soap opera" survived, reflecting the sponsorship of soap companies like P&G as well as the programs' dramatic excesses.[41]

Daytime serials, produced on lower budgets than those of prime time shows, nonetheless attracted large audiences, stimulating even more sponsorship of more serials by advertisers. As the genre expanded across the radio schedule, the Hummerts dominated serial production. Over the course of three decades, between 1932 and 1960, Frank and Anne Hummert produced nearly forty different daytime radio serials. By one count, during the peak of the Depression, 1932–37, B-S-H produced 46 percent of network daytime serials.[42] Between 1937 and 1942, serials were so popular on network radio that seventy-three new ones were introduced. By 1940, nine of every ten sponsored network programs were serial dramas.[43] Although many other agencies were active in soap opera production, including Benton & Bowles (*When a Girl Marries*, *Young Dr. Malone*), Young & Rubicam (*The Second Mrs. Burton*), and Compton (*The Guiding Light*), B-S-H produced by far the most. The Hummerts, as one journalist claimed, ran a soap opera "empire."[44]

The Hummerts' Reason-Why Formula

The Hummerts developed a simple formula, rooted in reason-why advertisements, for attracting daytime listeners.[45] Just as such advertisements usually identified a problem to be solved by a product, each Hummert program was based on a fundamental human problem, such as social division and its consequences.[46] One of the first Hummert serials, *Betty and Bob* (1932–40), sponsored by General Mills' Gold Medal Flour, concerned the marriage of a secretary, Betty, to her wealthy boss, whose father disapproved of the marriage and cut Bob off from the family wealth. *Stella Dallas* (1938–55), based on the best-selling novel by Olive Higgins Prouty, was "the true-to-life story of mother love and sacrifice, in which Stella Dallas saw her own beloved daughter marry into wealth and society and, realizing the differences in their tastes and worlds, went out of Laurel's life." American Home Products' Kolynos toothpaste sponsored *Just Plain Bill* (1933–55), about the "barber of Hartville, the story of a man who might be living right next door to you—the real-life story of people just like people we all know." *Just Plain Bill*'s initial problem was whether a barber like himself would be able to get on with a grown daughter who had been raised in a higher social class than he. Also sponsored by American Home Products, *Our Gal Sunday* (1937–59) was "the story of an orphan girl named Sunday from the little mining town of Silver Creek, Colorado, who in young womanhood married England's richest, most handsome lord, Lord Henry Brinthorpe. The story that asks the question: Can this girl from the little mining town in the West find happiness as the wife of a wealthy and titled Englishman?" A basic problem, reflecting the presumed social insecurities of the potential listener, is then given various solutions intended to assuage those insecurities.

Many Hummert serials revolved around the universal problems of mating: finding a mate, losing a mate, and maintaining marital relations. *The Romance of Helen Trent* (1933–60) was "the real life drama of Helen Trent, who, when life mocks her, breaks her hopes, dashes her against the rocks of despair, fights back bravely, successfully, to prove what so many women long to prove, that because a woman is 35 or more, romance in life need not be over, that romance can begin at 35." *Mary Noble, Backstage Wife* (1935–59), sponsored by Sterling Drug, was "the story of Mary Noble, a little Iowa girl, who married one of America's most handsome actors, Larry Noble, matinee idol of a million other women—the story of what it means to be the wife of a famous star." In *John's Other Wife* (1936–42), sponsored by American Home Products, John depends on both his wife and his "other wife," his secretary. Sterling Drug also sponsored *Young Widder Brown* (1938–56), introduced thus: "In the little town of Simpsonville, attractive Ellen Brown, with two children to support, faces the question of what she owes to them and what she owes to herself. Here's the story of life and love as we all know it." Would *Young Widder Brown* ever remarry? For the targeted housewife audience, the Hummerts believed that mating issues would rank high as a compelling problem.

As in reason-why advertising, the problem provided the bait with which to hook an audience. The characters were designed to appeal to typical housewives; serial writers, like reason-why copywriters, were to put themselves in the shoes of the typical consumer.[47] Hummert claimed, "Our stories are about the every-day doings of plain, every-day people—stories that can be understood and appreciated on Park Avenue and on the prairie."[48] His characters were thus unexceptional and accessible—a mother, a barber, a wife, a married couple. The central character, referred to as the "tentpole" of the narrative, often listened to the common, everyday problems of others and offered advice. The eponymous character of *Ma Perkins* (1933–60), "America's Mother of the Air," was a widow who ran a lumberyard and advised family and friends. The kindly and virtuous Bill of *Just Plain Bill* functioned "much like a super seltzer tablet relieving those in distress," according to one observer.[49] The tentpole character functioned much the way the reason-why advertisement did: to direct a person with a problem toward a solution.

Many Hummert serials addressed the problems facing Americans during the Depression without becoming explicitly political. When an unemployment rate of nearly 25 percent was a more likely cause of joblessness and poverty than shiftlessness or laziness, the Hummerts incorporated stories of struggle with which they hoped their audiences would identify. General Mills sponsored *Valiant Lady* (1938–46), which was "the story of a brave woman and her brilliant, but unstable husband—the story of her struggle to keep his feet planted firmly upon the pathway to success." Sterling Drug sponsored yet another challenging marriage in *Lorenzo Jones* (1937–55): "We all know couples like lovable, impractical Lorenzo and his wife, Belle. Their struggle for security is anybody's story, but somehow with Lorenzo, it has more smiles than tears." The lesson was that material success was not all that mattered. As Frank Hummert put it, their serials were "success stories of the unsuccessful," in which characters such as Bill the barber find success not by amassing wealth but "by endearing himself to others and winning their respect."[50] While their characters faced problems of social division, marital conflict, and individual economic hardship, the wider issues of political conflict were rarely touched upon. As James Thurber explained in *The New Yorker*, "Soapland, you see, is a peaceful world, a political and economic Utopia, free of international unrest, . . . the infiltration of Communists, and the problems of racism."[51] Injecting the narratives with specific contemporary political issues risked not only alienating listeners of different political views but, more to the point, distracting listeners from the point of the programs, which was to sell the product.

Critics often mocked the repetitive, slow, over-enunciated, and humorless quality of Hummert serials, but these features were intentional applications of the reason-why advertising strategy. Like reason-why practitioners who worried that audiences' presumed low cognitive abilities would prevent comprehension, the Hummerts unfolded plot-lines very slowly and always with repeated explanations of backstories by announcers. In a *Stella Dallas* episode, Stella suspiciously regards the yellow roses sent by her ex-husband, Stephen, telling her friend that the roses are supposed to distract her from Stephen's real interest, the "South American holdings." The narrator then explains:

The South American holdings Stella's talking about are those represented by a paper which Stephen jokingly presented to Stella at the time they were married giving her a title to all his holdings and properties in Brazil then practically worthless but today worth millions of dollars. Stephen has a business partner named Raymond Wiley and it was largely Raymond's work that created this empire and he's ordered Stephen to marry Stella again and regain ownership of the empire or Raymond says he will kill Stella.

Without the extensive exegesis provided by the narrator, it would have been difficult for the intermittent listener to follow the plot. The Hummerts also assumed that busy, distracted housewives, having missed some backstory while scrubbing pots or kneading bread, would appreciate the chance to catch up. Critics mocked the glacial pace of Hummert plotlines, such as the romances of the durable Helen Trent, who remained age thirty-five for decades as she lost or rejected one suitor after the other. But a Miss Trent who aged in real time or settled on a mate might confuse a distracted listener.

The Hummerts' concern for their audiences' presumed low cognitive abilities underlay their direction of actors' performances. They cast their serials with actors who would enunciate dialogue slowly and clearly, lest rapid dialogue, accented speech, overlapping dialogue, or too many sound effects confuse listeners.[52] Most scenes involved only two characters so as to make them as easy as possible for distracted housewives to follow. As reason-why practitioners, the Hummerts believed that humor detracted from the product and risked inviting the audience to make fun of the product itself. Thurber noted wryly that "the lack of humor . . . is so complete as to reach the proportions of a miracle of craftsmanship,"[53] but this, like the slow plots and portentous acting, was an intentional strategy originating in reason-why advertising. While the Hummerts were well aware that intellectuals and aesthetes might mock their serials' slow, repetitive humorlessness, they held to it in the belief that it best served their purpose, the delivery of audiences to advertisers.

Reason-why proponents stressed the didactic potential of advertising; so did the Hummerts in their serials—sometimes as specific, public-spirited advice, like the tips for dealing with the rationing of consumer goods during World War II, sometimes as more general embodiments of values regarded as traditional or American. Ma Perkins, for example, not only urged listeners to save foil and grease, but also lost a son in the war.[54] Critics resented the lecturing tone; some accused soap operas of brainwashing gullible and uneducated housewives. Dr. Louis Berg, a psychiatrist, went so far in the early 1940s as to accuse radio soap operas of "pandering to perversity."[55] In their defense, the Hummerts pointed out the positive effects of their moralizing tone. Anne Hummert argued that the morals of their narratives rewarded good behavior and punished the bad: "Ours is a religious country, so we try to embody the idea of right. Crime may appear, but either the annihilation or change of heart of the erring one must follow."[56]

The Hummerts' didacticism also functioned to naturalize the insertion of reason-why advertisements in and around the serials' narratives. In most of the Hummert serials, the advertising was neither "spot" (that is, textually separate) nor fully integrated into the program's narrative. Instead, they used what was called a "sandwich" style of advertising. After an organist played a musical signature, the announcer delivered the opening tag line and a minute-and-a-half-long commercial message, then introduced that episode, returning after nine and half minutes of dialogue with a closing commercial. The length and style of the commercials were typical of reason-why copy of the time. The language was simplistic and repetitive, and the brand names of products were repeated and usually spelled out to ensure brand recognition. The full text of the introductory commercial in a 1933 *Ma Perkins* episode illustrates these characteristics; this advertisement lasted for one minute and thirty seconds and was delivered by a narrator who introduced the day's episode.

Before we hear from Ma Perkins today though, I want to tell you about something else for a minute that will be of vital interest to every housewife listening, about a remarkable new laundry soap discovery that actually makes any other kind of laundry soap old fashioned and out of date. It's the new, improved Oxydol, spelled O-X-Y-D-O-L, Oxydol. It embodies the latest scientific discovery of the world's greatest soap makers, the Procter and Gamble Company. Whatever soap you've been using in the past, whether it's a granulated soap, a soap flake, or a bar soap, you owe it to yourself to try this new improved Oxydol. It makes washing easier, gets the washing done faster, and is safer for colors and fabrics than any other laundry soap now or ever known. Here's what Oxydol will do for you under guarantee of the world's greatest soap makers. Oxydol will wash your clothes 25 to 40 percent faster, whether you use a tub or the latest improved washing machine. It washes clothes four to five shades whiter by actual scientific tests than any other soap can do. And absolutely without scrubbing or boiling. And remember that even your best cotton prints and your children's dainty frocks are safe in mild thick Oxydol suds because it embodies a new discovery which keeps all the fast washing and white washing qualities in the soap and leaves all the harshness out. It's safe for colors, safe for fabrics, and yet so kind to your hands that, well, you're simply amazed at its cleansing power. And now, we find Ma Perkins just where we left her yesterday. . . .[57]

Reason-why tenets are reflected in the references to technological progress ("the latest scientific discovery"), quantification and unverifiable fact-like claims (cleans "25 to 40 percent faster"), scientism ("actual scientific tests"), and hyperbole ("remarkable," "greatest," "simply amazed").

The advertisement's length and repetitiousness, excessive by today's standards, suggest the degree to which advertisers were unsure that listeners were "getting" the selling message.

The lessons of the serial narratives were also integrated into the advertisements themselves. The episode of *Ma Perkins* begun above closed with a moral and an advertisement. The widow Ma Perkins, after at first refusing to mortgage her lumberyard to bail out her no-good son-in-law, finally gives in to her children's pleas. The narrator returns to report:

And so Ma Perkins has a change of heart at last. She realizes what mothers have found since the world began. You can't run other people's affairs for 'em, you can't make them do what you think is best. You've just got to help them. And speaking of help [*chuckle*], there's no household job that needs outside help more than washing clothes. Good intentions won't get clothes clean. If you don't use the best soap, well, you just wear yourself out and get a grey, disappointing wash. But suppose every time you washed clothes they came out fresh and sparkling white and colors unfaded and everything smelling sweet and fresh and clean. Heh, it's almost a joy to work then when you get the right results. And that's the kind of wash you will get if you use Oxydol laundry soap. . . .[58]

The announcer's chatty mode of address, which followed several minutes of folksy and plain-talking dialogue, helps to mitigate any sense of interference or disruption to the listener. Both the fictional narrative and the advertisement operate within a problem/solution structure. The character Ma Perkins dispenses advice on the management of family members, while the narrator dispenses advice on dirty laundry. The Hummerts' integration of reason-why strategies in both the narrative and advertising texts, a demonstration of the consistency of their beliefs about advertising and audiences, helped smooth over any disjunction between program and commercial.

The Hummert Assembly Line

The Hummerts' application of reason-why strategies to both story and commercial reassured advertisers that they were doing their best to sell and to sell hard; however, the Hummerts also innovated production processes and leveraged industry influence to create as many economic efficiencies as possible. They developed an "assembly-line system" of program production that made them the "Fords of the serial industry."[59] By economizing on airtime, talent, scriptwriting, and story development, they made their serials even more attractive to sponsors. In 1943 the top-rated prime time program, *Kate Smith Speaks*, cost $5,000 a week to produce; the Hummert daytime serial *Ma Perkins* cost only $1,300 a week. Because audience size was the same for both shows, the advertiser paid more than $600 per ratings point for *Kate Smith Speaks* but only about $165 per ratings point for *Ma Perkins*.[60] Hummert serials thus provided advertisers with access to listeners at a much lower cost per listener than other programming. Furthermore, unlike print media, which were limited by their print runs, radio had almost unlimited potential to expand its "circulation" or listenership, and thus to lower costs per thousand listeners. The size and power that resulted from their successes enabled the Hummerts to exert considerable influence within the industry, specifically in their relations with NBC, and so to increase yet more their economic efficiencies.

Some of these efficiencies arose from the policies of the Hummerts' agency, B-S-H, in buying airtime during the day, when it was cheaper and more easily available, and creating for it an audience that others had thought not worth building. To maximize this audience, B-S-H bought this airtime in blocks and scheduled a number of serial programs back to back, hoping to ensure continuous audience attention from one program to another. A one-hour time block could be programmed with four different fifteen-minute serials, each of which could lead in to another, so that a listener of one might easily become the listener of all. In the context for the programs thus established, B-S-H did not need to worry about adjacencies that might be perceived as inappropriate. This may have been the first attempt to shape what later would be understood as "audience flow," the movement of audience attention from program to program that would become the bedrock of future television network scheduling strategies. Buying longer blocks of time also won the agency price discounts from the networks, further improving economic efficiencies.

The Hummerts economized on talent costs too. They did not hire expensive "name" or star talent, and they routinely double- and triple-cast their actors, given that in radio, unlike theater or film, one actor could play multiple roles and the audience would be none the wiser. Actors might play in multiple serials, or even multiple roles in one serial. For example, James Meighan played Larry Noble on *Backstage Wife* and Kerry Donovan on *Just Plain Bill*. Karl Swenson played the title character in *Lorenzo Jones* and Lord Henry Brinthorpe in *Our Gal Sunday*.[61] Because radio did not require actors to memorize lines—they could read from the script during the broadcast—the Hummerts also kept rehearsals to a minimum. Their pay rates were relatively low for radio, but the Hummerts could defend themselves by pointing out that their multiple-role-casting policy meant that the actors they did hire usually worked more and earned more consistently than actors with less airtime on higher-paying programs.[62] The Hummerts also economized on music talent costs by hiring a single organist as musical accompaniment, rather than a band or orchestra or other group. The dramatically dirge-like organ chords opening every Hummert serial became infamous and have been endlessly parodied.

Compared with other advertising vehicles, radio serials were labor-intensive: They required the constant generation of new scripts, a costly and unavoidable expense. The Hummerts, however, innovated script production processes in order to speed them up and lower their cost. As daytime serials grew in popularity, advertisers targeting housewives demanded more serials like the Hummerts', and a number of other serial producers developed them. Irna Phillips, another major force in the development of the radio dramatic serial, began with the serial *Painted Dreams* in 1930 and went on to produce *Today's Children* (1933–38) and, most famously, *The Guiding Light* (1937–56 on radio), which continued as a television soap opera until 2009. However, as advertiser demand increased, the problem of simultaneously generating scripts and plots for multiple programs stymied serial creators. Phillips initially insisted on keeping creative control by writing all the scripts herself; however, the demands of serial production eventually led her to employ uncredited assistants.[63]

The Hummerts chose not to write all the scripts themselves. Instead, they maintained creative control through a scriptwriting "factory," in which they produced multiple serials simultaneously. This factory enabled them to introduce new serials every year throughout the 1930s. It generated, they claimed, up to 6.5 million words a year, and at least one hundred scripts per week; its serials were said to take up nearly one-eighth of all radio broadcast time in 1939.[64] Although this claim to "6.5 million words" is obviously hyperbolic and unverifiable in the reason-why tradition of advertising, it would have impressed potential advertising clients interested in such productivity and efficiency.

The process began with the invention or purchase of a title and character. Many Hummert soap operas were based on characters already proven popular in other media, such as *Stella Dallas*, from the 1937 film starring Barbara Stanwyck, which was in turn drawn from the popular 1923 novel by Olive Higgins Prouty. The pre-sold character franchise allowed the Hummerts to develop plotlines that "follow the lives of the characters after the last chapter of the book or the final curtain in the theatre."[65] Once the Hummerts decided on a title and a tentpole character, they would retreat to their house in Greenwich, Connecticut, and outline a theme in four or five pages and a storyline for five or six episodes. These they sent to teams of dialogue writers, one of whom would then write a draft, which was read by a script editor, who also kept the dialogue writers current with deadlines and plot shifts. The Hummerts stayed in Greenwich, communicating with the writers only by written memo, not in person or by telephone.[66] This way the Hummerts were able to oversee and control multiple serials at once.

Writers were expected to produce fifteen to twenty-five episodes a week, sometimes working on five serials concurrently.[67] They were paid by the script, usually $25 apiece, and so could increase their pay by working on more serials. The Hummerts' piece rate compensation was roughly half the going rate for scriptwriters who worked on other radio programs.[68] When criticized for this, the Hummerts responded that their writers, like their actors, were usually employed on more than one serial and that this multiple employment provided workers with a steady level of pay in an uncertain economy.[69] However, some observers believe that writers' resentment over the Hummerts' policies stimulated the formation of the Radio Writers Guild.[70]

The Hummerts prized writers for speed and efficiency, not for creativity. Writers were actively discouraged from contributing plot ideas or otherwise attempting to collaborate; they were expected to follow directions as to plot and characterizations.[71] The Hummerts often shifted writers around from serial to serial, ostensibly to keep their writing fresh but also to prevent too close an identification of any dialogue writer with any program.[72] They also insisted on anonymity for the dialogue writers.[73] Many of their serials included a narrator's spoken tag line "written by Anne Hummert," identifying them as Hummert creations and publicizing a Hummert brand, although anonymous writers produced the actual dialogue. This mode of script production continues today. Dialogue writers of present-day television soap opera scripts are employees of producers who conceptualize the plotlines. Soap opera writers do not function in collaborative groups; instead, they are intentionally isolated from other writers and the production process.[74] This specialization of labor promotes efficiency and speed, rather than authorial autonomy.

While the Hummerts were excoriated by critics like Dwight Macdonald for appearing to demean an ideal of creative autonomy for writers,[75] they were merely transposing the values of creative anonymity from advertising into radio programming. The Hummerts' control of a creative hierarchy was not unique to them; however, in the anonymity of their writers theirs differed from other assembly-line cultural production processes, such as those of the film industry. This was because anonymity was part of the ethos of the advertising industry. In advertising, copywriters did not sign their work; they were craftsmen, not artists, working for the advertiser's benefit, not their own. Drawing attention to themselves as creators of an advertisement might detract from the selling message. Reason-why advocates were particularly wary of any claims to artistry on the part of copywriters. To be sure, their strictures on anonymity did not prevent them from branding some of the serials with Anne Hummert's name; but, as Frank

Hummert had done in establishing his fame as a reason-why copy-writer, they were then advertising their own services like any other product.

In a 1938 ad in *Fortune* magazine, B-S-H explains to potential clients their success in radio.[76] Next to a graphic of many brand names, including Ovaltine, Oxydol, Wheaties, Swift, and Gold Medal Flour, the ad, headlined "Reflected Glory," begins with a paean to the brands: "Many are so universally known that they have become household words in every American community, large and small" (see Figure 5-1). After explaining that those brands represent the investment of "nearly *one billion dollars*," the ad notes, in the hard sell style of impressive enumeration, that these companies affect the "financial welfare of nearly *half a million* American citizens." B-S-H has been granted the "task of guiding these enterprises" with "strategies that will keep goods moving into the hands of the consumer." After claiming it has stimulated increased consumption of its clients' products, B-S-H demonstrates its ethos of modesty:

But famous as these products and their makers are . . . the name of Blackett-Sample-Hummert is totally unknown to all save a few. For whatever *kudos* an advertising agency may achieve comes under the heading of 'reflected glory' at best. And its fortunes are wholly contingent upon the prosperity of those clients whom it serves.[77]

Having established the success of its clients, the ad notes, B-S-H "can achieve our *own* financial objectives only by *indirection*—by helping to make money only for our clients *first*." This ad reminds potential clients of the agency's success and implies that the success is dependent on the agency's anonymity. For hard sell practitioners, the goal of advertising is not to glorify the copywriter's genius; the only goal that counts is increased sales. Unlike Young & Rubicam, which advertises itself as a creative force in advertising (see Chapter 6), B-S-H here underlines its pragmatic, bottom line–oriented approach, one that may not bring B-S-H fame but does bring its clients profits. This ethos of creative anonymity permeated both the copywriting and program production at B-S-H.

B-S-H's domination of daytime programming meant that it often had the upper hand when negotiating with networks and sponsors. At the bottom of the ad is a graph showing the dramatic upward growth of radio advertising handled by B-S-H. Mentioning that 1937 marks the "fourth consecutive year" that B-S-H "placed the largest radio volume of any agency," the ad notes a "302%" increase in dollar volume since 1929. If a sponsor tried to interfere in their program production, Frank Hummert would threaten to quit the account, claiming he did not tell sponsors how to manufacture soap, so they should not tell him how to write dramas.[78] Hummert's relationship with NBC was particularly fraught. As B-S-H increased its time-buying volume at NBC from about $4 million a year in 1930 to almost $10 million in 1934, Hummert became increasingly demanding of NBC staff.[79] By 1936 B-S-H oversaw the advertising accounts of Dr. Lyon's dentifrice, Bayer aspirin, Kolynos toothpaste, Anacin, Phillips' Milk of Magnesia, and Ovaltine, among others.[80] B-S-H and NBC clashed over continuity script control throughout the 1930s. B-S-H argued that its clients, who bought the airtime and financed the programming, should have final say over both. It threatened to withhold payment for time if the continuity script were not broadcast as written, or if there were any interruptions or technical problems. In one instance, B-S-H deducted $8,385 from its charges because it claimed some of its programs were not broadcast clearly; NBC denied there were any transmission problems and demanded payment.[81] B-S-H's resistance to NBC's efforts to regulate on-air content is exemplified in a 1932 order for time, in which it declared, "This continuity is written just exactly as we desire to have it broadcast, and our liability under this order is conditioned upon the continuity being broadcast as submitted."[82] NBC responded that "of necessity" it had "to retain the right of censorship in connection with any programs broadcast through our facilities" and that NBC would always politely "submit proposed changes to the agency or client prior to broadcasting."[83]

Janet MacRorie, the head of NBC's Continuity Acceptance Department, critiqued the Hummerts' programs in a 1939 memo to the then-president of NBC, Lenox Lohr. Pointing out that many Hummert serials had been on the air for more than five years, she noted that they had

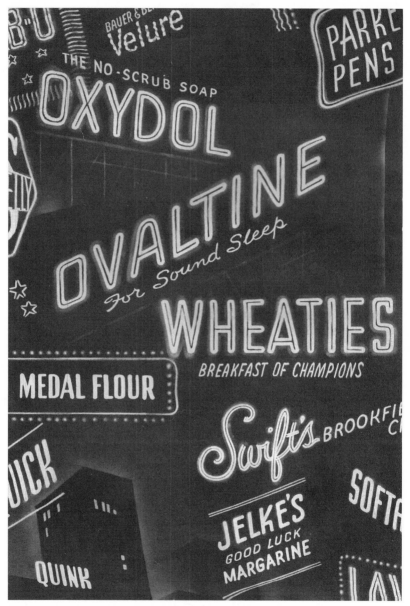

Figure 5-1 (*above and opposite*). Blackett-Sample-Hummert: "Reflected Glory." (*Fortune*, May 1938, 14–15.)

Reflected Glory

THE 15-YEAR RECORD OF
AN OUTSTANDING ADVERTISING AGENCY

ON the opposite page you will find some of the most illustrious names in American business. Many of them are so universally known that they have become household words in every American community, large and small. Collectively, these 24 products represent an investment of nearly *one billion dollars*. And the prosperity of the companies that make them is an important factor in the financial welfare of nearly *half a million* American citizens, including stockholders and employees.

The task of guiding these enterprises—of evolving plans and strategies that will keep goods moving into the hands of the consumer *in ever-increasing volume*, involves tremendous responsibilities. And the fact that those upon whom this obligation rests most heavily have appointed Blackett-Sample-Hummert as advertising agents to share these responsibilities is a matter of pride to us.

But famous as these products and their makers are—and importantly as they influence so many people's lives—the name of Blackett-Sample-Hummert is totally unknown to all save a few. For whatever *kudos* an advertising agency may achieve comes under the heading of "reflected glory" at best. And its fortunes are wholly contingent upon the prosperity of those clients whom it serves.

Thus—the recently published fact that in 1937 Blackett-Sample-Hummert placed the largest radio volume of any agency for the fourth consecutive year, is primarily

significant as a *barometer* of the unusual results achieved by our clients in this particular field. . . . And the fact that our dollar volume of business has increased 302% since the start of the first depression in 1929—is primarily a *reflection* of the prosperity achieved by our clients during these difficult years.

It is also interesting to note that 77% of our increased dollar volume since 1929 has accrued as a result of increased advertising appropriations on the part of clients we *already* served.

This is significant, since only those manufacturers who are reaping *tangible* results from their advertising investments are in a position to increase them appreciably with each succeeding year. And is a further substantiation of our conviction that, in our type of business, we can achieve our *own* financial objectives only by *indirection*—by helping to make money for our clients *first*.

Call this a materialistic attitude if you wish. But we believe that it has been a vital factor in our 15-year record of consistently increased dollar volume. And we believe that you will find this attitude definitely reflected in the financial statements of those clients whom we serve.

If our type of thinking appeals to you—if you feel that our experience with problems of advertising, merchandising and selling might profitably be added to that of your own organization—we should be glad to tell you more about our way of working. No obligation, of course.

The heavy line indicates the growth trend in dollar volume of Blackett-Sample-Hummert, Inc. from the date of its founding on May 1, 1923.

The dotted line indicates the trend of advertising in general since 1925. Figures prior to this time are not available.

NOTE:—Although more radio time was purchased in 1937 through Blackett-Sample-Hummert than through any other agency, percentage-wise there was a substantial increase in the amount invested by our clients in newspapers and magazines during this particular period.

BLACKETT-SAMPLE-HUMMERT, Inc.

NEW YORK
247 Park Avenue

CHICAGO
221 N. La Salle Street

turned sensationalist in order "to give them a new life through the introduction of child-birth, illness and death, murder, breach of promise cases, murder trials and constant misunderstandings between husbands and wives. For the most part, human happiness or contentment, according to these scripts[,] can never be attained." *Stella Dallas* was a "preposterously long–drawn out story" in which "Stella goes blind occasionally, suffers simply unbelievable illnesses but always comes out on top." The title of *John's Other Wife* "indicates the sex slant involved. The stupidity of the man, and the forebearance [sic] of his devoted and virtuous wife are past believing." *Just Plain Bill* "drips with woe and jealousy. Twice has Bill, depicted as a saintly philosopher, a barber by profession, been tried for murder." *Young Widder Brown* was a "sex story, pure and simple," which forced the Continuity Acceptance Department to stay "on its toes to keep bigamy and the more intimate personal relationships between men and women at a minimum."[84]

However, MacRorie's opinions notwithstanding, NBC treated B-S-H with the respect due a major client. Hummert insisted on special terms for dealing with NBC; he required that all negotiation of time sales and continuity script issues be conducted through salesman Roy Witmer. After NBC was sued for libel in 1932 because it had approved and broadcast a B-S-H advertisement for Bayer aspirin that implied a Bayer competitor was inferior, Hummert refused to negotiate future Bayer copy with anyone at NBC other than Witmer.[85] NBC was able to keep B-S-H and the Bayer account in 1933 only by continuing to agree that nobody at NBC other than Witmer would contact Hummert.[86] In 1934, trying to resolve the "battle of aspirin," Witmer asked Hummert to refrain from referring to competing aspirin brands as "bargain counter preparations."[87] Hummert claimed to be insulted, replying he had already ceased to use that phrase and that he didn't like being pushed around by NBC: "We place too much on the air for that, and propose to protect our clients in every possible way we can."[88] Hummert also threatened the then-president of NBC, Merlin Aylesworth, when NBC allowed a Bayer competitor to make competitive claims in its continuity copy. Hummert wrote to Aylesworth that another NBC executive (the future NBC president Niles Trammell)

has evidently taken the stand that he is stronger than Blackett Sample Hummert and I am afraid he is wrong because if this continues any further I
personally will see to it that every relationship between us and the National
Broadcasting Company is impaired to the best of my ability and I think you
know that I usually make good on these things.[89]

Ultimately, despite Hummert's fulminations, NBC continued to
cater to him. As Witmer explained to incoming NBC president Lenox
Lohr, "Hummert is the kind of man who likes fast action and minimum annoyances. He has almost a complex against 'hair splitting.' He
is a good friend of ours and can be of tremendous help to us in the
building of our daytime revenue."[90] Managing Hummert's demands
was simply part of the cost of building the business in commercial
broadcasting. Anne Hummert's strategy for dealing with NBC's objec-
tions to B-S-H copy was less combative. In a 1991 interview, Anne
Hummert described NBC executive Niles Trammell as "very gracious"
but as "always laughing at me, because he knew what I was doing."
She described a typical meeting regarding advertising copy: "If you
say, 'This is the fifth most highly paid beauty expert in America,' he'd
say, 'Have you got the figures on that, the statistics?' and I'd say, 'I'll
change it to probably one of the highest paid.'"[91]

In 1943, B-S-H reorganized, becoming Dancer Sample Fitzgerald
(DSF), and Frank and Anne Hummert spun off their own radio production company, Air Features, which continued to control the programs
and purchase airtime through DSF.[92] In 1948, at the peak of radio
advertising revenues, the Hummerts oversaw twelve serials simultaneously. Their stature in the radio industry was such that by the early
1950s, as Cold War red-baiting began to infect the entertainment industries, theirs was among the few production companies willing and
able to disregard the blacklists promulgated anonymously as "Red
Channels."[93] The Hummerts did not alter their approach to advertising
or programming to any great degree; however, as the text of this commercial aired during a 1948 *Young Widder Brown* episode indicates,
they had by this time softened their hard sell when it came to medicinal claims:

Ladies, in one respect, all tooth pastes are alike. That is, all of them will clean film from your teeth, will sweeten your breath, but Phillips' Milk of Magnesia Tooth Paste does more. Yes, Phillips' Tooth Paste also protects the beauty of your teeth by actually neutralizing on contact the mouth acids that many dental authorities say are a major cause of tooth decay . . . and remember, these acids are in everyone's mouths. . . . Today ask for P-H-I-L-L-I-P-S'—Phillips' Tooth Paste.[94]

Advertisers continued to sponsor radio soaps into the 1950s because they were produced at an extremely low cost for the number of listeners they attracted. As late as 1958, sixteen serials were broadcast on network radio and only ten on network television.[95] Although they remained on the air longer than most prime time radio programs, they succumbed at last in 1960, ending the Hummerts' hold on daytime programming. They had lost sponsors and audiences to television soap operas. Radio actress Mary Jane Higby has described the Hummerts' tenacity in the face of the shift to television: changing program times as better slots became available, experimenting with plotlines, and introducing new programs.[96] At some point in the 1950s, CBS bought the Hummerts' production company, Air Features, and they retired to a private life.

After the transition to television was complete by the end of the 1950s, not much of the Hummert dramatic "formula" survived in television soap operas. The television soap opera would develop a greater emphasis on characterization and move away from reason-why didacticism. The live, single-sponsored serial program with integrated or sandwiched advertisements was supplanted by the recorded program sponsored by multiple advertisers.[97] And yet the Hummerts' work in radio lay the groundwork for the collaborative, team-style production processes that typify most television program production today, an outcome of their adherence to advertising industry values and, more specifically, the hard sell strategy of reason-why advertising.

Sponsored radio programs reflected the advertising strategies of the agencies that produced them. The Hummerts created a distinct program style that reflected their belief in the efficacy of hard sell advertising strategies. Their serial dramas were designed to appeal to the target audience of housewives and keep their attention with open-ended narratives. Nearly every characteristic of Hummert soap operas that has been criticized or parodied, including the ponderous narration, the repetitive scripts, and the tentpole characters, is an intentional element of their reason-why advertising strategy. The Hummerts' success in producing the targeted audience for their clients was unequaled. For advertisers concerned about falling consumption during the Depression, the hard sell seemed a solution to their problem.

6 The Ballet and Ballyhoo of Radio Showmanship
Young & Rubicam's Soft Sell

While the hard sell strategies of the Hummerts dominated daytime soap operas, with their slow, repetitive, didactic, hyperbolic narratives, other agencies tacked toward the soft sell. These agencies tried to build "showmanship" in radio to attract and entertain audiences in both advertising and programming. In contrast to their hard sell counterparts, they sought to avoid exaggeration and repetition, often experienced as hectoring, so as to attract audiences and avoid giving offense. They embraced the entertainment value of radio and through their discussion of "showmanship" focused on what they saw as a natural overlap between good advertising and good programming, both designed to attract and to please. In both advertising and programming, soft sell agencies emphasized humor over didacticism, the aesthetically pleasing over the hyperbolic, and the emotional appeal over the rational.

While some advertisers and agencies may have been ambivalent about using entertainment to sell, sponsorship of radio programming forced them to confront the merging of selling and showmanship. In his autobiography, *Adventures in Advertising*, Young & Rubicam founder John Orr Young described the radio era as a time when advertising agencies brought "the show world to the world of commerce."[1] The advertising theorist Kenneth Goode described the adman's role in radio as "helping every businessman become his own showman."[2] The merger of "showmanship and salesmanship" would "spell success."[3] Even more romantically, the radio era was a time "when advertising joined hands with showmanship" to create commercial entertainment.[4]

Grappling with "showmanship" as both a theory and a set of practices, advertising agents debated conflicting approaches. And whatever theory agencies utilized, they also faced significant constraints that arose from internal agency divisions, pressures from sponsors, the mysteries of audience response, and the challenges of managing the "talent." Soft sell proponents were more comfortable with the merging of entertainment and selling than their hard sell counterparts. Among radio agencies, Young & Rubicam practiced in the soft sell tradition, and by the end of the 1930s Y&R oversaw some of the top radio entertainment programs, including *Jack Benny* and comedian Fred Allen's *Town Hall Tonight*. Like Blackett-Sample-Hummert, Y&R applied theories of advertising to radio programming, except that as soft sell practitioners, they emphasized humor, including reflexive humor about the products, and user-centered appeals.

Showmanship: Theory and Practice

A writer in the trade magazine *Broadcast Advertising* defined showmanship as "the ability to make people pay attention by giving them what they like,"[5] a definition typically flexible and vague. Admen defined "showmanship" in accordance with their outlook. A hard sell proponent defined showmanship as that which produces tangible results: "Showmanship is presenting any proposition *successfully* to the public."[6] A soft sell proponent, Robert Colwell at J. Walter Thompson, defined showmanship as a production ethos: "Showmanship is intelligence, imagination, taste. . . . Showmanship is doing everything just a little better than seems necessary. . . . Doing things supremely well."[7] In general, however, soft sell proponents thought more about showmanship than did their hard sell counterparts.

The problem of showmanship became so acute during the radio era that an entire trade publication was devoted to the topic, *Radio Showmanship* (1940–47) (see Figure 6-1), and "how to" books instructed admen on showmanship.[8] In their 1936 book *Showmanship in*

Business, Kenneth M. Goode and M. Zenn Kaufman argued that there was no real difference between showmanship and salesmanship: All selling is a form of showmanship and all showmanship a form of selling.[9] They sought to prove, among other things, that admen's skills were appropriate for producing entertainment because the basic principles for appealing to audiences applied to both advertising and entertainment. They urged businessmen to ignore showmanship's "doubtful repute businesswise" and to embrace it as a technique for producing results. Goode and Kaufman delineated the functions of showmanship: It "1. attracts attention . . . 2. emphasizes, 3. emotionalizes, 4. creates action."[10] To achieve showmanship, one must apply the tools of "suspense, pathos, humor," the basic Aristotelian elements of drama. In order to sell, however, these elements must be handled with "tact": "Showmanship, in short, is another name for 'tact.' Active, aggressive tact. Tact on a gorgeous scale. Tact blown up into a balloon. Painted like a barber pole!"[11] Goode and Kaufman did not specify how admen were to translate this ballooning, painted tact into effective advertising. Such vagueness is typical: Although promising in theory, the term provided not a set of consistent, workable rules and practices but a rubric under which admen might discuss the problem of how to integrate entertainment and advertising.

Critics of agency-controlled programming claimed that admen had no business passing themselves off as showmen. According to one critic, "Showmanship, the most important element in broadcasting, is likewise the rarest quality to be found in an advertising man." Admen are simply "not very adept at it."[12] Some entertainers resented admen's horning in on their territory; the Hollywood movie star Mary Pickford, for example, complained "that possibly many radio shows of today have been constructed by salesmen rather than showmen, and now that the novelty of 'tuning in' has worn off, I wonder if any production on the air can really succeed without the highest type of showmanship."[13] Others complained that admen were ruining radio by treating it not as entertainment but as advertising, "a thing entirely apart from show business."[14]

Admen defended their qualifications as radio showmen by insisting that their skills in advertising were transferable to entertainment. As

Figure 6-1. "Radio Showmanship." (*Radio Showmanship*, October 1940, cover.)

one writer put it, admen "are the chaps who have spent years dramatizing a bar of soap."[15] Advertising strategy has always included dramatics, though in print; radio simply offered admen a platform for extending those skills. A BBDO copywriter pointed out that showmanship came naturally to admen: "After all, showmanship is only brains plus imagination, plus the bravery to try something new. Brains—imagination—bravery—dramatic instinct and ability. Where will you find these qualities more necessary than in the advertising business?"[16]

Perhaps admen were better qualified than were established entertainers themselves: One BBDO executive sneered that "Ever since broadcasting began, broken-down vaudeville actors and ex-directors of ex–little theaters have been ranting that radio needed showmen."[17] The tensions between the people from show business and the people from Madison Avenue were exacerbated, as radio writer Robert Landry explained, by differences both in social background and in aims:

The gap between the conservatively tailored fraternity brothers from Dartmouth and Princeton and the sharp customers from the other side of Sixth Avenue was in part a social gap but it was also a matter of business conditioning. The admen said in horror, "They don't *think* advertising." The showmen said, also in horror, "They don't *think* show business."[18]

Even if admen's skills were transferable to entertainment, such differences maintained the divisions between admen and showmen.

Radio, of course, was not the first instance of entertainment as an advertising vehicle. Nineteenth-century patent medicine sellers traveled from town to town, putting on "medicine shows" to attract audiences. Observers within and without the advertising industry viewed the single sponsorship model as an updated version of the medicine show.[19] The entertainment of the medicine show had the same instrumental purpose as the sponsored radio program: to sell. For critics, and some admen, this impaired both the entertainment and the advertising. Others, however, rather than disown the legacy of the patent medicine trade, embraced it. Adman Carl Dreppert, for example, wrote:

The problems of the medicine showmen of yesterday are exactly the problems of the radio advertiser today. Call radio the macrocosm of mass showmanship to sell: the medicine showman is the microcosm. . . . Were these medicine showmen masters of all the entertaining arts they practiced? Not by a long shot. They were masters of but one art—the art of knowing the mental habits of the people who made up their market. . . . They weren't selling a show—they were *using a show to sell goods.*[20]

For Dreppert, the adman's purpose was not to produce a good show but to produce a good *enough* show to sell goods. If radio were a modern-day medicine show, that was not a compromise but a solution.

In contrast, Robert Simon argued in a 1932 JWT staff meeting that while the structure and goals of medicine shows and radio programs may be similar, the style of radio programs must evolve. Referring to an article comparing the two, Simon noted that while the similarities may have been obvious in 1930—"You had entertainment, you had an announcer who was virtually a barker"—audiences had changed, and so should radio program producers:

[T]he same thing has happened to radio that has happened to the medicine show. The patrons are getting wise to that racket. The doctor brings on his bottle and they go somewhere else. In short, we cannot continue indefinitely to sell our wares by the venerable combination of ballet and ballyhoo.[21]

Pursuing the medicine show strategy was increasingly risky for those advertisers seeking to establish long-term relationships with consumers.

In an article titled "Are We Selling Entertainment or Merchandise?" one adman cast doubt on the compatibility of entertainment and advertising, arguing that "a fact-smothering bombardment of cleverness does not help anyone to buy more sanely."[22] Selling and buying should be rational processes; entertainment was inherently irrational. In entertainment, the audience's response was unpredictable, the failure rate high, the risk of offense omnipresent. Entertainment as a selling strategy had pitfalls whether the program was successful with audiences or not; wrote one adman,

A radio program can "sell" so hard and so consistently that the listening audience will fade out in boredom or disgust. Or it may be an "impression" job with entertainment so fine that few people get, and none remember, the name and product of the sponsor.[23]

It was too easy to make either mistake: If the program sold too hard, the advertiser could lose the audience, but if the program entertained too well, he could lose the sale. Some admen, such as Howard Angus, worried that "advertisers have gone crazy and are selling stars instead of their products."[24] Arguing that expensive programming might please audiences but was a poor investment unless it helped sell products, adman L. Ames Brown wrote in 1932,

A $20,000 all-star program on a coast-to-coast network may get fine press notices and win the sympathetic applause of those self-appointed advertising critics who are working for high cultural standards—but it's a dead loss to the advertiser if it's all showmanship and no salesmanship.[25]

Was there a middle way between straight selling talks and high-priced star-filled entertainments?[26] Did the program have to be entirely dedicated to and identified with the sponsor's product, at the risk of alienating audiences? Or did the program have to be star-studded and expensive, at the risk of undermining sales?

Some admen, like JWT radio department head John Reber in 1932, began to question the assumption that the product and the program had to be closely associated. This assumption had operated since early radio, when advertisers such as ginger ale makers had sponsored bubbly, cheery music programs like *The Clicquot Club Eskimos*. Audiences, it was assumed, would associate the bubbly music with bubbly ginger ale. Reber argued that such an association was not necessary, that an effective radio advertising strategy began with identifying the product's target market, then building a program to attract that target market, whether or not the program resembled the product. As Reber explained in a staff meeting: "[T]he entertainment should be something which will attract an audience composed of the most likely people to whom the product can be sold. It need not have anything whatever to do with the product or advertising message."[27] In this view, an advertiser need not find or develop a program that was "keyed to his product."[28] Advertisers could buy or develop programs that simply attracted the audiences that would be interested in their products and so might consider a wider variety of programming options.

Admen and agencies had to find a way to mediate between the interests of advertisers (to sell more products) and audiences (to be entertained). As one trade magazine writer pondered: "Radio listeners want programs to be *interesting*, and sponsors want them to be *profitable*."[29] Showmanship, according to a Ruthrauff & Ryan executive, is a process akin to international diplomacy: "The problem is to mediate between the objective of social subjects and the practical task of selling soap. It is editorial statesmanship combined with the utmost concentration of showmanship."[30] While "statesmanship" may have been an exaggeration, admen certainly needed diplomatic skills. The radio department head of Young & Rubicam, Hubbell Robinson, described mediating between the selling needs of a sponsor and the entertainment aims of the program talent:

The question of entertainment versus advertising is fast reaching the state of a perennial bugaboo in connection with commercial radio broadcasts. . . . [M]ost clients . . . insist on as much direct selling talk as they can crowd in. Showmen, actors, script and continuity writers insist on cutting the selling talk to the minimum. On the horns of this dilemma the radio advertising men balance themselves as best they can . . . .[31]

Faced with the extremes of alienating audiences with too much advertising or not stimulating sales by overemphasizing entertainment, admen balanced themselves as best they could.

As a solution, some agencies integrated commercials into the program. As early as 1929, JWT used this approach in the Fleischmann's program starring Rudy Vallee. Reber explained to other JWT staffers how this allowed for the insertion of advertising while keeping the narrative frame of Vallee's nightclub act intact:

We have a little trick in Fleischmann which we feel is quite certain to work out well. . . . It provides for a conversation between Rudy and a friend of his. . . . He comes in and says, "Hello, aren't you going to show me around?" and Rudy takes him around, and as they walk around, and go into the kitchen, and meet the chef, it's "Hello," and "How do you do," and then they are out again, and as they walk along the tables, . . . the friend says, "You seem to have friends here," and [Rudy] replies, "There is a couple over there who don't even know I am here. I wonder what they are talking about. . . . Let's listen." And then, with enough of a change on the fader to indicate a change of microphone, you hear this conversation going on at the table. . . . The conversation is to the effect that this boy is doing better with his work, is getting more money, and the girl says, "How did you manage that, how did you do it?" and finally it ends by divulging the secret of his success, that he had been taking Fleischmann's Yeast, etc.[32]

This strategy was especially popular at the agencies that specialized in soft sell tactics. Young & Rubicam invented Jack Benny's famous invocation of his sponsor, "'Jell-O' again. This is Jack Benny speaking."[33] Benton & Bowles also used scripted backstage patter, having the performers shift out of the first fictional frame into another fictional frame of "real-life situations and settings" in order to identify more fully the product with the entertainers.[34] By eliding differences between the entertainment and selling texts, these strategies may have helped make commercialism more palatable to entertainers and their audiences alike.[35]

Radio advertising required "seductive selling coated with, or presented through the medium of, entertainment," as one adman put it.[36] But how to decide what kind of entertainment to use? JWT radio staffer Colwell sighed with exasperation in a staff meeting in 1930, "The question of what we are going to do for entertainment and how we are going to do it and who is going to do it is just endless."[37] In a 1931 JWT staff meeting, radio department head Reber acknowledged the increasing complexity of entertainment production, admitting he had given up his opinion that radio was "easy" to master. On the contrary, it was, he pointed out, increasingly labor-intensive as the agency tried "to make more of a performance, more of a show of the thing."[38] How to build showmanship into the shows themselves? What made a program a good program? Kenneth Goode defined good programs as those having "radiobility": the ability to have "an almost instantaneous attention catching-and-holding quality."[39] This was a difficult task. What did it take to create "radiobility"? What tools, methods, and strategies were useful?

Constraints on Showmanship

As agencies struggled to conceptualize showmanship and radiobility, they were already on the job, testing ideas as they went along. In doing so, they faced a number of constraints. First, they faced resistance from within the advertising industry itself and institutional limitations within agencies. Second, they faced the demands of their clients, the radio sponsors. Third, they were constrained by the difficulty of solving the mystery of audience desires: What did audiences want? Fourth, they had to manage the needs and demands of star talent, perhaps the most difficult of all these constraints.

Within the advertising industry, some admen never accepted radio or the sponsor model as an effective advertising vehicle; often detractors and proponents of radio co-existed within a single agency. For example, the head of N. W. Ayer thought so little of radio as an advertising medium that he undermined his agency's otherwise preeminent head start by moving its headquarters to Philadelphia, away from the burgeoning radio industry.[40] Young & Rubicam co-founder Raymond Rubicam never disguised his distaste for radio. However, Rubicam was a businessman, and radio was a good business for his agency throughout the 1930s and 1940s.

Agencies varied in the way their radio departments fit into their overall organizational structure. At Young & Rubicam, for example, the Radio Department was entirely separate from other departments, although it is unclear if that was due to Rubicam's attitude toward radio. In other agencies, a major problem was how to coordinate advertising on radio with advertising in print media: Usually the radio department was expected to pick up and use print advertising concepts. For some radio admen, this was problematic; print advertising strategies were not always appropriate on radio. At JWT, Radio Department head Reber criticized the print copywriters for providing poor advertising concepts the Radio Department was then required to execute. In a 1932 staff meeting, Reber complained: "The Radio Department leans very heavily upon the creative group because we expect you to work out the advertising message. . . . It is pretty difficult sometimes to accept some of the ramshackle platforms handed us by the creative group." Reber went on to disavow responsibility: "So don't blame us for what we say. You can blame us for the way it is said, but it is not our fault as to the basic advertising idea."[41] Clearly the Radio Department was under attack, and Reber was required to defend it. Tensions inside the advertising agency exposed the changing leverage of the Radio Department vis-à-vis other departments throughout the radio era. As a 1945 *Printers' Ink* article complained, "Why the wall between radio and other copy writers?" (see Figure 6-2). "The rigid barrier," argued adman Ralph de Castro, "is not conducive either to quality of production or to economy of operation."[42]

The second area of constraint for admen concerned their clients, the advertisers. Admen often complained that radio sponsors ignored their professional advice, meddled in issues of which they knew little, and stubbornly insisted on having their way.[43] Admen never aired their complaints directly, of course, but expressed their exasperation

Why the wall between radio and other copy writers?

Figure 6-2. "Why the wall between radio and other copy writers?" (Ralph E. de Castro, "Why the Wall between Radio and Other Copywriters?" *Printers' Ink*, 3 August 1945, 36.)

with sponsors in staff meetings, reminiscences, later interviews, and autobiographies. By the late 1940s, the problematic sponsor had become a character in popular culture, memorialized in Hollywood films such as *The Hucksters* and *A Letter to Three Wives*. Admen complained especially about the conservatism of many sponsors and their distrust of show business, which, according to then–NBC staffer and future ad agency president Mark Woods, "cramped and confined ingenuity."[44] Another adman somewhat dramatically claimed that sponsors "tramp with hobnailed shoes over the gossamer fabric of the entertainment."[45] In meetings JWT staffers complained repeatedly of sponsors whose demands were unrealistic, or meddlesome, or, worse, sabotaging. One client wanted close control over every detail of the program: "The client decides that Helen Kane ought to sing 'Annie Laurie' instead of 'That's My Weakness Now.'"[46] Another interfered with the talent: "I saw an eminent manufacturer of perfumery march up to a dull, middle-aged actress and tell her tearfully: 'My good woman, I'm paying for this program and I want you to put some passion into it!'"[47] Comedian Fred Allen openly complained about sponsor interference:

I think if I went in to Mr. Charles Luckman of Lever Brothers and showed him how to make some Lifebuoy soap, he'd resent it. He knows what goes in the vat there. I don't know anything about that. By the same token, I don't think he should come and tell me how to write the jokes.[48]

The most infamous sponsor of all, memorialized in the bestselling 1947 roman à clef *The Hucksters*, was George Washington Hill of American Tobacco. Hill oversaw the revival of the cigarette brand Lucky Strike, partly through the radio program *Lucky Strike Hit Parade* (1935–50). He demanded that the program feature what he considered the top ten popular dance numbers, although his method for ascertaining the popularity of songs was never revealed. In a pamphlet he wrote on American Tobacco advertising, Hill insisted on following hard sell formulas on radio.[49] As such formulas receded elsewhere in the industry during the 1940s, Hill's reputation as an obnoxious despot riding roughshod over his advertising advisors grew, until rumor and fact became difficult to separate.

For their part, sponsors who were accustomed to the more predictable practices of other industries were frustrated by the unpredictability of entertainment. It was difficult enough not knowing which advertising strategy would be effective, without the added uncertainty of show business. Admen, caught between entertainers' complaints and sponsor interference, were acutely aware of their uncomfortable position as mediators. Their flexibility was limited by their need to acknowledge, in the words of one adman, that the advertiser who "pays the piper" is able "to call the tunes."[50]

No one, neither ad agency, sponsor, nor entertainer, knew what would succeed as an advertising vehicle. Admen struggled to find a way through the entertainment options. One radio entertainer complained that the agencies promiscuously auditioned entertainers on a "hope-it-fits basis" instead of seeking talent that would suit the selling needs of their clients.[51] This was an exhausting, time-consuming process for both talent and talent buyers. Agencies rarely indicated what they were looking for, and they had plenty of options as the high rates of unemployment during the Depression had created an excess supply of talent. Some ad agencies tried to address this problem by bringing more discipline and order to the process.

John Reber at JWT argued that it was futile to buy an already existing program, such as a network-sustaining program, and then find a client to fit it. Instead, an agency should begin with the client, analyzing its needs and then building "a program for the particular client."[52] In JWT's case, its radio program *Lux Radio Theatre* (1934–55) grew directly out of a print advertising campaign begun in 1928 that used movie star testimonials to sell Lux Toilet Soap. On *Lux Radio Theatre*, movie stars such as Irene Dunne suggested that "9 out of 10" movie stars preferred Lux Toilet Soap.[53] Before introducing the setting for the radio play version of the film *To Have and Have Not*, the announcer of a 1946 episode of *Lux Radio Theatre* described how the newlyweds Humphrey Bogart and Lauren Bacall used Lux Soap in their new home.[54] By presenting radio play versions of films then in release, the program could more tightly bind the association of the movie stars with the product.[55]

In building programs from scratch, admen began with the targeted market. Their assumptions about their audience shaped their theories of showmanship. Kenneth Goode assumed that "Adults in the mass—even opera audiences—think slowly when at all. And are childlike."[56] Hard sell proponents assumed their audiences had short attention spans and that lowbrow culture would consistently attract more audiences than highbrow culture.[57] George Washington Hill, the American Tobacco sponsor, resisted the trend to use radio as a vehicle of cultural uplift, arguing, "Let's give the public what the public wants and not try to educate them."[58] William Benton, of Benton & Bowles, believed that his success in early radio rested on his relative ignorance of music, which coincided with what he perceived as his radio audience's ignorance of music. In an interview long after the fact, Benton claimed, "I have a tin ear. That's why my ear was so good for radio. Most people in the United States have a tin ear like mine. A totally tin ear."[59]

Members of corporate boardrooms shared the assumption that the radio audience lacked taste. Sponsors reliant on highbrow programming such as classical music for "good will" advertising sometimes feared that lowbrow strategies would be more effective and wondered if they should switch tactics. In at least one case, a major advertiser on NBC had to be reassured by the network's president that its highbrow strategy was indeed competitive. Alfred Sloan, the CEO of General Motors, wrote Merlin Aylesworth, president of NBC, that he was concerned that GM's musical program was not "tuneful" enough. Sloan worried that GM was "tremendously limiting the public appeal of our programs by making them so 'high brow' in character."[60] Aylesworth reassured Sloan, asserting that GM's chief competitor, Ford, relied on a "cheap" program and that GM would undermine its aims if it likewise lowered itself to "a common type of music."[61] Aylesworth was reiterating the public service rhetoric with which NBC defended its policies to critics and regulators; the more highbrow programs NBC carried, the less vulnerable it would be to accusations that it was defiling the lofty ideals of radio as cultural uplift. In the face of a major sponsor's fear that its programming repelled rather than attracted, Aylesworth had to resort to a thinly veiled assertion of class superiority.

However, sponsors who assumed that audiences were naïve risked underestimating and losing them. As early as 1930, one staffer at JWT, George Faulkner, argued against "dumbing down" programming to attract listeners. He contended, "The idea that the way to get a big audience is to play down to the moron is all wrong." In fact, Faulkner continued, "that is a theory even the movies have discarded."[62] Faulkner's comment was a backhanded compliment to radio's major competitor, the film industry, but it was a useful way to demonstrate the limits of the strategy, because, unlike the radio industry, which had little or no data with which to measure audience response, the film industry could use box office receipts as a clear measure of popularity.

On very little evidence, admen had to speculate about what radio audiences wanted. Hubbell Robinson of Y&R wrote an article for the trade press, "What the Radio Audience Wants," arguing that listeners want "entertainment which they can personalize," because the direct, intimate medium of radio was experienced not in a theater or concert hall but in a private, individualized setting, the home.[63] Movies were consumed in theaters with strangers, a much less intimate setting. Radio, then, might have a competitive advantage over competing forms of entertainment like the movies if it were to address listeners as individuals rather than as a large, undifferentiated mass.[64] Though his was a minority voice in the radio era, it reflected a growing awareness that audiences were far more complex than broadcasting institutions or advertisers had assumed initially. By the end of the 1930s, more admen attributed audience distraction to changing tastes rather than to lack of taste. The advertising theorist Warren Dygert, for example, recommended that radio programmers stay flexible and attuned to audiences: "If something new seems to be catching on, be ready to work fast. Skim the cream while the milk is fresh."[65] Programmers could not rest on any assumptions; they had to innovate constantly, to follow the audience rather than lead it.

Another constraint on admen was how to use stars from other entertainment fields, from vaudeville, Broadway, and Hollywood. Star testimonials had been effective in print advertising for beauty products (as in the JWT Lux campaign). However, few established stars were heard in early radio programming, for several reasons. First, many stars had little interest in the challenge of a new medium and none in radio's low or nonexistent rates of compensation. Second, in early sponsored programming the product was the star, with which actual stars were not allowed to compete. Thus, many early radio entertainers were anonymous, or identified by pseudonyms, or labeled as the "(product name) singers," such as *The Clicquot Club Eskimos*. The advertiser was spending money to promote the product, not the entertainer, so the personalities and identities of performers were obscured.[66] However, it soon emerged that stars attract audiences and might endorse products rather than compete with them. A famous performer almost guaranteed audience interest. A JWT staffer noted, "There is one sort of show that will always be good. That is a show on which you spend a great deal of money" for stars such as Clark Gable.[67] Free-spending clients, seeking guaranteed audience attention, competed for high-priced stars, driving up talent costs in the process.

This trend in turn provoked a backlash. Adman Leonard Lewis criticized advertisers' insistence on stars whatever their cost. He claimed that programming could be commercially effective without star power, as in American Home Products' *Easy Aces* and Colgate-Palmolive's *Clara, Lu 'n' Em*, programs featuring lower-cost radio-developed talent rather than Hollywood or vaudeville stars.[68] Using nonstar talent reduced production costs, whereas using stars, as Arthur Sinsheimer, the radio director at the Peck agency, complained, "serves rather to add to the glory of the featured artists than to increase materially the sales of merchandise of the sponsor."[69] Another adman stated flatly that "to place the entertainer in charge of your radio advertising is to subordinate the advertising viewpoint to the artistic viewpoint."[70] The blame for dependence on stars, according to Sinsheimer, rested not with the sponsors, because they could not be expected to know better, but with the advertising agencies and networks, which encouraged this star dependency.[71] In fact all were involved.

Agencies and networks, in their effort to keep advertisers interested in radio, looked to stars to reassure advertisers that they were reaching audiences. Many advertisers, worried that a no-name performer could not guarantee an audience, felt that expensive star talent was a relatively wise use of money. However, increased demand for stars, the supply of whom by definition is limited, also increased their asking prices: Talent costs went up. These costs "cast a chill over many a business mind"; some admen were concerned that radio would price itself out of being an effective advertising medium.[72] Still, on the whole, the use of stars as a selling strategy grew throughout the radio era.

In 1934 the advertising trade magazine *Printers' Ink Monthly* asked the stars themselves to weigh in on their significance to radio's commercialism and their relations with sponsors and agencies. The star Fred Waring represented a typical show business perspective when he argued that radio's "product" was entertainment, rather than advertising. Waring said he thought advertisers should give "radio artists" a freer hand in developing radio entertainment: "Advertisers should realize that people listen to the radio not for the advertising but for the entertainment."[73] Obviously Waring overlooked the fundamental economic fact that in radio, unlike in theater, the monetary transaction was between broadcaster and advertiser rather than between performer and audience. In contrast, other performers took a more realistic view of radio, acknowledging the truism that whoever pays the piper can call the tune. The entertainer Eddie Cantor "heartily" disagreed with Waring. Cantor, who rose to stardom in vaudeville's Ziegfeld Follies and whose radio program *The Eddie Cantor Radio Show* was sponsored by Chase & Sanborn coffee, was one of the top stars of the 1930s: He sang, danced, and told jokes with equal success on stage, radio, and screen. Cantor viewed radio as an entirely different commercial enterprise from "show business": "Radio is not the show business but the advertising business with the show business grafted on. Therefore, I say, that the star should listen sympathetically to the sponsor."[74] Other artists in this camp appealed to agencies and sponsors to allow them to become a more complete partner in the selling process. Radio entertainer Ray Perkins complained, "There is a tendency on the part of radio time buyers to look upon the performer as a piece of artwork rather than as an employee," as someone who is "incapable of any sympathetic understanding of business matters," whereas if performers were instructed as to the "selling strategy" they could work more effectively for the sponsor.[75] Clearly Perkins held no illusions of creative autonomy (see Figure 6-3).

Other radio performers were more reluctant to subordinate their art to the needs of the advertiser. Singer Jessica Dragonette gained stardom in a music program sponsored by Cities Service, *The Cities Service Concert*, and thought she enjoyed a measure of creative involvement in the program. However, she found that the producing admen had humiliatingly little interest in her contributions, and she was finally forced off the program. Describing a failed meeting about which songs to sing and which skits to perform, Dragonette complained in her autobiography, "[L]ooking up at the blank faces, I realized I was casting my pearls before agency men."[76] Radio stars also

Figure 6-3. "Radio—If the Stars Were Czars." (*Printers' Ink Monthly*, November 1934, 46.)

resented constraints they had not found in live performances. Comedians accustomed to ad-libbing in live performances resented the tight control of their scripts by agencies and sponsors as well as networks. The comedians of *Stoopnagle and Budd*, who specialized in improvised patter and running commentaries, complained that network and sponsor requirements for written scripts made them feel "restrained, unnatural."[77] Fred Allen infamously and flagrantly ad-libbed lines in his program *Town Hall Tonight* despite NBC's Continuity Department's efforts to stop him. Allen openly chafed at the layers of control in radio, referring to networks as "chains":

An air comedian works under tremendous handicaps. He has a sponsor who pays the bills. The sponsor has an agency to represent it. The radio chains have a flock of rules, all starting with "You Mustn't." In the secret heart of all these people—sponsors, agencies, and chain—is a belief that each of them is some sort of a kilocycle Ziegfeld.[78]

Radio-created stars—that is, stars whose first major breakout happened on radio—chafed less at sponsor and agency creative control. Kate Smith, another singer who gained fame on radio, characterized the best relations between performer and sponsor as mutually cooperative. A radio performer should not agree to be hired by just any sponsor; she should approve of the product she is to promote: "it is vital that the product must be one of mutual approval and admiration by both the artist and the sponsor. . . . There must be complete *esprit de corps* between sponsor, agency and artist."[79] In the case of JWT's production of *The Fleischmann's Yeast Hour* with Rudy Vallee, the star, whether or not he admired the sponsor's yeast, depended on the ad agency to craft his on-air persona. JWT radio director John Reber explained to staff in 1932 that JWT's current strategy for appealing to audiences was to make the scripts sound as if

Vallee did the whole thing himself, so that all who like Vallee will like the show because Vallee made it up. The facts are that Vallee doesn't know now what is going to be rehearsed this afternoon. He doesn't write one word of the script. All of the things about how he first met these people, etc., we make up for him.[80]

Radio, then, required artists as well as sponsors and agencies to reconceive their roles in creative production.

Sponsors employed stars not just to attract audiences but also to create an association between the product and the star. If audiences had a favorable attitude toward the star, perhaps that would carry over to the product. The Lux soap campaign was, as we have seen, based on this idea. But perhaps star association would not work. Radio star Eddie Cantor performed in a number of programs, including *The Chase & Sanborn Hour* and *The Eddie Cantor Radio Show*, with a variety of sponsors, including Old Gold cigarettes, Sunkist, Chase & Sanborn coffee, Camel cigarettes, and Texaco. How would audiences remember which product to associate him with?[81] Some surveys of listeners, asking them to identify the sponsors of major stars, concluded that for most listeners the association of stars with products or sponsors was weak.[82] Yet despite such evidence, general belief in star–sponsor association persisted, and sponsors continued the use of stars as an associative advertising strategy.

An obvious risk of star association was that a star might become involved in a scandal or other popularity-reducing circumstance and through this negative association hurt the sales of the product. This negative version of the persistent belief in star–sponsor association was one of the underlying assumptions behind the witch-hunts in Hollywood and radio in the late 1940s and early 1950s for suspected communist sympathizers.[83] Philip Loeb, who played Gertrude Berg's husband on the situation comedy *The Goldbergs*, was fired because of the presumed negative association of his leftist political beliefs. The problem of congruence between star image and product image continues to bedevil marketers, who still hope for branding efficiencies in star associations.

The flip side of negative associations was an excessively positive association between star and product. Once successful at promoting the brand, a star could demand higher compensation. The establishment of a radio performers' union in 1937, the American Federation of Radio Artists, threatened to shift more negotiating leverage to performing labor. These considerations led one adman to recommend to sponsors: "Don't hitch your business to a star. Hitch a star to your business—and then only as a part of your business and its promotional program."[84]

In addition to the problems of managing stars, sponsors, and intra-agency tensions, admen faced the basic problem of creativity in radio. On the one hand, admen needed to reach audiences where they were, using standard and recognizable appeals. On the other hand, they needed to innovate to build new markets. They aimed for "standard innovation," recognizable but new enough to be interesting.[85] Many admen saw advertising as a creative outlet, comparable to, or perhaps a variety of, high art; asserted one, "I do not know of any place in business where there is as much opportunity for original ideas and creative ingenuity as in advertising."[86] But advertising's commercial goals tended to undermine such claims. Admen were supposed to translate commodity into desire. Hill Blackett of Blackett-Sample-Hummert explained, "You must translate soap into how to get a decent complexion, just as you translate . . . cigarettes into how to keep a decent figure."[87] The entry of the advertising industry into radio expanded the range of such possibilities; it was a call to innovation.

Agencies debated issues of novelty, formula, originality, and plagiarism. In the earliest years of radio, admen relied on the novelty effect of a never-before-broadcast event. Agencies arranged stunts such as unseen tap dancers or the "first commercial program from an airplane."[88] However, by 1934, according to NBC staffer Art Hungerford, "The factor of novelty is no longer so important."[89] Like radio advertising, radio entertainment was often an amalgam of the tried-and-true with the novel.[90]

Vaudeville provided a large body of proven entertainment and talent to radio. Programs such as *The Fleischmann Hour, The Chase & Sanborn Hour,* and *Ziegfeld Follies of the Air* transferred the vaudeville "bill" more or less intact to radio: comedy monologue, skit, guest star, orchestra number, vocalist, and weekly visiting artists. Vaudevillian labor was also in good supply as the number of vaudeville theaters shrank from 2,000 in 1926 to fewer than 50 in 1933, victims of the

Depression and the new entertainment media of talkies and radio.[91] However, many vaudevillians relied on visual techniques, including pantomime, sight gags, pratfalls, dancing, ventroquilism, and visual novelties. Eddie Cantor and Ed Wynn both carried stage techniques over to radio and had trouble remaining within the strictures of the scripted, timed broadcast. They also had a tendency to play to the studio audience with facial expressions, sight gags, outrageous costumes, and other tools unseen by radio listeners.[92] The largest available labor pool was thus not perfectly suited to the new medium. Vaudeville veterans who did best on radio were those who adapted to it. Jack Benny's comedy, for example, shifted from vaudevillian puns and one-liners to comedic situations revolving around his character as a "braggart and skinflint."[93]

A key reason for vaudeville's prominence in radio was its potential to provide, for advertisers uncomfortable with the vagaries of show business and unsure how to draw audiences, both the tried-and-true and the novel. Vaudeville forms were familiar to audiences, and vaudevillians (unlike some film stars) were familiar with the demands of live performance. However, vaudevillians were accustomed to months of touring, giving them the opportunity to hone their acts over time in front of different audiences. On radio they had to perform new material weekly in the expectation that the radio audience was returning every week. Developing and refining new material that quickly was for many vaudevillians a daunting, if not impossible, prospect.[94] Vaudeville and Broadway performers and their financiers, the producers, also were accustomed to a high failure rate; they understood that not every act would be a hit, not every show would draw an audience. But radio sponsors expected hits and new material every week. Performers had both to meet audience expectations with the familiar and arouse audience interest with the new. As one observer reported, "This risk is intensified on the air, where a different show must be given for every broadcast. The advertiser must first build up his audience, and then hold them over periods of many weeks or months, in the face of shifting public tastes."[95] On the one hand, advertisers sought to create audience habits. In general, according to William Benton, "Every businessman wants a product that is habit-forming. That's why cigarettes,

Coca-Cola and coffee do so well."[96] However, unlike caffeine, entertainment can induce the same effect again and again only by means of something new. No single form of entertainment could solve the problem of audience appeal once and for all. As JWT's Robert Colwell pointed out, "The most popular programs on the air do not fall into any one type of entertainment."[97] Neither star nor genre alone could ensure a program's success, as one writer acknowledged in *Printers' Ink*: "The element of gamble cannot, of course, be wholly eliminated in entertainment building."[98] This copywriter went on to recommend that, "The advertiser can take a formula—even an existing program— . . . and adapt it to his needs," after "studying the experience and success of other programs."[99]

Imitation of success was a strategy not limited to radio, of course. The advertising industry can be seen as a cybernetic system or feedback loop of innovation and imitation. Almost every successful advertising campaign generates a host of copycat campaigns. In an article on plagiarism and radio, copywriter Don Gridley acknowledged that "advertising has had to depend partly on people whose genius lies almost wholly in the copying of other's ideas."[100] On radio, however, some admen complained about that most sincere form of flattery, imitation. Gridley asserted that "imitative" radio programs "undermine" the original program's effectiveness by diluting its appeal, hence forcing program producers to continue to innovate, at great labor and effort. Gridley concluded that "originators" of new program ideas must keep moving ahead of their imitators: "Their only hope lies in keeping ahead of the parade and creating something new a little faster than the imitators can imitate."[101]

Young & Rubicam: "Resist the Usual"

Young & Rubicam (Y&R), a well-known soft sell advertising agency, became a major force in radio. It produced some of the top prime time programs, such as *The Jack Benny Program* (1935–44), *The Kate Smith Hour* (1937–47), and *Town Hall Tonight* (1935–41) with Fred Allen, as well as serials such as *The Aldrich Family* (1939–51), *The Second Mrs.*

Burton (1941–60), and *When a Girl Marries* (1940–52), and the radio comedy *My Favorite Husband* (1948–51), the basis for the television comedy *I Love Lucy.*

Young & Rubicam was founded in Philadelphia in 1923 by two admen who broke away from N. W. Ayer. From the outset, Y&R resisted the conventional hard sell tactics. John Orr Young, the account executive whose task was to land accounts, or sell the agency to potential clients, claims he "never felt that bird-of-prey instinct" of the typical salesman. Concerned that "the techniques of seduction" would backfire when a customer resented being seduced, Young "tried to let the prospect sell himself" with the hope that the client would be more forgiving of mistakes "if he felt he had *bought* the service . . . instead of coming to the realization that a fast talker had sold him."[102] Young's partner, Raymond Rubicam, the chief copywriter and president of Y&R from 1927 until 1944, was well known as an adherent of the Theodore MacManus style of soft sell advertising.[103] His earlier career as a copywriter at the Philadelphia agencies F. Wallis Armstrong and N. W. Ayer included slogans for Steinway pianos ("The Instrument of the Immortals") and Squibb drugs ("The Priceless Ingredient of Every Product Is the Honor and Integrity of the Maker").[104] For Y&R's first account, Postum, a coffee substitute, they shifted away from warning about the "evils" of caffeine. According to Young, "Instead of haggard housewives, we pictured radiantly healthy and happy people enjoying the warmth, aroma, and satisfying flavor of a drink that was beguilingly good to taste—and that was good for them."[105] In the soft sell tradition, Y&R sought to entice rather than to bully or frighten.

Y&R's astute application of soft sell principles led to rapid growth. Their success at reviving the Postum brand brought more food accounts, including Borden and Heinz. After Postum was absorbed into the General Foods conglomerate, Y&R gained more General Foods accounts, including Grape-Nuts and eventually Jell-O, Minute tapioca, Calumet baking powder, and Swans Down cake flour.[106] By 1926, Y&R had relocated to New York. Its success in copywriting and then in radio increased its billings from $6 million in 1927 to $22 million in 1937, as it gained clients such as Norwich Pharmacal, Packard, and

Bristol-Myers.[107] For a Packard campaign, Y&R paid famed photographer Edward Steichen a record $1,000 fee for his photograph of a Packard automobile. This willingness to pay well for aesthetic quality also reflected Y&R's soft sell beliefs; as Young recounts, "We added salesmanship without sacrificing beauty."[108]

Y&R promoted itself to potential clients in the trade press as a unique agency specializing in creative solutions unbound by arbitrary rules. In a trade magazine advertisement, Rubicam wrote an ad promoting Y&R with the headline "Impact" over a photograph of a fighter being hit in the face (see Figure 6-4).[109] The copy read: "According to Webster: the single instantaneous striking of a body in motion against another body. According to Young & Rubicam: that quality in an advertisement which strikes suddenly against the reader's indifference and enlivens his mind to receive a sales message."[110] Rubicam himself argued that attention-getting was the first purpose of advertising: "The way to sell is to get read first. The way to get read is to say more about the reader and less about yourself and your product."[111] Under Rubicam's leadership, Y&R specialized in the attention-getting and user-centered strategies, such as humor and visuals, that hard sell admen distrusted. The advertisements should "say more about the reader," or user, and less about the product.[112]

Young & Rubicam was known as a creative agency, where copywriters and artists enjoyed some autonomy and control. In most agencies, the "creative" staff, those who wrote and illustrated the ads, was subordinate to the account executives, those who handled the clients; however, at Y&R the creative staff made decisions about campaigns and were eligible for partnership and equity ownership in the agency. In order to attract top copywriters from more established agencies, Y&R offered relatively generous shares of company stock in the belief that those "who carried the heaviest loads" should share the profits.[113] Y&R thus enjoyed tremendous loyalty from its relatively underpaid copywriters; as one adman recalled, it "was more of a religion than it was an advertising agency."[114]

Paradoxically, Y&R also became one of the key agencies during the Depression to come up with new market research techniques for radio. In 1932 Rubicam hired professor of marketing George Gallup after

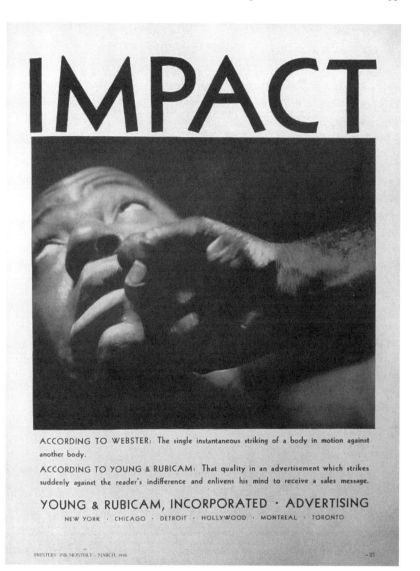

Figure 6-4. Young & Rubicam: "Impact." (*Printers' Ink Monthly*, March 1938, 25.)

noticing his groundbreaking magazine reader surveys.[115] Gallup helped develop radio audience measurement techniques, particularly the "coincidental method," in which researchers telephoned listeners and asked what radio station and program they were listening to at that moment (rather than what they had listened to the night before, as most telephone research had asked). By the end of the 1930s, Y&R's ratings measurement strategy had gained enough interest to be sold to C. E. Hooper, who rebranded the measurement technique as the Hooper Ratings.[116] Y&R's move into market research did not undermine its claim to being a "creative" agency; it simply gave the agency another tool for promoting itself to potential clients as knowledgeable about their markets.

Young & Rubicam on Radio

Y&R became a well-known radio agency despite Rubicam's open dislike of commercial radio; he believed that radio should be less dominated by advertising.[117] Rubicam assigned the initial foray into radio to Chester LaRoche (who would later become president of Y&R and an executive at ABC-TV). Its first radio program was probably the *Radio Household Institute* (1928–32), a kind of "domestic science" program filled with helpful information for housewives.[118] Young recounts buying cheap daytime-hour blocks and dividing them into four fifteen-minute periods "so that more clients might make an inexpensive experiment in this new kind of advertising."[119] Other early programs included *Johnson & Johnson Musical Melodrama* (1929) and *All American Football Show*. The radio department was officially inaugurated in 1930 under Hubbell Robinson and soon included other radio men such as Tom Lewis and Harry Ackerman. By 1936, Y&R was producing *The Jack Benny Program* for Jell-O, having won that and the Bristol-Myers *Town Hall Tonight* program away from Benton & Bowles. Both of these were variety-comedy programs built around the personae of their comedian hosts: Jack Benny's egotistic, penny-pinching deadpan and Fred Allen's bemused observations on the curious and unusual characters who populated *Town Hall Tonight*. In 1937 Y&R also produced the

Burns and Allen program for Grape-Nuts and *The Kate Smith Hour* for Calumet baking powder, both General Foods brands.

As a clear counterproposal to the hard sell school, Y&R advertised its commitment to sales through entertainment in a 1938 issue of *Fortune* magazine. Asking, "What makes a good radio show?" the ad discusses problems such as appealing to the wrong kind of audience or "inflicting dull or offensive product announcements" on listeners and concludes that "Young & Rubicam shows are proving daily that product announcements can have the *appeal of entertainment and the force of salesmanship at the same time*" (see Figure 6-5).[120] Entertainment, in other words, might support rather than obstruct selling, because both were aimed at the same result: attracting and pleasing audiences. Y&R openly criticized the hard sell for using "dull or offensive" advertising supposedly immune to the distractions of entertainment.

In order to generate the widest range of ideas and skills, according to one former employee, "Everyone had to write. Not just produce— write. Programs and commercials both."[121] Whereas Hill Blackett at B-S-H believed that the same copywriters should work in both print and radio, Y&R sought to develop radio copywriting specialists by hiring not admen but showmen with theatrical and radio backgrounds and training them in advertising techniques.[122] So one of the first radio commercial writers at Y&R was a man named Joseph Moran whose background was not in advertising at all; Moran had figured out how to win contests, often of the sort that asked readers to supply copy or slogans for new products, and had become well known for living off of contest winnings.[123] His cleverness qualified him more than any formal advertising training.

Unlike some agencies, such as Lord & Thomas, which left many production functions to network program departments, Y&R required total control over its programs and kept all radio workers in-house.[124] The agency opened an office in Hollywood in 1936 headed by LaRoche and staffed by Bill Stuhler and Don Stauffer. By 1938, 80 of 402 Y&R employees belonged to the radio department, which had become so important that it had its own writers (8), producers (14), talent managers (4), researchers (6), media planners, and accountants separate from the rest of the agency. The radio department functioned as an agency

Figure 6-5. Young & Rubicam: "What makes a good radio show?" (*Fortune*, May 1938, 93.)

within the agency; its large broadcast billings justified its autonomy. Y&R's estimated billings on NBC alone in 1938 were about $2.5 million a year.[125]

Between 1929 and 1956, Y&R served about thirty-five different radio clients.[126] It shuffled programs among clients, sometimes to keep clients pleased and sometimes to keep the talent happy. While some clients sponsored only one or two programs through Y&R—such as Life Savers' *Rendezvous* (1935–36), Pall Mall's *The Big Story* (1947–48), and Sterling Products' *Battle of the Sexes* (1940–45)—others tried a different program every year. General Electric sponsored four different programs between 1930 and 1936 and four different programs again from 1945 to 1948. The company must not have been fully satisfied with any of them; it is perhaps to Y&R's credit that the agency kept GE as a radio client as long as it did. Other advertisers found a program and stayed with it: Gulf Oil sponsored *We, the People* almost every year from 1942 to 1951 (after General Foods' Sanka ended its sponsorship, which had begun in 1937); Lipton sponsored *Arthur Godfrey's Talent Scouts* for eight years (1947–55); Energine sponsored *Manhattan at Midnight* for four (1940–44). Certain Y&R programs migrated among Y&R clients. For example, *Burns and Allen* was sponsored by General Foods' Grape-Nuts in 1937–38, Swan Soap in 1941–42 and 1944–45, then by other General Foods products in 1946–47 and 1948–49. Likewise, *The Adventures of Ozzie and Harriet*, about the bandleader Ozzie Nelson and his family, a show that would go on to a long television run, was sponsored by Johnson & Johnson in 1944–45, and then by International Silver in 1945–46 and 1947–49. *Duffy's Tavern* was sponsored by General Foods' Sanka in 1942–43 and then by Bristol-Myers from 1943 to 1950.

Y&R's two most significant radio clients were Bristol-Myers and General Foods. Bristol-Myers sponsored programs through Y&R every year between 1935 and 1953, some (such as *Town Hall Tonight*) inherited from rival agency Benton & Bowles. Bristol-Myers sponsored such top prime time programs as Fred Allen's *Town Hall Tonight* (1935–41), *The Eddie Cantor Show* (1940–47), *Duffy's Tavern* (1943–50), and *The Dinah Shore Show* (1941–42). General Foods, Y&R's first print client, was also its largest radio client. Between 1930 and 1956, roughly the entire radio era, Y&R oversaw at least thirty-five different programs for General Foods. In the 1944–45 season, a peak year for radio production, Y&R simultaneously oversaw eleven General Foods' programs and sixteen other programs for other clients. Sometimes different General Foods' products sponsored the same program: For example, *The Kate Smith Hour* was sponsored by Calumet baking powder in 1937–38, Grape-Nuts cereal in 1939–42, Jell-O in 1942–43 and 1944–45, and Sanka decaffeinated coffee in 1945–47. General Foods' Jell-O sponsored *The Jack Benny Show* in 1934–41, until its business was impaired by wartime sugar shortages, at which point General Foods' Grape-Nuts became the new sponsor from 1941 to 1944. In addition to star-studded variety and comedy prime time programs, General Foods sponsored daytime serials, including *Portia Faces Life* (1945–50), *The Second Mrs. Burton* (1945–51 and 1952–54), *When a Girl Marries* (1940–52), *The Aldrich Family* (1939–50), and *Young Doctor Malone* (1942–43). As radio began to lose audiences in the 1950s, Y&R even picked up some former Hummert serials for General Foods, including *Backstage Wife* (1955–56), and for Procter & Gamble, *Lorenzo Jones* (1951–52).

Young & Rubicam: Comedy and Integrated Commercials

Y&R's soft sell approach required an emphasis on entertainment on radio. JWT radio executive Robert Simon critiqued Y&R's combination of the soft sell with a "constant striving for novelty." Though he praised Y&R for not putting on an "act" for clients and for not being "married to" particular entertainers, he concluded that Y&R programs suffered not from staleness but from too much novelty: "There is so much straining for freshness that many an idea sounds forced and overworked."[127] This was attributed to the agency's employment of former actors and musicians, and to its radio director Hubbell Robinson's literary bent. Robinson disdained reason-why strategies, arguing in 1932, "One more thing the radio audience does not like, and that is to be fooled. They do not like their advertising delivered by sleight-of-hand methods."[128] While Robinson disagreed with competitor Hummert about advertising strategies, like Hummert he also used serials to build and retain audiences. For a 1930 program designed to promote the magazine *True Detective Mysteries*, Robinson used what he called "an old movie serial stunt" by providing a "tailpiece," or preview of next week's episode, as a "come-on" to audiences.[129]

Concerned that audiences would resent the sponsor for interrupting the program with commercials, Y&R promoted integrated commercials, which wove the sponsor's name or product mentions into the program text. While Y&R (and Benton & Bowles) did not originate the integrated commercial (JWT, as we have seen, used Rudy Vallee to discuss Fleischmann's Yeast), the strategy, in its indirectness and intended inoffensiveness, was typical of the soft sell. Integrated commercials developed naturally from the earlier indirect radio advertising strategies, such as naming programs after sponsors (*Ipana Troubadours*), personifying brands (the Coca-Cola girl), and associating highbrow culture with a company (*Cities Service Concert* and Jessica Dragonette).[130] But integrated commercials also incorporated direct selling methods: The characters of *Burns and Allen,* for example, discussed the merits of sponsor Swan Soap during a shopping expedition.[131] Integrated commercials were not a definitive solution; Robinson warned against badly executed integration, especially "selling talk" designed to "sound unlike selling talk": "The creaking of the machinery is so audible that it drowns out the selling point."[132]

The Jell-O Program Starring Jack Benny, beginning in 1934, included Y&R's best-known use of integrated commercials. In 1934, Benny claimed credit for it: "I believe I was the first" to "clown" about a sponsor's product "and in this way was able to weave the name of the product throughout the entire show."[133] Opening the program with a sung introduction spelling out the sponsor's product, "J-E-L-L-OOOOOOOOOOO," Jack Benny introduced himself with the line, "'Jell-O' again. This is Jack Benny talking," bringing the sponsor's name immediately into the program text.[134] The program included one commercial and several "plugs" integrated into the body of the show. The announcer Don Wilson, for example, worked in this plug for Jell-O mid-show: "I shopped around until I found half a dozen neckties, each one corresponding in color to a different flavor of Jell-O . . . you know, Strawberry, Raspberry, Cherry, Orange, Lemon, and Lime."[135] Or

Benny set up a commercial by discussing his upcoming Hawaiian cruise and asking, "Don, do you think I ought to take along some Jell-O with me?"[136] While Benny's proposal to take Jell-O on a cruise may have been a simple plug, it could also be heard as a joke at the expense of the sponsor, which carried some risks. During his appearances on the 1932 *Canada Dry Ginger Ale Program*, Benny's vaudevillian joke "Her father drank everything in the United States and then went up North to drink Canada dry" apparently displeased the sponsor, which dropped him at the end of the season.[137]

JWT radio executive John Reber disapproved of this strategy, naming Jack Benny and Ed Wynn as the worst examples of comedians who "kid the product and make fun of advertising on the radio." Comedian Wynn once interrupted the announcer Graham MacNamee's Texaco commercial thus: "Don't talk to me about gas, Graham. If a doctor ever operated on you for appendicitis, he'd find himself opening a gas station." At JWT, Reber announced, "Our precept is that we do not kid the idea of advertising itself at all. We do not kid the product. We do not allow the name of the product to be involved in the entertainment [aspect] of the program except in a few exceptions."[138] This view was shared by other comedic talent, including the writers/performers of *Amos 'n' Andy*, who insisted that it was "essential that we keep the entertainment part of the program entirely divorced from the advertising continuity."[139]

Instead, Y&R integrated the *Jack Benny* program into Jell-O's print advertising. In a 1938 ad, an illustrated panel of the program's characters is set into a backdrop of vividly colored Jell-O "whirls," a form of dessert.[140] Headlined "Jack Benny and the Mystery Girl," illustrated panels with dialogue in subtitles present a radio skit in print form (see Figure 6-6). Jack and his partner Mary Livingstone are dancing at a party and discussing the "mystery star" who is a "gorgeous blonde" who may be Swedish or Russian but nobody knows because her nationality is a "secret." Jack is frustrated because "she won't talk. I'll bet she's Polish though—something fascinating and exotic about her." Mary bets Jack that she can find out where "Delicia Velour" is from, and Jack bets she cannot. They invite Delicia to their table and serve her Jell-O, offering her "Strawberry, Raspberry, Cherry—Orange,

Figure 6-6. Jell-O: "Jack Benny and the Mystery Girl." (*Ladies' Home Journal*, April 1938, n.p.)

Lemon or Lime!" Delicia responds: "Um-m. It's real Jell-O all right—extra-rich. We used to have it back home. *Heavens!* I'm talking! *Please* don't tell. I'm really from Waukegan, Illinois." The mysterious star, pretending to be an exotic snobby European, turns out to be a nice Midwesterner who enjoys the quintessential American dessert. Jell-O disarms Delicia so completely that she forgets to play her role as the silent European and enthuses about the product. Meanwhile, the ongoing competition between Mary and Jack is resolved, temporarily, once again as Mary collects on her bet from Jack. At the bottom of the ad, readers are reminded to "Tune in Sunday night for the gayest, grandest show on the air!"

The huge success of Jack Benny's comedy and his strong association with Jell-O was somewhat of a surprise to Y&R. According to Y&R's General Foods account supervisor, Benny had not been Jell-O's or Y&R's first choice for comedy talent—other, better-known comedians were unavailable. But because Jell-O was suffering from competition from Royal Gelatin, which not only sponsored a program with Fanny Brice but also, according to Y&R executive Lou Brockway, "tasted better than Jell-O," Jell-O decided to introduce new, improved flavors in 1934 and wanted a new program to promote them. Benny "was available." The program became popular, and ratings grew; however, according to Brockway, General Foods decided to drop Benny nonetheless because the program ratings seemed to have "no discernible results" on sales. And then, suddenly, Jell-O sales rose, and General Foods' sponsorship of Benny continued another ten years.[141] Benny's show, one of the highest-rated radio shows of the 1930s, had a demonstrable effect on Jell-O sales, and Y&R could thus claim that its soft sell entertaining approach had succeeded where harder selling may have failed.

In 1935 Y&R took over Fred Allen's show, *Town Hall Tonight,* from Benton & Bowles, which was forced to drop the Ipana toothpaste account (sponsor of Allen) in favor of the higher-spending Colgate toothpaste account.[142] While Allen wrote most of the scripts of his own program, the agency was responsible for overseeing the scripts and dealing with network and sponsor issues—not an easy task, given Allen's notoriously negative attitudes toward NBC and his advertising agencies.[143] He characterized admen as "molehill" men: An adman is a "pseudo-busy executive who comes to work at 9:00 A.M. and finds a molehill on his desk. He has until 5:00 P.M. to make this molehill into a mountain."[144] Allen resented NBC's efforts to censor his scripts and hamper his ability to extemporize. The NBC Continuity Acceptance Department reciprocated this resentment. Janet MacRorie asked NBC program director John Royal if something couldn't be done about Allen: "Do you think it would do any good if we had a meeting with Young and Rubicam and Mr. Allen and discuss the possibilities of a change in Mr. Allen's sources of humor?"[145] Allen's relations with Y&R were similarly contentious; in his autobiography Allen complained that Y&R executive LaRoche, a former college football player, wanted him to change his comedy style: "The quarterback, being an advertising man, knew the importance of the word 'copy.' His solution was that all we needed to improve our show was to copy the Benny program in style and structure."[146] Sylvester "Pat" Weaver, who had already proven his facility in radio by producing the *Good Evening Serenade* and *Evening in Paris Roof* programs, was hired by Y&R specifically to oversee Allen's program, and he approached the task with trepidation. Weaver gained Allen's confidence during one of the first *Town Hall* shows he produced by asking some noisy gentlemen to leave the control room, unaware he was evicting executives from the sponsor and the network from their ordinarily privileged positions of oversight. Weaver was also willing to play himself in Allen's skits poking fun at the advertising and broadcasting industries.[147]

In one *Town Hall Tonight* episode, Fred Allen and his announcer, Harry von Zell, performed a commercial for Sal Hepatica, a laxative made by Bristol-Myers. While most radio commercials in hard sell style repeat the product name over and over, this commercial parodies that approach. After Allen sets up the announcer to deliver the commercial message, von Zell feigns forgetfulness as to the name of the sponsoring product.

Von Zell: "Don't ever neglect a cold. At the very first sign of a cold, get after it immediately with the faster help of sparkling . . . uh. . . . sparkling. . . . uh. . . . [*sotto voce*] What's the name?"

Allen: "Fred Allen, remember?"

Von Zell: "No, no, no [*laughter*], the name of the, I'm awfully sorry, that eagle has upset me. I can't remember the name of what it is that helps fight colds faster. It's slipped my mind."

Allen: "Well, it'll come to you. Go ahead, Harry."

Von Zell: "Well, yes, yes, of course. Ladies and gentlemen, this famous product acts very quickly, yet is exceptionally gentle, and since the progress of a cold is very fast, the greater speed of, uh, of what it is I'm talking about, is freshly important in fighting your cold. And that's not all. This, uh—the name will come to me in a minute—it also helps nature counteract the acidity that so often accompanies a cold. And ladies and gentlemen, you can check these facts with your own doctor."

Allen: "You'd better check the name, too, ladies and gentlemen."

Von Zell: "Fred, you know what I'm talking about."

Allen: "Why, certainly, Harry. You're talking about America's outstanding saline laxative."

Von Zell: "That's it, Fred, the name is. . . ."

Allen: "The name is . . . uh. . . . uh . . . So many physicians recommend it. . . ."

Von Zell: "Yes, yes, and it helps fight colds faster. But what is the name?"

Allen: "Oh, here's a pretty to-do. Wait, Harry, there must be somebody around here who knows. If there is, will you please tell us, confidentially?"

Audience (in unison): "Sal Hepatica!"

Fred: "That's it! Sal Hepatica! Thank you, ladies and gentlemen, thank you!"[148]

Having the star comedian "misunderstand" the announcer's question about the name integrated not only a joke but also Allen's star persona into the commercial. The audience, knowing the name of the product, can laugh in ironic knowingness at the expense of the announcer. Then, at the end of the commercial, Allen asks the audience to provide the sponsor's name, thereby reversing the usual order of hard sell advertising. Instead of the announcer's pounding the name repetitively into the audience's consciousness, the elision of the product name actually evokes the name in the minds of the listeners. By engaging in a scripted form of audience participation, both Allen and von Zell use self-reflexive humor, further softening the interruption caused by the commercial break.

In at least one instance, Allen incorporated his sponsor directly into his program. Lee Bristol, vice president of Bristol-Myers, was a guest on a 1939 broadcast of *Town Hall Tonight*. After the introduction, "Sixty minutes of fun and music brought to you by Ipana Tooth Paste and Sal Hepatica. Ipana for the Smile of Beauty. Sal Hepatica for the Smile of Health," Lee Bristol appeared as a guest in a segment about "odd occupations." When Allen insisted on calling his guest "Mr. Bristol," Bristol responded, "Yes. I've heard some of the names sponsors are called by certain radio comedians . . . when the sponsors are out of earshot" (ellipsis in original). Allen asked Bristol how one becomes a radio sponsor, the profiled job of the week, and Bristol replied, "Well, first you have to get a business, naturally," and then advertise it. "Advertising today involves radio. The first thing you know you wake up at an audition. A dotted line appears from under an advertising agency vice-president's coat. And the next thing you know—you're a sponsor." After a description of his typical day, Bristol mentioned he often listens to programs he sponsors, and Allen replied, "Gosh, a sponsor's life is sure tough. You not only pay for radio programs[,] you have to listen to them, as well."[149]

Occasionally Y&R's efforts to appeal to audiences pushed the limits of taste. In 1938 Y&R "auditioned" a program, *What Would You Have Done?*, at NBC; Program Department executive Bertha Brainard recommended against its airing. The show presented a different dilemma each week: A man driving with his family must choose between being hit by an oncoming truck or swerving to avoid the truck but hitting child bystanders instead; two sisters fall in love with the same man; a prison guard is taken hostage and his life threatened.

The fourth episode dealt with a doctor advising a young mother and father that their baby's life may be saved only by a major operation the result of which will be that he will be permanently a mental deficient and paralyzed. The father pleads that no operation be performed and the baby be allowed to die. The mother, screaming and sobbing, insists on the operation, and at the climax of this scene the announcer again asks "What would you have done?"

Three contestants answer what they would have done; the announcer holds a $10 bill over each as the audience applauds. "An applause-ograph meter registers the volume of applause and the ten dollar bill is awarded to the greatest volume-getter."[150] Brainard pointed out that the program is "built on horror, hysteria, and scare" and is therefore "not in the best interests of the Company"—that is, NBC.

By 1948, the peak year of radio revenues, Y&R was a top radio agency, overseeing twenty different radio programs in various genres: news (*News-Scope*, sponsored by Kaiser Frazer), soap operas (*Portia Faces Life*, General Foods), situation comedies (*The Goldbergs*, General Foods; *The Adventures of Ozzie and Harriet*, International Silver), star-studded variety shows (*Harvest of Stars*, International Harvester), and anthology dramas (*The Hollywood Star Theatre*, American Home Products). The advent of television in the 1950s led to a steep drop in radio production. By 1952, Y&R was producing only thirteen radio programs for six sponsors. Its last season of radio production was 1955–56, during which its programs had dwindled to only three: the former Hummert serial *Backstage Wife* for General Foods, the game show *Two for the Money* for P. Lorillard, and the drama *The Greatest Story Ever Told* for Goodyear Tire & Rubber. Y&R had shifted production to television, moving many of its radio programs over (and simulcasting some in both media). Beginning with experiments such as Gulf Oil's *Gulf Television News* in 1946–47, Y&R's television programs expanded rapidly in the early 1950s. By the last season of radio, Y&R was overseeing fifteen television programs, including *I Love Lucy* (General Foods), *The Life of Riley* (Gulf Oil), *What's My Line?* (Remington-Rand), and *Alfred Hitchcock Presents* (Bristol-Myers). Y&R's involvement in television production would continue through the 1960s, including *The Andy Griffith Show*, *Green Acres*, *Hogan's Heroes*, and *Gomer Pyle, USMC* during the 1965–68 seasons for General Foods, and the soap opera *Another World* and situation comedy *Family Affair* for Procter & Gamble.

Early in the radio era, admen debated the usefulness and necessity of showmanship, the problematic relationship between entertainment and advertising. Having struggled to bring a more sober, serious, and credible reputation to advertising, many admen feared that the entertainment could recall the old patent medicine shows and so undermine advertising's status as a respectable business. Humor, in particular, threatened to undermine the rational, reason-why, product-centered strategies of the hard sell proponents. While most admen acknowledged the need for entertainment to attract audiences for selling messages, they debated how to use it. They faced constraints in the advertising industry's institutional limitations, while dealing with the costs and demands of entertainment industries; the often competing demands of their clients; and, even more important, the unpredictable demands of audiences, whose desires were ever-changing and difficult to identify.

The soft sell dissidents against the hard sell orthodoxy embraced entertainment as a powerful attention-getting device. In this Y&R had great success on radio. Its close identification with major radio comedians such as Fred Allen and Jack Benny underscored its commitment to humor and entertainment as effective advertising strategies, though Benny's and Allen's humorous commentaries on their sponsors discomfited traditionalists like Hummert and JWT's John Reber. Benny's strategy of making humor out of advertising, encouraging the audience to laugh not only at the jokes but at the advertising too, laid the foundations for the self-reflexivity and humor that would characterize what became known as the "Creative Revolution" in the advertising industry of the 1960s. Y&R was a pioneer in the technique of disarming audience resistance to commercials by mocking their commercialism. More generally, its soft sell approach, dependent on positive associations between products and consumers' emotions, would become the dominant advertising strategy from the 1960s onward, when product-centered hard sell strategies receded in importance.

7

Two Agencies
Batten Barton Durstine & Osborn, Crafters of the Corporate Image, and Benton & Bowles, Radio Renegades

Successful advertising agencies differed from one another in more than just their advertising strategies. While the divide between the hard and soft sell is especially well illustrated by the contrasting practices of Blackett-Sample-Hummert and Young & Rubicam, many other agencies routinely relied on both strategies, emphasizing hard sell or soft sell more or less for particular clients or campaigns, or as advertising trends shifted. Batten Barton Durstine & Osborn, the agency whose name was compared to the sound of a trunk falling down the stairs on *Jack Benny*, was the foremost specialist in institutional advertising for large corporate clients seeking to improve their public image. Throughout the 1930s and 1940s, BBDO worked to convince consumers of the benevolence of U.S. Steel, General Motors, General Electric, and Du Pont.[1] Its reputation rested in part on the prominence of its famous copywriter Bruce Barton, who was best known for his bestseller about Jesus, *The Man Nobody Knows*, and who also served briefly as a Republican congressman. Benton & Bowles, on the other hand, was a maverick agency, forced by the exigencies it faced at its founding on the cusp of the Depression to break the rules and innovate agency practices. Led by two Yale-educated Democrats, William Benton and Chester Bowles, B&B was not a typical agency, and its leaders were not typical admen in certain respects, but their contributions to radio practices had far-reaching effects. By first challenging basic agency practices, and then the problem of the radio model of broadcasting itself, both Benton and Bowles helped undermine conventional wisdom and then, when each had gone on to careers in politics, education, and business, became vocal critics of commercial broadcasting, using their insider knowledge of the industry to suggest reforms. These two agencies, then, while both serving major corporate clients, approached radio differently. While each professed to tailor its work to the particular needs of each client, BBDO was clearly the establishment agency, known for its in-depth understanding of corporate institutional advertising strategies, while B&B was the maverick agency, inventing new solutions and challenging conventional wisdom.

BBDO Beginnings: Institutional Advertising Specialist

BBDO was the result of a 1928 merger of the George Batten Co., an agency founded in 1891, with the Barton Durstine & Osborn agency, founded after World War I by several former journalists.[2] George Batten, who died in 1918, had been well known in the trade for three decades as a reformer bent on bringing advertising into the mainstream of standard business practices. Batten had complained that agencies undermined their clients' trust by charging them for space they did not use and by retaining commissions from media they did not earn. Instead of buying space speculatively and trying to resell it to advertisers, Batten insisted on determining the clients' space needs first and finding space second, thus establishing a higher level of trust with clients.[3] As his agency expanded from one client, a kerosene lamp glass company that was absorbed by Corning Glass and became a decades-long client, Batten advocated increased standardization and transparency in advertising, such as "uniform commissions, published rate cards," and the founding of the Audit Bureau of Circulations, which distributed and verified the number of newspapers and magazines sold.[4] By 1910, the Batten Co. was successful enough that in one of its trade advertisements it boasted of its selectivity: "We go anywhere for business—but there is some business we do not want, and we haven't much time for 'scouting.'"[5] However, despite this respectability, by 1925 its billings were only half that of its neighbor and competitor, BDO. In 1928, when Batten merged with BDO, Batten's billings were only $7.8 million to BDO's $22.6 million.[6] Nonetheless, the strength of the Batten name gave it first place in the merger. Its culture was formal and paternalistic, in contrast to BDO's, which eventual BBDO president Charles Brower described as "swinging": Its executives were rumored to patronize a local "pleasure dome."[7]

The three former journalists who founded BDO in 1919 had met each other during the United War Work Campaign. Alex Osborn, who had also worked at the Remington agency, founded BDO's Buffalo office, where he stayed for the duration of his career. Roy Durstine, a Princeton graduate, had reported for the *New York Sun*, handled publicity for Teddy Roosevelt's Bull Moose Party in 1912, and worked with well-known adman Earnest Elmo Calkins; he became the founding business manager of BDO. Durstine, a major proponent of advertising on radio, helped found BDO's radio department in 1926, which was probably one of the reasons Batten merged with BDO. BDO's first clients included a number of publishers, including Scribner's, Condé Nast, and the *New York Tribune*, as well as the General Baking Co.

The chief copywriter of BDO was Bruce Barton, a magazine writer and editor. Having once aspired to be a historian, he had to be convinced to go into advertising, where he became one of the most famous admen of the era. His award-winning copywriting skill is evident in a 1926 institutional advertisement for General Electric, promoting the value of electricity generally. The headline above an image of a woman bending over a hand-cranked washer reads: "Any woman who does anything which a little electric motor can do is working for 3 cents an hour!"[8] Consumers suspicious of the increased costs of using electrical appliances were to conclude not only that using them would free women from the burdens of manual labor but also that not using them would result in their near-enslavement.

Like Batten, Barton was the son of a minister, in his case the well-known Congregationalist theologian William Barton, who wrote a biography of President Abraham Lincoln. After graduating from Amherst in 1907, Barton dropped out of graduate school to edit small magazines, write inspirational editorials, and sell Collier's Five-Foot Shelf of Harvard Classics. His success publicizing the Salvation Army during the United War Work Campaign (he is credited with the phrase "A man may be down but he is never out") convinced Barton that the pen was mightier than the sword. After joining BDO, potentially more lucrative than his other pursuits, Barton continued to write editorials, homilies, articles, and collections (such as *It's a Good Old World*, 1920).

Barton was best-known for his 1924 book about Jesus, *The Man Nobody Knows*, which was first serialized in *Woman's Home Companion* and stayed on the bestseller lists in 1925 and 1926.[9] Barton's Jesus, rather than a "'lamb of God' who was weak and unhappy and glad to die," was actually an "outdoor man" with muscles as "hard as iron," whose strong leadership demonstrated principles of effective "executive management."[10] Barton argued that Jesus's brilliance lay in his ability to communicate the Gospel effectively. Describing Jesus's parables as advertisements for Christianity, Barton urged admen to study the parables:

Take any one of the parables, no matter which—you will find that it exemplifies all the principles on which advertising textbooks are written. Always a picture in the very first sentence; crisp, graphic language and a message so clear that even the dullest can not escape it.[11]

Not only were the parables perfect advertisements, but Jesus also modeled excellent salesmanship in his preaching:

With his very first sentence he put himself in step with them; it was invariably a thought in line with their own thinking, easy for even the dullest to understand, and shrewdly calculated to awaken an appetite for more. Every salesman knows the value of being able to sense an objection and meet it before it is advanced.[12]

Barton found many ways to link Christianity to contemporary business practice. In a 1924 radio talk broadcast on RCA's WJZ station, Barton told a story of a shop owner's resisting an adman's proposal to place an ad because everyone knows "where I am and what I sell." Barton's adman asks about the church across the street and how long it had been there. The shop owner answers, "'Oh, I don't know; seventy-five years probably.' 'And yet,' exclaimed the advertising man, '*they ring the church bell every Sunday morning.*'"[13] Human nature is forgetful; even the church must remind its worshippers, and advertisers must do likewise for their customers. Critics then and since have excoriated Barton for conflating Jesus with salesmen and the Gospel with advertising.[14] In trying to reconcile the apparently competing discourses of Christianity and modern business, to elevate everyday business practice into an important and valuable calling, a form of "service" to "human progress," Barton was, however, typical of the admen of his time in their efforts to shed their profession's disreputable associations. Although he may have reached his greatest celebrity during the 1920s, Barton's stature as bestselling author, speaker, and, from 1937 to 1940, elected congressman from the "silk stocking" district of the Upper East Side of Manhattan, helped BBDO maintain its reputation as a particularly effective agency for institutional advertising clients whose needs for polishing their corporate image were well served by his progressive advertising ideals.

The merged BBDO became one of the most successful advertising agencies on Madison Avenue, though like other agencies it suffered during the Depression. Immediately after the merger, it posted record high billings of $32.6 million in 1929; thereafter these declined to a low of $14.8 million in 1933 and did not recover their 1929 volume until 1944, when as a result of the war economy they reached $34 million.[15] Despite these reductions, BBDO attracted new clients throughout the 1930s, including Hormel (1931), Consolidated Edison and Schaefer Brewing (1932), Continental Can and Curtis Publishing (1933), New York Telephone and Remington Arms (1934), Liberty Mutual and First National City Bank of New York (1935).[16] It enjoyed unusually stable relationships with some of its clients; in 1966 it could boast of virtually unbroken relationships with Armstrong Cork since 1917, General Electric since 1920, and United Fruit since 1925.[17] BBDO claimed to continue Batten's commitment to honesty and transparency in advertising, operating with the highest ethical standards. (Barton's extramarital affair and the resulting trial in 1932 apparently had no lasting effect on his or BBDO's reputation.)[18]

Barton's copywriting philosophy reflected some of Theodore MacManus's soft sell, user-centered precepts when he wrote that an advertising theme "should be based on two principles—a man's interest in himself and his interest in other people."[19] In a 1930 campaign, BBDO copy tested two different headlines for a life insurance company. The first headline, "What would become of her if something happened to you?" lost to the second, which addressed itself more directly to the needs of the potential buyer: "To men who want to quit work some-day."[20] Emphasizing "interesting headlines," good "visualization," and succinct copy, Barton also clearly valued aesthetics.[21]

BBDO's best-known campaigns applied these strategies to institutional advertising for large corporations. When U.S. Steel became a client in 1936, it sought to counter public perceptions that it was a monopoly, unfair to labor. Barton devised what BBDO called a "sympathetic consumer campaign to show how the corporation had contributed to the progress of the country."[22] In a print advertisement overseen by Barton, an image of U.S. Steel's founder, Andrew Carnegie, was headlined: "He came to a land of wooden towns *and left a nation of steel*,"[23] thus demonstrating with a few choice words the progressivism of the client (see Figure 7-1). This type of image advertising was designed not to spur readers to buy things from U.S. Steel but to change their perception of the company and of Carnegie, from a strike breaker and predatory monopolist to an engineer of progress and modernity. Barton's ambitions to raise advertising and business practice to the lofty goal of "service" and general progressive ideals found their perfect outlet in this kind of advertising.[24] However, unlike some soft sell proponents, who sought only to get attention and entertain, Barton still very much believed in advertising's power to educate. BBDO's institutional advertising approach, though less hectoring in tone than reason-why advertising, nonetheless emphasized the instructional.

BBDO and Radio

While Barton had extolled the "magic" of radio as early as 1922, Roy Durstine was more eager and effective in involving his agency in radio.[25] While the Batten Co. investigated radio and then finally hired George Podeyn from NBC in 1927, BDO had already entered radio in 1925, when its client Atwater Kent began broadcasting Metropolitan

He came to a land of wooden towns
and left a nation of steel

IN AN ATTIC in Dunfermline, Scotland, he was born on November 25th a hundred years ago—the son of a man and woman who later dared the great adventure of crossing the Atlantic to find opportunity.

They sailed seven weeks in a wooden ship and landed in a country of wooden towns.

From New York to Pittsburgh was another three weeks' journey, by the Erie Canal and the Lake to Cleveland, thence down a canal to Beaver, and up the Ohio River. Andrew was thirteen years old. Before he had reached middle age, steel rails had joined New York and Pittsburgh, and steel Pullmans rolled over them in ten hours. He lived to see automobiles of steel travel from city to city in a day. Now airplanes, powered by gasoline explosions inside cylinders of steel, span the distance in a hundred minutes; and the Atlantic crossing has changed from seven weeks of danger to a hundred hours of comfort in a floating steel hotel.

Great eras are the work of great men. And great men flourish only when they are needed. When a country ceases to need them, it is no longer great. Andrew Carnegie became a master builder because America needed him and welcomed him.

Does our country no longer need great builders? Have we no frontiers left, as some would assert?

Andrew Carnegie, if he were alive, would be the first to deny it. United States Steel, which carries forward the industry he helped to create, protests against any such counsel of despair.

The economic pains we have had are the pains of adolescence—not the pains of old age. America is built, but men are dreaming of building it better. Those vital arteries of national life, the railroads, are to be rebuilt. New steels—rustless, stronger, lighter—will lift the burden of dead weight from rolling stock and make transportation more economical and efficient.

Twenty-five million homes are to be rebuilt, and steel will be there to hold comfort and health within the walls—to lift the threat of fires that have wiped out whole communities, from country villages to cities as large as Chicago.

Twenty-five million automobiles are to be replaced with lighter, stronger, safer cars. Already thousands of miles of steel and concrete highways have been laid, and thousands more miles must be added. Will America ever be finished? Never as long as American ingenuity begets ideas and American ambitions remain unsatisfied.

The nation that Andrew Carnegie helped to build will be rebuilt and *rebuilt* again. Always with more and more steel.

AMERICAN BRIDGE COMPANY · AMERICAN SHEET & TIN PLATE COMPANY · AMERICAN STEEL & WIRE COMPANY · CARNEGIE STEEL COMPANY · CARNEGIE-ILLINOIS STEEL CORPORATION · COLUMBIA STEEL COMPANY · CYCLONE FENCE COMPANY · FEDERAL SHIPBUILDING & DRY DOCK COMPANY · NATIONAL TUBE COMPANY · OIL WELL SUPPLY COMPANY · SCULLY STEEL PRODUCTS COMPANY · TENNESSEE COAL, IRON & RAILROAD COMPANY · U.S. STEEL PRODUCTS COMPANY · UNIVERSAL ATLAS CEMENT COMPANY · *United States Steel Corporation Subsidiaries*

UNITED STATES STEEL

ANDREW CARNEGIE ······· *Born one hundred years ago*

Figure 7-1. U.S. Steel: "He came to a land of wooden towns *and left a nation of steel*." (Reproduced in the seventy-fifth anniversary edition of the *BBDO Newsletter*, February 1966, 34, courtesy of BBDO.)

Opera performances to promote its radios. Although BDO did not directly produce these broadcasts, their apparent success stimulated Durstine's interest. Having been in Princeton's drama society, he felt qualified to oversee BDO's radio efforts. In 1927, BDO hired the son of a famous bandleader, Arthur Pryor Jr., expecting to use his connections to the entertainment industries. Pryor directed the first dramatic radio programs produced by BDO, *Soconyland Sketches*, which undertook a series of broadcasts in 1929 called "The Seven Governors" that featured governors from eastern states and New York mayor Jimmy Walker.[26] In addition to this and the Atwater Kent programs, BBDO in 1929 produced *General Motors Family Party, The Aeolian Hour, National Home Hour, Lehn & Fink Serenade, Happy Wonder Bakers, The Armstrong Quakers, The Gillette Program, The Blackstone Plantation,* and *The Scadertown Band.* General Electric promoted electricity with a special broadcast from Niagara Falls with announcer Graham MacNamee on the International Bridge and Phillips Carlin broadcasting from the Cave of the Winds.[27] According to an in-house BBDO history, "From then on, client after client sponsored Big Name after Big Name. The world of opera, concert, musical comedy, vaudeville, motion pictures and, yes, baseball flocked to BBDO's Radio Bureau."[28] Meanwhile, Durstine gave speeches and wrote articles urging agencies and advertisers to become more involved in radio. Calling radio "this lusty infant," Durstine exhorted advertisers to rely on the wisdom of their agencies and take it seriously as an entertainment medium that sells. He also, however, warned advertisers of the risks of offending engaged listeners: "But dare to be dull or stupid or uninteresting with your radio programming and you will hear from them, because you are doing it *on their air!*"[29]

In a 1930 trade advertisement headlined "Audible Advertising," BBDO featured photographs of eight of its twenty-three radio department employees and listed its programs, which had expanded to include the *Johnson & Johnson Musical Melodrama, The Raleigh Revue,* and *The Fuller Brush Man Program* (see Figure 7-2). With the exceptions carefully noted, BBDO announced that "the creative work of writing, rehearsing and directing . . . is all ours." Comparing radio work to print media, BBDO pointed out: "We buy talent anywhere, just as we

April 16, 1930   ADVERTISING & SELLING   31

MARY SCANLAN SPIER
Secretary, Radio Department
New York

ARTHUR PRYOR, JR.
Manager, Radio Programs
New York

HERBERT SANFORD
Program Director, Radio Department
New York

GEORGE J. PODEYN
Manager, Radio Promotion
New York

WILLIAM SPIER
Program Director
Radio Department
New York

KENNETH M. FICKETT
Program Director and Announcer
Radio Department
New York

WILLIAM R. STUHLER
Program Director
Radio Department
New York

THOMAS HARRINGTON
Director of Morning Programs
Radio Department
New York

Audible Advertising

OUR EXPERIENCE in radio broadcasting covers five years. We plan, write, rehearse and direct more programs than any other agency.

This radio activity is a service to our clients. It is not offered separately, because we believe that unless an agency is intimately acquainted with an advertiser's entire business, it cannot

—*intelligently advise whether broadcasting should be used, or*
—*successfully plan a program adapted to the advertiser's special needs.*

Our Radio Bureau, containing 23 people, works with the rest of our organization, which is becoming as familiar with this new art as it is with any of the older forms of advertising.

We buy talent anywhere, just as we buy drawings anywhere. We engage the facilities of the broadcasting stations just as we engage the facilities of the publishers.

The creative work of writing, rehearsing and directing the following evening programs is all ours—with the three exceptions noted below.

Atwater Kent Radio Hour
General Motors Family Party
**Soconyland Sketches*
Blackstone Plantation
Johnson & Johnson Musical Melodrama
Happy Wonder Bakers
Atwater Kent Mid-Week Program
The Armstrong Quakers
The Raleigh Revue
The Fuller Brush Man Program
***General Electric Hour*

In addition to these evening programs we write, rehearse and direct eight periods of morning broadcasts, and a considerable number of spot programs.

* * *

*John T. Adams, vice-president of the Judson Radio Program Corporation, has been associated with us as a program director on this series since it started in 1925.
**The dialogue of this program is written by Henry Fisk Carlton and William Ford Manley and directed by Gerald Stopp in association with our own program directors.
***Placed every other week, alternating with another agency. The National Broadcasting Company builds this program. We write the scripts for the programs every other week.

BATTEN, BARTON, DURSTINE & OSBORN
INCORPORATED
ADVERTISING
383 MADISON AVENUE · NEW YORK

CHICAGO, McCormick Building... BOSTON, 10 State Street... BUFFALO, Rand Building... PITTSBURGH, Grant Building... MINNEAPOLIS, First National-Soo Line Building

Figure 7-2. BBDO: "Audible Advertising." (*Advertising & Selling*, 16 April 1930, 31.)

buy drawings anywhere. We engage the facilities of the broadcasting stations just as we engage the facilities of the publishers": In both media BBDO sought out the best for its clients. Claiming to "plan, write, rehearse and direct more programs than any other agency," BBDO also noted that radio services are "not offered separately, because we believe that unless an agency is intimately acquainted with an advertiser's entire business, it cannot intelligently advise whether broadcasting should be used, or successfully plan a program adapted to the advertiser's special needs."[30]

By 1931, BBDO claimed to be producing seventy-seven programs for twenty-nine clients, some of which aimed for high-minded goals. For General Motors' *The Parade of the States*, Barton wrote a "testimonial" to each state with the purpose "to sell America to Americans by a weekly radio tour of each state."[31] According to BBDO's historian, "A handsomely printed, framed copy of Bruce Barton's tribute was sent to each State's Historical Society."[32] BBDO took over *Time* magazine's news program, *The March of Time*, in 1933 when *Time* could no longer justify the airtime expense. Under Pryor's direction, BBDO produced the program jointly with *Time* for its client Remington Rand, a manufacturer of typewriters and adding machines. Though at first concerned that "a new sponsor was taking over an old and well-established program—lock, stock and barrel," and that this form of dual sponsorship—promoting both *Time* and Remington Rand—was risky, BBDO announced that its advertising continuity for Remington Rand had successfully enabled audiences to identify the new sponsor without undermining *Time*'s formula. An observer describes a production process that began on the fiftieth floor of the Chrysler Building, where *Time* staff choose the news items "most suitable for dramatization"; then Arthur Pryor Jr., "crack production man . . . gives the program form and meaning"; he concludes that the coordination among "editors, agency, and network engineers" is "so complete" that "listeners are probably quite unaware of the rush, the glamour, the continual excitement which envelopes [sic] the program's production."[33] The high-minded seriousness with which BBDO approached radio was mocked by a JWT executive, Robert Simon, in a 1932 staff meeting: "Production men dash about, whispering mysterious instructions to conductors . . . others sit in the control room and frown wisely . . . and always a tense atmosphere, a brooding, a sense of heavy thinking." Barton's scripts, according to Simon, were "panting panegyrics."[34]

Cavalcade of America: Educating the Public

Cavalcade of America (1935–53) was perhaps the best-known BBDO radio program.[35] An anthology drama based on historical events, vetted by historians, written by well-known authors, performed by stars, it was sponsored by Du Pont, which trumpeted it as "a new form of entertainment." According to an early press release, *Cavalcade* "offers a new and absorbing approach to history, the incidents being re-enacted so as to emphasize the qualities of American character which have been responsible for the building of this country."[36] *Cavalcade's* function extended beyond the didactic, of course; it was intended to provide effective institutional advertising for Du Pont.[37]

Du Pont, founded in Delaware as a gunpowder manufacturer in 1802, had long since expanded into other areas of manufacturing, such as paints, pesticides, plastics, and fertilizers, yet in 1934 it found itself on the defensive when it was called before the Nye Hearings in the U.S. Senate and investigated for inciting wars to sell munitions. As Du Pont president Walter Carpenter later recalled, Du Pont "undertook to find ways and means of dissipating the evil effects of this slander operation and in that connection instituted the 'Cavalcade of America' program on the radio" (see Figure 7-3).[38] Although the threat of further hearings investigating "merchants of death" gradually receded, Carpenter recalled that an institutional advertising effort like *Cavalcade* seemed a good way to "offset" what Du Pont viewed as the Roosevelt administration's "policy to assail industry, particularly so-called big business."[39] Like U.S. Steel, Du Pont made many products not directly sold to individual consumers and so faced the problem of how to communicate to consumers so as to improve their attitudes toward it. In 1935 BBDO offered Du Pont a variety of potential slogans, including "The Age of Chemistry is an age of plenty," "Chemistry creates comfort," and "Chemistry—the servant of progress." One slogan, "Chemistry Finds Better Things," evolved into "Better Things for Better

THE CAVALCADE OF AMERICA

● Du Pont is pleased to announce to educators of the United States that The Cavalcade of America will return to the air on January 2, 1940, over a nation-wide network of the National Broadcasting Company.

The Cavalcade, already a "must" on lists of those who have looked to radio for dramatic, entertaining programs distinguished by their contributions to education, gains added authority through the addition of these American scholars to the Cavalcade staff:

MARQUIS JAMES, famous author and twice the winner of the Pulitzer prize for biography, is a new member of the Cavalcade staff. He is the author of *The Raven, A Biography of Sam Houston; Andrew Jackson; They Had Their Hour;* and other important books in the field of American historical biography. He is also a frequent contributor to leading magazines, including The Saturday Evening Post. Mr. James is supplying unusual and stirring story material for Cavalcade dramas.

CARL CARMER, noted author who now aids the preparation of Cavalcade, is an able story-teller whose best sellers include *Stars Fell on Alabama; Listen For A Lonesome Drum;* and *The Hudson.* Mr. Carmer has also been a college professor and editor, and is well-known as a popular

lecturer. To Cavalcade Mr. Carmer brings a fresh and exciting approach to American history.

DR. FRANK MONAGHAN. Serving as historical consultant and supervisor for all Cavalcade programs is Professor Frank Monaghan of the Department of History at Yale University and Fellow of Calhoun College. Dr. Monaghan, who has written and lectured widely on American history, was formerly assistant editor of the Dictionary of American Biography. John Jay: Defender of Liberty and French Travellers in the United States are notable among his publications.

With its return to the air on January 2, Cavalcade of America, winner of many radio awards, promises unexcelled entertainment for all members of the family. The brand-new series is featuring many little-known stories of notable characters and high-spot events in American history. Radio's best dramatists and actors are cooperating in the production of vivid, informative dramas. One interesting feature, continued by popular demand, is the brief story of chemical research, at the close of the program. Advance synopses of Cavalcade dramas are available to teachers on request. Write Du Pont, Wilmington, Delaware.

Preparing to return to the air January 2, the staff of historical experts holds a story conference. From left to right, Dr. Frank Monaghan, Marquis James and Carl Carmer.

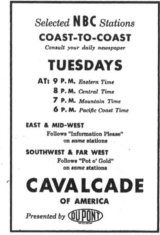

Selected **NBC** Stations
COAST-TO-COAST
Consult your daily newspaper

TUESDAYS

AT: **9 P.M.** *Eastern Time*
8 P.M. *Central Time*
7 P.M. *Mountain Time*
6 P.M. *Pacific Coast Time*

EAST & MID-WEST
Follows "Information Please" on *same* stations

SOUTHWEST & FAR WEST
Follows "Pot o' Gold" on *same* stations

CAVALCADE
OF AMERICA

Presented by DUPONT

Figure 7-3. Du Pont: *Cavalcade of America.* (Box 67, Folder 81, NBC Records.)

Living—Through Chemistry."[40] In the best BBDO tradition, the slogan appeals to a consumer's self-interest: how to get better things through the wizardry of Du Pont's chemical research. The slogan shifts the audience's focus from Du Pont's potentially dangerous products (explosives and the like) to "better living."

BBDO offered Du Pont two radio program ideas to go along with the slogan. The first, played from a record for a group of Du Pont chemists, was a half-hour monologue program, "a sort of sentimental diary," but according to an in-house account of the presentation, "the expression on [the chemists'] faces as the record came to a stop indicated acute pain." The second, a drama based on the Pilgrims' landing in the New World, was better-received, and BBDO was instructed to find more topics that would reflect "the widespread belief among thinking people that America should be brought back to first principles and given a new realization of the sturdy qualities and stamina and character which built this country."[41] Over the course of its eighteen-year run on radio, *Cavalcade* presented a different story each week, usually about heroic historical figures, ranging from obscure inventors and scientists to explorers, reformers, and politicians; one season focused on composers. The titles of episodes in the early years indicate earnest seriousness; dramas entitled "Heroism in Medical Science" (1935), "Tillers of the Soil" (1936), "Mary Lyon, Pioneer Woman Educator" (1937), and "Child Welfare in the United States" (1938) could not possibly have been mistaken for entertainment. However, by the 1940s, when production had shifted west to Hollywood and film stars were commonly featured, evidence of the lessons of the entertainment industry become apparent.[42] Consequently, while earlier episodes about Lincoln were simply titled, "Abraham Lincoln in Illinois" or "Abraham Lincoln: The War Years," a 1944 Lincoln episode featuring Raymond Massey was titled "Prologue to Glory."

Du Pont and BBDO intended *Cavalcade of America* to exceed existing standards for radio; *Cavalcade* was to be more than simply a drama series or a corporate image campaign. It was to be a cultural event and an effective educational vehicle reflecting actual scholarship. *Cavalcade* would simultaneously prove radio's capacity for uplifting the public through engaging educational entertainment while reshaping public perceptions of a misunderstood corporate patron. Signs of quality were regularly employed and promoted. Initially, Roy Durstine at BBDO went to the trouble to consult with historians to suggest subjects and vet scripts, including Arthur M. Schlesinger Sr. of Harvard, Frank Monaghan of Yale, biographer Marquis James, and James Truslow

Adams (editor, *Dictionary of American History*). The historians were prominently featured in program promotion, as in a 1939 advertisement that includes a photograph of conferring historians captioned "the staff of historical experts hold a story conference."[43] Despite trumpeting their role, eventually Du Pont stopped paying historians for their contributions to scripts.[44]

Some scripts were written by well-known authors, including Carl Sandburg, Alexander Woollcott, Stephen Vincent Benét, Robert Sherwood, and Arthur Miller, while others were written by radio writers, such as Erik Barnouw, Arch Oboler, and Norman Corwin, who would become well established in the industry.[45] As evidence of the quality and significance of *Cavalcade*, in 1937 the president of the New-York Historical Society, Dixon Ryan Fox, and Arthur Schlesinger edited and collected fifteen *Cavalcade* scripts into a book. The collection included "The Story of Rubber," about Charles Goodyear's efforts to vulcanize rubber, and "The Story of Dynamite," about Alfred Nobel's experiments with nitroglycerin. In an Introduction, the editors explained that *Cavalcade* had "made a broad and deep contribution to America's understanding of its heritage."[46] But *Cavalcade* not only drew upon top writers and historians, it also brought in top performers, a signifier of quality more obvious to the casual listener. It initially depended on mostly unknown radio actors (with a few exceptions such as the first program star, in October 1935, Walter Hampden, a "famous character actor"), but by the 1940s expensive film stars had become a regular feature, especially after production shifted to Hollywood in 1943: These included Claude Rains, Fredric March, Henry Fonda, Errol Flynn, Irene Dunne, Charles Boyer, Bette Davis, Tyrone Power, Loretta Young, Clark Gable, Lana Turner, and Humphrey Bogart.[47]

The advertising talk in *Cavalcade*, written by BBDO, was usually inserted near the opening of the program and generally resembled the indirect selling talks more common in early radio. Avoiding the specific product information hammered on repetitiously by hard sell practitioners, these talks were sometimes labeled "News from the Wonderful World of Chemistry" or "A Story from the Wonder World of Chemistry" to distinguish them from regular advertising. Du Pont vetted the BBDO copywriters' work; the commercials were "checked for scientific accuracy by as many as twenty chemists, physicists, plant pathologists and other technical experts."[48] In a 1940 episode about Thomas Jefferson, the announcer explained at length the role of Du Pont explosives in the building of railroads, tunnels, and roads, such as the Pennsylvania Turnpike, and pointed out how they "have played a pioneer part in helping build America." In another episode, about Nathan Hale, the talk concerned the role of venture capital for creating jobs, according to which the $21 million Du Pont invested in new facilities in 1938, "courageously spent, found their way into countless pay envelopes—yours and mine, perhaps—and thence moved across counters into store cash registers—from there into the pockets of farmers and factory workers—marched on to make a happy circle, and did good wherever they went." In a 1937 episode featuring the story of Elmer Ambrose Sperry, "last of the old-time inventors," the talk concerned several Du Pont products, including ammonia, made from "coal, air and water" and used as "a refrigerant for the manufacture of ice." Through Du Pont's "constant chemical research," the price of ammonia had been cut in half, and the effect on the listener's life was that "Many of the fruits, vegetables and meats you serve are brought to your table from long distances because refrigeration of this type protects them en route and during storage."[49]

By June 1947, Du Pont had sponsored 12 seasons—528 episodes—and was facing the problems of increasing costs (especially of star talent) and relatively low audience ratings. Listenership had peaked in 1945 at what was estimated by Hooper Ratings to be about 7.5 million. The expense of Hollywood stars, useful for attracting listeners to the relatively low-rated program, became less bearable once radio audiences began to migrate to television. A 1951 BBDO memo notes that the $10,000 weekly talent budget could be slashed by nearly $3,500 if an unknown were substituted for a star.[50] The program had moved to CBS, then been bumped in 1939 when demand for airtime allowed CBS to schedule a more popular program, and relegated to the lower-power NBC Blue network in 1940, then to the more powerful NBC Red in 1941. Meanwhile, Du Pont had temporarily suspended the program twice, in 1938 and 1939. Du Pont's advertising manager, William Hart, had often considered changing the format but hesitated, fearing that typical radio entertainment, such as comedy, variety, or purely fictional drama, would undermine Du Pont's serious purpose or lose its advantage of distinction.[51] Du Pont's strategy of association with heroic historical figures seemed appropriate for a company that produced few direct-to-consumer products.

Nonetheless, by 1947, Du Pont made the decision to make a "slow transition from institutional copy to that using a more direct selling technique."[52] BBDO and Du Pont debated when and if to shift *Cavalcade* to television; the greater expense of television and the wider coverage of radio kept *Cavalcade* on radio until 1953. However, radio ratings kept falling steadily, and although the radio *Cavalcade* drew as many listeners as other institutional programs on radio, Du Pont began to experiment with television starting in 1951. Less historical and more contemporary subjects appeared on *Cavalcade*'s television run; by 1956, the program name was changed to *Du Pont Theater*, jettisoning the historical altogether in order to compete for television audiences.[53]

Did *Cavalcade of America* do the institutional job for which it was designed? Ratings were not the sole measure of success. Du Pont executive William Hamilton noted that ratings numbers do not reflect the "intangible values" such as "impact," or the fostering of "favorable attitudes toward the Company."[54] Regular surveys by the Psychological Corporation documented an improvement of public attitudes toward Du Pont: While only 47 percent had a favorable attitude toward Du Pont in 1937, by 1950 that number had increased to 76 percent. Likewise, of those surveyed who could identify Du Pont as *Cavalcade*'s sponsor, 86 percent had a favorable attitude toward Du Pont, whereas of those who never listened to *Cavalcade*, only 66 percent had a favorable attitude.[55] By 1953, the Psychological Corporation found that 92 percent of lower-income listeners had a favorable attitude toward Du Pont.[56] Du Pont executive Hamilton was pleased that rather than sell specific products, with BBDO's help radio was "used by Du Pont to make friends" and promote "Positive Americanism."

BBDO's radio specialty was the institutional advertising program designed to help a large corporation "make friends" with listeners and, as the historian William L. Bird argues, counter political adversaries. Beside Du Pont, BBDO's institutional advertising clients included U.S.

Steel, Armstrong Cork, General Electric, and General Motors. However, it was also in the mainstream of commercial radio, overseeing many entertainment programs, including Schaefer Beer's *The Schaefer Revue*, Hormel's *It Happened in Hollywood*, General Motors' *Hit the Jackpot*, and Ne-Hi/Royal Crown Cola's *Believe It or Not*. As president of BBDO, Durstine, who resigned in 1939 to start his own agency, continually promoted the significance of the evolving technology of radio in an effort to overcome the residual resistance among agencies and advertisers. In a 1938 speech to the Advertising Federation of America, Durstine claimed, "Big business has learned a new vocabulary. It has grabbed a new sales tool, absorbed a new technique, adopted a new medium. It's now in show business." And whether or not advertisers wanted to be in show business, Durstine pointed out they would have to be anyway:

And even if there had been no such thing as radio, showmanship would have been applied to business over the past decade. The stepped-up pace of life today clamored for it. Whether we like it or not, masses of people today can be influenced only by the dramatic, the exciting, the graphic, the simple smash.[57]

Benton & Bowles: Innovator

During the radio era, Benton & Bowles was a close competitor to Y&R. The two agencies shared an affinity for soft sell approaches, and they both produced some of the same programs (usually because the sponsor changed agencies), including programs featuring Jack Benny and Fred Allen, *Portia Faces Life*, and *Young Doctor Malone*. B&B also produced *Maxwell House Show Boat*, *Ziegfeld Follies of the Air*, and *Palmolive Beauty Box Theater*. Like Y&R, B&B was a relatively new agency, founded in 1929, that approached the challenges of the Depression and radio with unconventional strategies. As founder Chester Bowles explained in a 1963 interview, "[B]ecause no one knew anything about [radio], you could improvise and the standards weren't very good, and we were able to do a lot of things that looked quite fresh and new."[58] Advertisers hired B&B for their innovative problem-solving abilities rather than for specific rule-bound solutions to the problems of radio advertising. The propensity of B&B's founders, William Benton and Chester Bowles, to question standard practices and implement innovations influenced the industry, and B&B thrived as a major radio agency even after its founders left.[59]

Both Benton and Bowles were Yale graduates who fell into advertising in the mid-1920s despite interests in politics and education. While at the George Batten agency, Bowles worked as Benton's assistant and remained after Benton was fired.[60] Benton sought to learn from the best in the advertising industry: He worked under master salesman John Patterson at the National Cash Register Company in the early 1920s, and in 1928 he joined Lord & Thomas in Chicago in order to work under Albert Lasker, the famous proponent of "salesmanship in print." While there, he grew interested in new research methodologies. By going out and speaking directly with consumers about products, he impressed Lasker, who had been dissatisfied with earlier market research efforts that tended to focus on retailers.[61] Benton was also interested in the new medium of radio. In a 1970 interview he claimed that one night leaving Lord & Thomas he was struck on the walk home by "these colored voices leaping out into the street, from all the apartments." Walking back up the street, he counted seventeen radios tuned into the local program *Amos 'n' Andy* and returned to Lasker insisting he sell the program to their client, Pepsodent, for national network broadcast.[62] *Amos 'n' Andy* went on to become one of the greatest hits of early network radio. Benton's claim to recognize the program's appeal may be apocryphal; however, his interest in radio as a commercial medium clearly developed earlier than that of many others in the advertising industry.

By the time Benton decided to join with Bowles and set up their own agency in 1929, both had become frustrated by the relatively low standards of education and professionalism in the advertising industry.[63] Bowles had carefully analyzed the advertising strategies of General Foods, a large advertiser that gave several of its accounts to Y&R, thereby making it possible for that agency to survive its first year. Bowles reasoned that General Foods could do the same for his and Benton's new agency, so, in June 1929, he approached the company, promising new ideas and new forms of consumer research, and convinced it to transfer some of its accounts from the more established J. Walter Thompson agency.[64] Once the Depression hit, Benton & Bowles grew rapidly by taking advantage of advertiser dissatisfaction. As Bowles put it, "[C]ompanies were examining their old relationships and were very critical of them and looking for anything new that might be helpful."[65]

B&B focused on a small number of large-budget advertisers in the drug and food industries; along with General Foods, their early clients included Bristol-Myers and Colgate-Palmolive, and each account billed more than $1 million a year. This gave B&B a wider margin for profit than if it had been servicing a larger number of smaller accounts.[66] With the idea that an agency had to do more for its clients in the economic climate of the Depression, B&B also developed new marketing, merchandising, and consumer research strategies. In a time of deflation, B&B recommended that its clients lower prices and improve quality to stimulate consumption. This was a relatively radical idea for consumer goods manufacturers, who had enjoyed wide profit margins on relatively high prices during the 1920s. Client Maxwell House lowered the price on its coffee, while improving its packaging and the quality of its coffee beans, and thus reaped a large increase in sales, capturing market share from its competitor Chase & Sanborn.[67] Bowles (along with partner Atherton Hobler, who joined in 1932) insisted that improving value through pricing and quality would work better than any advertising campaign.[68] In order to convince a client to finance such a change, Bowles also suggested that clients spend less on advertising appropriations—in the case of Maxwell House, by lowering its annual expenditures from $3 million to $1 million.[69] This tactic helped cement Benton & Bowles' reputation, according to Bowles:

You see, the interesting thing about this deal was that it included a recommendation for a reduction of the advertising budget, even though the agency made all its money on a percentage basis [of the advertising budget]. So, I think this persuaded people that we had integrity. What we had really was not integrity but a sense of long-range interest. If you could build up long-range relationships, you'd be better off than with the short-range ones.[70]

B&B also recommended that Maxwell House put *all* of its advertising spending into radio, rather than print, another radical idea at a time when radio was still relatively unproven. According to B&B partner Hobler, radio offered an opportunity to reach "three times the audience of any other media" at a much lower cost than that of print.[71] As radio became a larger part of their business, Bowles oversaw all of the radio programs, including *Palmolive Beauty Box Theater*, Bristol-Myers' *Town Hall Tonight*, and *Maxwell House Show Boat*. During the severe downturn of 1932–33, when many agencies cut their staffs, B&B recruited some of the best-known copywriters and radio men in the industry, including Walter O'Meara, Tiny Ruffner, and Tom Revere, to build their radio department.[72] By 1936, B&B oversaw seven different national network broadcasts a week, three of which (*Town Hall Tonight*, *Maxwell House Show Boat*, and *Palmolive Beauty Box Theater*) accounted for three of the top four shows on the national networks.[73] That year, Benton wrote his mother, Elma Benton, that B&B's success in show business made it one of the largest "employers of entertainers in the country," which was "a rather anomalous position for a bunch of advertising men."[74]

B&B claimed credit for innovative strategies. While many agencies routinely double- or triple-cast one actor for several parts in order to save on labor costs, B&B's high production budgets enabled them to do the opposite: cast more than one person for a single role. According to Benton, "We'd get a sexy singer, who might not be a good actress, then we'd get the sexiest actress we could find and we'd give her the speaking lines, softening the audience up, getting it warm and ready to melt. Then the girl would come in and sing." For example, on *Maxwell House Show Boat*, the role of "Mary Lou" was sung by Muriel Wilson and acted by Rosaline Greene.[75] Using the listening audience's blindness to such advantage would never have occurred to "people in the theater," argued Benton. "The advertising men made radio. We weren't inhibited. We didn't know you couldn't put two people in one part."[76]

Benton & Bowles consistently sought to reach audiences at their perceived taste levels. Benton claimed that he had a "tin ear" for music, giving him an everyman perspective on radio programming despite his educated background.[77] Bowles pointed out, "If people don't listen, they don't buy. They'll listen only to what they like." Bowles argued against trying to shape the audience's taste:

We can't give the farmer's wife and the grocer's daughter a taste for Beethoven and Brahms; we can't make them like Shakespeare or Greek tragedy; we can't stop them from enjoying "The Music Goes 'Round," or "Robins and Roses." We can't ask them to agree with our own tastes in music, entertainment and education.[78]

Not imposing tastes also extended to not assuming that any one programming strategy was the "best kind." B&B developed programs in a variety of genres and lengths, differentiated for a variety of targeted audiences and products. According to an agency presentation memo, "The success of most programs varies in direct proportion to the ability of the people who write them and the skill with which they are produced."[79] B&B, then, unlike B-S-H, believed that there were no formulas for attracting audiences; instead, a program's success depended most on the talent of the participants.

B&B's most important program, *Maxwell House Show Boat*, not only became a top prime time program but, according to Hobler, also increased Maxwell House coffee sales by 70 percent.[80] The program opened with the announcement "Come aboard, folks. Your ticket of admission is just your loyalty to Maxwell House Coffee," indicating the hope that audience gratitude would translate into product sales.[81] *Maxwell House Show Boat* was one of the most expensively produced programs on radio, costing about $6,500 a week for airtime and production in 1932, well above average.[82] B&B, as the producer using a budget supplied by Maxwell House, paid the performers relatively well in 1932, reasoning that skimping on talent fees would undermine the program.[83] *Maxwell House Show Boat* was a variety show, with featured guest stars as well as a returning cast of singers and musicians, including a minstrel act named Molasses 'n' January, which traveled by boat up and down the river doing shows. It was built from pre-sold elements: *Show Boat*'s title and some of the songs came from the composer Jerome Kern's Broadway musical *Show Boat*.

Maxwell House Show Boat used integrated commercials in which the performers plugged Maxwell House coffee both in and out of character, both within the program text and also in interstitial "backstage" moments. According to Hobler, "What [the performers] did and discussed back-stage became an integral part of the show and as much a source of entertainment as the songs and music they performed."[84] Like Young & Rubicam, B&B attempted to prevent audience alienation by naturalizing the commercial pitch. According to an article in the trade magazine *Advertising & Selling*, "Good radio copy and radio talent, of course, are a sister-act. Talent collects the crowd, and 'softens' it. Copy picks up from there." For proof, the writer cites a B&B commercial. Tiny Ruffner, the well-known radio announcer for *Maxwell House Show Boat*, talks with the program's chief character, Captain Henry, in a team effort to sell Maxwell House during a 1935 broadcast:

Captain: "And now, I'm going to ask Tiny Ruffner a question. Tiny, exactly what do you mean when you say that everybody who buys Maxwell House Coffee gets full value for his money?"

Tiny: "Well, I refer to three separate things when I say that—three things that added together *mean* full value. You might get one or two of these three advantages in other coffees—but in Maxwell House you get all *three*—First, there's the Maxwell House blend of choicest coffees—for more than fifty years the favorite of people who really enjoy good coffee."

Captain: "And the favorite of all of us!"

Tiny: "Right you are, Captain Henry. The second, there's the new improved method of grinding that assures you a more perfect cup of coffee by any method of coffee making—by drip, percolator, or boil. Third, there's that marvelous exclusive Vita-fresh method of packing which always brings Maxwell House coffee to you roaster fresh . . . and no coffee can be fresher than that! And it's this combination of all three points that assures you *full* value in every pound of Maxwell House Coffee you buy. The stage is yours, Captain Henry!"[85]

Captain Henry's polite interrogation, as well as enthusiastic confirmation, brings a softer sell to the otherwise direct rational appeal employed here ("three things" that "mean full value"). B&B also used sound effects to great effect. As Benton later described it, "When we had Captain Andy [sic] drink coffee and smack his lips, you heard the coffee cups clinking and the coffee gurgling as it was poured. It put action and actors into commercials."[86]

B&B's integrated advertising carried over into some print advertising as well. In a 1935 ad that appeared in the *Saturday Evening Post*, a comic strip provides a narrative that integrates the ad into a putative episode of *Maxwell House Show Boat* and demonstrates the technique of the "backstage" strategy (see Figure 7-4).[87] In first pane of the comic strip, two performers on the show are dancing together: Lanny Ross, the tenor, and the character Mary Lou. Mary Lou says, "Isn't this heavenly, Lanny?" Lanny responds, noticing two men sneaking away, "Marvelous, Mary Lou, but I wonder what those men are up to. Let's follow them." In the next pane, the couple see the suspicious men down a dark hallway, and Mary Lou says, "Oh, Lanny, I feel something terrible is going to happen." Lanny replies, "I know—and the Captain brought the payroll aboard to-day. You get Conrad and Tiny. I'll follow them." The suspicious men go into a room, and in the next pane Mary Lou and police officers are peering into the room with surprised looks on their faces: "Well, I'll be—" because the suspicious men are drinking coffee, not stealing the payroll. One says, "Ah, the same wonderful coffee we had at intermission," and the other says, "Yes, I hope the captain didn't see us sneak off. But it's worth the risk to get another cup of coffee like this." The next panel shows Lanny Ross, in a captain's hat, explaining, "That's the way it goes, folks . . . One taste of our delicious Maxwell House coffee and folks just naturally come back for more."

B&B produced comedian Fred Allen's program *Town Hall Tonight* until 1935, when the agency gave up the Bristol-Myers toothpaste account in order to keep the higher-budget Colgate toothpaste account.[88] In this show B&B experimented with the issue of product identification. Most sponsors advertised only one product per program, not wanting to confuse prospective purchasers and blur the positive association of star with product. However, B&B convinced Bristol-Myers to combine the advertising of two of its products into *Town Hall Tonight*, integrating the marketing through the interlinked slogans: "Take Ipana

Figure 7-4. *Maxwell House Show Boat*: "The Two Men in Black." (*Saturday Evening Post*, 23 March 1935, 4.)

for the Smile of Beauty. Take Sal Hepatica for the Smile of Health."[89] The risk of audience confusion was worth the ability to market two products for the cost of one. As Fred Allen recalled, Benton pitched the idea to Bristol-Myers by reminding them that combining two programs would "save the expense of one orchestra."[90] Multiple sponsorship would not become standard until the television era, when the savings were more important to both advertisers and broadcasters, given increased production costs. However, this early attempt at a kind of multiple sponsorship illustrates B&B's willingness to try new strategies and go against conventional wisdom.

B&B's strategy of focusing on a few large clients rather than on many small ones was also reflected in its focus on a few rather than many radio programs. And though the success of these programs gave B&B more leverage with the networks than their sheer number would have suggested, the agency could not wield the power of other agencies with higher radio volumes, such as JWT and B-S-H. Whereas JWT received its own direct telephone line to NBC and B-S-H executive Frank Hummert was powerful enough to be able to turn down a request to lunch with the new NBC president, NBC quickly dismissed Hobler's complaint that the network was undercutting B&B's Palmolive operetta program by allowing other advertisers to sponsor similar programs. NBC program director John Royal pointed out that the agency was disingenuous in claiming an exclusive on the operetta format because its other program, *Maxwell House Show Boat*, had also put on operettas.[91] And when B&B radio executive Tom Revere complained about having to pay a music clearance fee and demanded NBC pay it instead, one NBC executive complained in an internal memo to another, "For every single job we do for Benton & Bowles we do ten for J. Walter Thompson. I do not quite see the necessity for changing a system satisfactory to all agencies except Benton & Bowles when they cause endless trouble and give us small thanks for our pains."[92]

In 1933 Benton proposed that NBC provide more publicity support for itself and its programs through cross-promotion. He suggested that broadcasters, like their counterparts in the film industry, might invest in a "large number of competent publicity men" who could work on getting magazine articles placed despite print publishers' resistance to promoting the competing medium. Benton also pointed out that "NBC doesn't take sufficient advantage of its own facilities in order to publicize itself."[93] He suggested, for example, having Jack Pearl, the then-star of the Lucky Strike program, pretend to come on the air accidentally during *Maxwell House Show Boat*, which preceded it: "This ought to do a lot to carry the Maxwell House audience over into the Lucky Strike audience."[94] Benton's interest in the "flow" of audience attention from program to program, even those of another agency's client, was ahead of its time. In the television era, networks schedule programs in order to build "audience flow" from one program to the next with lead-ins and cross-promotions. But in 1933 NBC sought to avoid complaints that it was favoring one advertiser over another. In its efforts to stay neutral among advertisers, NBC did not understand that it was in both the network's and the advertisers' interests to build audiences for the overall program schedule and thus improve broadcasting's effectiveness as an advertising medium.

William Benton and Chester Bowles: Beyond Commercial Radio

Benton's effort to convince NBC to consider the overall schedule of programming was of a piece with his efforts to improve broadcasting in general. While he was still at B&B, and for decades afterward, he lobbied network chieftains David Sarnoff, Niles Trammell, and William Paley to consider ways to upgrade the programming and reformulate the business model of commercial network broadcasting. In a 1933 presentation at NBC, Benton argued that "[b]roadcasting must be improved or lose its listeners."[95] He proposed that the networks change their business model. Instead of selling blocks of time to an advertiser, who then had programming control over that "time franchise," the networks should take editorial control over programs, selecting and producing and controlling them as magazine publishers did editorial content, and selling interstitial minutes to advertisers, as magazine publishers sold advertising pages between articles.

Why would Benton, whose livelihood depended on serving his clients by producing radio programs, argue that the networks should take over the task of production? He feared that a lack of overall editorial guidance undermined audience interest in radio and that advertiser abuse of airtime could alienate audiences. He pointed out to NBC, "Advertising programs [are] not built for listeners, but to suit client whims." He was all too aware of advertisers' small concern with the overall success of the broadcast medium or with the "public interest." If the government was not going to become a programmer, as it had in the United Kingdom, then, to admen like Benton, the networks were best situated to rationalize, centralize, and professionalize radio and thereby maximize its commercial effectiveness. In retrospect, Benton's proposal anticipated the television-era business model, in which the networks are the program producers, purchasers, and schedulers, while advertisers (for the most part) simply purchase interstitial minutes within programs. In 1933, however, NBC executives regarded the existing radio business model, in which advertisers controlled a "time franchise" and produced, purchased, and scheduled programs, as too well established to change. Wrote NBC executive Wayne Randall in response to Benton's proposal: "Not a chance. Development of present sponsored program has gone too far."[96]

As NBC's negative reaction to Benton's proposals indicates, he had gained a reputation as a maverick in the industry, and in fact neither he nor his partner, Bowles, was typical of it. Both were Democrats in a predominantly Republican industry, and each would eventually pursue political careers, including service in the Roosevelt, Truman, and Kennedy administrations. Each worried that the Great Depression threatened American capitalism. Bowles believed that the New Deal "was the only thing that would save the system"; without it, "the whole country would blow up."[97] In 1932 Benton attended a secret series of conferences with corporate leaders about how to respond to the Depression. He condemned their lack of interest in reform: "It is astounding, however, how narrow the viewpoint of such men. . . . How limited their vision. . . . How unconscious, apparently, of the broad social problems which underlie so many of the economic questions the business world is facing."[98] Capitalism, wrote Benton in 1935, has "its back to the wall."[99]

Benton's disillusionment with the business world of 1932 reflected not rebellious opposition but a concern that narrow self-interest could undermine the future stability of the American economy. Both Benton and Bowles subscribed to what some historians call corporate liberalism.[100] Corporate liberals struggled to reconcile bureaucratic and oligopolistic corporate practices with liberal notions of individualism, the sanctity of private property, and free markets. In his concern that the pursuit of short-term profits by selling airtime to the highest bidder would undercut the overall value of broadcasting, while a longer-term perspective attuned to the public interest would benefit it, Benton represented a reformist wing of corporate liberalism. As himself a producer of commercial radio programming, he was better positioned than and more credible to his peers than the typical radio critics who made some of the same complaints from the outside.

Frustrated by the reluctance of then-stakeholders to change the business structure of radio, Benton sought to develop commercial alternatives. For example, he proposed to NBC in 1933 that it broaden its programming mission beyond advertisers' needs to include a "Special 'highbrow' network for 'class advertising'; self-improvement and cultural education material."[101] NBC declined to develop this suggestion also, focusing instead on selling out its prime time slots. In 1936 Benton left his agency and went on to a career as promoter for the University of Chicago and its Great Books curriculum, which emphasizes foundational texts of Western culture, and as overseer of its radio program *The University of Chicago Round Table*. The *Round Table* gathered experts of the day to discuss pressing issues such as "the need for opposition in government" and usefully allowed NBC to claim that it provided educational programming, though it kept the program ghettoized in a Sunday morning time slot where it reached few listeners.[102]

Benton explored other alternatives to advertising-supported broadcasting. In 1939 he invested in Muzak, a wired music subscription service, and expanded it beyond hotels and restaurants into banks, hospitals, and department stores. Believing that there was an even greater market in individual households for a wired subscription radio service without intrusive commercials, in 1944 Benton set about establishing one, in direct competition with the broadcast networks. He proposed offering subscribers several channels of musical, cultural, and educational programming, uninterrupted by commercials, for about five cents a day. NBC and CBS were alarmed at the potential competition; they did not want their ad-supported business model undermined by a commercially viable alternative. The *New York Times* editorialized against subscription radio as "inject[ing] a poll tax on radio—the payment of a fee in order that the public might enjoy what is already free and their property—the air. This is hardly a liberal conception of the 'freedom to listen.'"[103] Benton's response was informed by his experience in commercial radio:

"The air" may be free. But broadcasting certainly is not. It must always be paid for . . . somehow. Under our present system, people pay for radio through their purchase of radio-advertised goods, all listeners having to submit to the interruptions of commercial announcements. . . . We propose to give the listener, for the first time, an opportunity to pay for some radio programs *directly* rather than indirectly.[104]

Noting that no federal broadcast regulations, such as the Communications Act of 1934, include "any suggestion that advertising should prevail in this field," Benton pointed out the historical contingency of the commercial broadcasting system: "Certainly there is nothing in legal theory and very little in tradition that makes broadcasting solely a venture for advertising." The more choice offered to listeners, including the choice of direct payment, Benton concluded, "the greater the freedom of the air."[105] A subscription-based service, Benton hoped, would offer more audience-responsive programming than the advertiser–sponsorship model. This service did not come to fruition at the time, but it prefigures cable television just as his magazine subscription model prefigured broadcast television.

Both Benton and Bowles entered public service after they left advertising. Benton's career included the founding of the *Voice of America*, a short stint as a U.S. senator from Connecticut, and involvement in the founding of UNESCO. During his senatorial career, Benton wrote legislation for closer public oversight of broadcasters, proposing a Citizen's Advisory Board to ensure that they served the public interest; however, this initiative failed. Bowles likewise became deeply involved in politics, joining the Roosevelt administration as head of the Office of Price Administration and the Truman administration as the postwar director of Office of Economic Stabilization and becoming governor of Connecticut, ambassador to India, congressman from Connecticut, and Undersecretary of State in the Kennedy administration.

Although Bowles and Benton had sold the rights to their names to the agency, they made efforts to dissociate themselves from advertising. Both claimed to avoid listening to commercial radio after leaving the agency. Bowles later characterized his time at the agency as "not a particularly pleasant period."[106] The feeling was mutual at B&B. Remaining B&B partner Hobler later declared, "I had no idea that the names of my partners would come to stand for philosophies far afield from advertising—and from the feelings of some of our clients!"[107] In a 1963 interview, Bowles was asked, "What intrigues me was that you said that both you and Mr. Benton weren't very interested in business and yet you had these creative ideas about advertising which no one seems to have anticipated, and you make a marvelous success of your career. How do you account for that?" Bowles replied, "Oh, you try to run away from it."[108] Bowles's comment implies that some of the people who contribute the most innovative ideas to a field or industry may be the people who have the least stake in its conventions and verities.

These two successful radio agencies of the 1930s could not have been more dissimilar in attitude, outlook, and goals. BBDO, renowned for its institutional and corporate image advertising, famous for its copywriter Bruce Barton, was a "white shoe" firm serving large corporate clients in the tradition of Republican progressivism. While many of BBDO's radio programs provided standard entertainment fare, their longest-running and best-known program, *Cavalcade of America*, was a docudrama tracing the history of American business and innovation for the Du Pont Company. Serving the progressive goals of cultural uplift, public education, and good corporate citizenship, *Cavalcade* represented some of the ideals of BBDO. B&B, on the other hand, founded by Yale-educated Democrats, ran against the grain of accepted industry practice from its inception. Forced to innovate in order to survive its founding at the beginning of the economic crisis, both Benton and Bowles sought to use radio creatively and hoped to appeal to audiences without talking down to them. They broke rules; they tried to innovate solutions to advertisers' problems. Despite their success, focused on a limited number of clients and popular programs, Benton and Bowles were dissatisfied with the commercial radio industry. Benton idealistically proposed reforms to the radio business model; each was disillusioned with advertiser control of programming. Both went on to careers in public service, and the gap between them and their former colleagues at B&B grew wider. Their status as former insiders informed their later critiques of commercial broadcasting. Benton's 1933 suggestion that networks take editorial control of programming would, of course, come to pass by the 1960s.

8   Madison Avenue in Hollywood
J. Walter Thompson and *Kraft Music Hall*

In early radio networking, Chicago and New York were the centers of program production; well-known serials such as *Clara, Lu 'n' Em* were originally broadcast from Chicago. Chicago production gradually shifted to New York, where facilities such as Rockefeller Center and its Radio City became epicenters of radio; and then, by the late 1930s, a new center of program production arose: Hollywood. Home to the film industry at least since entrepreneurs had fled west to escape Thomas Edison's onerous patent fees in the 1910s, Hollywood evolved from chief competitor to closest collaborator with the New York–based radio industry. The center of radio programming shifted to Hollywood for various technical and economic reasons; however, the primary impetus was the availability of star talent. Advertising agencies set up branch offices to manage Hollywood-originated programming; the resulting culture clashes between Madison Avenue admen and their counterparts in Hollywood reflected different attitudes about the role and function of entertainment. J. Walter Thompson, one of the largest radio ad agencies, established a strong beachhead in Hollywood in order to produce star-studded programs. *Kraft Music Hall*, hosted by Bing Crosby, the singer and movie star, exemplified JWT's advertising strategy of associating celebrities with their clients' products.

Radio and Hollywood

From their beginnings, the development of sound and broadcast technologies had led to interactions between the film and broadcasting industries. Even in early commercial radio, film star extravaganzas were broadcast from Hollywood; the film studio Paramount tried to start a network in 1927 and then allied itself with CBS in 1929; and RCA moved into film when it founded RKO studios in 1928.[1] Although a few programs, such as *The Fleischmann's Yeast Hour*, hosted by Rudy Vallee, were broadcast regularly from Hollywood as early as 1932, such broadcasts increased dramatically during the "Swing to Hollywood" of 1936–38.[2] By the latter year, twenty-five major transcontinental radio programs originated from Hollywood. Because advertising agencies dominated program production, the result was that Madison Avenue–based agencies became, according to the trade magazine *Sales Management*, "as much a part of the Hollywood scene as Metro-Goldwyn-Mayer studios, high salaried glamour girls or blossoming ingénues."[3]

The symbiosis between radio and Hollywood peaked in the late 1930s and the 1940s for several reasons: improvements in transcontinental transmission, shifting economic incentives, and changing use patterns of radio and film talent. Until 1935–36, broadcasts originating from Hollywood were more expensive than those originating in New York or Chicago. Network broadcasts were carried on AT&T phone lines, the charges for which AT&T structured according to a cost-per-circuit-mile calculation. AT&T's policy that any broadcast originating in Hollywood or outside New York had to be transmitted to New York first before going back out on long lines to other stations increased transmission costs considerably,[4] until a federal regulatory investigation of AT&T's pricing policies forced a downward revision of long-line rates. Another obstacle to Hollywood-originated programming was NBC itself, which had initially established its West Coast facilities in San Francisco rather than in Los Angeles. Because of this, until the AT&T rate revision, NBC had little incentive to encourage Hollywood-originated broadcasts.[5] In 1935, once the pressure from sponsors for Hollywood-based broadcasts had increased and the economic viability of transcontinental transmissions had improved, NBC president Merlin Aylesworth finally went to Hollywood to scout for new facilities. However, according to John Swallow, manager of the NBC Hollywood studios, parochial attitudes within the broadcasting industry still hindered Hollywood's role in radio:

Most of the trouble was that New York still didn't believe Hollywood would or could ever be a radio center. New York was the spot and talent would always be available there. As a matter of fact, it was harder to try and convince the top radio executives of the day that money should be spent in Hollywood than it was to get motion picture studios to accept radio.[6]

Nonetheless, as transmission costs were finally lowered and it became increasingly clear that Hollywood talent could not always travel to New York for broadcasts, this attitude underwent revision. While in 1932 NBC broadcasts originating from Hollywood had totaled about 12 hours, by 1937 such broadcasts totaled about 700 hours.[7]

The film and radio industries during this period shared many characteristics and business strategies: Both prosecuted patent wars in order to control technologies; both tended to form oligopolies; both used stars for branding; and both, through self-regulation and trade organizations, resisted increased governmental oversight.[8] But the industries also differed in many ways: Radio was increasing its profitability during the Depression just when the film industry was suffering narrowing margins, the result of declining ticket sales and increased capital costs because of the transition to sound. Despite the film industry's greater revenues, the radio industry was actually attracting larger audiences at much lower costs.[9] While the film studios welcomed the publicity that radio could offer films, they were reluctant to anger film exhibitors, who, in the face of the declining ticket sales of the early 1930s, feared loss of box office revenue if film stars and material were accessible for free on radio.[10] However, broadcasters attempted to increase the film industry's awareness of their mutual interests. RCA, for example, established RKO pictures, and the president of both NBC and RKO, Merlin Aylesworth, pushed for greater cross-promotion between the two media, working to overcome the film industry's resistance.[11] Nonetheless, radio may have been the primary beneficiary of these efforts to promote films on radio, because attracting larger radio audiences with programs featuring film stars allowed the networks to increase time charges.[12]

The nadir of the relationship between film studios and broadcasters was probably in 1932–33, when the studios banned their contracted stars from performing on radio. Even during this short-lived ban, the studios signed and recruited radio talent for films, including Kate Smith, Bing Crosby, and George Burns and Gracie Allen. Clearly, they objected not to cross-promotion between the two media but to the risk of losing the monopolistic control over the "talent" the studios enjoyed via restrictive contracts.[13] So when advertising agencies negotiated for talent affiliated with film studios, they met with resistance. When J. Walter Thompson executive Cal Kuhl reported his failure to convince MGM to allow its star Jean Harlow to guest star on its Fleischmann's program, his supervisor, John Reber, instructed him to find "movie stars who are restive in their studio contract jails."[14] Referring to the film studios, one unhappy adman claimed, "Deep down they resent radio."[15] Eventually, as radio attracted larger audiences, the studios realized they had more to gain than to lose from radio exposure. Radio's increased exploitation of "presold" talent—that is, talent already proven to attract audiences—was probably inevitable.

At least one film studio attempted to extend its monopoly control over film talent into radio: MGM in 1937 sold access to all of its stars, writers, and producers as a package to a radio sponsor, Maxwell House, which paid $20,000–$25,000 a week to MGM for access to its talent and $15,000–$18,000 a week to NBC for time charges but subcontracted the actual program production to MGM. The program, which was initially broadcast as *The Maxwell House MGM Hour*, then as *Film Stars on Parade*, and finally as *Good News of 1938/1939*, featured MGM stars such as Robert Young, Judy Garland, Joan Crawford, Frank Morgan, and Fanny Brice, performing in a comedy-variety format. The deal spurred other studios to consider package deals with radio sponsors. However, competing endorsement deals, such as the one MGM star Clark Gable had with Maxwell House arch-competitor Chase & Sanborn, made such package deals unwieldy and fraught with potential conflicts.[16] Despite studio contracts, the film studios simply did not have total monopoly control over their stars.

Advertising Agencies in Hollywood

During the rush to California in the late 1930s, most of the major advertising agencies opened Hollywood offices to oversee Hollywood-based programming. By 1938, 30 percent of Young & Rubicam's revenues reportedly derived from its Hollywood radio shows, including *The Jack Benny Program, Al Pearce and His Gang* (a comedy program), *Lum and Abner* (a serialized situation comedy), and *Passing Parade* (a docudrama-style anthology series). Lord & Thomas produced *Pepsodent Presents Bob Hope.* Ward Wheelock produced *Amos 'n' Andy* and *Hollywood Hotel*, based on Hollywood gossip columnist Louella Parsons' reporting. Lennen & Mitchell produced *Hollywood Playhouse* and *Old Gold Hollywood Screen Scoops*, the latter another star-centered gossip program. William Esty produced *Eddie Cantor's Camel Caravan*, the vaudeville and film star having moved on to yet another sponsor, a cigarette company. Ruthrauff & Ryan produced *The Big Town*, a crime drama starring Edward G. Robinson, and an Al Jolson program. Benton & Bowles produced four Hollywood programs: the Maxwell House–sponsored MGM program; a program featuring the vaudeville comedian Joe E. Brown; *The Joe Penner Show*, featuring a comedian who had risen to fame on Rudy Vallee's program with the catchphrase "Wanna buy a duck?"; and *The Wonder Show*, a comedy-variety program sponsored by Wonder Bread and starring Jack Haley, the actor subsequently best known for his role as the Tin Woodman in *The Wizard of Oz.*[17]

During World War II, radio's dependence on Hollywood talent increased dramatically, as did talent costs. There were few disincentives to reduce such costs during the war; as Young & Rubicam radio director Tom Lewis noted, "Star-studded, dollar-studded Hollywood creations" had "blossomed in wartime loam, fertilized by paper shortage and excess profits tax."[18] Advertisers were more willing to pay higher prices for talent, thereby increasing their advertising expenditures, in order to avoid booking revenues as profit to be taxed at high rates. The profit margins for broadcasters widened, increasing from about 20 percent of revenues in 1937 to about 33 percent in 1944.[19] Once the war ended, talent and network prices seemed too high to many sponsors: "Talent is often priced out of proportion to its values," one complained.[20] Top comedians earned as much as $25,000 a week.[21] According to BBDO executive Charles Hull Wolfe, at war's end "more realistic fiscal policies replaced feverish wartime spending," resulting in a wave of cancellations of radio talent contracts.[22] Lewis of Y&R reported that Hollywood talent recognized the "new economy trend" and would reduce fees accordingly, being "more appreciative of the value of radio to the box office" than before.[23]

Despite increasing audience demand for Hollywood-originated programming, some admen criticized Madison Avenue's embrace of Hollywood values and reliance on Hollywood glamour as a sales strategy. Such a marriage, in the view of one adman complaining about "Hollywooden Idols" in the trade press, was doomed. Pointing out the absurdity of promoting Hollywood films to sell unrelated products, P. H. Erbes wrote a satirical set of instructions to an advertiser:

In order to sell, for example, canned peas, you should devote the large part of your program to selling the latest output of one of the big motion picture studios. You allot twenty-eight minutes of a half hour for the stars to build themselves up, glorify the men who manufacture the pictures and announce selling points about the latest product of the studios. Naturally the listener becomes so accustomed to being sold on things that she is a pushover for the two minutes which are devoted to selling the peas.[24]

Erbes's intention was to criticize the use of unrelated entertainment as a selling strategy; however, his description foreshadowed the television era, when programs produced in Hollywood without any design to sell a particular product would be interrupted by unrelated sixty- or thirty-second commercials. Erbes's assumption that programming unrelated to advertising could never be an effective vehicle for advertising would be overturned within the decade.

For the most part, the Hollywood offices took direction from their New York headquarters. Most of the primary program conceptualizing, as well as most of the continuity or commercial writing, was generated in New York and transmitted to Hollywood for production. Agency radio directors often had to commute regularly between Hollywood and New York to meet with agency and sponsor executives, usually by train. By the 1940s, it was a regular circuit for admen involved in radio. After the war, Y&R executive Lewis noted that the traditional relationship of New York offices to Hollywood offices was beginning to change, as responsibility for advertising copy shifted to Hollywood rather than being "teletyped in toto from New York."

The shift of program production to Hollywood exacerbated the differences between the print and radio departments in many agencies. Especially in those, like J. Walter Thompson and Young & Rubicam, where radio departments functioned quasi-autonomously within the larger firm, the differences in attitude, style, and work habits became pronounced. Adman James Webb Young recalled running into agency radio men heading to Hollywood by train during the war and commented that "our radio people are more showmen than salesmen," a distinction some admen still found discomfiting in the second decade of agency involvement in programming.[25] "Salesmen" thought themselves businessmen operating within acceptable norms of business; they suspected "showmen" of having no norms or ethics at all. Hollywood seemed rife with showmen who could not be trusted. One adman warned his peers about negotiating in Hollywood: "The cross, the double cross, and the triple cross with fancy fixings are every-day routine."[26] At an agency staff meeting in 1932, JWT staffers were warned by a visiting Los Angeles newspaper reporter that the film industry was "[a] billion-dollar industry exploited by the cunning few, run by ignoramuses, [and] thronged with the stupid mob."[27] The prevalence of such attitudes toward Hollywood helps explain why the N. W. Ayer agency, according to house historian Ralph Hower, "recognizing that Hollywood's show atmosphere tends to warp business judgement in men working there . . . arranged for a regular and frequent exchange of top personnel between New York and Hollywood."[28] Some admen had resisted their agencies' entry into radio precisely because of radio's association with show business; the establishment of agency outposts in Hollywood brought to the fore the risks of ever-deeper involvement in the entertainment industry.

J. Walter Thompson and Radio

J. Walter Thompson, one of the most established and longstanding advertising agencies on Madison Avenue, took the lead in early radio and then in Hollywood-based programming. In order to understand why, we must briefly consider how the agency came to prominence.[29] Founder J. Walter Thompson had apprenticed with a small agency in the 1870s and had noticed that magazines, unlike newspapers, rarely ran advertisements despite their greater prestige and access to decision-making housewives. Persuading both advertisers and magazine publishers of the value of the medium, Thompson soon developed a near-monopoly on magazine advertising as he convinced publications such as *Scribner's*, *Harper's*, the *Atlantic*, and *Godey's* to sell advertising only through his agency.[30] By 1878 he had taken over the small agency and was soon credited with inventing the position of account executive, the person who mediates between the client and the agency staff who produce and place advertising. Although Thompson maintained his agency's lead with further innovations and a reputation for customer service that included overlooking bad debts, by the turn of the century his account executive–dominated agency was beginning to lose ground to competitors expanding their expertise in copywriting and art direction.[31] In the 1910s, the team of Stanley Resor and his copywriter, Helen Lansdowne, working at JWT's Cincinnati branch, had remarkable success with their campaigns for clients such as Crisco (Procter & Gamble) and Lux soap (Lever Bros.) in reaching the targeted female markets. Resor bought out Thompson in 1916 and married Lansdowne, and the two oversaw JWT's expansion during the 1920s. Stanley Resor encouraged market research: He hired the behavioral psychologist John B. Watson to study consumers in an effort to make advertising a more scientific process.[32] Helen Resor oversaw the advertising; she believed in the power of the visual appeal and user-centered copy but also used the reason-why tactic of offering free samples or coupons, most famously in her Woodbury Facial Soap ad headlined, "A skin you love to touch," with an accompanying coupon for a 10-cent bar of soap.[33] Although denying there was any such thing as an advertising formula, JWT's copywriters, according to JWT historian Howard

Henderson, made sure their copy was "keyed primarily to interest women," who were assumed to be intelligent and able to "decide for herself"—unlike reason-why copywriters who tended to underestimate the consumer's intelligence. More important, unlike reason-why copy, which stressed the "educational," JWT copy "makes specific *emotional promises* like these: *You, too, can have.*"[34]

One advertising strategy developed by Helen Resor in 1927 employed testimonials, not from average consumers, but from "screen stars," and relied on the power of celebrity association. Association is a soft sell advertising strategy that aligns a product with desirable attributes, such as wealth, social status, or celebrity, in order to create positive feelings in the consumer about the product. Headlined "Nine out ten Screen Stars care for their Skin with Lux Toilet Soap," one ad features the photographs of sixteen film actresses and the names of another fifty, just in case the reader needed more convincing that screen stars "use this soap in their luxurious bathrooms" (see Figure 8-1).[35] Instead of the product information found in hard sell ads, this ad promotes a positive association between soap and celebrities and implies magical effects—perhaps the stars' beauty will rub off on the users of Lux soap, or, at least, the users may *feel* glamorous. The naming of sixty-six actresses to get the point across is, on the other hand, a hard sell repetition strategy.

JWT's involvement in radio grew rapidly. Under the leadership of John Reber, the radio department carved out its own territory within the agency; by early 1930 it oversaw thirty-one programs a week and radio had become a $3 million business for JWT.[36] The agency claimed to account for 14 percent of the commercial radio "business" in general, and radio accounted for nearly a fifth of its total billings by 1932.[37] Because roughly 75 percent of its business was placed on the two NBC networks, in 1933 NBC staff installed dedicated telephone lines for JWT.[38] In 1936, JWT spent $5.14 million on radio network airtime, ranking third in airtime spending after Blackett-Sample-Hummert ($6.29 million) and Lord & Thomas ($5.6 million).[39] Top JWT programs included *Major Bowes' Amateur Hour* (Chase & Sanborn coffee), *The Fleischmann's Yeast Hour with Rudy Vallee, The Jergens Program, Kraft*

Figure 8-1. Lux Toilet Soap: "9 out of 10 Screen Stars care for their Skin with Lux Toilet Soap." (Reproduced in Julian Lewis Watkins, *The 100 Greatest Advertisements* [New York: Dover, 1959], 82.)

Music Hall, *Lux Radio Theatre* (Lever Bros.), *One Man's Family* (Royal Desserts), and *Shell Chateau* with Al Jolson, among others.

In his unpublished reminiscence about Reber (entitled "The Grim Reber"), JWT radio producer Cal Kuhl argued that Reber was "the first to dismiss the 'radio experts'" as supplied by the networks and insist that the agencies could do better by using their own personnel to write, direct, and produce radio programs.[40] Reber's logic was simple; unlike the networks, the agency would put the advertisers' needs first. In a 1936 trade magazine advertisement, JWT boasted not only that it produced thirteen programs simultaneously but that the programs illustrated "the two steps necessary to radio advertising success: 1. They gather audiences suited to the ends of the products advertised. 2. They move these audiences to action with sales messages that sell."[41] NBC, or even CBS, supplying directors and writers from Broadway and vaudeville, could not promise advertisers service so closely tailored to their needs.

In a 1933 advertisement in *Fortune* magazine, JWT uses stars as a marketing tool, just as in its print Lux soap campaigns, not to sell soap but to attract new clients. In one ad, head shots of twenty-four major radio stars—including Al Jolson, Rudy Vallee, Eddie Cantor, Burns and Allen, Joe Penner, and Ozzie Nelson—fill the page, surrounding a short piece of text: "These artists appear for our clients in radio programs whose design, construction, presentation, and direction are controlled entirely by the J. Walter Thompson Company" (see Figure 8-2).[42] Aiming to impress advertisers with the strength of the star power JWT could wield on their behalf, this ad illustrates how important star-centered entertainment is to JWT's advertising strategies. Although the text of this ad announces just how much power JWT has over stars, the visual effect is of a multiplicity of stars—comedians, musicians, singers, and bandleaders—whose power to catch the potential client's attention is being employed in the same way stars are used to attract radio or film audiences.

JWT client Standard Brands began on radio in 1928 with *Ida Bailey Allen's Radio Homemakers' Club* for Royal Gelatin and Royal Baking Powder, in which the products were integrated into the recipes executed live on the air with running commentary.[43] Each program was

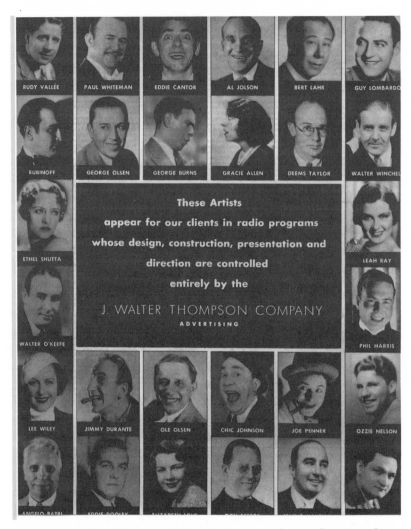

Figure 8-2. J. Walter Thompson: "These Artists appear for our clients in radio programs whose design, construction, presentation and direction are controlled entirely by the J. Walter Thompson Company." (*Fortune* [no month], 1933, 85.)

built around a theme, such as "When Your Mother Comes to Visit" or "Commencement Parties." Other Royal Gelatin programs featured Fanny Brice and Jack Pearl. For the 1934 program *One Man's Family*, which cost $2,500 a week including talent and airtime, the copy theme was "smell your gelatin," emphasizing the product's freshness and natural flavors. In 1936, Royal Desserts became the sponsor of *The Rudy Vallee Variety Hour*; the copy theme included claims such as "When you pour on the hot water, you get only the aroma of fruit—never any unpleasant odor." In mid-1938, Vallee's program was split between two sponsoring products: Royal Desserts and Fleischmann's Yeast.

Chase & Sanborn coffee was another early JWT radio client. JWT began *The Chase & Sanborn Hour* in 1929 with an orchestra and then featured headliners, including Maurice Chevalier, Rubinoff and His Violin, Nelson Eddy, Oscar Levant, Eddie Cantor, Jimmy Durante, Major Bowes, Abbott and Costello, and finally Edgar Bergen and his puppet sidekick, Charlie McCarthy.[44] Bergen's ventriloquism act, originally developed in vaudeville, was first launched on the Rudy Vallee program. Radio audiences could not see Bergen's ventriloquism, but Charlie McCarthy's irreverent, skirt-chasing, childlike narcissist provided a comic foil to Bergen's straight man and proved so popular that JWT moved him to headline *The Chase & Sanborn Hour* until 1956. While the program featured a wide variety of talent, from crooners to comedians to orchestra leaders, JWT's chief strategy for *The Chase & Sanborn Hour* was to make it "first of all a Chase & Sanborn program—not Eddie Cantor's" or any other star's program.[45] So, in this case the sponsor's identity was carefully kept foremost, and the headlining stars rotated in and out as JWT saw fit.

Rudy Vallee, on the other hand, as the headliner for *The Fleischmann's Yeast Hour*, became closely linked to the sponsor. Fleischmann's Yeast ran two advertising campaigns. Yeast for Bread sponsored Ripley's *Believe It or Not* and a program headlined by comedian Joe Penner and bandleader Ozzie Nelson. Yeast for Health, focused on promoting direct yeast consumption to cure acne, indigestion, low energy, and constipation, sponsored Vallee's program.[46] The leader of the Yeast for Health campaign, JWT staffer Robert Simon, pointed out, "To many people, Rudy Vallee spells yeast."[47] Beginning in 1929 as a musical program, Vallee's program featured him at first as the orchestra leader and crooner, a singer better heard on microphone than live stage, but gradually the personality around whom the program revolved. His crooning style discomfited traditionalists but seemed more suitable for radio than that of singers trained to project to the back of the auditorium. Vallee, with his insouciant whistling and his interpretations of hits such as "I'm Just a Vagabond Lover," did not try to "educate the public to higher musical standards," as Abbott Spencer explained to other JWT staffers.[48] JWT staffer Cal Kuhl explained to his colleagues that to hire someone like Vallee and then try to change him is "like hiring John Barrymore and telling him you like his work very much but that he should be more like Charley [sic] Chaplin."[49]

However, JWT had had serious doubts about Vallee in 1932 when his temporary replacements, a comedy team known as Olsen & Johnson, received better Crossley ratings. As JWT considered introducing more variety in Fleischmann's Yeast all-music program, Reber stressed the importance of the choice of talent: "You will put up with an act you don't like in a theater, but not on the radio." His solution, as he explained to Helen Resor in a staff meeting, was to script the program as if Vallee "did the whole thing himself, so that all who like Vallee will like the show because Vallee made it up." Vallee, of course, did not make up anything: "He doesn't write one word of the script." Reber kept him on nonetheless because he believed that the "ominpresence of Vallee takes away the impression of unrelated acts," smoothing over the discontinuities of the variety show format and encouraging the audience to tolerate the weaker acts.[50] The production of Vallee's program moved to Hollywood in 1932, earlier than that of many other programs, to take advantage of easier access to Hollywood talent. As yeast sales began to diminish in the late 1930s, Vallee gained another sponsor, Royal Desserts, also made by Standard Brands, before leaving the air in 1939.

J. Walter Thompson in Hollywood

As more and more radio shows originated in Hollywood, JWT transferred key personnel west. Writer Carroll Carroll was sent there very suddenly when a resignation left a key program writerless. While radio admen were used to being regarded with suspicion by their colleagues in print advertising, by moving to Hollywood they also faced suspicion from the "showmen" of Hollywood. Carroll described how JWT employees experienced their transfer to Hollywood:

Members of the J. Walter Thompson office, all from New York . . . huddled together for company and protection the way British colonists once did in Africa and Asia. Radio people, considered by the Hollywood picture colony not only as "the enemy" but also as "upstart punks," "no status bums," and "unwelcome invaders," were forced to rely on each other for warmth and comfort.[51]

Condemned sometimes as "showmen" in New York, admen were condemned as "not showmen" in Hollywood. It was true that JWT staff could not make many claims to show business experience. George Faulkner had been a drama critic; Robert Simon a music critic; Cal Kuhl had worked for Victrola, the recording company; John Reber's show business background consisted of participating in Amherst College's drama club; and Carroll Carroll had written poetry and done public relations before he was recruited into comedy and advertising writing at JWT.[52]

Nonetheless, Carroll indignantly objected to the characterization of admen as lacking showmanship, writing to a friend that it was time to say "a few words in defense of the guys responsible for most of the good radio programs, Advertising Men." Arguing that advertising was "a certain kind of showmanship" and that "National advertisers and their agents, do, today, exercise about 90 percent of the showmanship in radio," Carroll went on to point out that the film industry was developed "in spite of many famous showmen, not with their cooperation"; radio was likewise scorned by "showmen" who "ignored it, laughed at it." Carroll was especially sensitive to the accusation that admen were less creatively autonomous than were, say, Broadway or Hollywood writers: "If advertisers sometimes butt into the jobs of the [radio] writers and directors, so, too, does the money on Broadway and in Hollywood dictate to the creative echelon. But advertising men are attacked for doing what bankers and other angels do" ("angels" being Broadway investors).[53] For Carroll, the commercial imperatives of radio were no more or less overt than those of other entertainment industries—a point overlooked by those who blamed commercialism for radio's lack of high-mindedness.

At JWT the tension between Madison Avenue and Hollywood was reflected in the longstanding rivalry between radio department head John Reber and Hollywood office president Daniel "Danny" Danker. Reber oversaw all of JWT's radio programs from the New York office, managing the Hollywood programs by telegram, letter, and telephone. The JWT Hollywood office opened in 1934, but Danker had been representing JWT in Los Angeles since 1930, procuring movie star testimonials for Lux Toilet Soap. Danker, described by Rudy Vallee as "a mean, arrogant, pugnacious, hard-drinking Irishman," was known as the "Lux Playboy": His method was to offer free soap and free publicity to aspiring stars if they consented to appear in print advertisements testifying to the benefits of Lux soap.[54] Clara Bow, Janet Gaynor, and Joan Crawford all appeared in Lux advertisements; Crawford is quoted as saying, "Never have I had anything like it for keeping the skin smooth."[55] A Lux starlet who became famous owed a debt to Danker, which usually included appearing in future advertisements for free.

Danker's Hollywood connections began to prove indispensable once JWT moved *Lux Radio Theatre* and *Kraft Music Hall* to Hollywood in 1936. *Lux Radio Theatre*, an anthology drama program, had begun in 1934 when Lever Bros. rather belatedly and precipitously asked JWT to build it a top-rated radio program right away. At first airing on Sunday afternoons and featuring unknown New York actors, *Lux Radio Theatre* moved to Monday nights in 1936 when a slot opened on CBS, and production moved to Hollywood because of the "greater availability of 'top name' talent" there.[56] Its one-hour radio plays were from that time based on Hollywood films then in exhibition.[57] Airtime costs rose because of the move to prime time, but talent costs rose even more dramatically, from $10,500 per program in 1935 to $15,800 in 1936 and to $25,300 in 1937, as Reber sought through an infusion of movie stars to raise the ratings high enough to merit the increased costs.[58] Danker spent money freely in order to attract stars; his expense account made it easier for Hollywoodites to "find it pleasant to do business with Thompson people"; he was able to get stars for JWT programs whom other agencies could not get at all.[59]

It was rumored that Danker's leverage in Hollywood had an unsavory underpinning. According to notes from an unpublished history of JWT, "Danny Danker was the power in Hollywood and was said to operate very much like dear Louella [Parsons, the gossip columnist], getting any talent he wanted through blackmail. He also ran a procuring service for visiting executives and had a stable of starlets handy at all times."[60] Despite his distaste for Danker, Reber understood earlier than most the need to cooperate with Hollywood, the usefulness of the star system to radio, and the fact that radio had to go where the talent was.[61] Carroll later recalled, "Mr. Reber did not want Danny to have anything to do with 'his' department. But Danny's power was such in Hollywood that—as our needs for guest stars grew—Danny became more and more essential to the operation. . . . Naturally, as Danny's power grew[,] the seething feud between him and Reber boiled harder,"[62] until Danker's death from a heart attack at age forty-one in 1944 ended the conflict.

Kraft Music Hall (1936–46)

In addition to the star-studded *Lux Radio Theatre*, JWT produced another top Hollywood program, *Kraft Music Hall*. Kraft, originally known as Phenix Cheese, had been a JWT client since 1922 and had begun experimenting with radio fairly early. A morning program, *Woman's Magazine of the Air*, premiered in 1929; a fifteen-minute "food talk" called *Mrs. A. M. Goudis* aired from 1929 until 1933.[63] As Kraft's advertising manager, John H. Platt, explained, "though skeptical at first" about radio advertising, "we are becoming more and more convinced that the age of radio is here."[64] In 1933, Kraft approached JWT to devise a high-impact strategy for introducing its mayonnaise substitute Miracle Whip. Reber decided to book an unprecedented two hours of airtime on NBC Red's eastern affiliates, hire the top dance band Paul Whiteman Orchestra and stage and screen star Al Jolson, and call it *The Kraft Program*.[65] When Miracle Whip's sales exceeded expectations, Kraft continued it as a one-hour program, *The Kraft Music Revue*, which again featured Jolson and Whiteman, along with many guest stars, performing a musical variety show on the roof of the New Amsterdam Theater in Times Square. Jolson, whose previous radio performances had been disappointing probably because of his unfamiliarity with playing to a microphone instead of to a live audience, was allowed to continue his signature show ender: asking for song requests from the audience with his trademark, "Folks, you ain't heard nothin' yet!"[66]

After it was retitled *Kraft Music Hall*, the program lost Jolson, and Reber sought another baritone. By the end of 1935, he had decided on Bing Crosby, but Crosby was based in Los Angeles, where his film and recording careers were already well underway. Reber tried out Crosby for several broadcasts by cutting in his California-based performances during a New York–originated broadcast, then decided to move the program west, where the talent was. From the beginning of 1936 until 1946, Crosby hosted *Kraft Music Hall* in Hollywood, helping to create a distinctive program with his casual crooning style and the assistance of major stars of screen, stage, and concert hall as guests.[67] Crosby was accompanied by a series of comedians (Bob Burns, Jerry Lester, and Victor Borge); an announcer named Ken Carpenter, who had also announced for other JWT programs such as *Lux Radio Theatre*; and a music director, John Scott Trotter. Platt promised that Kraft would not interfere with JWT: "Let the experts do their jobs." Platt wanted the program to be "acceptable in the many millions of homes" so that customers would "accept your selling message with best grace." The program, he thought, sounded like "a group of congenial people, talking and acting very much as they would talk and act if they were to drop in on one of their member's houses for an evening visit."[68]

JWT writer Carroll Carroll was the lead writer on *Kraft Music Hall*, which was a musical variety show. Unlike most other programs of this type, it always featured classical music artists, which Kraft hoped would "give the show some cultural tone," as Carroll put it.[69] He avoided any highbrow stuffiness by scripting guests such as Jascha Heifetz so as to "let their hair down" and allow the audience to "look upon them as human beings." According to Carroll, "our copy platform was 'treat opera as if it were baseball and baseball as if it were opera.'"[70] But the best-known element of the program was the casual, apparently ad-libbed dialogue of Crosby and his guests. Carroll, however, carefully scripted the program each week; his lack of on-air credit, following agency and network policy, helped to sustain the illusion of friendly spontaneity, as did his strategy for making Crosby sound more like Crosby. Carroll had observed Crosby closely and incorporated Crosby's known fascination with slang, hip talk, and nicknames into the scripts, which were filled with such Crosbyesque locutions as "prayer bones" (knees), "zingy" (quick), "I seem to be playing infield" (I'm confused), and "a whingdinger" (superlative).[71] Carroll also interviewed each guest before writing the week's script in order to ascertain their interests and speech style, which he then incorporated into his scripts.[72] Crosby, who insisted he had no acting ability and preferred singing, needed loosening up; Carroll decided to create a "louse up," in which Crosby's guests were given a slightly different script so that, when they spoke a line Crosby did not anticipate, he was forced to improvise.[73] The lack of an actual full dress rehearsal also contributed to the casual sound of the show. The guests, moreover, had little rehearsal—they were also paid some of the lowest rates of any major radio show—but Carroll insisted that because his scripts were designed to showcase them rather than their host, the guests benefited despite their low pay. Whether it was because of the quality of the program, or the free Kraft cheese given to every guest, or Danker's leverage, *Kraft Music Hall* secured the services of major Hollywood stars, including Bob Hope, David Niven, Joan Fontaine, Cary Grant, John Barrymore, James Cagney, Joan Crawford, Bette Davis, Humphrey Bogart, Jackie Coogan, Betty Grable, George Raft, Mary Astor, and Fay Wray. Securing star talent without, as Platt proudly claimed, being "guilty of succumbing to the 'bidding-up' hysteria which frequently affects the radio world," kept the budget down while executing Reber's basic strategy of using stars to attract audiences.

Inside JWT, Reber oversaw the program from New York. His tight long-distance control via telegrams occasionally caused dissension among the program's staff. The workload was backbreaking; Carroll complained of having to contribute to the scripts of other JWT programs as well as *Kraft Music Hall.* In one letter to Carroll, Reber instructed him to focus on *Kraft Music Hall*: "If that takes 7 days a week and results in your blood pressure looking like a thermometer on a wintry day, your blood count like the short end of a baseball score and your stomach like a piece of tripe in strong vinegar, then that's all right with me. We will take care of you, nurse you back to health and put you back on the Kraft again."[74] Reber's terse telegrams and telephone calls sometimes enraged Carroll. After pulling double duty on *Kraft Music Hall* and the Old Gold program, Carroll exploded in a lengthy telegram to Reber: "I certainly do not think that either Cal [Kuhl] or I merited the implication of incompetence and stupidity that you projected to us over the phone this evening."[75] In a 1943 instance, Carroll made a point-by-point rebuttal of a Reber telegram regarding a cast member named Leo "Ukie" Sherin. To Reber's "Ukie good but not enough of him," Carroll responded, "Ukie was not good. He had only a few lines and he fluffed some of them."[76] Reber not only critiqued each show, he also ran interference with Kraft executives in Chicago. Reber explained some of his comments in an earlier telegram to Carroll:

I get a certain amount of criticism from Chicago that the talk spots are "too long." . . . Chicago's way of criticizing such spots is to say that there isn't enough music, or that it ought to be broken up with a song by Bing. I don't pass on these things to you very often because I realize what you're attempting to do, and usually it comes off successfully enough so that I can hold Chicago in line.[77]

Kraft Music Hall's advertising reflected the views of JWT and Kraft. Kraft's Platt insisted that the advertising be "palatable" and that it not alienate audiences.[78] As one of its advertising managers later put it, Kraft's target is "Mrs. Consumer": "She's your wife! She is first rate and high class and Kraft advertising is fashioned to meet those attributes."[79] Reason-why exaggeration or too much hard sell could alienate potential customers. Kraft declined to require the talent to present the commercials. "Crosby and [Bob] Burns," noted Platt, "are artists . . . valuable as entertainers. When they step out of character—become commercial salesmen—we think that the listening audience may resent it, and with some justification."[80] Instead, the announcer, Ken

Carpenter, presented the "straight, selling commercials—short, but always straight. . . . No tricks, no furbelows, no kidding."[81] In a 1941 episode featuring Hopalong Cassidy, at the midpoint of the program, after singing "And the Band Played on," Crosby provided a segue to the commercial by mentioning Eddie Cantor's big wedding anniversary party the next day: "And by the way, it will probably be a long party, so if you haven't ordered all the groceries yet, here's a hint." Carpenter then began the actual commercial:

Planning three meals a day, week after week, month after month, certainly can't be called easy. But maybe it's a little bit easier now than it is in winter. For instance, thinking up good salads, isn't that less of a trick with the new green vegetables and fruits? For the salad dressing, well there's no need to ponder about that. You just open a jar of Miracle Whip and everyone'll be happy. All the time, more and more women are discovering that Miracle Whip salad dressing is the kind their families like best. Because this salad dressing isn't the least bit too bland or too oily and yet it's not too sharp. Miracle Whip really is deliciously different from other salad dressings, different in its flavor and its texture too. To make it, Kraft combines fine mayonnaise and old-fashioned boiled dressing by a secret recipe, then blends them to marvelous smoothness in an exclusive patented beater. Salads made with Miracle Whip are so popular that this creamy zestful salad dressing outsells the next twenty leading brands combined. It sells so fast that most food dealers get fresh supplies every few days. If you want your family to really gobble up their salads, and you do because salads are so good for them, ask your dealer for Miracle Whip salad dressing. Remember you save if you buy the large size jar.[82]

While this commercial follows the familiar format—an announcer speaks for more than one minute about the product—several elements distinguish it from the type of commercial the Hummerts wrote. First, the announcer speaks with a casual tone, in the *Kraft Music Hall* style of modest self-effacement, rather than with rushed urgency, so as to maintain the tone of the program rather than deviate from it. Second, despite the product-centered elements—Miracle Whip's "secret recipe" and "patented production process"—the commercial begins with a user-centered strategy, appealing to mothers seeking to tempt their families to eat healthful foods and make them happy. Third, unlike reason-why advertisements, it does not belabor the product name or spell it out. All these strategies were designed to avoid audience alienation; if audiences were to complain about radio advertising, Kraft advertising would not be singled out for obnoxiousness.

Although Crosby rose to stardom on stage, screen, and recordings, JWT would take credit for building his stardom through *Kraft Music Hall*. In an advertisement to attract new advertising clients, JWT depicted Crosby bathing and singing in a shower: "Suppose Bing sang only in the shower," asked the headline (see Figure 8-3).[83] If Bing were only a "bathroom baritone," his wife and children might enjoy his singing but it "wouldn't keep them in shoesies." Crosby is able to keep those children "in shoesies," a phrase chosen to reflect Crosby's slangy style, because of his successful career, aided specifically by JWT. "It isn't the fact that Bing can sing, but the fact that somebody found out that people want to hear him sing and then gave them a chance to hear him, that put him where he is today." The ad, describing what JWT does for its clients, explains:

There is a distinctive "something" in most commercial products that makes people want to buy them, just as Bing's talent makes people want to hear him. It is the discovery and the focusing of public attention on this "something" . . . that makes them *headliners*. The J. Walter Thompson Company has made it its business to uncover these "somethings" in commercial products, to direct buyers' attention to them, to cultivate a demand for them.[84]

Crosby, then, illustrated JWT's ability to identify and shape the cultural forms that could be harnessed for commercial gain. Implying that Crosby's talent would be hidden in his shower without JWT's creation of *Kraft Music Hall* as his vehicle may have stretched the truth about Crosby's career. However, what this ad clearly shows is that JWT understood advertising as the successful mediation of commerce and culture.

Crosby left *Kraft Music Hall* in 1946 and, to Carroll's surprise, did not take with him the writer who had done so much to polish his public persona. At issue was NBC's insistence on live broadcasts, which

Figure 8-3. J. Walter Thompson: "Suppose Bing sang only in the shower." (*Fortune* [no month], 1941, 107.)

Crosby disliked, and from which he hoped that the Ampex magnetic tape recording technology might free him (and in which he had, not incidentally, invested).[85] JWT's efforts to retain Crosby failed, as did an effort to legally enforce its contract.[86] After various guest stars filled in as host, JWT recruited Al Jolson to return to the program in 1947 with the pianist Oscar Levant as his sidekick. Kraft later became an early television sponsor with *Kraft Television Theater*, an anthology drama program that was eventually replaced by a new version of *Kraft Music Hall* in 1958. However, Crosby's association with the program marked its height; his cool, casual persona and his easy banter with guest stars of film, theater, and music, while scripted by Carroll to sound improvised and natural, executed Kraft and JWT's purpose of using Hollywood stars for effective advertising.

———————————

The entertainment industries of radio and film always overlapped to some degree. But competition between them, their different institutional structures, and federal regulation prevented their full integration. However, by the 1940s, audience and advertiser demand for star-studded entertainment pushed more and more radio program production westward to Hollywood, where stars were more accessible. As the primary program producers, Madison Avenue–based advertising agencies had to open branch offices in Hollywood, where their culture clashed with that of Hollywood denizens. J. Walter Thompson led this trend, producing major Hollywood-based programs, such as *Lux Radio Theatre* and *Kraft Music Hall*, both of which reflected its advertising strategies. Unlike the programs of Fred Allen or Jack Benny, both of whom employed their own stables of writers, *Kraft Music Hall* relied on agency writers to build the performers' personae. JWT's Carroll Carroll's role in creating and sharpening Bing Crosby's radio performances was never credited on the air because he was an advertising agency employee and thus precluded from making a public claim of authorship. JWT would go on to produce programs on television, where Reber's effort to fully import the radio model of agency control would fail; [87] during the radio era, JWT was the foremost producer of star-studded popular entertainment derived from the Hollywood film industry.

9   Advertising and Commercial Radio during World War II, 1942–45

World War II, like the crisis of the Depression, forced the advertising industry to justify its methodologies, even its very existence, to critics and clients alike. Although the Depression had emboldened its opponents among the critics of capitalism, the rise of radio helped the advertising industry prove its continuing usefulness to advertisers. In some ways, however, World War II presented even greater threats to the advertising industry. A war economy could cripple the advertising industry if corporate advertising budgets shrank drastically. The federal government could nationalize the advertising or broadcasting industry to control propaganda efforts. The federal government could also change the tax codes, set prices, and seize private assets for the war effort, all of which could threaten the health of the advertising industry. In the few years between the war's beginning and the United States' entry, the anxiety about how the war could affect government's relation to industry was reflected in part in the prominence of many business leaders in organizations such as America First, which lobbied against overseas involvement. But after the attack on Pearl Harbor in December 1941, the resistance to the war in the business world rapidly eroded. BBDO principal Alex Osborn reported to Bruce Barton in March 1942 that "within the past 30 days the philosophy in regard to the war has undergone a radical change. More and more of our clients have recently revealed that they don't care what happens to them as long as we win the war, and they want to do everything they can to aid the war effort."[1]

As it happened, they had nothing to worry about. The war years were a period of close cooperation of government and industry; the advertising industry and commercial radio became closely associated with the federal war effort. Despite the war economy, both industries grew and thrived. Although the conversion to a war economy reduced the availability of consumer goods, advertisers promoted their contributions to the war effort. The advertising industry created the Advertising Council, renamed the War Advertising Council, to help coordinate participation in the war effort. Commercial radio donated time for war programming and star talent, such as Kate Smith, who raised millions for war bonds singing on the radio. The commercial radio industry also helped develop the Armed Forces Radio Service. Radio played a key role in the federal war propaganda effort.[2] William B. Lewis, a CBS executive who had also worked at J. Walter Thompson, became the chief of the radio division at the Office of War Information and worked to integrate propaganda into popular commercial radio programming. Because he preferred such integration to didactic documentary programming, Lewis has been attacked as favoring commercial interests over U.S. propaganda needs;[3] however, he was motivated by a sincere belief that such integration was the best available communication strategy.

World War II and Madison Avenue

The climate in Washington immediately before the war was not particularly friendly to the advertising industry. The Federal Trade Commission had been investigating monopolistic trade practices in advertising, and Congress had been considering the Voorhis bill, which would have restricted the ways in which businesses could have deducted advertising costs against income.[4] Many feared that the federal government would nationalize many industries once war was declared; on the contrary, it relaxed antitrust enforcement and stimulated some industries through federal war contracts, based on a cost-plus formula that guaranteed profitability, plus low-interest loans and a reformed tax structure.[5] In general, it sought cooperation rather than conflict with industry.

The advertising industry particularly benefited from this new government attitude, which encouraged advertising spending. The Voorhis bill was abandoned, and a reverse effect was produced by the wartime excess profits tax, which allowed advertisers to deduct advertising expenses against income even when they were producing only war materiel for the government. The tax, then, gave advertisers an incentive to advertise even when they had no consumer goods to sell, and, of course, this helped keep ad agencies in business. In fact, the agencies helped defeat a few attempts to disallow advertising as a deductible against profits, a move that would have led many businesses to cease advertising for the duration, crippling ad-supported media.[6] Thus, tax policy helped stimulate some advertising expenditures, despite a relative dearth of consumer products to advertise.[7] Some product advertising increased in direct response to war conditions. For example, Kraft's advertising budget for Velveeta ballooned from just under $200,000 in 1939 to more than $600,000 in 1942, taking advantage of an opening in the market for replacements for dairy products that were increasingly scarce and requisitioned for the military. Kraft's radio expenditures rose in proportion, from about $150,000 in 1939 to $535,000 in 1942, while its magazine expenditures grew less dramatically, from $42,000 in 1939 to $57,000 in 1942, indicating the increased desirability and perceived effectiveness of radio advertising.[8] Though overall the advertising industry suffered a severe contraction during the first half of 1942—immediately following Pearl Harbor—reaching a low point in June, thereafter advertising spending steadily increased, until by the end of the war it exceeded the heights of the pre-Crash era.[9]

The agencies and networks that controlled the radio industry adhered to this general trend. BBDO's billings, having peaked at about $32.6 million in 1929 and bottomed out at $14.8 million in 1933, climbed rapidly from $25.6 million in 1942 to $42.8 million in 1945.[10] The networks' billings in 1940, before the United States entered the war, totaled $39.9 million for NBC's Red network, $10.7 million for NBC's Blue network, $41 million for CBS, and $4.7 million for Mutual, or roughly $96.4 million altogether.[11] By 1945, those billings had roughly doubled to $197.9 million.[12] So, although many industries had to wait for the postwar expansion for a thorough recovery from the Depression, the advertising and commercial radio industries were well on their way during the war itself.

Admen made several arguments for the importance of advertising during the war. First, because wars are expensive, the domestic economy needs to grow, and advertising could increase business activity. Second, the commercial press embodies the freedoms that the United States was defending overseas, and advertising is what keeps the free press free from government control. Advertising revenue, in contrast to state subsidy, guarantees that media can remain independent of the state. Third, advertising is, in the historian Frank Fox's words, the "spiritual essence of freedom itself," the necessary practice of a free economy and a free people, providing freedom of choice and the framework within which the free enterprise system could flourish.[13] In this view, advertising is not a side effect of the American system but a fundamental element; to disallow or restrict it during the war would undercut morale, undermine the war effort, and deny the very principles for which American troops were fighting. Finally, although there were fewer goods to sell, advertising could inform the public of industry's contribution to the war effort and explain how to contribute to it.

Supporting the war effort was a good strategy for businesses anticipating the postwar economy. Bruce Barton pointed out to a General Motors executive that war-related revenues "ought to be used to keep alive a consciousness of the institution in the public mind which will make it easier for you to get back to making money out of the automobile business when the war is over."[14] The N. W. Ayer agency approached advertising during the war as a "demand management" tool, building demand, especially for goods that were in short supply, for future availability. Advertising was a "communications device" that had a "broader function than sales," as N. W. Ayer historian Ralph Hower pointed out.[15] For example, an ad headlined "How Can a Bomber Part Improve Tomorrow's Typewriter?" ties the war effort directly to future consumer goods and their benefits. A 1943 General Electric advertisement likewise connects its war production to future consumer goods. Under an illustration of soldiers fighting from a tank, the headline announces: "A tank destroyer is plenty rough on radio" and then, "One more reason why your post-war G-E electronic radio will be better than ever!" (see Figure 9-1). The ad copy explains that GE radio parts, although many are "fragile and delicate" electronics, "undergo the most grueling tests" in order to meet the needs of the military. The illustration of one test, a "vibration test," is set into the corner of a larger illustration. "A radio has to be *good*, to stand that punishment!" Having established both visually and textually that GE products are of high quality and are supporting the war effort, the ad then reminds the reader, "Your own General Electric radio, after the war, will be finer because of these rigorous wartime standards." The ad executes an institutional strategy that links GE to the war effort and postwar consumer goods and manages demand by promising consumers that although new radios may be unavailable during the war, after the war GE radios will be even better than before. With the tagline "General Electric: Leader in radio, television, and electronic research," the ad reminds readers to tune into the GE *Mazda Lamp* radio program on Sunday nights.[16]

Businesses could demonstrate their patriotism through advertising. Willard Chevalier, in a 1943 speech to the Advertising Federation of America, touted advertising's potential for playing a special role during war: "In times of peace, [advertising] appeals to [consumers'] individual desires and aspirations. War transforms it into a powerful instrument of education and community action for the common good."[17] Bruce Barton made a similar argument when he urged a General Motors executive to "seize the opportunity" in the shift to a war economy by using advertising "to make the public feel that industry really has a service spirit and ideal." The prevalence of "hard hitting selling" during the Depression, complained Barton, had emphasized the "profit motive" instead of service.[18] Patriotic advertising could refocus consumers on corporate ideals and offset criticisms of big corporations and obnoxious hard sell advertising. Large corporate advertisers worked patriotic themes into institutional campaigns; a 1943 Westinghouse ad claimed that Westinghouse products are "On every front—in every battle!" including North Africa, Russia, "in the Pacific," "on the seven seas," and "in the bombing of Germany." But not just abroad, also at home: "Day

Figure 9-1. General Electric: "A tank destroyer is plenty rough on radio." (*Life*, 5 July 1943, 5.)

and night, the search goes on in our laboratories and engineering departments to find still more effective ways of bringing victory nearer and surer."[19] Advertisers of packaged goods also used patriotic themes for products ranging from whiskey to soap, antacids to cereal, often urging consumers to support home-front war efforts by recycling, buying war bonds, planting victory gardens, and accepting war rationing cheerfully. A Pepto-Bismol ad proposes that war workers on the night shift could avoid "lunch-box stomach" with "soothing Pepto-Bismol."[20]

Commercial Radio and the Military

Though there was not a full political consensus to go to war, preparations began in earnest in 1940–41.[21] Commercial radio was involved in these. As Edward Kirby, a public relations director for the National Association of Broadcasters, recalled, the new draft in 1941 had caused some resistance to military service. The United States had not yet entered the war, and the bombing of Pearl Harbor, which galvanized public opinion in favor of war, was still to come. The newly forming Army then tried to raise morale among resentful draftees through military broadcasts of commercial programs such as Lucky Strike's *Kay Kyser and His Kollege of Musical Knowledge*. Kirby claimed these broadcasts gave draftees "a recognition and a living assurance they were not forgotten."[22] Each program had to open and close with a disclaimer that the military origination of the broadcast "in no way implies or is an endorsement for the product advertised."[23]

Soon after the United States declared war on December 8, 1941, a more coordinated effort to deliver commercial programs to troops evolved. The Armed Forces Radio Service (AFRS) was established in May 1942; sponsors and networks supplied recordings of major programs free of charge to be aired overseas to troops. The AFRS gradually expanded its radio stations until it was operating in about 300 bases. It broadcast only well-known popular programs because hearing a familiar program was thought to lift the morale of overseas troops. But not all programs were welcome. According to a War Department survey, soldiers preferred to hear dance music, news, comedy, and sports. Soldiers were not interested in serial dramas, opera, symphonies, or "hillbilly music." This led Du Pont, for one, to drop the idea of sending its historical drama *Cavalcade of America* overseas for live production in front of servicemen; comedians and musical entertainers such as Bob Hope, Jack Benny, Fred Allen, and Eddie Cantor would have more appeal than *Cavalcade*'s histories of American scientists and businessmen.[24] Nonetheless, recordings of hundreds of hours of sponsored radio programming were donated to the AFRS, including programs such as *The Bob Hope Show*.

The AFRS also produced its own programs. Radio executives to help produce these were of course recruited from the advertising industry. Young & Rubicam executive Tom Lewis, who was married to film star Loretta Young, oversaw the effort in Hollywood. AFRS programs included *Are You a Genius?*, a quiz show conducted by Mel Blanc; music variety programs *G.I. Journal* and *Command Performance*; and *Mail Call*.[25] *G.I. Journal* followed a newspaper format, alternating reports and letters sent in by G.I.s with comic sketches and musical numbers. In a 1944 broadcast featuring Bob Hope and a "star reporter," the Italian-accented "Professor Colona," the humor was clearly designed to appeal to young men, some of whom may have been flying B-21 bombers:

Bob Hope: ". . . and Professor Colona, who ought to be calling in with a big story any minute now."

[ringing telephone]

Bob Hope: "Hello?"

Professor Colona: "Hello, Hope? I'm flying over enemy territory with a B-17."

Young Woman [petulantly]: "Professor, I've got to go home now."

Bob Hope: "Colona, what's a girl got to do with a B-17?"

Professor Colona: "It won't be long now until she'll be 21."[26]

Many Hollywood and radio stars donated time to AFRS programs, including Jack Benny, Loretta Young, Bob Hope, Bing Crosby, Clark

Gable, and the Andrews Sisters. Many admen did the same. J. Walter Thompson writer Carroll Carroll was recruited to the AFRS by Elmer Davis of the Office of War Information, who noted that Carroll's "services will be without compensation from the United States Government."[27] Carroll described the AFRS radio studios, located on Western Avenue in Los Angeles, as "Fort Western Avenue," staffed by multiple advertising agency employees, including Nat Wolff and Cornwell Jackson, who corralled musicians and stars and writers into volunteering.[28] Most of the radio workers at the AFRS facility simultaneously worked on already existing commercial programs and so carried a double load, maintaining their volunteer war work while continuing their regular radio work. Carroll complained of being overtaxed as a writer for Bing Crosby, because Crosby, along with Bob Hope, was in high demand to entertain the troops from organizations such as the USO and Red Cross; these organizations, according to Carroll, "never thought any further about talent than 'We'll get Crosby and Hope.' And, naturally, they always did."[29]

Toward the end of the war, another former Young & Rubicam executive, Sylvester "Pat" Weaver, joined AFRS in Hollywood. Weaver had produced Fred Allen's program while at Y&R and had worked for American Tobacco head George Washington Hill and before the war for Nelson Rockefeller when he was Coordinator of Inter-American Affairs, as director of a Latin American radio propaganda project. Tom Lewis assigned Weaver supervision of *Command Performance*, in which servicemen "were invited to 'command' their favorite stars to perform on the program, and the stars would comply, as if the command had come from the President of the United States or the King of England."[30] Every week a different star would perform without pay; apparently no stars refused to appear. Featured stars included Judy Garland, Groucho Marx, Betty Grable, Deanna Durbin, Ginger Rogers, Irene Dunne, and Bette Davis. Later, Weaver described the most famous *Command Performance*, a two-hour special broadcast based on the "Dick Tracy" comic strip and featuring Bing Crosby, Bob Hope, Jimmy Durante, Judy Garland, and Dinah Shore, attributing its success in part to the quality of its writers. Although the writers were volunteers, "nobody felt sorry for them, because they had almost complete freedom," presumably from the need to satisfy advertising clients.[31] *Mail Call*, another AFRS-produced program, "featured a young woman with a sexy voice who answered letters from servicemen everywhere." Weaver also recalled a program, *G.I. Jive*, sometimes hosted by a female disc jockey nicknamed G.I. Jill; these female voices clearly were intended to appeal to homesick servicemen.[32]

This strategy of giving servicemen a taste of home extended to nonprogram material too. After an unfortunate incident, perhaps apocryphal, recalled by Edward Kirby in which starving and despondent U.S. soldiers trapped on the Bataan Peninsula heard a commercial program announcing "the ease with which you could go to the family ice box for some delicious cheese and cold drinks," commercial programs were routinely "de-commercialized."[33] Instead, alternative announcements were inserted into them. Kirby recalls "commercials" to promote war bonds, personal cleanliness, recycling, and security measures. Many of these relied on conventional advertising techniques. For example, the slogan for American Tobacco, a hard sell advertiser, "LSMFT: Lucky Strike Means Fine Tobacco," was adapted in an announcement: "VDMT: Veneral [sic] Disease Means Trouble: For a moment of play you may have to pay."[34] Another announcement broadcast in the South Pacific promoted a prophylactic for malaria with the reason-why tactic of spelling out the product name:

This program was brought to you by Atabrine, spelled A-T-A-B-R-I-N-E, endorsed by leading Army medical authorities as just the thing to keep you healthy and vigorous. They may taste awful, but fellers, they're healthful—they're wonderful–they're free. . . . Reach for Atabrine instead of dessert.[35]

The last phrase is an obvious allusion to another Lucky Strike slogan, "Reach for a Lucky instead of a sweet," intended to promote cigarettes as a healthful and slimming alternative to calorie-laden desserts. The strategy built on soldiers' familiarity with advertising techniques in order to impart information they might otherwise ignore. While ad industry critics decried the use of such reason-why strategies as obnoxious, Kirby believed that "[t]he soldier rather welcomed these because they sound 'more like home.'"[36] Such claims may have been somewhat self-serving; however, it is not hard to imagine that these "commercials," with their parodic, satirical undertones as well as their familiarity, might have attracted soldiers' attention.

William B. Lewis, Director of the Radio Division, Office of War Information, 1942–43

One of the most remarkable aspects of the advertising industry's war effort was its cooperation with the federal government in disseminating propaganda. The general story of propaganda in film and radio has been well told elsewhere, as has the history of the advertising industry during the war.[37] But the wartime career of one adman, William B. Lewis, exemplifies some of the ideas and beliefs underlying the ad industry's cooperation in radio war propaganda in this period. Lewis's success in organizing and mobilizing the advertising and broadcasting industries together to contribute to the war propaganda effort was unsurpassed. His background as an adman at J. Walter Thompson and, since 1936, program director at CBS fully informed Lewis's work at the two government information bureaus he joined, the Office of Facts and Figures, where he led the Radio Division from the fall of 1941, and the subsequently reorganized Office of War Information, where he became chief of the domestic radio bureau from July 1942 until July 1943. Lewis went on to run the radio/television department at the advertising agency Kenyon & Eckhardt from 1944 to 1967.

Before the United States entered the war at the end of 1941, the federal government had already begun to mobilize propaganda campaigns in anticipation of eventual involvement. Seeking to avoid an overly centralized propaganda agency, such as the Creel Committee during World War I, the Roosevelt administration scattered propaganda efforts across a variety of offices and departments.[38] Among the myriad offices created was the Office of Facts and Figures (OFF), led by Archibald MacLeish, poet and Librarian of Congress. To lead its radio division, Lewis took a leave of absence from CBS in the fall of 1941.[39] While program director at CBS, Lewis had reorganized the program department and commissioned several unsponsored ("sustaining") programs, including MacLeish's *Fall of the City*, Norman

Corwin's *Words without Music,* and Orson Welles's *Mercury Theater of the Air,* programs considered by some to be the apogee of "golden age" radio.[40] While Lewis also directly commissioned some pure propaganda programs for the government, such as Corwin's *We Hold These Truths,* which was broadcast the week after the attack on Pearl Harbor, these had to be slotted into unsold network times at odd hours, reaching smaller audiences than sponsored prime time programs.[41] Lewis's role at CBS in supporting programming by writers like MacLeish and Corwin may have contributed to the decision to select him to lead the OFF radio division.

Arriving at the OFF, Lewis found the propaganda effort to be scattershot, uncoordinated, and lopsided. An unsigned OFF memo, either written or supervised by Lewis, complains that multiple government agencies are bombarding networks and stations with multiple requests for propaganda without coordination or direction as to the priority of these requests, and that much of this government-produced material is not only duplicated by multiple government agencies but "inferior": "repetitive announcements have irritated the audience, and [they have] reacted *against* the war effort."[42] Lewis later described the audience-alienating effects of well-intentioned but uncoordinated war propaganda:

It wasn't at all unusual then to hear a network program end up with a boost for War Bonds, followed after a brief pause by a local station-break plug for War Bonds, and then, ten seconds later, to have the next network show start off with an admonition to buy War Bonds. Listeners have been known to pitch their radio sets through parlor windows because of things like that.[43]

Lewis planned to prevent such audience alienation by using popular entertainment rather than pure propaganda programs spreading war information. In January 1942, Lewis spoke at a meeting that included representatives from the federal Treasury, Labor, and Justice departments, and members of the broadcasting and advertising industries, in order to begin coordinating the propaganda effort. He had to convince the government representatives that he and his adjutant,

Douglas Meservy from NBC, were not simply representing the interests of networks and advertisers: "Neither of us is representing the radio industry, nor any part of it. We are not here, as I have heard it rumored in Washington, to act as a bulwark for the networks against government requests for time."[44] Instead, Lewis argued that the radio industry was willing to help and that "properly mobilized and organized" it had vast potential "to shape and maintain the morale of the American people." And then Lewis explained how his approach would differ from the already existing plan to air government-produced propaganda: The government would supply information about the war effort to the radio industry, which would then use the information as they saw fit in already existing programs, whether sponsored or sustaining. The information "may take the form of a curtain speech by their star; it may be the subject of an entire dramatic show; it may replace a commercial announcement; it may be treated humorously, emotionally, seriously, or musically."[45] Radio, according to Lewis, "is primarily an *entertainment* medium, and must continue to be if it is to continue to deliver the large audiences we want to reach."[46]

In a subsequent speech in March 1942 to the Advertising Council, the trade organization formed to help coordinate the war effort within the advertising industry, Lewis explained that instead of inventing propaganda programs from scratch, programs that would have to build new audiences, "it is important to use those audiences already established instead of starting a whole new program structure."[47] As Archibald MacLeish explained in a letter to President Roosevelt, Lewis believed that "a radio chain is not only a network of wires and broadcasting stations but also an audience," an audience "already established."[48] Lewis's insights, that broadcasting organizes audiences and that radio's greatest strength was not necessarily in its apparatus but in the appeal of its programming to large audiences, reflected his experience in advertising, as organizing the largest audiences possible was the primary goal of radio sponsors.

In another speech, Lewis explained that audiences would best be wooed by the familiar: "Consequently, we fell back on the time-tested formulas—the methods we had devised and used so successfully in getting across sponsored messages." Advertisers had developed strate-gies to attract, not repel, audiences, and the government propaganda campaign needed to do the same. Lewis noted it was important "not to disrupt the pattern of broadcasting," or deprive audiences of well-loved programs. He described his plan as a way "not to *displace* [pro-gramming] with the war, but rather to *superimpose* the war" on already existing broadcast programming. He was careful to make a distinction, however, between the typical "selling job" and the propaganda job of building morale: "It's not, you see, like you were out to create public acceptance of a new soap, or trying merely to win customers for a new breakfast food. While we're building morale, we still have to keep repairing the fences against destructive forces that want to tear it down."[49]

During the winter of 1941–42, Lewis oversaw a number of efforts at the OFF. He met regularly with assigned liaisons from advertisers, agencies, and broadcasters: One meeting, for example, included Paul Kesten, Pat Weaver, Ed Klauber, Niles Trammell, William Paley, Mark Woods, Edgar Kobak, Frank Mullen, and George Faulkner.[50] And he oversaw coordinated "War Information Fact Sheets" to focus and stan-dardize war propaganda. These were sent to radio writers and produc-ers, who were to incorporate them into programs. For example, one Fact Sheet explained why salvage is important:

FIRST: *Tell Them How Urgent It Is. And Why.* By pointing out such things as: *It Takes* 100 lbs. of scrap paper *To Make* Containers for eighty 75mm shells . . . *SECOND*: *Tell Them HOW* To HELP By pointing out the general type of articles which contain the scrap America *needs* . . . *IN THE ATTIC*: *Rubber*: mats, heels, overshoes, rubbers . . . *Beds:* made of brass or iron . . . *IN THE CELLAR*: *Coal stoves* that are worn out . . . *Radiators* . . . *IN THE GARAGE*: *Tires*, tubes, floor mats . . . *Bicycles and tricycles* . . . *THIRD*: *Tell Them What To Do With The Scrap They Collect.* Donate the material to the local community scrap collection cen-ter . . . *FOURTH*: *Some Do's and Don'ts To Tell the Radio Audiences.* The Govern-ment does *not* buy this scrap . . . Don't call for a collector until you have at least 100 pounds of salvage material.[51]

These Fact Sheets, typically covering issues such as recycling, car pool-ing, and sugar rationing, were each prefaced: "*NOTE TO WRITERS AND*

PRODUCERS: *Everybody . . . without exception . . . is a part of the war effort. In producing the material for your broadcast you can make your listeners feel and recognize that what they do is important. They, by following your suggestions, can actively contribute to winning the war, and beating the Axis."*[52] The Fact Sheets were designed to allow writers to pick and choose which elements to use, while providing consistent and complete information about a specific issue.

Yet the OFF struggled. In April 1942, Lewis recorded in his diary: "Present status of OFF: Operations Bureau only one getting anywhere. Intelligence behind; Liaison not well administered; Production a mess. Reorganization of government information services stalled. MacLeish, a bad executive, trying hard; [associate director Allen] Grover not doing his part, because he can't or won't."[53] Shortly after this, the management of government propaganda was reorganized; the Office of War Information was established, and Lewis was appointed chief of its radio bureau in July 1942. At the OWI, Lewis continued to implement the plans he had been developing at the OFF.

By the end of 1942, Lewis had created the Network Allocation Plan for existing national network programs carrying "action messages" (or "what to do" to help the war effort); the Announcement Plan for local stations to synchronize local announcements with network messages; the Transcription Plan for local stations using prerecorded government propaganda programs; the Special Assignment Plan for existing network programs carrying "understanding themes," or messages explaining the war effort rather than providing information on what to do; and finally, the Special Features Plan, for new network programs focused on the war but emphasizing "understanding themes" rather than "what to do" themes.

The Network Allocation Plan, begun in April 1942 at the OFF, was Lewis's first major effort to implement his ideas about integrating propaganda into existing entertainment. Having consulted with the Advertising Council and the Association of National Advertisers, he oversaw a survey of every network radio sponsor for information on the type, audience, and writing staff of its programs. Then his staff selected themes or messages from various government agencies, assigned priority to the messages, selected appropriate audiences for those messages, and assigned time periods for those messages to be carried. For example, as Lewis noted, "[I]nformative messages can be well handled on certain quiz programs; inspirational messages on various dramatic and musical shows; the part of women in the war on some of the daytime serials; comedy programs can treat certain subjects with good results while themes like disemployment would be quite out of place."[54] Hard sell advertising proponents had always conceived advertising as a form of consumer education; so the Hummerts, for example, easily and willingly integrated war information into their serials, such as suggestions for victory gardens and recycling, as part of their didactic discourse.[55] But all program producers, having received information sheets about those messages, would be free to use the material *however they saw fit*. Lewis was eager to point out that neither the OFF nor the OWI was "a policing group. American broadcasting is still free enterprise and we want to see it stay that way. We are coordinating not only radio with Government—but Government with radio."[56] From Lewis's perspective, the government was helping coordinate information for the radio industry only so that commercial radio could support the war effort more effectively.

Focusing on popular network programs, the Network Allocation Plan first identified the message themes of the week (see Figure 9-2). For example, one week the themes were automobile pooling, salvage, and war bonds. Each participating program was then assigned one of those themes. Multiple themes were assigned for every day and for every network, and the themes were organized to rotate, so that the following week a different group of themes was distributed among programs. This way, audiences would hear not the same information repeatedly but each theme in turn as they listened to different programs. Moreover, because each program was expected to present the theme in its own way, audiences who did chance to hear information repeatedly would not hear it in the same way. For example, on Monday, the NBC Blue program *I Love a Mystery* (8:00 P.M.) was assigned war bonds; the CBS program *Blondie* (7:30 P.M.) was assigned salvage; and the Mutual Broadcasting System program *Music That Endures* (10:30 P.M.) and the NBC Red program *Firestone Hour* (8:30 P.M.) were both assigned automobile pooling. On Thursday, NBC Blue's *Mr. Keene*

346-14

MESSAGES ASSIGNED ON NETWORK ALLOCATION PLAN

COLUMBIA BROADCASTING SYSTEM

(All times are EWT)

MONDAY APRIL 27	PROGRAM	MESSAGE
11:15 am	Sustaining Fill	Automobile Pooling
12:30 pm	Helen Trent	War Bonds
3:30 pm	Sustaining Fill	Salvage
7:30 pm	Blondie	Salvage

TUESDAY APRIL 28		
10:30 am	Stepmother	War Bonds
1:00 pm	Life Can Be Beautiful	Automobile Pooling
3:00 pm	David Harum	Salvage
6:30 pm	Sustaining Fill	Salvage
8:00 pm	Missing Heirs	War Bonds
10:00 pm	Sustaining Fill	Automobile Pooling

WEDNESDAY APRIL 29		
12:15 pm	Big Sister	Salvage
5:45 pm	Scattergood Baines	Automobile Pooling
6:15 pm	Hedda Hopper	War Bonds
9:30 pm	Ranson Sherman	Salvage

THURSDAY APRIL 30		
12:45 pm	Our Gal Sunday	War Bonds
1:30 pm	Vic and Sade	Automobile Pooling
4:45 pm	Sing Along	Salvage
7:30 pm	Maudie's Diary	War Bonds
10:15 pm	First Line	Automobile Pooling

FRIDAY MAY 1		
9:15 am	American School	War Bonds
11:30 am	Bright Horizon	Salvage
2:15 pm	Joyce Jordan	Automobile Pooling
5:30 pm	Sustaining Fill	Salvage
6:45 pm	The World Today	Automobile Pooling
7:30 pm	How'm I Doing	War Bonds
10:00 pm	Glenn Miller	Salvage

SATURDAY MAY 2		
9:30 am	Garden Gate	Automobile Pooling
1:00 pm	Buffalo Presents	Salvage
4:00 pm	Meadowbrook Cnty Club	War Bonds
6:00 pm	Frazier Hunt	War Bonds
8:30 pm	Hobby Lobby	Salvage

SUNDAY MAY 3		
2:00 pm	Sustaining Fill	Automobile Pooling
8:30 pm	Crime Doctor	Automobile Pooling

Figure 9-2. "Messages Assigned on Network Allocation Plan." (April 1942, Lewis Collection.)

(7:15 P.M.) had the salvage theme; CBS's *Maude's Diary* (7:30 P.M.) had the war bonds theme; and NBC Red's *The Aldrich Family* (8:30 P.M.) had the automobile pooling theme.[57]

While Lewis was successful in convincing the advertising and radio industries of the efficacy of this plan, he faced resistance from other quarters. A Treasury Department official complained to MacLeish that "this scheme is benefiting nobody but the advertising agencies and sponsors, and is doing real harm to the Government."[58] Lewis vigorously defended the plan. Pointing out that the Treasury Department, through its "more aggressive staff," had nearly monopolized the messages on commercial programs before the Network Allocation Plan, Lewis argued that other government agencies needed time as well to transmit other messages, such as information about price controls, nurse enrollment, salvage, and sugar rationing. He also pointed out that the average number of war bond announcements on commercial programs, which Treasury complained had fallen, had in fact grown under the plan from about eight to twenty-nine. He then defended the efforts of the advertisers: "$140,000,000 is spent yearly by sponsors for time and talent on the national networks. Under the Allocation Plan approximately $28,000,000 worth of that time and talent is very effectively carrying war messages to the American people, a figure that matches the current yearly budget the government is spending for *all* its information services."[59] In other words, government would be foolish to expect that all war information should be funded by taxpayers; voluntary advertiser contributions in time and talent to support the war effort not only saved taxpayers money, but, Lewis would argue, worked more effectively in the long run because, instead of replacing the public's favorite programs, the important information was *integrated* into them. The Network Allocation Plan reached already existing audiences, bringing them into the war effort and maintaining their morale with star power and familiar entertainment.

The effectiveness of this led to the creation of the others, such as the Announcement Plan, the Transcription Plan, the Special Assignment Plan, and the Special Features Plan. In a memo to the chiefs of the major networks, Lewis explained how the last of these would complement the others.[60] The networks, he noted, had voluntarily aired special war programs; he proposed that the OWI coordinate these. Pointing out that some of the programs lacked clarity or quality, he insisted he was not finding "fault" with the effort but was "suggesting that you devote fewer but *better* programs; fewer but better time periods; and that the whole effort be synchronized among the networks." He presented the proposal as if the government "were an advertising agency placing the business" but said that the OWI was not intending either to buy time or produce programs like an advertising agency: "But the fact that we cannot buy—and thus control—the time and programming does not lessen one whit the need." Instead, Lewis analyzed existing network war programs for how they presented "war aims," the "nature of the enemy," "the fighting forces," and the "home forces" and made recommendations for each. For the MBS program *This Is Our Enemy*, serving "the enemy" theme, airing at 10:30 P.M. on Sundays, Lewis suggested "better time; better talent." For the CBS program *Soldiers with Wings*, serving the "fighting forces" theme and airing at 10:15 P.M. on Saturdays, Lewis recommended, "Kill in lieu of other[,] more important needs." For NBC Blue's *Meet Your Navy*, airing at 10:00 P.M. on Fridays, Lewis recommended, "Less entertainment; more information." Analyzing the overall efforts of each network, Lewis concluded that of NBC Blue's eighty-nine quarter-hours of war programs, only seventeen met "special features specifications"; NBC Red did better with thirteen of twenty-eight quarter-hours, CBS best with twenty-five of forty-six. Lewis proposed that quality rather than quantity would be appropriate for war programming and reiterated his belief that the entire commercial radio industry was committed to doing its best to disseminate war information.

Because big-budget sponsored programs featuring major stars attracted the largest audiences, Lewis urged the networks to develop war programs as such, with advertisers as sponsors. The OWI, Lewis said, "will do everything in our power to persuade advertisers who want to help that nothing could be more helpful than the sponsorship of these programs," with the proviso that any sponsorship of war information programs be presented with "good taste and a disclaimer of Government product endorsement."[61] Again, Lewis thus sought to carry out his belief that war propaganda would be most effective if it were well integrated into already existing commercial forms. To create separate war programs scheduled at obscure times and staffed with unknown talent would be far less effective than to integrate war themes into programs scheduled during prime time, featuring stars, and supported by advertisers.

However, Lewis faced resistance from yet another quarter. In mid-1943, a long-simmering conflict within the OWI led to the resignation of fifteen writers and editors who had overseen propaganda pamphlets, the production of which was curtailed under the leadership of Lewis and newspaper publisher and radio station owner Gardner Cowles Jr. Lewis and his commercial colleagues, such Seymour Morris from the Compton agency and William Spine of McCann-Erickson, were derided by these protesting writers as "dollar a year men" (their official salary for their war work) whose real allegiance was only to the advertisers and industry that paid them.[62] The protestors, including the biographer Henry Pringle and the future historian Arthur M. Schlesinger Jr., believed that Lewis and his assistants had transformed the OWI into an "office of war ballyhoo" controlled by "high-pressure promoters who prefer slick salesmanship to honest information."[63] In their statement to the press, the resigning writers accused Lewis's cohort of being "promoters [who] would treat as stupid and reluctant customers the men and women of the United States. They delude themselves that the only effective appeal to the American public in wartime is the selfish one of 'what's in it for me?'"[64] One writer claimed that advertising strategies had the effect of "dimming perception, suspending critical values, and spreading the sticky syrup of complacency over the people."[65]

In complaining that the OWI was preventing them from telling the "full truth" about the war effort, the protesters assumed that the techniques favored by Lewis could not be truthful. OWI director Elmer Davis responded by accusing the protesters of making "completely incorrect" statements and by asserting that the OWI provided "one plain commodity—the facts the people of this country need to win the war."[66] Like many critics of advertising, the quitting writers assumed that advertising techniques could never be anything but manipulative and that appealing to audiences through entertainment was not "honest." The historian Jackson Lears notes that many critics of advertising have assumed that the only honest speech is "plain speech"; following Thorstein Veblen's somewhat puritanical critique of consumerism, these critics believe that advertising's emotional and associative appeals must therefore undermine rational discourse.[67]

Although the writers' resignations have since been validated as a principled stand for New Deal ideals against reactionary commercial interests,[68] this view, promulgated by the resigning writers, sidesteps the actual issue, which was a debate over how to get audiences to pay attention to war propaganda. The resignees may have felt their New Deal views were compromised by the cancellation of their textually dense pamphlets in favor of the "sticky syrup" of radio entertainment and other media. But Lewis and his cohorts were focused on the question of how to attract and appeal to the *audience*. Would the audience prefer to read textually dense pamphlets or listen to radio entertainment? The protesters claimed that Lewis was assuming audiences were "stupid," but Lewis was assuming that in order to reach audiences, the information had to go to where the audiences had already been drawn: to commercially produced entertainment. The protesters implicitly assumed that audiences *ought* to pay attention to their serious prose *instead of* entertainment.

In the face of these critics, Lewis and his colleagues in advertising and commercial radio persisted in viewing the problem of educating the public on the war as one solvable not by avoiding commercialism but by embracing it. Cowles, who had acknowledged that his leadership in giving priority to advertising strategies at the OWI had helped galvanize the writers' protest,[69] gave a speech on "Advertising and the Home Front" to the National Association of Broadcasters in 1943, emphasizing the importance of commercial media in war propaganda. For Cowles, "even with the help of all the editorial and news channels open to us in OWI today, we need advertising. Advertising is the only force powerful enough to do the job." Furthermore, as Lewis had pointed out that the effort should not fall entirely on taxpayers' shoulders, Cowles argued that the war effort required that the OWI "mobilize the resources of private advertising behind government information problems." Because taxpayers cannot fund the war advertising, "we must turn to private business."[70] To Cowles and Lewis, it was foolish and naïve to overlook the resources of the commercial media and its advertisers. If as much was at stake in this war as many claimed, then the commercial media industry had at least as much to lose in defeat as any other, and so galvanizing and organizing its cooperation was an obvious, and effective, strategy.

Was the OWI hijacked by commercial interests that put profits before the national interest?[71] Or was Lewis's approach a practical, inventive, cost-efficient, and culturally relevant set of solutions to the problem of audience attention?[72] As an experienced adman and radio programmer, Lewis understood the challenges of attracting audience attention, yet he was careful not to oversimplify the problem of making effective war propaganda as merely an advertising problem. By centralizing through the Network Allocation Plan the decision-making process of message selection while simultaneously decentralizing the form of the messages (program producers could incorporate the idea any way they chose), Lewis cannily built on the existing relationships between audiences and programs while allowing for individual program creativity. This decentralization of the form of the message was hugely significant to creating effective propaganda. Allowing audiences to learn about how they could support the war effort through recycling, say, in a variety of program formats, whether soap opera drama, comedy skits, song lyrics, and even advertising texts, not only opened up more opportunities for audiences to comprehend but also, and more crucially, gave audiences a set of alternatives from which to choose how to hear war information. Lewis, far from holding radio audiences in contempt, catered to their interests not only in refusing to replace entertainment with centralized, uniform, purely didactic state-controlled propaganda programming but also by trusting audiences to learn what they needed to know within the context of what they already enjoyed: radio entertainment.

Lewis resigned from the OWI in July 1943, after its appropriation was deeply slashed by Congress, and William Paley hired him to study the state of radio in America that fall. He traveled all over the country, spoke with people in and out of the industry, and wrote up a report of recommendations for Paley to consider for network radio in the post-war era.[73] In 1944, Lewis joined the Kenyon & Eckhardt agency as radio director, where he oversaw radio programs and the transition into television, eventually becoming president of the agency and retiring in 1967. Posterity has not been kind to him: Historians and critics have echoed his contemporary detractors, seeing a defeat for the New Deal in his ascendancy and a corruption of the true role of the government.[74] Ironically, or not, at Lewis's death in 1975, Norman Corwin, radio writer and staunch New Dealer, wrote a heartfelt reminiscence of Lewis's "generosity" and commitment to nurturing the "creative people" of radio. Corwin explained how at CBS Lewis went out of his way to support new creative work and, in Lewis's words, to make "creative people . . . feel cherished and important . . . praise good work and extraordinary effort on the part of creative people, and—above all—see that they get credit for it."[75]

Commercial Radio Programs and War Propaganda

Lewis's plans were implemented in network and local programs, and in all program genres, so that his goal of having all radio listeners aware of the most important war messages was well met.[76] Sometimes war messages replaced the commercial messages, sometimes they provided a subject for a sketch, and sometimes they provided a subject for the plotline of a dramatic serial. One form of programming presented particular difficulties for advertisers: How were advertisers to sell their wares adjacent to war news?

Musical variety programs, such as *Kraft Music Hall*, easily integrated war themes and messages into sketches, songs, and announcements.[77] The use of major stars to carry the message was especially common. In this 1943 broadcast, after singing "You Are My Sunshine," Bing Crosby spoke at length about the war effort:

This is the old *Kraft Music Hall*, friends, battle station bound to every spot on the globe; where men are digging for victory in Tunisia, and in the Solomons they're digging foxholes, and from the skies above Germany they're digging up Berlin streets. The least we can do is dig a little too. We've got to dig for war bonds and we've got to be doing a little digging for that victory garden. There's any number of cartoons and [unintelligible] about victory gardens but nobody's kidding about the urgent need for them. The more groceries we grow ourselves for our own uses the more our farmers can send to our fighting men and our allies. So when you have a little time off, get your exercise in the garden. Climb into some old clothes—

Crosby is interrupted by other guests, who continue a comedy sketch about victory gardens, including one gag about a garden running on motors: "No, it's just a little buggy."[78]

Commercials themselves often incorporated war themes. During a 1943 *Jack Benny* broadcast, announcer Don Wilson delivered a Grape-Nuts Flakes commercial, jokingly introducing it as a "cereal serial in three acts":

Act 1. The scene is breakfast. Mom, Pop, and Little Willy are seated at the breakfast table. And notice, please, in the spotlight, a big, 12-ounce, economy size package of delicious, malty, rich Grape-Nuts Flakes. Act 2. The next day and it's lunch time. Pop's just come home from the war plant, and Mom's just come home from Red Cross. But Willy beats them both home and his teacher told him that whole grain cereals make a swell luncheon dish nowadays. And here he comes, bearing those grand tasting nourishing Grape-Nuts Flakes. Act 3. One more day, it's suppertime for our dear little Willy. And Mom's there with those crisp, tempting, toasty brown Grape-Nuts Flakes. They're just as delicious, they're just as nutritious at breakfast, at lunch, or at supper.

Grape-Nuts Flakes becomes part of the war effort as a nutritious, eco-nomical meal for war workers, volunteers, and their children.

This strategy of associating the advertiser with the war effort can also be heard in a 1944 *Texaco Star Theater* commercial, when the program featured comedian Fred Allen:

This is Jimmy Wallington reminding you that there may be more miles left in your car than you realize. Countless cars have served more than 100,000 miles with proper care and lubrication. And the chances are yours can do as well when you take it to your Texaco dealer for systematic Texaco lubrication and a regular Texaco stem to stern check up. The first rule to making your car last is seeing your Texaco dealer regularly.[79]

In the face of rationing and scarcity, cars must be made to last; Texaco identifies itself as eager to help in the effort and thereby support the war.

Fred Allen also integrated the nightly "dim out" of electric lights in New York City into his "March of Trivia" interview of a "Broadway character" named "Sharp Sherman":

Allen: "What about this dim-out, Sherman?"

Sherman: "I got a coupla gimmicks operatin' already, Chum."

Allen: "What gimmicks?"

Sherman: "I got a dim-out Racin' Form."

Allen: "What is that?"

Sherman: "Hundreds of horseplayers used to stand in front of restaurants and read their Racin' Forms by the light of the restaurant windows. Today, them windows is dimmed out."

Allen: "Oh. And your—"

Sherman: "My Racin' Form's got a lightnin' bug tied on it. A horseplayer can read it anyplace."[80]

The daytime serials, already structured as didactic vehicles of reason-why advertising strategy (see Chapter 5), were a natural fit for the transmission of messages about how to support the war effort.[81] In a contemporaneous interview, Anne Hummert asserted that many women had difficulty grasping some of the issues raised by the war: "You know how most women shudder when the word 'inflation' is mentioned? The average woman will say, 'I've tried so hard to learn what it's all about, but, it's so involved, I've just given up!'" The solution, in Hummert's view, was to explain the issue in "terms of everyday conversation, between characters whom the listeners know." The character Stella Dallas, for example, according to Hummert, says, "'After all, the thing that concerns us is—how much money we get in our pay envelope at the end of the week and *how much we can buy with it*. . . . If we don't *all* work to keep prices down . . . if we just bid against each other for things, 'cause we're makin' good money now—we can reach the place where all prices go sky high.'"[82] Many other Hummert characters joined the war effort, including the character of Mary Noble's famous actor husband; the program title was temporarily changed from *Mary Noble, Backstage Wife* to *Mary Noble, War Wife*.

The Hummerts also created a soap opera specifically for the War Department, *Chaplain Jim USA*. Broadcast in the mornings as a sustaining program on NBC Blue, it featured the character Chaplain Jim relating the problems and concerns of servicemen to audiences at home. According to Edward Kirby, it was designed to appeal to "the little educated, anxious ones, who couldn't quite understand why their son, or husband or sweetheart had been taken from them by Uncle Sam and sent to some 'far-away' place." Audiences were encouraged to write to Chaplain Jim, who would read and respond to audience letters on the air, becoming a "real 'Living Friend' in the minds of thousands."[83] A *Time* magazine radio critic wrote, "[T]his khaki serial may well explain many perplexing army matters to womenfolk who are worried about their men in the armed forces."[84] The Hummerts' characters were designed to encourage identification on the part of listeners; the Hummert production style, as discussed in Chapter 5, emphasizing plain speech, instructional texts, and clear enunciation, made them well suited to disseminate war propaganda. Their war effort was their most effective response to the advertising and commercial radio critics, who excoriated their soaps in particular for their relentless reason-why tactics and longwinded repetitiveness. In the case of Hummert soaps, critics did not need to fear that humor might be inappropriately applied to war topics.

One form of programming was especially problematic for advertisers: news. In the 1930s the major news wire services had boycotted radio stations at the behest of newspaper publishers fearful of losing paying subscribers to free radio, and many advertisers had avoided sponsoring news for fear that listeners would make negative associations with their product. But by the onset of the war, news had nonetheless become established on radio, especially after the radio news coverage of the Munich Crisis of 1938 and London Blitz of 1940 attracted large audiences. As a percentage of programs, news increased from around 5 percent in the 1930s to nearly 20 percent by the mid-1940s.[85] However, having convinced some advertisers to advertise during news and news commentary, broadcasters faced complaints that advertising during war news was inappropriate. Hoping to head off criticism, even if the critics were only "the small minority who would like to have all commercials eliminated," in 1942 the National Association of Broadcasters immediately formulated a voluntary code for broadcasters, in which advertising announcements would not interrupt the middle of the news but be placed "after the body of the news has been given." Furthermore, as NBC Blue news director G. W. Johnstone pointed out, because "the news today is almost always far more exciting than any advertising could possibly be," the code recommended that advertisers avoid words such as "flash," "bulletin," and even "good news." CBS went further, mandating that during news broadcasts "Neither opening commercial nor any other commercial is to be in the form of a jingle or any other device manifesting undue gaiety, humor, or excitement." Johnstone concurred, noting that "a cheerful announcement about the beautifying effects of a new soap, for example, is all very well when it follows the rendition of swing music but is definitely annoying when it comes after the announcement that a ship has been sunk with 'all hands on board.'"[86] Thus, as radio grew into a greater war information resource, broadcasters and advertisers negotiated strategies for preventing audience alienation while maintaining the commercial structure of advertising-supported programming.

World War II, dreaded by many in advertising as a potentially fatal disruption, actually provided the advertising and commercial radio industries with the opportunity to expand audiences, contribute to the war effort, and demonstrate their centrality to American culture and business. During the war, unprecedented coordination between government agencies and business interests helped disseminate war information not just as separate didactic propaganda programs but also as specific themes interwoven throughout commercial radio entertainment. William B. Lewis, adman and CBS executive, spearheaded this effort at the OWI to integrate propaganda and entertainment in order to reach audiences where they were, gathered around their favorite programs on the radio. Criticized for protecting commercialism, Lewis actually leveraged commercial interests to serve the larger need to mobilize all Americans for total war. Once the war ended, radio had proven its centrality to American popular culture; audiences and profits were at high tide. Few in the industry were aware just how suddenly and dramatically that tide would turn.

10 On a Treadmill to Oblivion
The Peak and Sudden Decline
of Network Radio

The radio broadcasts of national network star-studded entertainment programs to nearly all American homes had its greatest reach during the 1940s. The war effort, rather than undermine radio, had helped make it even more central to American popular culture. Its strength and continued growth throughout the 1940s seemed unstoppable. Commercial radio had become practically synonymous with advertising itself. Cartoonist H. T. Webster makes the point in a 1945 cartoon showing a balding, bespectacled gentleman in a living room with a large radio set explaining to his nine- or ten-year-old daughter, "When I was a boy *nobody* owned a radio. There weren't any." The young girl, quizzically positioned with her chin on her hands, objects: "But, Daddy, how did they sell soap?" (See Figure 10-1.)[1]

Critics of radio continued to rage against its commercialism, gathering a "revolt against radio" among those concerned about mass cultural degradation, or deceptive advertising, or the brainwashing of gullible housewives. One of the most articulate critiques of commercial radio, however, came from within. The bestselling novel *The Hucksters* expressed an adman's frustration with a tyrannical sponsor. Meanwhile, the economics of radio and advertising shifted during the 1940s, leading to the development of new strategies of sponsorship and program control well before television upended the radio system. Many were aware that television, which had been invented in the 1920s, might someday reach audiences and compete with radio; but few anticipated that the system of national network radio would be almost entirely dismantled by the end of the 1950s. In the late 1940s many in the ad

Figure 10-1. "But, Daddy, how did they sell soap?" (*The Best of H. T. Webster: A Memorial Collection* [New York: Simon & Schuster, 1953], 227.)

industry expressed ambivalence about television—was it an opportunity or a threat? As television began to gain ground, one adman in particular lobbied for a reordering of the existing broadcast business model. NBC-TV president Sylvester "Pat" Weaver, former Young & Rubicam executive, argued for network control of programming and the relegation of advertisers to the purchase of interstitial minutes. Accused of betraying his advertising background, Weaver actually applied the lessons he learned as an adman in radio to the evolving business model of television.

The Revolt against Radio

Although the advertising industry had proven its good corporate citizenship by providing time, labor, and services to the war effort, it was still dogged by criticism for its role in commercial radio. Advertising agency dominance over programming was undisputed: In 1945 five agencies were responsible for 46 percent of CBS's billings; as clients of the networks, their needs were paramount.[2] According to one critic, radio programming was in consequence "either corny, strident, boresome, florid, inane, repetitive, irritating, offensive, moronic, adolescent, or nauseating."[3] Daytime serials were a particular target of critics who found serials' reason-why advertising to be obnoxious and serial plotlines to be "pandering to perversity."[4] Famed radio inventor Lee De Forest fulminated in 1947 that commercial interests had ruined his creation: "You have debased this child, you have sent him out on the street in rags of ragtime, tatters of jive and boogie-woogie to collect money from all and sundry for hubba hubba and audio jitterbug."[5] The rise of the radio jingle further inflamed critics, who cautioned that the repetition of advertising jingles could "create ill-will among listeners."[6] The Pepsi-Cola jingle, which became a hit record heard in jukeboxes everywhere, signaled the ubiquity of radio advertising:

> Pepsi-Cola hits the spot,
> Twelve full ounces, that's a lot,
> Twice as much for a nickel, too,
> Pepsi-Cola is the drink for you.[7]

Although many in the industry, according to adman Charles Hull Wolfe, were "inclined to close their ears to censure and let the opposition shout itself hoarse," admen and broadcasters had some compelling reasons to address their critics' complaints.[8] Foremost was the ongoing threat of federal intervention. The *FCC Report on Chain Broadcasting* of 1941 had accused RCA of monopolistic practices by running two networks, NBC Red and NBC Blue, simultaneously. FCC Chairman James Fly believed that this gave NBC too much market control; perhaps more competition would improve radio programming. The FCC regulated not networks but only local stations, which depended on the Commission for broadcast licenses; however, Fly was able to force NBC to sell off one of its networks by ruling that the FCC would not renew the license of any station affiliated with any network owned by a company that owned more than one network. So, having first picked off its best stations, NBC sold the Blue Network in 1943 to Life Savers candy magnate Edward J. Noble, who renamed it ABC.[9]

However, the addition of another commercial network had the unintended effect of intensifying commercialism. While affiliated with NBC, the Blue Network had been able to provide more "public service" and educational programming than other networks because it was cross-subsidized by the Red Network's commercial success. But as ABC, the network had to compete for advertisers by programming as commercially as possible.[10] A 1946 FCC report, known as the Blue Book, reiterated many critics' concerns about the state of commercial broadcasting.[11] It asserted that there were not enough public service programs and live local programs, that there was not enough discussion of public issues, and that advertising "excesses" needed to be eliminated or reduced.[12]

CBS head William Paley responded with a speech to the National Association of Broadcasters in 1946 expressing contrition for "advertising excesses," but most admen and broadcasters vociferously defended their practices and policies.[13] Competing studies drew different conclusions about the level of listener irritation at radio advertising: Paul Lazarsfeld's 1946 study, *The People Look at Radio*, suggested that listeners do not resent commercials, while a McCann-Erickson report by Herta Herzog and agency head Marion Harper Jr. was more concerned about audience alienation, concluding that up to one-fourth of listeners were critical of radio advertising.[14] Admen also cited a National Opinion Research Center survey which claimed that 62 percent of listeners preferred programs with commercials and that only 7 percent wanted programs without them.[15]

Such studies helped defenders of commercial radio marginalize their critics as unrepresentative of the American public and therefore irrelevant. JWT adman Carroll Carroll argued that "the critics of commercial radio are critics not of art, not of intrinsic goodness, but of the national taste."[16] In other words, "elitist" critics simply did not share the tastes of the majority of Americans; admen, on the other hand, catered to that "national taste" rather than degrade it. Fellow JWT adman Robert Colwell argued that radio's "economic function" of "selling more goods to more people" was far more important than "whether the Little Mother's Club of Split Lip, Nevada, happens to like the commercials." Critics of radio advertising were just "people to whom the commercials are not directed."[17] The critics were not the market; their opinion was irrelevant. NBC president Niles Trammell took another tack when he pointed out that while nearly 50 percent of magazine space is routinely devoted to advertising, "only 6.8% of the network's total program time is devoted to commercial announcements."[18] If critics wished to decry the predominance of advertising, they should turn to print media, which uses the majority of its space for advertising. Trammell neglected to mention that advertisers in print media do not normally control the editorial content, as they did in commercial radio.

Accusations that commercial radio was not fulfilling the compact to serve the public interest by providing "public service" programming underlay some of the criticism.[19] Defenders reacted by redefining commercialism and "public service" until the two seemed interchangeable. While others may have defined "public service" as, say, airing educational programs, NBC executive Phillips Carlin defined it as "practically everything that we are doing in radio. . . . A comedian lifts people, gets them out of the dumps. I think that is a public service program."[20] Carlin's populism was echoed by Trammell, who feigned doubt as to what constituted a public service program: "Opinions may differ as to which kinds of programs are most heavily weighted with public interest . . . a debate between two college professors or a debate between Fibber McGee and Molly," two popular radio stars.[21] Clearly aimed at elitist critics in academe, Trammell's point, echoed by many others, was that the public interest is simply what interests the public. Trammell also found advertising in the public interest: "Not only is advertising *in* the public interest, but it is the very *expression* of that interest." Advertising expresses "interest in all that is new, all that is better, all that inspires, stimulates, and drives us to make this a world of peace, of strength, of freedom, of equal opportunity for all."[22] Not only, then, is radio entertainment itself in the public interest, but the advertising that supports radio is itself an expression of American values. Rather than some foreign parasite debilitating American culture, advertising is a sign and source of its health.

The Hucksters: Admen Critique Sponsor Control

Frederic Wakeman, a former adman at Lord & Thomas who had worked on the American Tobacco account, in 1946 published a thinly veiled roman à clef of his experiences in radio, *The Hucksters.* The novel sold more than 750,000 copies and was selected by the Book-of-the-Month-Club. The MGM film of the same name starring Clark Gable followed almost immediately in 1947. In both novel and film, *The Hucksters* follows the fortunes of adman Vic Norman, who, after war service, joins an ad agency to oversee the radio programming of the Beautee soap account. The sponsor, named Evan Llewellyn Evans, was understood by industry readers to have been modeled on Wakeman's former client, American Tobacco head George Washington Hill. In the novel, Evans, like Hill, demands total fealty and obeisance from his agency and intimidates underlings by performing such stunts as spitting on a conference table to introduce himself to Norman. He lectures Norman on advertising strategy:

Remember, two things make good advertising. One, a good simple idea. Two, repetition. And by repetition, by God, I mean until the public is so irritated with it, they'll buy your brand because they bloody well can't forget it. All you professional advertising men are scared to death of raping the public; I say the public likes it, if you got the know-how to make 'em relax and enjoy it.[23]

Initially Norman, though repelled by Evans and his advertising strategies, goes along and invents a radio commercial in which a "colored maid" repetitiously chuckles, "Love that soap."[24] However, Norman eventually regrets such hack work; when he realizes that he actually wants Evans's approval, he is so disgusted with himself that he quits. And this resistance to the crude and manipulative sponsor becomes Norman's path to redemption. The mainstream press regarded the novel as a literal report on what was wrong with commercial radio. The broadcasting and advertising industries were concomitantly concerned that the novel, and its popularization in a film, would generate enough negative sentiment to inspire further federal regulation.

Wakeman, as a former adman, was indicting radio sponsors, whose ability to intimidate and browbeat men of integrity such as Norman made them the clear villains in the degradation of radio. In an interview by the trade magazine *Printers' Ink*, Wakeman insisted his novel was not a condemnation of advertising or the "American system of sales and distribution" but simply an "indictment of despotism in industry, *any industry*, that prohibits the creative function," and in this case, the despot was a radio sponsor. The radio sponsor as despot was a familiar enough type to admen, some of whom had written Wakeman congratulating him on "the fine job he did of portraying their particular pain-in-the-neck client."[25] The novel, then, articulated a frustration common in the advertising industry: Although the industry was blamed for obnoxious programming, many admen believed the fault was actually the sponsor's. Admen would produce better advertising and programming if only their clients the sponsors were more reasonable, or knowledgeable, or cultured. Complaints about radio, according to these admen, actually reflected sponsor interference; these complaints would disappear if sponsors stopped interfering.

Wakeman's caricature of George Washington Hill was especially pertinent on Madison Avenue because Hill was infamous for intimidating subordinates and insisting on repetitive reason-why radio programs and advertising strategies. Hill oversaw the program *Lucky Strike Hit Parade*, which was based on his notion that only hit tunes played up-tempo would appeal to listeners.[26] Apocryphal stories circulated of Hill's insisting on selecting tunes by dancing to them in his office.[27] CBS chief William Paley claimed Hill made NBC president Merlin Aylesworth dance to the *Hit Parade* with his secretary—a clear demonstration of an advertiser's power over the networks.[28] Independent radio producer Dan Golenpaul recalled that his fearlessness in standing up to Hill in some confrontation earned him gratitude from ad agencies. Admen told Golenpaul that they "found Hill's methods a thorn in their side, because he was getting away with horrible commercials," but they could not openly disagree with Hill without losing the large American Tobacco account. These admen also worried that "their clients were actually in danger of the same thing"—that is, engaging in crude, repetitive hard sell tactics instead of moving toward less audience-alienating strategies.[29]

Although Wakeman's critique of the radio sponsor may have been secretly welcomed on Madison Avenue, concerns over the novel's popularization in a 1947 MGM movie starring Clark Gable as Vic Norman and Sydney Greenstreet as Evan Llewellyn Evans "hit ad alley with a sickening thud."[30] A JWT staffer worried that "the picture will do more widespread and popular harm to advertising than the good of all our basic contributions and fine deeds placed end to end from now until Christmas 1950."[31] The film, however, reduced Wakeman's lengthy analysis of the pitfalls of sponsor control of programming to a few brief speeches by Norman and transformed the plot to revolve around a romance between Gable's adman and Deborah Kerr's character (a married woman in the novel but conveniently widowed in the film). The advertising trade magazine *Tide* accused Hollywood of losing "most of the plot and some of the people."[32] Nonetheless, the diminution of Wakeman's insider critique of broadcasting and advertising in favor of the love story did not placate admen who viewed the film as another effort on the part of Hollywood to smear Madison Avenue as the refuge of hacks and craven opportunists.

NBC executives, in particular, were outraged by the film's implication that, as one reported, "sponsors wouldn't be pulling this kind of thing on the air if the broadcasters controlled the programs."[33] NBC executives were so angered by MGM's adaptation of *The Hucksters* that they considered smearing the filmmakers by accusing them of suspicious politics. In 1947, NBC executive Syd Eiges prepared statements of varying degrees of vehemence for NBC president Niles Trammell to choose from. The most outraged of these, never published or released, described the film as a "vicious and untruthful attack on our American system of advertising" which is "in keeping with the best traditions of the left wingers which Hollywood has so warmly clasped to its ample bosom."[34] Eiges' obvious red-baiting of Hollywood was in line with growing efforts to intimidate entertainment industry denizens with accusations of communist sympathies, which reached their peak in the House Un-American Activities Committee investigations of Hollywood between 1947 and 1954.

The sense of outrage was perhaps more pronounced because Wakeman's direct experience in broadcasting informed his critique. *The Hucksters* underlined the fact that the NBC executives' view of sponsor control of programming as an inherent and necessary condition for commercial broadcasting was a view not entirely shared by the advertising industry. In a 1947 interview Wakeman argued that broadcasters ought to take control of programming precisely to prevent sponsor abuses:

[Y]ou radio people should take back your programs from the hucksters. Take back your networks. Take back your stations and do your own programming without benefit of what any sponsor thinks any program should be . . . commercials can then be sold to advertisers on a dignified, properly controlled basis that will protect the program, not destroy it. It works with newspapers and magazines—why not with radio?[35]

Wakeman articulated one of the key issues admen had identified over and over: that sponsor control of programs mixed up the editorial and advertising functions of the medium. By allowing those functions to be conflated, the radio networks had lost editorial control; as a result, bad programming and inept advertising had undermined the advertising value of the medium overall. Wakeman's reference to magazine and newspaper business models echoed the point made by admen before him, including William Benton and William B. Lewis, that the sponsorship model might not actually be the best way to use broadcasting as an advertising medium.[36]

In response to these various public criticisms of commercial radio, within the industry many debated how to improve it. To encourage higher-quality advertising and programming, NBC considered bestowing awards for "the best handling of advertising copy each year" or an Oscars-type award for soap operas that would make "daytime radio socially and culturally acceptable."[37] The film industry had created the Academy Awards for this purpose and had enjoyed positive promotional effects. A producers' trade association adjudicated those awards and included votes from other areas of the film industry, thus allowing for industry-wide participation and the appearance, at least, of objective judging of films. NBC, however, enjoyed no such neutrality in relation to its clients, the advertisers and agencies, and so declined the opportunity lest it be exposed to accusations of client favoritism.

Others sought to improve radio advertising in reaction to a shift in their views of their audiences. BBDO radio department head Charles Hull Wolfe posited that the postwar radio era needed a "new approach to radio advertising" that is "more business like," "more socially conscious," and "more research-minded."[38] Admen's assumptions about their audiences could be challenged by actual research. Reason-why strategies were based on retrograde notions of audience intelligence. Famed adman Bruce Barton declared in an agency memo that "This formula by which the listener is treated as a moron was unquestionably effective when it was evolved by Mr. [George Washington] Hill [of American Tobacco] and Mr. [Albert] Lasker [of Lord & Thomas] but those were the days when radio was new, when passenger trains ran at 40 miles an hour and airplanes at 90."[39] Reason-why advertising, then, was as old-fashioned as out-of-date technologies. But what should replace reason-why strategies? Wolfe surveyed radio directors, who declared, "The new approach calls for shorter, quieter, less razzle-dazzle radio copy and more straightforward honesty."[40] Internally, then, industry insiders acknowledged critics' complaints about the obnoxiousness of hard sell advertising and sought to soften or eliminate it.

Meanwhile, the new emphasis on audience research provided an opportunity for quantifying advertising's effects and demonstrating its utility. McCann-Erickson agency head Marion Harper Jr. bought the "program analyzer," a device that recorded audience reactions while listening, from Frank Stanton and Paul Lazarsfeld at CBS and used it in new business presentations for selling clients on radio. Harper then hired Herta Herzog for qualitative radio research and marketed McCann-Erickson as employing a scientific approach to the problem of radio audiences.[41] Sponsors like General Foods, having accepted radio's effectiveness, wanted more specific information about audiences than just their size. Who was listening and how likely were they to buy the product? Unfortunately for sponsors, there was no definitive way to identify the effects of radio advertising, whether they tried to measure audiences or advertising "impact" or the "action-factor" of how many listeners actually bought. Broadcast signal receipt was untraceable. Unlike movie theaters, which can count tickets sold to determine audience size, broadcasters could not measure audiences accurately. The dispersion of audiences in their individual homes, not to mention the privacy inherent in home listening, left advertisers dependent on sampling techniques vulnerable to error, bias, and measurement limitations. Advertiser pressure to more accurately measure audiences and the impact of advertising would increase over the following decades.

Shifting Strategies of Sponsorship and Program Control

Commercial network radio reached its peak in the late 1940s and then, to the surprise of many in the industry, went into inexorable decline. In 1948 network radio advertising revenues reached $210 million; 94 percent of American households owned radios; and the FCC began issuing new radio station licenses, increasing the number of new radio stations on the air.[42] In 1947, of a total of 1,062 stations, 1,028 (97 percent) were affiliated with a network. By 1952, the FCC had issued twice as many station licenses, 2,331. Although there were more network affiliates, 1,247, they made up a smaller proportion (53 percent) of the whole.[43] By 1952, network radio's percentage of advertising revenues had slid from 46 percent of all radio advertising revenues at the end of the war to 25 percent.[44] The dominance of network radio as a national advertising medium thus eroded rapidly. Advertisers had shifted their national radio network appropriations into television, newspapers, and local "spot" radio. Over the course of the 1950s and into the 1960s, radio turned away from networking and toward more local station control, away from nationally sponsored entertainment programs and toward less expensive recorded music and talk formats designed for local advertisers.[45]

However, well before the impact of network television, radio advertisers and agencies had already begun to shift strategies in response to the increasing costs of network radio; program packaging, cooperative programming, spot advertising, syndication, and transcriptions allowed agencies and sponsors to bypass the national networks. Independent production specialists, called program packagers, became more important in the late 1940s: Often they produced a particular genre, such as quiz shows, and could reap economic efficiencies through specialization. Agencies such as JWT, although itself one of the largest program producers, began subcontracting production to program packagers, in part to address the needs of their clients for different types of programs without having to add more radio staff.[46] Cooperative programming, in which more than one advertiser paid production costs for one program, gained favor during the war, when some advertisers began to seek cheaper alternatives to national network airtime and high talent costs. This form of sponsorship was also sometimes called "participating sponsorship," indicating multiple participating advertisers.

As the prices of national network airtime pressed upward in response to increased advertiser demand, lower cost non-network, or spot, advertising, also grew steadily from 46 percent of radio revenues in 1939 to 65 percent in 1949.[47] Spot buying allowed advertisers to target specific local markets rather than pay for access to the entire national market. While the networks provided huge efficiencies for reaching the national market, some advertisers found better economic efficiency in spot buying for specific regions.[48] Thus spot buying began to rise in importance in the agencies.[49] By 1950, at the cusp of the television era, Frederic Ziv, an independent producer of syndicated radio, argued that spot time buying and syndication were the future of radio.[50] He probably did not know he was predicting the end of network radio as the single largest advertising medium, but he was essentially correct.[51]

Syndicated programming, prerecorded programs distributed directly to individual stations rather than through networks, allowed an advertiser to buy a preexisting program and choose either regional or national distribution. Syndicated programs were usually recorded on discs, similar to record albums, called transcriptions. For advertisers the advantages of syndicated transcriptions included the ability to repeat episodes, to allow for differential scheduling in various locations, and to target specific local markets. NBC and CBS had banned transcriptions from their national broadcasts, insisting on live broadcasts primarily as a means of maintaining control over affiliates. If affiliates were not required to carry live network feeds, the networks worried, stations could leave networks, and transcribed programming might replace live network programming.[52] The use of recordings on radio broadcasts was not a new development and is traceable at least back to the Pittsburgh garage of radio pioneer Dr. Frank Conrad in 1920, if not Lee De Forest's similar experiments a decade earlier in Riverdale, New York. Furthermore, transcribed syndicated programs had been key to commercial radio's development. *Amos 'n' Andy*, for example, was distributed as a transcribed syndicated program and attracted large audiences before it was aired nationally on NBC in 1929. The network insistence on live broadcasts undermined program quality as millions heard botched or imperfect performances. Performers complained about the increased workload of repeating the same program several times in one evening to reach different time zones. By the mid-1940s, radio stars Bing Crosby, Jack Benny, and Edgar Bergen all advocated the use of transcriptions, at least for their repeat broadcasts. As network radio rapidly lost ground in the late 1940s and as the networks redirected their resources toward television, the radio networks began to relent on the transcription ban. The weaker national networks, ABC and Mutual, already allowed transcriptions in order to attract advertisers interested in more economical programming options, as well as performers interested in greater quality control.[53] The ban next crumbled at CBS, and finally at NBC in 1947. At first NBC allowed transcriptions only on a case-by-case basis, and JWT interpreted this as a temporary rather than a permanent change.[54]

The advent of the Ampex tape format in 1948 eliminated the possibility of returning to a live-only broadcast policy on network radio. Audiotape improved sound quality; more important, unlike previous forms of audio recording, such as the wax disc recording, which required one long single take, audiotape permitted editing. It became possible to cut and paste together an error-free recording. By the end of 1948, NBC had not yet allowed its performers to prerecord on Ampex tape. Radio star Ozzie Nelson wrote NBC executive Sydney Strotz asking if the real reason for the tape ban was that RCA had not yet developed its own tape recording format. Although Strotz denied that was the case, he took the matter to NBC president Trammell, asking, because NBC would have to give in on this point sooner or later, why not do so now?[55]

Meanwhile, at CBS, William Paley had decided to pursue an aggressive policy of network program packaging; he began offering packaged programs to sponsors in 1946. Paley believed the network needed to take more control over programming, especially over talent, reasoning that stars brought audiences to networks, not the other way around. He helped convince a number of radio stars to form corporations to save on tax liabilities; CBS then purchased the services of the star-corporations, pulling them away from NBC. Some of the stars Paley won over in what were called the "talent raids" of 1948 included Jack Benny, Bing Crosby, and Red Skelton. However, these gains came at a high cost and just as the network was about to lose the bulk of its audiences to television.[56] Looking back, Paley claimed he was trying to secure talent for television. But in 1948, network radio was at its peak, and television had yet to find an audience: It is more likely that Paley's "talent raids" were designed to build the CBS radio network.

NBC also sought increased program and scheduling control. In 1943, NBC suspended its waiting list for prime time availabilities, citing not only wartime exigencies but also its interest in controlling the schedule, heretofore dictated by each sponsor in its time franchise. In its notice to advertising agencies NBC pointed out that it was faced "with a far greater responsibility than ever before with respect to the character and quality of our programs" and thus would assign time slots according to the quality of the program offered by a sponsor rather than the sponsor's position on the waiting list.[57] NBC, rather than the sponsor, would thus determine what a "quality" program would be. Thus, by the end of the 1940s, both networks and advertisers were working to modify the radio model of sponsor control of programming. Throughout the 1940s, the peak of the radio era, both CBS and NBC moved toward increased network control of programming and scheduling. With the arrival of television, the networks would pursue these strategies even more aggressively.

The Coming of Television: Ad Agencies' Ambivalence

In audience size and advertising revenues, network radio reached its zenith in 1948, the same year television network broadcasts began. Less than 1 percent of households had a television receiver in 1948; by 1952, that figure had risen to 34 percent, and by 1954 to 55 percent.[58] In hindsight, television's rapid dissemination appears foreordained; it was poised to pick up the stars, programs, advertisers, and audiences built by radio and carry on. However, the actual transition to television was extremely complex; it was politically, economically, and technologically contested at every step. The broadcasting industry was internally conflicted over how to make the transition. While networks were poised to seize greater programming control, they still hoped to shift television's higher production costs onto sponsors. While sponsors mulled the increased costs and smaller audiences, their agencies faced financial losses overseeing television programming as long as their compensation was limited to commissions. Meanwhile, both agencies and sponsors balked at any diminution of their program control at the same time they sought alternatives to the single sponsorship model, which had become unsustainable in the higher-cost medium of television. Because the shift from radio networking to television networking was so complex, a full accounting of the transition is beyond the scope of this book; however, the ways in which the advertising industry in the late 1940s debated the shift to television is addressed here.

JWT was one of the few agencies that had eagerly anticipated television. As early as 1928, radio director William Ensign reported, "Television is a lot further developed than I thought," and in 1930 another staffer argued that the agency had been too slow to get into radio and so hoped, "[W]e will get going on television from the first."[59] The advertising theorist Edgar Felix wrote an article in 1931 predicting that "television will be the greatest advertising medium" yet.[60] Others were skeptical: One adman pointed out in 1947, "Television has been 'in the air' for twenty years. Its enthusiasts have cried 'Wolf!' so often that most people are skeptical about its imminence."[61] Such skepticism was especially typical of admen deeply involved in radio production. Carroll Carroll wrote other JWT staffers in 1944 that "television will never be the world force radio is, because television will leave little or nothing to the imagination, and it is imagination that gives radio its power." Referring to his own work writing Bing Crosby's patter between songs on *Kraft Music Hall*, Carroll continued, "Bing Crosby's singing will be enhanced by television, but he won't sound nearly so convincing when everyone sees him reading those casual ad libs."[62] Nonetheless, JWT, which had begun conducting television experiments in 1930, oversaw the first regularly sponsored one-hour television program, *Hour Glass*, in 1946–47 and was producing a television version of the Kraft music program by 1947.[63]

In approaching television as an advertising medium, admen debated its advantages and disadvantages. Like radio, television had the potential for "tremendous intimacy," believed BBDO executive Bob Foreman.[64] Another adman claimed that television would improve on radio's feeling of "personal contact": "It more closely approximates person-to-person selling than any other medium."[65] Yet the use of actors to sell was precisely what worried another adman; Fred Coe believed it possible for still photographs in print ads to appear "sincere," but he wondered if a commercial would still seem "sincere" if it were dependent on actors' demonstrating products enthusiastically on live television: "[I]t's just too hard to believe even for a sophisticated eight year old."[66] Admen debated the primacy of hearing or seeing. Would audio or video be more important for capturing audience attention? In 1944, Edgar Kobak, former adman and then an NBC vice president, wondered, "Which is more important in television—the eye or the ear?"[67] In 1936, an adman speculated that although audiences could listen to radio for hours at a time, they wouldn't want to watch many hours of television at a time because "the [eye] seems to tire of objects more quickly than the ear does of sounds."[68] The requirement that audiences watch, as well as listen, worried an adman in 1937, who complained, "The point is, I like entertainment, but I don't want to make a job of it. And that's exactly what television is asking me to do. It's a job to drop one's evening paper, dim the lights, and then concentrate on a few images doing a tap dance or harmonizing in a duet."[69] Another adman also assumed that television would demand much greater attention from audiences than radio: Television "will require a dark or darkened room. That means that father cannot read his newspaper; mother cannot sew or mend; little brother can't sprawl on his stomach and look at comics."[70] According to this adman, however, all this was advantageous: It would make audiences more attentive, thereby increasing the selling impact of any advertising.[71]

Unlike print or radio, television would be a multimedia advertising vehicle; as one adman pointed out, television "combines sight. It combines sounds. It combines motion, and it also combines immediacy."[72] As early as 1935, an adman predicted that "A vast increase in selling power may be anticipated for a medium which actually shows Rootie-Tooties on the breakfast table, a Zub-Zero Refrigerator full of food . . . each surrounded by a circle of characters registering intense consumer satisfaction."[73] E. P. H. James, having moved to the Mutual Broadcasting System from NBC by 1948, tried to reassure admen concerned about the visual nature of television by pointing out that it would be a "sound" medium too: "Television includes among its ingredients the full power of the human voice for *spoken salesmanship.*"[74] Thus, television could be the ultimate medium for demonstrating products, according to one advertiser, offering "the opportunity to show and demonstrate merchandise actually in use."[75] Claiming that "a product well demonstrated is more than half sold," JWT executive Fred Fidler predicted television's effectiveness as a demonstration medium because "television utilizes the *conviction* of sight, the *interest* of action and movement for demonstration, combines these with the *persuasiveness* of the human voice, and will some day 'plus' the formula with the *appeal* and *realism* of color."[76] Early television advertisers who took advantage of television's demonstrative quality included car and appliance makers, such as Buick and Westinghouse. Most famously, actress Betty Furness demonstrated Westinghouse washers, dryers, ovens, refrigerators, and television sets on the anthology drama *Studio One.* The risks of live demonstrations, as when a refrigerator door did not open in a 1954 live commercial, or when a cigarette spokesman coughed after announcing "never an irritation," led to a greater reliance on filmed demonstrations, at greater expense.[77]

However, despite the promises of television's ability to demonstrate action visually, many early television commercials relied on existing radio commercial techniques, such as a lengthy verbal commercial delivered by the star, extolling the reasons-why to buy. At the opening of a 1949 live television episode of *The Goldbergs*, the character Molly Goldberg raises the window shade, leans out her window, and confidentially chats to the audience about Sanka decaffeinated coffee in a single simple medium shot. "Hello everybody. Excuse me for talking to you from my kitchen window," she explains, but she is preparing supper for cousin Simon, who she complains is not their favorite cousin. Simon is unpleasant to be around, Molly explains:

Sometimes I really think that maybe it's something in which he really indulges. I mean that. I once read a book, you are what you eat, you are what you drink. That's something to ponder. For instance, let us say, just for instance, if you drank Sanka coffee, it's a marvelous coffee, it's a delicious coffee, with a wonderful flavor, and 97 percent of the caffeine is removed and the sleep is left in and you can drink as much as you like and sleep. What is the logical conclusion to conclude? That it's good for restlessness, it's good for irritability, and then, look, restlessness and irritability, what that can do to the natural environment of the system, don't ask. And if it does cost a penny more, what's money? If in the morning you can rise and shine and brighten the corner where you are? I mean it, if you're still without Sanka, it comes in the Regular and it comes in the Instant, the Instant comes in a little bottle, and 1, 2, 3, with a little boiling water you have the most delicious cup of Sanka, so don't linger. After all, a word to the wise, shouldn't it be sufficient? I've got to go now to serve the supper. . . .[78]

This commercial announcement was made in the traditional radio "sandwich style," when ads were heard before and after the program text, as in Hummert serials. Like Hummert ads, this one included product information and many reasons-why to buy. By being carefully integrated into the narrative about cousin Simon and delivered in Molly

Goldberg's folksy Yiddish accent and confidential tone, the ad's hard sell tactics are somewhat ameliorated. As this commercial indicates, the risks of staging live demonstrations and the expense of filmed demonstrations meant that many early television commercials simply replicated radio strategies.

In the late 1940s, many still assumed that sponsor identification was the ultimate aim of television advertising, and that the radio model of single program sponsorship, predicated on audience gratitude to the sponsor, would survive intact. Some were concerned that the visual nature of television would disrupt viewer identification.[79] Others actively resisted the first steps toward multiple sponsorship. For example, adman Ned Midgley objected to adjacent commercials for different products, arguing that if gratitude were the basis of radio advertising, "the listening public was so confused it could not tell what product to buy!"[80] And in 1948 a BBDO staffer noted that programs under multiple sponsorship on network radio had not worked out because of disagreements about program control.[81] Ad industry attachment to sponsor identification was thus still strong at the cusp of the television era. But at the same time, many were increasingly skeptical of the old model. JWT staffer Robert Colwell, for example, had much earlier already dismissed the impact of gratitude on sales. Participating sponsorship, two or more sponsors per program, had been increasing, initially as a cost-savings measure; its success on a number of daytime radio programs (e.g., *Breakfast Club*, *The Marjorie Mills Hour*) reassured many advertisers that audiences could distinguish among different advertised products, that a program and a product did not require tight association for the advertising strategy to be successful. Eventually radio admen were forced to concede, as did Charles Brower of BBDO in retrospect, that the sponsor identification strategy was ineffective in television: "One sacred cow that we all believed in was ground to hamburger. That was 'sponsor identification.'"[82]

What forced this concession, more than any other factor, was the most pressing issue facing ad agency entry into television: the high costs of television production. One reason the advertising industry had been able to lure advertisers to radio was the very low cost-per-thousand audience members that radio offered, compared with more established media such as newspapers. Its production costs were low (except for high-priced talent), and its national reach was impressively broad by the end of the 1930s. Early television, on the other hand, had tenfold higher production costs and no proven national reach.[83] It would take years before a television broadcast could reach a truly national audience. An agency could cover its radio programming costs by charging the sponsor a commission on talent in addition to its commission on time costs. However, the entirely different scale of cost for television production made this impossible: Not even both commissions could cover programming costs. In 1949, a trade magazine article claimed that only one agency was making a profit from its involvement in television; for the rest, according to an anonymous agency head, "When we get into television, we lose our shirt."[84] A vice president of the Ted Bates agency concurred but hoped in a 1949 trade press article that the agency commission would soon be extended to "all costs of television production," not just time and talent, and that the reduced profits agencies were suffering would be a "temporary profit loss" that would "be well worth the extra effort and trouble involved" once television matured.[85]

In a 1949 memo regarding the General Electric television program, a BBDO staffer explains that BBDO was splitting the commission for the time with the producing agency, Young & Rubicam, but that Y&R would recoup its production costs in part from BBDO's share of the commission, potentially resulting in a net loss to BBDO for the account. The staffer believed that Y&R was also not able to cover all its production costs with its share of the commission. While BBDO executives were hesitant to continue this economically unrewarding arrangement, the BBDO staffer believed Y&R "seems, at present, to regard television as a 'loss leader'" and thus more willing to lose money on television program production.[86] Nonetheless, Y&R advertised its commitment to television in a 1949 advertisement in *Television*, a trade magazine. Headlined "The newest medium," the ad claims that "Of the ten top-rating television shows . . . five are produced by Young & Rubicam" next to an image of a serious camera operator in suit and tie (see Figure 10-2).[87]

Figure 10-2. Young & Rubicam: "The Newest Medium." (*Television Magazine,* February 1949, 4.)

Television's higher costs were directly attributable to its being a visual medium, requiring a multiplicity of elements unnecessary for radio production, including sets, cameras, lights, blocking rehearsals, a different actor for each part, makeup, and costumes. As adman Victor Armstrong warned in 1936, "No longer will the cast be able to stand around a microphone and deliver." Armstrong went on to point out, "Producing a television program is going to be more like producing a movie" and wondered whether television would become "nothing more than the broadcasting of movies from the film?"[88] Another adman predicted in 1935 the shift of television program production to Hollywood precisely because of the film industry's greater skills for visual media (he assumed the entire advertising industry would move to Hollywood as well).[89] Thus, well before the advent of national television broadcasting, some admen anticipated both the increased costs and complexity of television production and the impending significance of Hollywood as its chief competitor in program production.

The agencies' clients, the advertisers, likewise were concerned about the drastically higher costs of television. This concern was summarized succinctly in 1953 by Du Pont's advertising director William Hart: An episode of Du Pont's docudrama program *Cavalcade of America* cost $17,000 on radio and $57,000 on television.[90] How much should an advertiser invest in television programming before audiences had fully migrated from radio? Companies such as Du Pont resolved to buy television time whatever the cost, with the aim "to secure for the future a choice spot"; Du Pont assumed that the sponsor "time franchise," in which an advertiser would control the time, would dictate television scheduling as it had radio.[91]

Despite agency interest in serving accounts by continuing to oversee programming, the future profitability of such service on television seemed dim. JWT continued under John Reber to maintain the radio model of agency control in the 1947 television production of *Hour Glass*, fighting with NBC over script approval, yet as early as 1946 other JWT staffers, such as Robert Colwell, realized that Reber's radio formula was declining in usefulness.[92] In a *Variety* article reporting on problems with JWT's *Kraft Television Theater*, NBC program director John Royal claimed that JWT controlled the production only because

NBC was "giving the advertising men a chance to learn the new medium" and that eventually the network would probably have to take over. Royal went on to cite approvingly the agencies that "have already turned over all phases of production to the networks."[93] In fact, even in radio production, agencies' increasing disinclination to take on the costs of production led them to the view that "no harm" would come from allowing networks and independent producers to package programs, so long as the agencies could retain supervisory or script control.[94]

In an undated memo most likely written around 1956, an N. W. Ayer staffer described how and why advertising agencies left television program production. The first factor was the networks' "attitude" toward gaining control over the schedule and their desire to remove the threat of sponsor and program defection to rival networks. As long as the networks did not own the programs, they would be vulnerable to the threat of a program owner's taking it elsewhere and thereby benefiting a competing network. The networks, then, were beginning to understand that their success depended on program control. Rather than view program ownership primarily as a cost center—their attitude in the early radio era—networks realized that program ownership could allow them through scheduling to build a "flow" of audience attention from one program to the next, increasing audience aggregation, and, ultimately, prices for airtime.

The second factor, according to this N. W. Ayer staffer, was the "agency profit margin," which was drastically reduced by the increased costs of television production. Agencies could not recoup these costs through the "price" they charged clients—that is, the 15 percent commission.[95] Yet any agency proposal to change the 15 percent commission model for television production ran the risk of bringing into question the commission model in general: Most agencies preferred not to rework this in order to deal with what was still a small proportion of their business. Agencies served multiple clients requiring multiple advertising services; they could not devote their resources solely to program production. The commission model also limited the resources available to them. Unlike film studios, for example, which were able to raise financing for production from a variety of sources, agencies were able to finance production only out of their commissions. This had the effect of limiting production budgets just as costs were increasing. Furthermore, agencies did not have ownership stakes in the programs they produced—their clients, the advertisers, owned the programs—and so they could not benefit from the long-term returns of program ownership. Other program producers, such as film studios and independent producers, could own programs, and the benefits of ownership would increase with the eventual shift to prerecorded programs and the potential for multiple resales in syndication markets.

The last factor pushing the agencies out of program production was the ever-increasing importance of program packagers such as Goodson-Todman and Barry-Enright. As we have seen, these were specialists who could reap economies of scale by producing several programs in the same genre or format, such as quiz shows. Such packagers could get by with a much smaller staff than an advertising agency, which had to serve multiple clients and their various program needs. And, unlike agencies (but like film studios), they could also benefit from shares in program ownership.[96] Consequently, just as the agencies had stepped into the breach to serve the production needs of advertisers on radio in the early radio era, the program packagers did the same for early television. The independent program packager could produce the television programming demanded by networks and sponsors more efficiently and economically than the advertising agencies could.[97]

Pat Weaver: Adman as Broadcast Reformer

As the pressures to manage the changing economics of television increased in the earliest years of the television era, one of the key leaders in reconceiving broadcasting's business model was Sylvester "Pat" Weaver, who was president of NBC Television from 1949 to 1956.[98] Weaver's experiences in advertising strongly shaped his views of television. By the time he accepted his position at NBC, where he was to oversee the development of NBC Television, his experience at Young & Rubicam and at American Tobacco had exposed him to some of the worst and best of the radio business model. At Y&R, Weaver produced

Fred Allen's *Town Hall Tonight* (1935–38), a job that required him to mediate among Allen, whose distaste for advertising and network executives was well known, and NBC and Y&R. When Weaver was promoted to supervising producer at Y&R, he clashed with NBC personnel over studio scheduling. He complained to NBC president Lenox Lohr, and when Lohr responded by scolding him for challenging NBC, Weaver moved a Y&R program from NBC to CBS, demonstrating the agency's power over the networks.[99] In his autobiography, Weaver claims to have been troubled by this. He understood that whoever controlled the programming controlled where and when an audience might gather; if networks did not begin to assert this control, they would never develop effective audience management strategies. After Y&R, from 1938 to 1941, Weaver worked for the most infamously difficult radio sponsor, George Washington Hill, of American Tobacco, caricatured in *The Hucksters.* Although Hill was dedicated to the hard sell, the opposite of the Y&R soft sell approach, Weaver was intrigued by the challenge of working directly for an advertiser who needed to turn around a declining brand, in this case Lucky Strike cigarettes. Weaver cleverly managed Hill by suggesting ideas that Hill could claim as his own and by refusing to toady to him. He pushed Hill to try new broadcast advertising strategies, including sponsoring more radio programs. After serving in the Navy during the war, Weaver returned to Y&R, interested in how new technologies such as audiotape and television would affect radio. Concerned about television's higher production costs, he actually proposed that agencies form a production cooperative to share costs.[100] When he found few agency heads willing to rethink the radio model, he went to the networks, hoping to convince them they were best positioned to control and shape programming in the television era. In Weaver's view, the networks could take a "broader" view of programming, unlike an individual advertiser and its agency, "whose chief aim was to sell his commodity."[101]

Weaver was hired by NBC in 1949 to develop its television division in part because of his ideas for reforming the radio model. In a speech to NBC executives at the outset of his NBC career, Weaver noted his extensive experience in all facets of broadcasting: "I have been mixed up in a lot of radio and television, but I was not concerned only with these media, but rather with the entire scope of selling products and services through advertising." Television, Weaver went on, "serves the public by providing a means of effective mass selling at lower cost than other media . . . and thus lowers the cost of products and services to the American home."[102] Weaver viewed television foremost as an advertising medium, one that had the potential to avoid some of the problems of radio, but only if the flaws of the radio business model, such as advertiser control of programming, were not carried over.

Weaver's first concern was how to manage the high costs of television; he proposed multiple sponsorship. In a 1949 memo ("Memorandum Number One" as NBC executive), he argued that television could not follow the radio "pattern" because "There is not enough money to put on full programs for a single product (as [is] generally the case in radio)."[103] He advocated increasing the number of programs with multiple "participating" sponsors, rather than a single sponsor, in order to spread the costs among advertisers and to allow advertisers with lower budgets access to television audiences. Like other admen before him, Weaver used the term "magazine plan" to suggest that participating sponsorship was merely the application to broadcasting of an already successful advertising model: Advertisers might buy interstitial "pages" of time within a program and leave the editorial content, or program, to the network. This required abandoning the notion of sponsor identification as the key benefit of broadcast advertising.

Weaver suggested rethinking programs as "projects," shows that would attract viewers but not with the intention of promoting a single advertiser. He described his idea for what would become *The Tonight Show* as a partly ad-libbed studio program appearing at 10 or 11 o'clock every night that would be "a sort of spontaneous, casual show, largely musical and easy going." "The public will easily identify the show," he said, not by sponsor but "by name or by NBC."[104] He summarized his approach as a shift in advertising strategy: "In short, these plans all try to approach the television medium as if the parallel were more like the magazine field than the radio field."[105] In addition to *Tonight*, Weaver championed *The Today Show* and NBC *Spectaculars*, all participating sponsorship programs designed to attract audiences without depending on sponsor identification. Weaver's idea that the networks should function like magazine editors, overseeing content while selling "pages" of advertising time, was shared by many prominent admen at the time, including agency heads Fairfax Cone (Foote Cone & Belding, previously Lord & Thomas) and Raymond Rubicam (founder of Y&R), both of whom believed that advertiser control of radio had undermined both advertising and radio.[106]

However, some admen viewed Weaver as a turncoat, confused by his shifting allegiances. The *New Yorker* quoted one adman complaining, "Who does Pat think he is, anyway? Hell, in the old days he was the greatest believer in agency programming! What does this plan offer the agencies?"[107] Advertisers resisted Weaver as well. In a blistering letter to the NBC Sales Department, Firestone's advertising manager described wanting to "poke [Weaver] in his handsome kisser."[108] Weaver was well aware of the resistance to some of these ideas; in an unsent letter to the complaining advertising manager, Weaver listed his extensive experience in the field as the basis for his shift in strategy, claiming, "In short, I know what I'm doing."[109] In order to implement some of these changes, Weaver handpicked a number of former radio admen to assist him at NBC, including Fred Wile, George McGarrett, Sam Fuller, Carl Stanton, and Tom McAvity, explaining, "I hired ad men because there was no other place to find people with wide program experience."[110] Weaver, then, helped facilitate the transition of many admen from radio to television, a path many others followed, including Edgar Kobak, Hubbell Robinson, and Mark Woods.

Weaver did not invent participating sponsorship out of whole cloth, but his background and experience in advertising informed his ideas about changing the broadcast business model; the ideas he promoted had already circulated through the advertising and broadcasting industries.[111] From the earliest days of the radio model of single sponsorship, some admen had questioned its utility and proposed "magazine"-style models instead. But Weaver did become the point man, so to speak, in instituting and articulating the rationale for network control of programming and the shift to the "magazine plan." And Weaver, unlike other would-be reformers such as William Benton, another adman who argued for network program control in order to build broadcasting as an advertising medium, was in a position to execute some of these ideas. As Weaver rather grandiosely claimed in his first memo as NBC Television president, "The development of television, in my judgement, will depend not on what we all think about it, but what a few people do about it."[112] Weaver's career at NBC is practically a reply to Frederic Wakeman's complaint about the ruination of radio by sponsor control. Unfortunately, as the historian James Baughman points out, some of the same problems Weaver attributed to sponsors—their disinterest in public service and resistance to innovative programming—would soon be attributable to the networks themselves.[113]

Radio comedian Fred Allen titled his autobiography *Treadmill to Oblivion* to describe the years of a desperate work pace of writing and producing a weekly radio program that ended suddenly; postwar commercial network radio, enjoying its largest listenership, deepest cultural impact, and widest profit margins, was likewise on a treadmill to oblivion. Even at its peak in the late 1940s, commercial network radio was subject to vociferous critique, both from outsiders worried about the degradation of culture and from insiders, like Frederic Wakeman, who identified the "despotic" control of advertisers as undermining it as a medium. Commercial radio was also undergoing shifts to new program distribution and financing models, such as cooperative programming and recorded programming, shifts that would gain momentum during the television era. The advertising industry viewed the advent of television with ambivalence—reluctant to give up program control, yet critical of single sponsorship; unable to imagine how television would keep audience attention, yet boosterish about a new visual medium; concerned about how to manage production costs, yet worried about maintaining a key role in the new medium.

Pat Weaver, former radio adman at Young & Rubicam, producer of Fred Allen, and advertising executive for George Washington Hill, brought his experiences in advertising and radio into television in order to build it as a more effective advertising medium than radio. Weaver, like others, identified sponsor control of programming as a key weakness in the radio model and used his position as president of NBC-TV to push for "magazine"-style network-owned programs. By decoupling program from advertisement and program owner from advertiser, this model of broadcast advertising provided far more flexibility and mobility for advertisers and programmers. Once advertisers were not locked into tight associations with their sponsored programs and stars, or locked out of prime time because of limited airtime, they were free to buy interstitial minutes among different network-controlled programs. More important, instead of sponsoring programs in order to draw audiences in to their advertising message, advertisers could seek out and *follow their targeted audiences* by buying commercial time in any program where that audience had gathered. By the end of the 1950s, single sponsorship was all but dead, and television had surpassed radio as the most effective advertising medium ever.

Conclusion

Radio became a national advertising medium and a platform for popular culture in the 1930s; by the 1940s, its centrality in American culture seemed assured. Yet, by the late 1950s, television had supplanted it. In cultural memory, radio's seminal contribution to the development of television is often obscured. The behind-the-scenes role of the advertising industry, which helped build broadcasting as both an advertising and an entertainment medium, is even less known. In one sense, the involvement of advertising agencies in programming during the radio era was an anomaly, because once the economic incentives shifted during the television era, agencies left program production. In another sense, however, their involvement was *not* an anomaly. A new medium must develop a functional business model; crucial to doing so is to develop audiences. The historian David Potter points out in 1954 the central role of advertising in the development of any new medium:

> Students of the radio and of the mass-circulation magazines frequently condemn advertising for its conspicuous role, as if it were a mere interloper in a separate, pre-existing, self-contained aesthetic world of actors, musicians, authors, and script-writers; they hardly recognize that advertising *created* modern American radio and television, *transformed* the modern newspaper, *evoked* the modern slick periodical, and remains the *vital essence* of each of them at the present time.[1]

Although such encomiums have fallen from fashion, Potter brings out a key point: Advertising is not separate from American "mass" culture;

it is symbiotically engaged in it. A more recent historian, James Livingston, compares advertising's relation to its medium to that of recording technology to music: Each is an "essential component" of the other.[2] Without understanding this symbiotic relationship, we cannot understand the evolution of American radio and television and, by extension, American popular culture. In this book I have analyzed that relationship in all its complexity and, I hope, challenged assumptions about both advertising and culture.

Over the roughly twenty-five years of advertising agency involvement in national network radio that I have documented here, certain issues and concerns recur, rising and falling in prominence in intra-industry discourses, all of which help shape the emerging television industry: first, the relationship between advertising strategies and programming strategies; second, the problem of sponsorship; third, the relations and tensions among various media industries; and, finally, the problem of reaching and connecting with audiences. In what follows, I examine these briefly, then consider the post–network radio era, showing how the shift to a different business model for television was ultimately beneficial to the advertising industry. I end by considering how some of the issues facing the advertising industry at the advent of a new medium in the 1920s and 1930s are similar to those facing various media industries at the advent of yet another great shift—that to digital media in the early twenty-first century.

Advertising Strategies and Programming Strategies

As we have seen, agencies consciously applied their theories of advertising to entertainment. The Hummerts employed "reasons why" hard sell strategies to daytime serials designed to sell household products to housewives. Young & Rubicam relied on soft sell traditions in programs such as *Jack Benny*. Corporate image specialist BBDO produced the docudrama *Cavalcade of America*, celebrating American industrial innovation, to improve Du Pont's image. J. Walter Thompson, one of the largest buyers of radio airtime, became a key agency in Hollywood, so that it might recruit film stars for its programs and associate those celebrities with clients' products. Each of these agencies applied specific advertising strategies not just to the commercial announcements but to the form, format, and style of the programming they oversaw. BBDO's didacticism was designed to create cultural uplift, reflecting the progressivism of its founders, as well as to polish its clients' corporate image and improve consumer attitudes toward big business. Blackett-Sample-Hummert's didacticism, its hectoring repetition and lists of "reasons why" to buy, was based on its own theory of effective advertising. Criticism of commercial radio in the 1930s and 1940s was often actually criticism of hard sell advertising strategies, which was then and has been since wrongly applied as criticism of the medium as a whole.

Partly in reaction to the hard sell, and in response to its critics, agencies such as Young & Rubicam wooed audiences with humor, associations, emotional appeals, and user-centered advertising. Today, the soft sell approach is so completely dominant that advertising from any time before the 1960s looks unsophisticated to us. Y&R's approach prefigured the major shift in advertising in the 1960s, as advertisers realized markets are segmented not mass, that audiences are smart not stupid, and that audiences resist advertising and have to be coaxed into attentiveness. During the economic crises of the Great Depression and World War II, however, many advertisers wanted proof that their agencies were trying hard to sell. They wanted to hear the names of their product repeated, the benefits they conferred directly asserted. Only after the anxieties of economic failure were tempered by the sustained postwar economic boom that culminated in the 1960s did the soft sell come to predominate.

The Problem of Sponsorship

Although radio critics blamed sponsorship for commercializing broadcasting, some members of the advertising industry blamed it for eroding broadcasting's *commercial effectiveness*. Sponsored entertainment might serve advertisers' needs, but if audiences were alienated by heavy-handed advertising, broadcasting would not be able to sell them things. Many stakeholders in early radio feared that "lowbrow" direct advertising would prevent radio from becoming a medium of cultural uplift and so did not allow sponsors to advertise at all, except by announcing that they had paid for the programming. The economic stresses of the Depression did away with such prohibitions and led, as we have seen, to the hard sell.

Nonetheless, many in the advertising industry saw that advertiser control of programming had drawbacks. First, each hour was controlled by a different advertiser, so no central editorial authority could ensure that one program flowed naturally to another. Adjacencies, the principle by which advertisers chose which magazines to advertise in, could not be controlled in radio. Second, advertisers chose programs based on selling goals rather than on audience interests. A program that did not seem to create a close enough association with a sponsor's product could be cancelled despite its popularity. Third, advertisers, applying their own interests or values, could and did suppress program innovation. By the late 1940s, the overcontrolling, obnoxious sponsor had become a popular culture figure in films and novels such as *The Hucksters*.

Throughout the radio era, members of the advertising industry, aware of these problems, sought reform. Some, such as William Benton and Pat Weaver, proposed moving to a "magazine" plan, in which networks would act as the "editors" and oversee appropriate program content and then sell interstitial minutes to advertisers. This model would eventually allow television to develop as the largest advertising medium in the 1960s and 1970s.[3]

Inter-industry Relations

The role of the advertising industry in radio was shaped by the economic exigencies of the Depression, during which broadcasters sought to shift the cost of programming onto advertisers, who then hired ad agencies to ensure that programming served the purpose of selling soap, or cereal, or gasoline. The economic contraction, paradoxically, allowed radio to grow exponentially because sponsors sought increased sales and audiences wanted "free" programming. World War II provided a different although no less difficult challenge. The war economy provided fewer goods to advertise; however, radio, now the nation's central medium, grew in the face of a national crisis. Instead of nationalizing radio, the federal government, through the OWI, encouraged the integration of war propaganda into entertainment programming, thus preserving the industrial structure of commercial radio. So, despite economic conditions that caused structural contraction overall, radio and, by extension, the advertising industry, grew.

This undue expansion of the advertising industry, unsurprisingly, led to conflict with other industries. Broadcasters, though they had happily shifted the costs of program production, regretted their resulting loss of control and struggled with advertisers and their agencies. Licensed by the FCC to serve the "public interest," broadcasters were accountable to regulators and audiences and yet had little power over the actual content of many broadcasts. We have seen how NBC and CBS both negotiated terms and practices in the 1930s and 1940s: NBC treating all advertisers the same, CBS preferring the best-paying ones. Both felt the lack of program control by the early 1940s and from then on struggled for it with agencies and advertisers; the eventual result was the television model of broadcasting, which finally took hold by the end of the 1950s. Logically, the television networks recruited their key personnel from ad agencies because they had extensive radio programming experience.

The entertainment industry likewise both struggled and collaborated with the advertising industry. Theatrical and vaudeville entertainers claimed expertise that made them suitable for developing radio entertainment. Advertisers trusted their agencies instead to prevent these performers from hijacking or undermining their selling goals. The oversupply of vaudeville talent allowed radio sponsors to pick and choose, and vaudevillians had to adjust their visual techniques to the aural medium of radio. The entertainment industry that became most symbiotically engaged in radio was Hollywood. Advertisers increasingly believed in the power of stars to attract audiences to their commercial message and the strength of a positive association between star and product to sell. Consequently, the center of radio program production shifted west from Chicago and New York to Hollywood. However, "Hollywood-ites" resented the incursion of Madison Avenue onto their turf, and admen likewise regarded the denizens of Hollywood with distrust. Neither believed the other could fully understand the needs of audiences: Advertising agencies believed Hollywood was out of touch with families gathered around the home radio set; members of the film industry resented the interference of sponsors and the interruptions of commercials.

Reaching Audiences

Advertising, like any "culture industry" or "media industry," is in the business of converting audience attention into profit. What is particularly fascinating about the radio era is that the advertising industry was forced, against Albert Lasker's principle that advertising is "salesmanship in print," to engage in a wider forum of culture. National network radio programming outstripped any other single medium during the Depression in gaining audience attention and at a very low cost per listener. To convert these audiences into profits, advertising agencies were required to build programs appealing to audiences yet lucrative to advertisers. How to do so was a mystery.

Industry discourse fluctuated between two poles: first, the fear of alienating audiences with poor programming and advertising; and second, the hope of penetrating the intimacy of the home and reaching audiences in a state of private relaxation, where they might be persuaded to buy anything. Much has been made of these hopes. Critics of the medium sometimes assume that the wildest of them were fully realized, that advertisers and broadcasters shaped minds and dictated consumer behavior at will.[4] In fact, ad agents were acutely conscious of struggling, not always successfully, with risks and doubts. As Roland Marchand points out, admen claimed extraordinary powers in order to convince their clients that their work was valuable. At the same time, admen were "courtiers" to the throne, in that their work was done at the dispensation of their patron, the advertiser, and they had no actual control over either the process or the outcome.[5]

The advertising agent, like most participants in commercial culture industries, works collaboratively, for hire, to glorify the product, not the creator. Many an agent has been frustrated by this anonymity, which opposes a romantic notion of the artist as an inspired genius working alone. Most cultural production is neither original nor unique; most of it is based on ideas, themes, images, and beliefs already commonly accessible and therefore recognizable to its audiences. If we merely dismiss advertising as debased, derivative, and empty, we overlook what is, for our times, a central cultural form, one that arises from a constant struggle to connect with audiences without alienating them, to build new meaning with common themes and tropes and images.

The Post-Radio Era

By the end of the 1950s, after a series of technological, regulatory, industrial, economic, and cultural changes far too complex to summarize adequately here, the television model was well established.[6] The networks finally took over editorial control of broadcasting—selecting, producing, and scheduling programming—and made their profits from the spread between what they paid for programming and what they charged advertisers for airtime.[7] Programs were supplied not by advertising agencies but by in-house producers or specialized program packagers, who could focus on program production exclusively. By the end of the 1950s, the film studios had become key program suppliers, especially of filmed episodic series.[8] The major Hollywood film studios had suffered severe setbacks in the 1940s and 1950s: Their efficient, vertically integrated oligopoly was broken up by the requirement of the Paramount Decrees (1938–48) that they sell off their theater chains; their ability to enter the nascent television industry was blocked by rules barring them from owning television stations; and their audiences shrank as television's increased. The studio system's eventual reorganization into a "New Hollywood" industry structure included the recycling of film techniques, sets, and talent into television program production. The studios' greater access to capital and their retention of program ownership gave them a much better chance at profiting from the highly risky business of television program production than the advertising agencies would ever have enjoyed. Consequently, the oligopolistic television networks were able to forge a partnership with the oligopolistic film studios, one in which the film studios sold their television programs to networks at a price lower than their costs ("deficit financing") in return for the majority of syndication revenues when the program moved into the aftermarket of reruns and international sales.

Advertising agencies, relieved of the burdens and expenses of program production, focused on their core businesses, media buying and advertisement production—that is, commercials. Advertisers and agencies could bring greater resources to bear on the advertisements themselves once they were no longer responsible for producing the entertainment as well. The sixty-second commercial would evolve into the most expensive (if measured by cost per minute) and elaborately produced of television forms. Agencies' media-buying skills—advising advertisers on where and when to place commercials—depended on their continuing sensitivity to audiences' tastes and viewing habits. Although agencies no longer selected and produced entire programs for their clients, their expertise in predicting and evaluating audience response increased in importance with the expanding range of choices facing their clients. Once advertisements were unlinked from programs, advertisers no longer had to look for a program to fit the commercial message; advertisers and their agencies looked for *audiences* and were free to follow them to whichever program they viewed.

The television model of commercial broadcasting built upon and modified the radio model. It rested on the same premises: that programming would be subsidized by advertisers, and that the primary economic relationship was not between producers and consumers of programming but between distributors (the networks) and advertisers. In both broadcast business models, consumers received "free" programming in exchange for tolerating advertising messages. The television model, however, improved upon the radio model in key ways. By detaching advertisement from program text and by centralizing editorial control in networks, the television model allowed advertisers and networks to develop far more flexible strategies for attracting audience attention, and so broadcasting continued its development into the single most important and effective advertising medium of the twentieth century.

During the 1960s and 1970s, the three networks (NBC, CBS, and ABC) enjoyed a tripartite oligopoly, controlling producer and advertiser access to airtime and audiences and therefore prices for both airtime and programs. While radio at its peak in 1948 accounted for 12 percent of all advertising spending, by 1976 television accounted for 20 percent, becoming the single most important national advertising medium.[9] But networks, not advertisers, wielded the most power over programming. Advertisers could no longer create or destroy programs at will; they only either bought in or cancelled out of a program a network chose to air. As one advertising executive lamented in the late 1970s, "An advertiser's power to control or affect programming is reaction rather than action."[10] The limited inventory of airtime, enforced through a trade association code that capped the number of minutes available during prime time, helped propel airtime prices upward, from an average of $30,000 per minute in the early 1960s to more than $100,000 in the late 1970s.[11] The sixty-second commercial spot rapidly evolved into a significant cultural form in its own right, as advertisers and their agencies shifted their resources into capturing audience attention in this brief moment. As Jonathan Price notes in 1978, commercials adapted a variety of cultural forms: "In an hour of TV we are likely to see all these aftertraces from several generations of myths—the primitive, the print, the modern film, and the post-modern scene, all jumbled up. Commercials move in fast; tightly edited, quickly paced, their style fits TV better . . . than the programs."[12] The commercial became a cultural form of its own; festivals, museums, and awards acknowledge the most "creative" work, adding prestige, fame, and status to those associated with successful commercials.[13]

Advertising and New Media: Evolving Strategies

The era of the broadcast television business model, which depends entirely on advertising revenues, is ending. At first it seemed threatened by subscription multichannel television services—that is, cable and satellite television—but in effect the two television models integrated: Broadcast networks relying on advertising for revenue became sister companies with cable networks that also receive subscription fees. Now it is threatened by digitized online distribution platforms. Television is no longer an appliance watched by the entire family in the living room. Audiences have become more mobile—both spatially and temporally. No longer bound by network schedules, viewers "placeshift" and "timeshift" on multiple devices, threatening legacy distribution channels, audience measurement systems, and scheduling strategies. The streaming of digital media over the Internet "disintermediates" the relationships between broadcast networks and local station affiliates and between cable operators and cable networks, and it undermines traditional business models as viewers seek to avoid both advertising and the paying of subscription fees.

In consequence, the clear demarcation between advertising and program texts that was established with the magazine plan in early television is blurring, as advertisers once again seek new strategies for locating and engaging audiences. Some of the "new" strategies are closely related to the "old" strategies of the radio era: product placement, integrated advertising, and single sponsorship. However, these strategies reintroduce the problems of the radio era: Advertisers risk negative associations (say, if a star misbehaves) and lose the mobility of advertising that is separable from the program. Furthermore, product integration may be effective only for some products, such as automobiles and packaged goods; the makers of laxatives or tampons, for example, may not find the strategy of much use. "Brand integration" promises to be subtler than product placement. Instead of inserting a product into a scene, a producer may incorporate a character who is employed by a brand or otherwise allude to it in a manner that maintains the program's claim to creative legitimacy.

As television networks and advertisers struggle to reorganize the way they reach, measure, value, buy, and sell audiences, they face an even greater challenge than audiences' increased mobility: the mobility of programming itself. Media industries have been built on revenue from advertisers' purchasing access to time and space adjacent to exclusive content by which they enjoyed guaranteed access to that content's audience. In a digital networked environment, not only are audiences more mobile, so is *content*. Just as audiences are no longer captive, content is no longer exclusive. Digital copies are instant, perfect, and easy to distribute outside copyright owners' control. Controlling content in order to organize and then buy and sell the audiences that congregate around it is thus becoming difficult, if not impossible. As one observer notes, "Marketers are in a slow, denial-laden shift from buying content-attached audiences, like those of television shows, to buying intent-attached audiences, like those of search engines and personal video recorders."[14]

The advertising industry is reconceiving advertising media as "owned," "paid," or "earned."[15] Owning media is similar to sponsorship, wherein the advertiser owns the content or the platform or the site and so controls the advertising *and* its context. Paid media is the traditional form of advertising media, in which advertisers buy airtime or page space adjacent to other content in order to reach audiences and must evaluate the adjacent content for appropriateness. In earned media, the advertiser's message is spread not by purchase or ownership but by other means, usually social media. Advertisers hope that social media users spread advertising message to their social networks without being paid to do so. This form of recommendation may be powerful, yet it remains almost entirely out of the control of the advertiser. Advertisers are also developing more "native" advertising, once called "advertorials," that blend advertising into other content.

Although they create the buzzwords, slogans, and entertaining commercials that continue to become part of popular culture, advertising agencies neither own nor distribute content, having always allowed their clients to do so. Some agencies are reconsidering this policy. According to one agency director, Ben Jenkins, "Advertising is a massively old model based on the 1950s [*sic*]. As media has [*sic*] proliferated, it's become a lot harder for us to earn enough money off our ideas." Jenkins's agency "is about creating the properties ourselves from scratch and having 100 percent of it."[16] Some agencies hope to build and create a brand that they can control themselves. One advertising analyst promises that "the creation of intellectual property and new products is something you're going to see a lot more of."[17] These agencies are resisting the subordinate role of the traditional agency, hoping that new media give them the opportunity to produce cultural products and control their use. When radio was a new medium, agencies increased in cultural importance, producing the majority of programming. It remains to be seen if the upheavals in traditional media caused by digital networking will provide similar opportunities to advertising agencies, or if an industry that first developed in the 1840s will succumb at last as new media, new mediators, and new strategies displace it.

My own guess is that the current crisis, like the crises of the past, will in the end turn to the advantage of the advertising industry. The Internet, like the airwaves, cannot be parceled out and sold, but an ingenious ad industry will probably again discover a means of making money of its public use. In the future as in the past, as I hope this study has demonstrated, American popular culture cannot be understood without the industry that funds and is funded by it, shapes and is shaped by it. We may long for a perfect culture, in which our authentic selves participate directly in a rhapsodic community on which no mercenary motives ever intrude; but if we want to understand the culture we have, we will have to understand the advertising industry.

Notes

Introduction

1. *The Lucky Strike Program Starring Jack Benny*, "Jack Tries to Reach His Advertising Agency," broadcast on 11 November 1948.

2. Michele Hilmes, *Hollywood and Broadcasting: From Radio to Cable* (Urbana: University of Illinois Press, 1990), 89; Michele Hilmes, *Radio Voices: American Broadcasting, 1922–1952* (Minneapolis: University of Minnesota Press, 1997), 114.

3. *Kraft Music Hall*, broadcast on 14 December 1942.

4. Michele Hilmes, "Nailing Mercury," in Jennifer Holt and Alisa Perren, eds., *Media Industries: History, Theory, and Method* (Malden, Mass.: Wiley-Blackwell, 2009), 24.

5. Jennifer Holt and Alisa Perren, "Introduction," in Holt and Perren, eds., *Media Industries*, 4. The classic statement of the Frankfurt School position is Max Horkheimer and Theodor Adorno, "Culture Industry: Enlightenment as Mass Deception," in M. Durham and D. Kellner, eds., *Media and Cultural Studies*, 2d ed. (Boston: Blackwell), 41–72.

6. John Hartley, "From the Consciousness Industry to the Creative Industries," in Holt and Perren, eds., *Media Industries*, 232; Ian Connell, "Fabulous Powers: Blaming the Media," in L. Masterman, ed., *Television Mythologies* (London: Boyars, 1984).

7. John Thornton Caldwell, *Production Culture: Industrial Reflexivity and Critical Practice in Film and Television* (Durham, N.C.: Duke University Press, 2008).

8. Holt and Perren, "Introduction," 5; Christine Gledhill, "Pleasurable Negotiations," in E. Deidre Pribram, ed., *Female Spectators: Looking at Film and Television* (New York: Verso, 1988).

9. John Thornton Caldwell, "Cultures of Production: Studying Industry's Deep Texts, Reflexive Rituals, and Managed Self-Disclosure," in Holt and Perren, eds., *Media Industries*, 201.

10. Alexander Russo, *Points on the Dial: Golden Age Radio beyond the Networks* (Durham, N.C.: Duke University Press, 2010), 7.

11. Stuart Ewen, *Captains of Consciousness: Advertising and the Social Roots of the Consumer Culture* (New York: McGraw-Hill, 1976); Judith Williamson, *Decoding Advertisements: Ideology and Meaning in Advertising* (London: Marion Boyars, 1978); Charles F. McGovern, *Sold American: Consumption and Citizenship, 1890–1945* (Chapel Hill: University of North Carolina Press, 2006); Katherine J. Parkin, *Food Is Love: Advertising and Gender Roles in Modern America* (Philadelphia: University of Pennsylvania Press, 2006); Inger Stole, *Advertising on Trial: Consumer Activism and Corporate Public Relations in the 1930s* (Urbana: University of Illinois Press, 2006).

12. Paul Baran and Paul Sweezy, *Monopoly Capital* (New York: Monthly Review Press, 1966); Raymond Williams, "Advertising: The Magic System," in *Television: Technology and Cultural Form* (New York: Schocken Books, 1977).

13. Roland Marchand, *Advertising the American Dream: Making Way for Modernity, 1920–1940* (Berkeley: University of California Press, 1985); Stephen Fox, *The Mirror Makers: A History of American Advertising and Its Creators* (New York: William Morrow, 1984).

14. David M. Potter, *People of Plenty: Economic Abundance and the American Character* (Chicago: University of Chicago Press, 1954).

15. For example, Neil H. Borden, *The Economic Effects of Advertising* (Chicago: Irwin, 1942); K. Rotzoll, J. Haefner, and C. Sandage, *Advertising and Society* (Columbus, Ohio: Copywright Grid, 1976).

16. William Leiss, Stephen Kline, Sut Jhally, and Jackie Botterill, *Social Communication in Advertising: Consumption in the Mediated Marketplace*, 3d ed. (New York: Routledge, 2005). For a view that advertising is a less effective form of social communication than either its critics or practitioners may acknowledge, see Michael Schudson, *Advertising, the Uneasy Persuasion: Its Dubious Impact on American Society* (New York: Basic Books, 1984).

17. Nick Browne, "The Political Economy of the Television (Super) Text," in Horace Newcomb, ed., *Television: The Critical View* (New York: Oxford University Press, 1987).

18. Jackson Lears, *Fables of Abundance: A Cultural History of Advertising in America* (New York: Basic Books, 1994); Jennifer Wicke, *Advertising Fictions: Literature, Advertisement, and Social Reading* (New York: Columbia University Press, 1988); Ellen Gruber Garvey, *The Adman in the Parlor: Magazines and the Gendering of Consumer Culture, 1880s to 1910s* (New York: Oxford University Press, 1996).

19. Marchand, *Advertising the American Dream*; Fox, *Mirror Makers*; Daniel Pope, *The Making of Modern Advertising* (New York: Basic Books, 1983); Pamela Walker Laird, *Advertising Progress: American Business and the Rise of Consumer Marketing* (Baltimore: Johns Hopkins University Press, 1998).

20. Caldwell, "Cultures of Production," 201.

21. Marshall Sahlins, *Culture and Practical Reason* (Chicago: University of Chicago Press, 1976), 117.

22. Examples of the so-called "consensus" history they reject include Gleason Archer, *History of Radio to 1926* (New York: American Historical Society, 1938); William Peck Banning, *Commercial Broadcasting Pioneer* (Cambridge, Mass.: Harvard University Press, 1946).

23. Erik Barnouw's three-volume history includes *A Tower in Babel*, *The Golden Web*, and *The Image Empire* (New York: Oxford University Press, 1966, 1968, 1970); Susan Douglas, *Inventing American Broadcasting, 1899–1922* (Baltimore: Johns Hopkins University Press, 1987); Susan Smulyan, *Selling Radio: The Commercialization of American Broadcasting, 1920–1934* (Washington: Smithsonian Institution Press, 1994); Robert McChesney, *Telecommunications, Mass Media, and Democracy: The Battle for the Control of U.S. Broadcasting, 1928–1935* (New York: Oxford University Press, 1993); Kathy M. Newman, *Radio Active: Advertising and Consumer Activism, 1935–1947* (Berkeley: University of California Press, 2004).

24. See also Clayton R. Koppes, "The Social Destiny of Radio: Hope and Disillusionment in the 1920s," *South Atlantic Quarterly* 68, no. 3 (1969): 363–76; Daniel Czitrom, *Media and the American Mind: From Morse to McLuhan* (Chapel Hill: University of North Carolina Press, 1982); Mary S. Mander, "The Public Debate about Broadcasting in the Twenties: An Interpretive History," *Journal of Broadcasting* 20 (Spring 1984): 167–85. For a nuanced view of the "civic ambition" of commercial radio, and how liberal ideals were debated and enacted through programming and network policies, see David Goodman, *Radio's Civic Ambition: American Broadcasting and Democracy in the 1930s* (New York: Oxford University Press, 2011).

25. Michele Hilmes, "Beating the Networks at Their Own Game: The Hollywood/Ad Agency Alliance of the 1930s," unpublished paper, 2.

26. Hilmes, *Radio Voices*, 18.

27. Clifford J. Doerksen, *American Babel: Rogue Radio Broadcasters of the Jazz Age* (Philadelphia: University of Pennsylvania Press, 2005), x.

28. Ibid., 17.

29. Russo, *Points on the Dial.*

30. Hilmes points this out in her foreword of Michele Hilmes, ed., *NBC: America's Network* (Berkeley: University of California Press, 2007), xii.

31. For an example of struggles over credit in the advertising industry, see the interview with agency head Julian Koenig on the radio program *This American Life*, originally broadcast on 19 June 2009: http://www.thisamericanlife .org/radio-archives/episode/383/transcript.

32. Marchand, *Advertising the American Dream*, ch. 2.

33. Smulyan, *Selling Radio.*

34. Julian Lewis Watkins, *The 100 Greatest Advertisements* (New York: Dover, 1959), 4.

35. *Kraft Music Hall*, broadcast on 1 April 1943.

36. See James L. Baughman, *Same Time, Same Station: Creating American Television, 1948–1961* (Baltimore: Johns Hopkins University Press, 2007); William Boddy, *Fifties Television: The Industry and Its Critics* (Urbana: University of Illinois Press, 1990); Michael Mashon, "NBC, J. Walter Thompson, and the Evolution of Prime-Time Television Programming and Sponsorship, 1946–58" (PhD diss., University of Maryland–College Park, 1996).

37. For example, see Stuart Elliott, "An Old Industry Name Signals a Shift into a New Era," *New York Times*, 22 November 2010, B6.

1. Dramatizing a Bar of Soap: The Advertising Industry before Broadcasting

1. In the large literature of this area, the best known include Raymond Williams, "Advertising: The Magic System," in *Problems in Materialism and Culture* (London: New Left Books, 1962, 1980); Judith Williamson, *Decoding Advertisements: Ideology and Meaning in Advertising* (London: Marion Boyars, 1978); Stuart Ewen, *Captains of Consciousness: Advertising and the Social*

Roots of the Consumer Culture (New York: McGraw-Hill, 1976); William Leiss, Stephen Kline, Sut Jhally, and Jackie Botterill, *Social Communication in Advertising: Consumption in the Mediated Marketplace*, 3d ed. (New York: Routledge, 2005); and Sut Jhally, *The Codes of Advertising: Fetishism and the Political Economy of Meaning in the Consumer Society* (New York: St. Martin's Press, 1987).

2. Jackson Lears, "Some Versions of Fantasy: Toward a Cultural History of American Advertising, 1880–1930," *Prospects* 9 (1984): 350.

3. The scholarly "effects" literature, using social scientific methodologies, is designed to identify behavioral responses to specific advertising strategies or the potential effects of advertising on vulnerable populations, such as children. Samples of this vast literature can be found in journals such as *Journal of Advertising Research, Journal of Advertising, International Journal of Advertising, Journal of Applied Communication Research, Journal of Consumer Research, Journal of Marketing*, and others.

4. Michael Schudson, *Advertising, the Uneasy Persuasion: Its Dubious Impact on American Society* (New York: Basic Books, 1984), makes this argument.

5. Frank Presbrey, *The History and Development of Advertising* (New York: Greenwood Press, 1929, 1968).

6. Susan Strasser, *Satisfaction Guaranteed: The Making of the American Mass Market* (New York: Pantheon, 1989); Daniel Pope, *The Making of Modern Advertising* (New York: Basic Books, 1983); Pamela Walker Laird, *Advertising Progress: American Business and the Rise of Consumer Marketing* (Baltimore: Johns Hopkins University Press, 1998); William Leach, *Land of Desire: Merchants, Power, and the Rise of a New American Culture* (New York: Pantheon, 1993). For a history of salesmanship, see Walter A. Friedman, *Birth of a Salesman: The Transformation of Selling in America* (Cambridge, Mass.: Harvard University Press, 2004).

7. Richard Ohmann, *Selling Culture: Magazines, Markets and Class at the Turn of the Century* (London, New York: Verso, 1996); Ellen Gruber Garvey, *The Adman in the Parlor: Magazines and the Gendering of Consumer Culture, 1880s to 1910s* (New York: Oxford University Press, 1996).

8. Jackson Lears, *Fables of Abundance* (New York: Basic Books, 1994), 92–93; Ohmann, *Selling Culture*, ch. 6; Pope, *Making of Modern Advertising*, ch. 4.

9. Laird points out that early ad agents discouraged clients from using media that did not pay them commissions, such as chromolithographs and posters. *Advertising Progress*, 158.

10. Ibid., 232–33.

11. Ibid., 246.

12. Timothy B. Spears, *100 Years on the Road: The Traveling Salesman in American Culture* (New Haven, Conn.: Yale University Press, 1995).

13. James H. Young, *The Toadstool Millionaires* (Princeton, N.J.: Princeton University Press, 1961).

14. The following relies on Pope, *Making of Modern Advertising*, 198, 157, 191, 172.

15. Laird, *Advertising Progress*, 242.

16. Stephen Fox, *The Mirror Makers: A History of American Advertising and Its Creators* (New York: William Morrow, 1984), 75–76.

17. Otis A. Pease, *The Responsibilities of American Advertising: Private Control and Public Influence, 1920–40* (New Haven, Conn.: Yale University Press, 1958), 20.

18. Kenneth M. Goode, *How to Turn People into Gold* (New York: Harper, 1929), 215.

19. Quoted in Presbrey, *History and Development of Advertising*, 625.

20. Fox, *Mirror Makers*, 79.

21. Donald Meyer, *The Positive Thinkers*, rev. ed. (Middletown, Conn.: Wesleyan University Press, 1965, 1988), 179.

22. William Benton, "The Reminiscences of William Benton," 73, Oral History Research Office, Columbia University, New York.

23. C. Wright Mills, *White Collar: The American Middle Classes* (New York: Oxford University Press, 1951), 139; Pope, *Making of Modern Advertising*, 173.

24. Roland Marchand, *Advertising the American Dream: Making Way for Modernity, 1920–1940* (Berkeley: University of California Press, 1985), 29.

25. Ibid., 36–37, 66.

26. Ibid., 33.

27. Fox, *Mirror Makers*, 83, 91.

28. On the professionalization of salesmanship, see Friedman, *Birth of a Salesman*.

29. Marchand, *Advertising the American Dream*, 13.

30. Lears, "Some Versions of Fantasy," 366.

31. Irwin Rosenfels, Address to Annual Meeting of Association of National Advertisers, "How Much Sincerity Does Advertising Want?" 1 November 1927, New York, Box 1, Bruce Barton Papers, Wisconsin Historical Society, Madison.

32. Earnest Elmo Calkins, "The Practical Ethics of Sincere Advertising," *Advertising & Selling*, 2 November 1927, 20.

33. Fox, *Mirror Makers*, charts the swing back and forth between the two tendencies decade by decade.

34. Albert Lasker, *The Lasker Story: As He Told It* (N.p.: Advertising Publications, 1963), 21. See also Jeffrey L. Cruikshank and Arthur W. Schultz, *The Man Who Sold America: The Amazing (But True!) Story of Albert D. Lasker and the Creation of the Advertising Industry* (Boston: Harvard Business Review Press, 2010).

35. Marchand, *Advertising the American Dream*, 67.

36. Claude Hopkins, *My Life in Advertising; Scientific Advertising* (Lincolnwood, Ill.: NTC Business Books, reprinted 1966), 22.

37. Reproduced in Julian Lewis Watkins, *The 100 Greatest Advertisements* (New York: Dover, 1959), 80.

38. Emphasis in original. *Printers' Ink*, 6 September 1905, n.p.

39. For example, see Inger Stole's criticism of admen who defended the use of emotional appeals: *Advertising on Trial: Consumer Activism and Corporate Public Relations in the 1930s* (Champaign: University of Illinois Press, 2006), 31, 61.

40. Reproduced in Frank Rowsome Jr., *They Laughed When I Sat Down* (New York: Bonanza Books, 1959), 70.

41. Hopkins, *Scientific Advertising*, 242–43.

42. *Saturday Evening Post*, 2 January 1915, n.p. Reproduced in Watkins, *100 Greatest Advertisements*, 22.

43. J. George Frederick, ed., *Masters of Advertising Copy* (New York: Frank-Maurice, Inc., 1925), 119.

44. *Printers' Ink*, 22 January 1914, n.p.

45. Reproduced in Robert Atwan, Donald McQuade, and John W. Wright, *Edsels, Luckies, and Frigidaires: Advertising the American Way* (New York: Dell, 1979), 337.

46. Reproduced in Watkins, *100 Greatest Advertisements*, 24.

47. *Printers' Ink*, 11 February 1915, n.p.

48. Lasker, *Lasker Story*, 81.

49. Jennifer Wicke, *Advertising Fictions: Literature, Advertisement, and Social Reading* (New York: Columbia University Press, 1988), 16; Lears, *Fables of Abundance.*

50. John Thornton Caldwell, *Production Culture* (Durham, N.C.: Duke University Press, 2008); Jackson Lears, "The Concept of Cultural Hegemony: Problems and Possibilities," *American Historical Review* 90 (June 1985): 587.

51. Marshall Sahlins, *Culture and Practical Reason* (Chicago: University of Chicago Press, 1976), 117.

52. Barbara Rosenblum, *Photographers at Work* (New York: Holmes and Meier, 1978), 81.

53. Eileen Meehan, "Conceptualizing Culture as Commodity: The Problem of Television," *Critical Studies in Mass Communication* 3 (1986): 450.

54. Michele H. Bogart, *Artists, Advertising, and the Borders of Art* (Chicago: University of Chicago Press, 1995).

55. Advertising workers in "creative" departments often analogize themselves with artists like Michelangelo, whose work was supported by a patron/client. Aimee L. Stern, "Selling Yourself on Madison Ave," *New York Times,* 1 October 1989, F4.

56. Lears, "Some Versions of Fantasy," 361.

57. James Webb Young, *How to Become an Advertising Man* (Chicago: Advertising Publications, Inc., 1963), 93.

58. "Agency Air Credit Gets NBC 'No' as CBS Tries It Out," *Variety,* 25 July 1933, 37.

59. JWT Staff Meeting Minutes, 21 December 1932, 9, John W. Hartman Center for Sales, Advertising and Marketing History, Duke University, Durham, North Carolina.

60. Charles F. McGovern, *Sold American: Consumption and Citizenship, 1890–1945* (Chapel Hill: University of North Carolina Press, 2006), 48.

61. Marchand, *Advertising the American Dream,* 67, 49.

2. The Fourth Dimension of Advertising: The Development of Commercial Broadcasting in the 1920s

1. Charles Hull Wolfe, *Modern Radio Advertising* (New York: Printers' Ink Publishing Co., 1949), 612.

2. Ibid., 620.

3. Joseph H. Jackson, "Should Radio Be Used for Advertising?" *Radio Broadcast*, November 1922, 76.

4. Sean Street, *Crossing the Ether: British Public Service Radio and Commercial Competition, 1922–1945* (Eastleigh, UK: John Libbey Publishing, 2006). For a nuanced approach to the contrasting and complementary UK and U.S. broadcasting systems, see Michele Hilmes, *Network Nations: A Transnational History of British and American Broadcasting* (New York: Routledge, 2011).

5. H. D. Kellogg Jr., "Who Is to Pay for Broadcasting—and How?" *Radio Broadcast*, March 1925, 863ff.

6. Susan Douglas, *Inventing American Broadcasting, 1899–1922* (Baltimore: Johns Hopkins University Press, 1987), ch. 6.

7. Michele Hilmes, "Beating the Networks at Their Own Game," unpublished paper, 3. Station owners in 1922 included Gimbel's department store, the Ford Motor Company, the Alabama Power Company, and the Omaha Grain Exchange; J. Fred MacDonald, *Don't Touch That Dial! Radio Programming in American Life from 1920 to 1960* (Chicago: Nelson-Hall, 1979), 3; Ronald J. "Noah" Arceneaux, "Department Stores and the Origins of American Broadcasting, 1910–1931" (PhD diss., University of Georgia, 2007).

8. Austin Lescarboura, "How Much It Costs to Broadcast," *Radio Broadcast*, September 1926, 367.

9. William Peck Banning, *Commercial Broadcasting Pioneer: The WEAF Experiment, 1922–26* (Cambridge, Mass.: Harvard University Press, 1946), 56.

10. Mark Woods, "Reminiscences," 14, Oral History Research Office, Columbia University, New York (hereafter Woods Reminiscences).

11. Quoted in Gleason Archer, *History of Radio to 1926* (New York: American Historical Society, 1938), 397.

12. Banning, *Commercial Broadcasting Pioneer*, 109.

13. Clifford J. Doerksen traces the fault line between the corporate-owned stations, like WEAF, that avoided direct advertising, and entrepreneur-owned stations that embraced commercialism, arguing that those overtly commercial stations more directly served their audiences' tastes whereas AT&T was attempting to impose a standard of cultural uplift on radio. *American Babel: Rogue Radio Broadcasters of the Jazz Age* (Philadelphia: University of Pennsylvania Press, 2005).

14. Banning, *Commercial Broadcasting Pioneer*, 90, 152.

15. Ibid., 100, 154.

16. Edgar Felix, "The Reminiscences of Edgar Felix," 1962, 33, Oral History Research Office, Columbia University, New York.

17. Gleason Archer, *Big Business and Radio* (New York: American Historical Company, 1939), 274.

18. Banning, *Commercial Broadcasting Pioneer*, 262.

19. Woods Reminiscences, 14.

20. Laurence Bergreen, *Look Now, Pay Later: The Rise of Network Broadcasting* (Garden City, N.Y.: Doubleday, 1980), 30; see also Daniel Czitrom, *Media and the American Mind* (Chapel Hill: University of North Carolina Press, 1982), 79.

21. Roland Marchand, *Creating the Corporate Soul: The Rise of Public Relations and Corporate Imagery in American Big Business* (Berkeley: University of California Press, 1998), 64.

22. Warner S. Shelly, interviewed by Howard Davis, 2 October 1985, transcript 1.5, N. W. Ayer Archives, New York.

23. Frank Arnold, "Reminiscences," 5, Oral History Research Office, Columbia University, New York (hereafter Arnold Reminiscences).

24. Woods Reminiscences, 44.

25. Ibid., 44; Doerksen, *American Babel.*

26. Banning, *Commercial Broadcasting Pioneer*, 271.

27. Carl J. Friedrich and Jeanette Sayre, "The Development of the Control of Advertising on the Air," *Studies in the Control of Radio*, no. 1, November 1940, 6.

28. Opening address by Herbert Hoover, "Recommendations for the Regulation of Radio Adopted by the Third National Radio Conference," 6–10 October 1924, 4.

29. I take issue with Czitrom, *Media and the American Mind*, 76.

30. *Proceedings of the Fourth National Radio Conference, and Recommendations for the Regulation of Radio*, 9–11 November 1925, 10.

31. Federal Radio Commission, *Second Annual Report of the Federal Radio Commission*, 1 October 1928, 168.

32. For more on how "free speech" claims shaped early broadcast regulation, see Thomas Streeter, *Selling the Air: A Critique of the Policy of Commercial Broadcasting in the United States* (Chicago: University of Chicago Press, 1996). For an analysis of how commercial broadcasters in the 1930s proceeded to demonstrate their commitment to public service and civic

engagement, see David Goodman, *Radio's Civic Ambition: American Broadcasting and Democracy in the 1930s* (New York: Oxford University Press, 2011).

33. H. A. Batten, "A Confidential Statement of Policy and Practice in Radio Broadcasting," 5 January 1938, 9, N. W. Ayer Archives.

34. Ralph M. Hower, *The History of an Advertising Agency: N. W. Ayer & Son at Work, 1869–1939* (Cambridge, Mass.: Harvard University Press, 1939), 166; Warner S. Shelley, former chairman of N. W. Ayer, interview with Don Sholl, 2 October 1985, N. W. Ayer Archives.

35. Susan Smulyan, *Selling Radio: The Commercialization of American Broadcasting, 1920–1934* (Washington: Smithsonian Institution Press, 1994), 38. For an alternative narrative focusing on the non-network and local development of commercial radio, see Alexander Russo, *Points on the Dial: Golden Age Radio beyond the Networks* (Durham, N.C.: Duke University Press, 2010).

36. Hower, *History of an Advertising Agency*, 164. Broadcast signals are geographically limited; reach varies depending on the strength or wattage of the transmission.

37. Arnold Reminiscences, 8.

38. Russo, *Points on the Dial*, 37.

39. Herman S. Hettinger, *A Decade of Radio Advertising* (Chicago: University of Chicago Press, 1933), 112–13.

40. Tim Wu, *The Master Switch: The Rise and Fall of Informational Empires* (New York: Knopf, 2010), 76.

41. Smulyan, *Selling Radio*; Doerksen, *American Babel*; Russo, *Points on the Dial*.

42. For more on the regional networks, see Russo, *Points on the Dial*, ch. 2.

43. Roland Marchand, *Advertising the American Dream* (Berkeley: University of California Press, 1985), 90; Doerksen, *American Babel*, ch. 1.

44. Archer, *Big Business and Radio*, 33.

45. E. P. H. James, interview, 29 March 1963, 14, Box 1, Folder 1, James Papers, Wisconsin Historical Society, Madison (hereafter James Interview, James Papers).

46. Archer, *Big Business and Radio*, 32.

47. William Paley, *As It Happened* (Garden City, N.Y.: Doubleday, 1979), 35.

48. Archer, *Big Business and Radio*, 400.

49. Erik Barnouw, *A Tower in Babel: A History of Broadcasting in the United States*, vol. 1 (New York: Oxford University Press, 1966), 251.

50. Adrian Forty, *Objects of Desire: Design and Society since 1750* (London: Thames and Hudson, 1986).

51. Russo, *Points on the Dial*, 9.

52. Christopher H. Sterling and John M. Kittross, *Stay Tuned: A Concise History of American Broadcasting* (Belmont, Calif.: Wadsworth, 1978), 533.

53. Roy S. Durstine, "Function of the Agency in Broadcast Advertising," *Broadcast Advertising*, June 1929, 15.

54. John Benson, "The Advertising Agency and Broadcasting," *Broadcast Advertising*, January 1931, 4.

55. E. P. H. James claimed that most of NBC's advertisers in the earliest days "had themselves taken an interest in radio, either over the head job or against the objection of or at least in spite of the apathy of their advertising agencies." N. W. Ayer and Rankin were the exceptions. James Interview, 27, James Papers.

56. Banning, *Commercial Broadcasting Pioneer*, 149.

57. Charles F. Gannon, "The Agency's Place in American Broadcasting," *Broadcast Advertising*, August 1931, 28; Benson, "The Advertising Agency and Broadcasting," 4; Durstine, "Function of the Agency in Broadcast Advertising," 29.

58. Dick Dunne, "What Is Advertising Agency's Real Function?" *Printers' Ink Monthly*, July 1937, 14–15.

59. Howard W. Dickinson, "Radio Broadcasting and the Advertising Agent," *Advertising & Selling*, 6 February 1929, 92.

60. Banning, *Commercial Broadcasting Pioneer*, 149; Woods Reminiscences, 42.

61. Archer, *Big Business and Radio*, 294–95.

62. Arnold Reminiscences, 34, 19.

63. Ibid., 32.

64. James Interview, James Papers.

65. Ibid.

66. Woods Reminiscences, 39.

67. James Interview, 13, James Papers.

68. Arnold Reminiscences, 67.

69. Frank A. Arnold, "Commercial Broadcasting: The Fourth Dimension of Advertising" (New York: National Broadcasting Co., 1927), 4–5.

70. E. P. H. James, "The Reminiscences of E. P. H. James," 1963, 3–4, Oral History Research Office, Columbia University, New York (hereafter James

Reminiscences). His career would take him from NBC to the Mutual Broad-casting System and, by the 1960s, to the A. C. Nielsen Company.

71. NBC promotional pamphlet, ca. 1926, Box 1, Folder 7, James Papers.

72. Wolfe, *Modern Radio Advertising*, 627.

73. James Interview, 14, James Papers.

74. Arnold, "Commercial Broadcasting," 11.

75. Sally Bedell Smith, *In All His Glory: The Life of William S. Paley* (New York: Simon & Schuster, 1990), 63; Bergreen, *Look Now, Pay Later*, 53.

76. CBS, "Broadcast Advertising," 16. Or as Bergreen puts it, they were "refugees from advertising agencies"; Bergreen, *Look Now, Pay Later*, 8.

77. Hugh K. Boice, "Radio—The Network," in Alden James, ed., *Careers in Advertising* (New York: Macmillan, 1932), 464.

78. "Broadcast Advertising: The Distinguishing Characteristics of Broadcast Advertising," CBS pamphlet, 1929, 9.

79. "Broadcast Advertising: The Sales Voice of America," CBS pamphlet, 1929.

80. Paul W. Kesten, "Radio—The Network: Research and Sales Promotion," in James, ed., *Careers in Advertising*, 469.

81. At CBS Paul Kesten first directed promotion, then later helped shape television standards as "vice president in charge of the future" and ultimately ran the network during Paley's absence in World War II. Jack Gould, "P. K. of CBS," *New York Times*, 4 November 1945, X5.

82. Kesten, "Radio—The Network," 470.

83. "And All Because They're Smart," *Fortune*, June 1935, 163.

84. Paley, *As It Happened*, 67.

85. Hugh K. Boice, "Radio: A Discussion for Executives Who 'Already Know the ABC's of Radio,'" CBS pamphlet, 1937, Library of American Broad-casting, University of Maryland, College Park (hereafter LAB).

86. Boice, "Radio."

87. Hettinger, *A Decade of Radio Advertising*, 35.

88. Edgar Felix, "Small Time Radio Advertising Brings Big Time Results," *Advertising & Selling*, 19 September 1928, 72.

89. "You Do What You're Told," CBS pamphlet, no date, 5, 7.

90. "Broadcast Advertising: The Sales Voice of America," CBS pamphlet, 1929, 7; Edgar Felix, "To Broadcast or Not to Broadcast," *Advertising & Selling*, 9 February 1927, 23; Felix, "Small Time Radio Advertising Brings Big Time Results," 34.

91. Felix, "To Broadcast or Not to Broadcast," 23.

92. Letter from Henry O. Philips to H. B. Harvey, 19 December 1928, Box 3, Folder 81, NBC Records, Wisconsin Historical Society, Madison.

93. Smulyan, *Selling Radio*, 75–77.

94. Martin P. Rice, "Radio Advertising," *Advertising & Selling*, 30 June 1926, 72.

95. Frank A. Arnold, "High Spots in Broadcast Technique," *Broadcast Advertising*, May 1929, 7.

96. "Broadcast Advertising," NBC promotional booklet, 21, Box 1, Folder 9, James Papers.

97. M. H. Aylesworth, "Radio's Place in the Advertising Career," in James, ed., *Careers in Advertising*, 449.

98. J. H. P., "Good Morning, Everybody!" *Cheesekraft*, vol. 8, no. 2, May 1929, 6, Kraft Archives, Morton Grove, Illinois.

99. Association of National Advertisers, "What About Radio Advertising?" May 1928, 3, LAB.

100. James Interview, 28, James Papers.

101. Special Radio Report No. 1, *Ayer News File*, 10 April 1939, 5, N. W. Ayer Archives.

102. Martin P. Rice, "Radio Advertising," *Advertising & Selling*, 30 June 1926, 72; "Broadcast Advertising," CBS pamphlet, 1929, 5.

103. Hettinger, *A Decade of Radio Advertising*, 122.

3. They Sway Millions as If by Some Magic Wand: The Advertising Industry Enters Radio in the Late 1920s

1. Stephen Fox, *The Mirror Makers* (New York: William Morrow, 1984), 118.

2. "And All Because They're Smart," *Fortune*, June 1935, 82.

3. E. P. H. James, interview, 27, James Papers, Wisconsin Historical Society, Madison (hereafter James Interview, James Papers).

4. *Printers' Ink*, 27 April 1922, 201.

5. "Radio an Objectionable Advertising Medium," *Printers' Ink*, 8 February 1923, 175–76.

6. Fox, *Mirror Makers*, 153.

7. "Inland Newspapers Demand Pay for Radio Programs," *Printers' Ink*, 2 March 1933, 33.

8. Roland Marchand, *Advertising the American Dream* (Berkeley: University of California Press, 1985), 26–28.

9. Ralph Starr Butler, "Radio Tomorrow," *Printers' Ink Monthly*, July 1936, 73; J. Walter Thompson Staff Meeting Minutes, 5 January 1932, 18, John W. Hartman Center for Sales, Advertising and Marketing History, Duke University, Durham, North Carolina (hereafter JWT Staff Meeting Minutes).

10. "National radio broadcasting with better programs permanently assured by this important action of the Radio Corporation of America in the interest of the listening public." Advertisement reproduced in Erik Barnouw, *The Sponsor: Notes on a Modern Potentate* (New York: Oxford University Press, 1978), 23.

11. "Agencies View Radio Advertising in Survey by Station," *Advertising & Selling*, 30 April 1930, 90.

12. Alexander Russo, *Points on the Dial* (Durham, N.C.: Duke University Press, 2010), 7.

13. S. H. Giellerup, "It's Time We Took the 'Blue Sky' out of the Air," *Advertising & Selling*, 16 October 1929, n.p.

14. From a Batten agency memo, ca. 1924, quoted in Ed Roberts, "Radio and Celebrities," unpublished manuscript, commissioned by BBDO, ca. 1966.

15. John Gordon Jr., "Says Mr. Gordon to Mr. Giellerup," *Advertising & Selling*, 13 November 1929, 32.

16. Lawrence Doherty, "Adman Sample? He's Florida Land Tycoon," part 2, *Advertising Age*, 7 May 1962, 66.

17. Robert Colwell, JWT Staff Meeting Minutes, 8 July 1930.

18. JWT Staff Meeting Minutes, 13 January 1931, 8.

19. George Lewis, "Audit Bureau for Radio Organized by ANA," *Advertising & Selling*, 19 March 1930, 83.

20. "Agencies View Radio Advertising in Survey by Station," *Advertising & Selling*, 90.

21. "Acute Inflammatory Radioitis," J. Walter Thompson *Newsletter*, 15 February 1928, 81, 82, JWT Newsletter Files, John W. Hartman Center for Sales, Advertising and Marketing History, Duke University, Durham, North Carolina (hereafter JWT *Newsletter*).

22. Ibid., 82.

23. Clayton R. Koppes, "The Social Destiny of Radio: Hope and Disillusionment in the 1920s," *South Atlantic Quarterly* 68, no. 3 (1969): 367.

24. Clifford Doerksen argues that this class divide played out in early radio as AT&T/WEAF, seeking to protect commercialism in a "highbrow" context, went so far as to sue the local commercial station WHN, broadcaster of jazz and other "lowbrow" programs, for patent infringement for airing advertising. *American Babel: Rogue Radio Broadcasters of the Jazz Age* (Philadelphia: University of Pennsylvania Press, 2005), ch. 2.

25. Edgar H. Felix, "Broadcasting's Place in the Advertising Spectrum," *Advertising & Selling*, 15 December 1926, 19.

26. Letter from L. A. Jenkins to B. F. Goodrich Company, 26 May 1925, Box 3, Folder 126, NBC Records, Wisconsin Historical Society, Madison (hereafter NBC Records).

27. Letter from L. A. McQueen, Advertising Manager, B. F. Goodrich Company, to L. A. Jenkins, The Kolynos Company, 3 June 1925, Box 3, Folder 126, NBC Records.

28. "Less Radio Advertising Asked," *Advertising & Selling*, 27 November 1929, 73.

29. "Broadcasters and Agencies Condemn Blatant Advertising," *Broadcast Advertising*, May 1930, 20ff.

30. An Advertising Agency Executive, "When Will Radio Quit Selling Its 'Editorial Pages'?" *Advertising & Selling*, 22 July 1931, 17.

31. Martin P. Rice, "Radio Advertising," *Advertising & Selling*, 30 June 1926, 72.

32. "When Will Radio Quit Selling Its 'Editorial Pages'?" 17ff.

33. "Acute Inflammatory Radioitis," 83.

34. "When Will Radio Quit Selling Its 'Editorial Pages'?" 18.

35. Ibid., 18.

36. Gordon Best, "Radio Has Brought a New Responsibility to Advertising Agencies," *Broadcast Advertising*, July 1932, 6.

37. L. Ames Brown, "Radio Broadcasting as an Advertising Medium," in Neville O'Neill, ed., *The Advertising Agency Looks at Radio* (New York: D. Appleton, 1932), 7.

38. Robert Colwell, "The Program as an Advertisement," in O'Neill, ed., *Advertising Agency Looks at Radio*, 26.

39. John T. Flynn, "Radio: Medicine Show," *American Scholar* (Autumn 1938): 430–37; Peter Morrell, *Poisons, Potions and Profits: The Antidote to Radio Advertising* (New York: Knight Publishers, 1937). For more on radio's critics, see Kathy M. Newman, *Radio Active: Advertising and Consumer Activism, 1935–1947* (Berkeley: University of California Press, 2004).

40. George Faulkner, JWT Staff Meeting Minutes, 12 August 1930, 2.

41. Mark Woods, "Reminiscences," 11, Oral History Research Office, Columbia University, New York (hereafter Woods Reminiscences).

42. William Banning, *Commercial Broadcasting Pioneer* (Cambridge, Mass.: Harvard University Press, 1946), 103.

43. Edgar H. Felix, "Organizing Broadcasting and Publicity Bureaus in Advertising Agencies," *Advertising & Selling*, 20 February 1929, 25; Edward L. Bernays, "What Future for Radio Advertising?" *Advertising & Selling*, 8 February 1928, 27.

44. M. Lewis Goodkind, "How Radio Department Can Add to Its Importance as Agency Adjunct," *Printers' Ink*, 23 December 1937, 83. Raymond Rubicam, founder of Young & Rubicam, a successful agency in radio, avoided listening to Y&R programs. Fox, *Mirror Makers*, 157.

45. JWT Staff Meeting Minutes, 2 February 1932, 3.

46. Ibid., 2.

47. JWT Staff Meeting Minutes, 8 July 1930, 3.

48. Roy Durstine, "Function of the Agency in Broadcast Advertising," *Broadcast Advertising*, June 1929, 29.

49. Felix, "Organizing Broadcasting and Publicity Bureaus in Advertising Agencies," 84; Durstine, "Function of the Agency in Broadcast Advertising," 15.

50. Ralph M. Hower, *The History of an Advertising Agency: N. W. Ayer & Son at Work, 1869–1939* (Cambridge, Mass.: Harvard University Press, 1939), 167.

51. "Why Writers Flop," *Variety*, 5 September 1933, 57.

52. Woods Reminiscences, 51–52.

53. Charles F. Gannon, "The Agency's Place in American Broadcasting," *Broadcast Advertising*, August 1931, 15.

54. Robert Simon, JWT Staff Meeting Minutes, 2 February 1932, 2, 3.

55. Chester Bowles, "Agency's Responsibility in Radio," *Printers' Ink Monthly*, July 1936, 82.

56. J. Fred MacDonald, *Don't Touch That Dial!* (Chicago: Nelson-Hall, 1979), 32.

57. Christopher Sterling and John Kittross, *Stay Tuned: A Concise History of American Broadcasting* (Belmont, Calif.: Wadsworth, 1978), 516.

58. Woods Reminiscences, 48.

59. "The News Digest," *Advertising & Selling*, 13 November 1929, 104.

60. Woods Reminiscences, 49.

61. H. A. Batten, "A Confidential Statement of Policy and Practice in Radio Broadcasting," 5 January 1938, 4–5, N. W. Ayer Archives.

62. Ibid., 9–10.

63. *The Literary Digest*, 17 December 1927, n.p. Author's collection.

64. Remarkably, N. W. Ayer kept AT&T as a client until the early 1990s.

65. Ralph M. Hower, *The History of an Advertising Agency: N. W. Ayer & Son at Work, 1869–1949*, rev. ed. (Cambridge, Mass.: Harvard University Press, 1949), 178.

66. James Hanna, interviewed by Howard Davis, 2 May 1988, 33a.1, N. W. Ayer Archives.

67. Hower, *History of an Advertising Agency*, rev. ed., 179.

68. Fred McClafferty, interview with Howard Davis, February and March 1989, 29, N. W. Ayer Archives.

69. JWT Staff Meeting Minutes, 2 February 1932, 8.

70. Charlie Brower, *Me, and Other Advertising Geniuses* (Garden City, N.Y.: Doubleday, 1974), 87.

71. BBDO *Newsletter*, February 1966, 16.

72. *Printers' Ink*, 7 July 1932, 38–39.

73. Bernays, "What Future for Radio Advertising?" 59.

74. Robert Simon, JWT Staff Meeting Minutes, 2 February 1932, 5.

75. Ed Roberts, "Radio and Celebrities," unpublished manuscript commissioned by BBDO, ca. 1966, 4.

76. "Audible Advertising," *Advertising & Selling*, 16 April 1930, 31.

77. Ibid.

78. Quoted in "'Variety' Tells All," *Printers' Ink*, 24 August 1933, 90.

79. JWT Staff Meeting Minutes, 2 February 1932, 12.

80. One claim is that Pepsodent sales increased 100 percent in the first year of its sponsoring *Amos 'n' Andy*. Jeffrey L. Cruikshank and Arthur W. Schultz, *The Man Who Sold America* (Boston: Harvard Business Review Press, 2010), 275.

81. Melvin Patrick Ely, *The Adventures of Amos 'n' Andy: A Social History of an American Phenomenon* (New York: The Free Press, 1991).

82. *Amos 'n' Andy* continuity script, 1 April 1932, Box 13, Folder 1, NBC Records.

83. Quoted in "'Variety' Tells All," 90.

84. And both *The Goldbergs* and *Amos 'n' Andy* would go on to television, albeit with less successful results. For an interesting analysis of these ethnic

programs, see Michele Hilmes, *Radio Voices* (Minneapolis: University of Minnesota Press, 1997).

85. William Ensign, JWT Staff Meeting Minutes, 11 July 1928, 3.

86. "The Story of Lennen & Mitchell," *Advertising Agency and Advertising & Selling*, August 1949, 62.

87. Robert Simon, JWT Staff Meeting Minutes, 2 February 1932, 9.

88. Ruth Cornwall, "McCann Practice: What About Radio?" Pamphlet, McCann Company, 1930, 31.

89. Ibid., 44.

90. "'Variety' Tells All," 90.

91. Joan Hafey, "Young & Rubicam and Broadcasting," in *Y&R and Broadcasting: Growing Up Together* (New York: Museum of Broadcasting, n.d.), 21.

92. Robert Simon, JWT Staff Meeting Minutes, 2 February 1932, 10.

93. JWT *Newsletter*, 15 May 1928.

94. William Ensign, "Radio-Raze," JWT *Newsletter*, 5 May 1928, 17; William Ensign, "What Price Radio," JWT *Newsletter*, 18 November 1928, 1; William Ensign, JWT Staff Meeting Minutes, 11 July 1928, 4.

95. William Ensign, JWT Staff Meeting Minutes, 11 July 1928, 5.

96. JWT Staff Meeting Minutes, 14 January 1930, 7.

97. JWT Staff Meeting Minutes, 2 February 1932; Roy Witmer to Mark Woods, 21 July 1933, Box 22, Folder 28, NBC Records.

98. "'Variety' Tells All," 90.

99. Goodkind, "How Radio Department Can Add to Its Importance as Agency Adjunct," 26ff.

100. JWT Staff Meeting Minutes, 2 February 1932, 4.

101. For a different perspective on the struggle over who would run JWT's radio department, see Hilmes, *Radio Voices*, 144–46.

102. JWT Staff Meeting Minutes, 12 August 1930, 2. The censorship issue is addressed in Chapter 4, "Who Owns the Time?" and the need for showmanship is addressed in Chapter 6, "The Ballet and Ballyhoo of Radio Showmanship."

103. J. T. W. Martin, "Copy for the Ear," in O'Neill, ed., *The Advertising Agency Looks at Radio*, 69. Pamela Laird argues that the distrust of the visual within the advertising industry had led to the earlier shift away from chromolithography as a major advertising medium. *Advertising Progress* (Baltimore: Johns Hopkins University Press, 1998), 293.

104. JWT Staff Meeting Minutes, 21 December 1932, 2.

105. JWT Staff Meeting Minutes, 8 July 1930, 6; Robert Colwell, "The Program as an Advertisement," in O'Neill, ed., *The Advertising Agency Looks at Radio*, 38.

106. Hubbell Robinson, "What the Radio Audience Wants," in O'Neill, ed., *The Advertising Agency Looks at Radio*, 53.

107. George W. Smith, "Continuity's the Name," *Radio Showmanship*, September 1942, 301.

108. Martin, "Copy for the Ear," 72.

109. Ibid., 73.

110. F. B. Ryan Jr., "Copy on the Air," *Printers' Ink Monthly*, March 1934, 55.

111. Hill Blackett, "Agency Operation," *Printers' Ink*, 12 August 1937, 38.

112. John Archer Carter, "But Do They Really Listen?" *Printers' Ink Monthly*, March 1936, 45.

113. *The Coca-Cola Top Notchers*, broadcast on 19 March 1930.

114. Victor Ratner, "Maybe It's 'Copper and Brass'?" *Advertising & Selling*, 29 March 1934, 40.

115. *Chase & Sanborn Hour*, broadcast on 12 December 1937.

116. Robert Colwell, JWT Staff Meeting Minutes, 8 July1930, 7.

117. Colwell, "The Program as Advertisement," 39.

118. Ernest S. Green, "What 'Typeface' for Your Radio Commercials?" *Printers' Ink Monthly*, May 1938, 18–19.

119. JWT Staff Meeting Minutes, 8 July 1930, 5.

120. Norman Brokenshire, "Announcer—or Advertising Man?" *Broadcast Advertising*, October 1930, 20.

121. Robert Colwell, JWT Staff Meeting Minutes, 8 July 1930, 8.

122. JWT Staff Meeting Minutes, 11 August 1931, 9.

4. "Who Owns the Time?" Advertising Agencies and Networks Vie for Control in the 1930s

1. Herman Hettinger, *A Decade of Radio Advertising* (Chicago: University of Chicago Press, 1933), 42.

2. Stephen Fox, *The Mirror Makers* (New York: William Morrow, 1984), 118.

3. James Rorty, "Advertising and the Depression," *The Nation*, 20 December 1933, 703.

4. *Printers' Ink*, 25 July 1935, 76.

5. Warren B. Dygert, *Radio as an Advertising Medium* (New York: McGraw-Hill, 1939), 7.

6. JWT Staff Meeting Minutes, 15 September 1931, 14, John W. Hartman Center for Sales, Advertising and Marketing History, Duke University, Durham, North Carolina (hereafter JWT Staff Meeting Minutes).

7. Frank Allen Burt, *American Advertising Agencies: An Inquiry into Their Origin, Growth, Functions and Future* (New York: Harper, 1940), 1.

8. Ralph M. Hower, *The History of an Advertising Agency: N. W. Ayer & Son at Work, 1869–1939* (Cambridge, Mass.: Harvard University Press, 1939), 184; Studs Terkel, interview with William Benton, *Hard Times: An Oral History of the Great Depression* (New York: Pantheon, 1970), 62; Peggy J. Kreshel, "The 'Culture' of J. Walter Thompson, 1915–1925," *Public Relations Review* 16, no. 3 (Fall 1990): 80–93.

9. Donald S. Shaw, "The Policy Racket in Radio," *Advertising & Selling*, 12 August 1937, 31, 63.

10. Michele Hilmes, *Radio Voices: American Broadcasting, 1922–1952* (Minneapolis: University of Minnesota Press, 1997), 97.

11. Howard Angus, "Preparation of Commercial Copy Is Hardest Task of Radio Advertiser," *Broadcast Advertising*, December 1931, 8.

12. For more on the differences between NBC and CBS, see Michael J. Socolow, "'Always in Friendly Competition': NBC and CBS in the First Decade of National Broadcasting," in Michele Hilmes, ed., *NBC: America's Network* (Berkeley: University of California Press, 2007), 25–43.

13. Paley's family manufactured La Palina cigars and sponsored a radio program. The opening announcement of a 1929 (circa) program began:

Once more, a program to express the good-will of the Congress Cigar Company, Manufacturers of La Palina, America's largest selling high-grade cigar—over a million a day. The slogan for La Palina cigars is "Made good," and "Made good" is the term *you* have applied to the entertainment given at the Casino in Havana—so we invite you there again this evening.

N. W. Ayer Staff, *Classes of Advertising*, Book I (Scranton, Penn.: International Textbook Company, 1929), 28.

14. JWT Staff Meeting Minutes, 13 January 1931, 7.

15. Laurence Bergreen, *Look Now, Pay Later: The Rise of Network Broadcasting* (Garden City, N.Y.: Doubleday, 1980), 54.

16. Sally Bedell Smith, *In All His Glory: The Life of William S. Paley* (New York: Simon & Schuster, 1990), 131, 152, 155.

17. Letter from Roy Durstine to David Sarnoff, 28 April 1936, Box 44, Folder 29, NBC Records, Wisconsin Historical Society, Madison (hereafter NBC Records).

18. Memo from R. C. Patterson to Edgar Kobak, 20 August 1935, Box 40, Folder 42, NBC Records.

19. Memo from Roy Witmer to Frank E. Mullen, 29 May 1945, Box 114, Folder 71, NBC Records.

20. Ibid.

21. Bergreen, *Look Now, Pay Later*, 50, 52, 53.

22. E. P. H. James interview, 29 March 1963, Box 1, Folder 1, James Papers, Wisconsin Historical Society, Madison (hereafter James Interview, James Papers).

23. Memo from Wayne Randall to Frank E. Mason, 24 April 1933, NBC Records.

24. Letter from William Benton to Merlin Aylesworth, 25 August 1933, Box 16, Folder 12, NBC Records.

25. Memo from Wayne Randall to Frank Mason, 11 July 1935, Box 34, Folder 34, NBC Records.

26. "Radio Network Billings," *Printers' Ink*, 27 January 1938, 88.

27. Trade-Ways, Inc., *Selling Broadcast Advertising: A Handbook for NBC Network Salesmen*, III-7, NBC, 1933; Edgar Felix, "Radio for the Advertiser," *Advertising & Selling*, 28 October 1931, 48.

28. Memo from Roy Witmer to R. C. Patterson, 2 February 1933, Box 16, Folder 8, NBC Records.

29. Memo from Walter Duncan to Harry Kopf, 19 March 1935, Box 42, Folder 69, NBC Records.

30. Memo from E. P. H. James to George Frey, 20 December 1933, Box 22, Folder 28, NBC Records.

31. Letter from Chet LaRoche to Roy Witmer, 3 April 1933, Box 23, Folder 19, NBC Records.

32. Walter E. "Hap" Myers interview, 4 December 1965, Library of American Broadcasting, University of Maryland, College Park (hereafter LAB).

33. Memo from D. U. Bathrick to Edgar Kobak, 12 September 1934, Box 24C, Folder 59, NBC Records.

34. Memo from Art Hungerford to Lee B. Wells, 24 May 1934, Art Hungerford Scrapbook, 1, LAB.

35. Memo from John Royal to Don Shaw, 18 June 1934, Box 29, Folder 35, NBC Records.

36. Atherton Hobler, "The Triangle of Marketing Success," n.d., Box 19, Benton & Bowles Files, 48, Hartman Center for Sales, Advertising and Marketing History, Duke University, Durham, North Carolina (hereafter Benton & Bowles Files); JWT Staff Meeting Minutes, 2 February 1932, 10; Calvin Kuhl, "The Grim Reber," unpublished manuscript, 1971, 34 JWT Writings and Speeches Files, Hartman Center, Duke University.

37. Howard Angus, "The Importance of Stars in Your Radio Program," *Broadcast Advertising*, February 1932, 26.

38. JWT Staff Meeting Minutes, 2 February 1932, 12.

39. Trade-Ways, Inc., *Selling Broadcast Advertising*, VIII-18.

40. Dygert, *Radio as an Advertising Medium*, 8.

41. Letter from Joseph Vessey, Kenyon & Eckhardt, to NBC, 28 January 1936, Box 47, Folder 35, NBC Records.

42. C. E. Hooper, "Radio Program Ratings and Sales: Their Relationship," *Printers' Ink Monthly*, October 1939, 52.

43. Robert Landry, *This Fascinating Radio Business* (Indianapolis: Bobbs-Merrill, 1946), 276.

44. Ralph Starr Butler, "I Believe in Broadcast Merchandising," *Broadcast Merchandising*, September 1933, 17.

45. Letter from Leonard T. Bush to Niles Trammell, 6 September 1939, Box 67, Folder 37, NBC Records.

46. Letter from Arthur Sinsheimer to Merlin Aylesworth, 30 October 1935, Box 40, Folder 22, NBC Records.

47. Memo from C. E. Rynd to K. R. Dyke, 30 November 1938, Box 63, Folder 50, NBC Records.

48. Letter from Edgar Kobak to Roy Witmer, 7 October 1936, Box 47, Folder 56, NBC Records; letter from Roy Durstine to Edgar Kobak, 13 September 1934, Box 24, Folder 8, NBC Records.

49. Hettinger, *A Decade of Radio Advertising*, 24.

50. Memo from R. C. Patterson to David Sarnoff, 15 July 1935, Box 40, Folder 17, NBC Records.

51. Correspondence between Pedlar & Ryan and NBC staffers, October–November 1934, Box 31, Folder 14, NBC Records; telegram from Niles Trammell to John Royal, 30 November 1934, Box 27, Folder 27, NBC Records.

52. Letter from Edgar Kobak to Roy Witmer, 7 October 1936, Box 47, Folder 56, NBC Records.

53. Bergreen, *Look Now, Pay Later*, 78; Alexander Russo, *Points on the Dial* (Durham, N.C.: Duke University Press, 2010), ch. 3.

54. Memo from C. Lloyd Egner to Niles Trammell, 2 December 1937, Box 52, Folder 37, NBC Records.

55. Trade-Ways, Inc., *Selling Broadcast Advertising*, VIII-13.

56. Letter from A. Pryor to H. Slingo, 7 October 1932, Box 6, Folder 56, NBC Records.

57. For a nuanced analysis of how the tension between public service (educational, highbrow, and civic) programming and commercial entertainment evolved through the 1930s, see David Goodman, *Radio's Civic Ambition* (New York: Oxford University Press, 2011).

58. Memo from I. E. Showerman to Janet MacRorie, 19 December 1938, Box 59, Folder 28, NBC Records.

59. Matthew Murray, "Broadcast Content Regulation and Cultural Limits, 1920–1962" (PhD diss., University of Wisconsin–Madison, 1997), 18, 117.

60. Memo from Jack Van Nostrand to Grimm, Stauffer, et al., 13 January 1939, Box 66, Folder 55, NBC Records.

61. "Oppose Federal Radio Station," *Printers' Ink*, 1 July 1937, 54.

62. Emphasis in original. JWT Staff Meeting Minutes, 8 July 1930, 8.

63. Donald S. Shaw, "The Policy Racket in Radio," *Advertising & Selling*, 12 August 1937, 31, 63.

64. Ibid., 31, 63. For more on the PCA, see Thomas Doherty, *Hollywood's Censor: Joseph I. Breen and the Production Code Administration* (New York: Columbia University Press, 2007).

65. *Printers' Ink Monthly*, March 1936, 65.

66. "Commercial Radio Advertising," letter from Chairman of Federal Radio Commission in response to Senate Resolution No. 129, 8 June 1932, 190.

67. Ibid., 191.

68. "Permits Price Mention on Radio," *Printers' Ink*, 15 September 1932, 33.

69. JWT Staff Meeting Minutes, 14 April 1931, 6.

70. Letters from A. K. Spencer to Merlin Aylesworth, 3 May 1935, and from George Frey to A. K. Spencer, 3 May 1935, Box 42, Folder 9, NBC Records.

71. Memo from D. S. Shaw to John Royal, 15 March 1935, Box 34, Folder 34, NBC Records.

72. "Radio Notes," *Advertising & Selling*, 6 June 1935, 62; Smith, *In All His Glory*, 142.

73. Gifford Hart, "Are Laxative Programs Objectionable?" *Advertising & Selling*, 9 May 1935, 58.

74. Bernard Grimes, "To Improve Radio," *Printers' Ink*, 23 May 1935, 28.

75. Memo from Janet MacRorie to Edgar Kobak, 24 September 1935, Box 34, Folder 25, NBC Records.

76. Reproduced in Frank Rowsome Jr., *They Laughed When I Sat Down: An Informal History of Advertising in Words and Pictures* (New York: Bonanza Books, 1959), 171.

77. Memo from Janet MacRorie to John Royal, 11 October 1935, Box 40, Folder 25, NBC Records.

78. "Regulating Radio," *Business Week*, 8 February 1936, 13.

5. The 1930s' Turn to the Hard Sell: Blackett-Sample-Hummert's Soap Opera Factory

1. Kenneth M. Goode, "Is Advertising Big Enough to Meet Today's Emergency?" *Advertising & Selling*, 27 November 1929, 18.

2. "Will Advertising Appropriations for 1930 Be Cut?" *Advertising & Selling*, 13 November 1929, 17.

3. Goode, "Is Advertising Big Enough . . . ?" 18.

4. For accounts of the consumer movement, see Inger Stole, *Advertising on Trial: Consumer Activism and Corporate Public Relations in the 1930s* (Urbana and Chicago: University of Illinois Press, 2001), and Kathy M. Newman, *Radio Active: Advertising and Consumer Activism, 1935–1947* (Berkeley: University of California Press, 2004).

5. Ralph M. Hower, *The History of an Advertising Agency: N. W. Ayer & Son at Work, 1869–1939* (Cambridge, Mass.: Harvard University Press, 1939), 185.

6. Ibid., 187.

7. James Rorty, "Advertising and the Depression," *The Nation*, 20 December 1933, 703; James Rorty, *Our Master's Voice* (New York: The John Day Co., 1934).

8. Although NBC was approached, its executives were not interested in buying any advertising in *Ballyhoo*. Box 6, Folder "Ballyhoo," NBC Records, Wisconsin Historical Society, Madison (hereafter NBC Records).

9. John Benson, "What About the Future of Advertising?" *Advertising & Selling*, 28 January 1937, 32.

10. Stole, *Advertising on Trial.*

11. Arthur Kallet and Frederick J. Schlink, *100,000,000 Guinea Pigs* (New York: Grosset and Dunlap, 1933).

12. Untitled script (no date, "early 1930s"), Dorothy Dignam Papers, Wisconsin Historical Society, Madison.

13. Daniel Horowitz, *The Morality of Spending: Attitudes toward the Consumer Society in America, 1875–1940* (Baltimore: Johns Hopkins University Press, 1985), 159; Stephen Fox, *The Mirror Makers* (New York: William Morrow, 1984), 169; Otis Pease, *The Responsibilities of American Advertising* (New Haven, Conn.: Yale University Press, 1958), 92. Stole dismisses the Wheeler-Lea Act for not outlawing advertising that causes a "misleading impression," arguing that all advertising should be product information only. *Advertising on Trial,* 157, see ch. 6.

14. For a thorough recounting of the broadcast reform movement of the early 1930s, see Robert McChesney, *Telecommunications, Mass Media, and Democracy: The Battle for the Control of U.S. Broadcasting, 1928–1935* (New York: Oxford University Press, 1993). Clifford Doerksen, on the other hand, highlights the class divide that animated this reform movement, noting that much of the criticism of commercial radio was also a criticism of the popular culture forms, such as "hot jazz," of which middle-class reformers disapproved. *American Babel: Rogue Radio Broadcasters of the Jazz Age* (Philadelphia: University of Pennsylvania Press, 2005).

15. Peter Morrell, *Poisons, Potions and Profits: The Antidote to Radio Advertising* (New York: Knight Publishers, 1937), 59, 9. For more on Morrell, see Newman, *Radio Active,* ch. 2.

16. John T. Flynn, "Radio: Medicine Show," *American Scholar* (Autumn 1938): 433.

17. Bruce Barton, "Human Nature in Advertising" (University of the Air series), broadcast on WJZ, New York, 4 March 1924, Bruce Barton Papers, Wisconsin Historical Society, Madison.

18. "Barton, on Banks' Radio Program, Says Big Man in Picture Today Is Little Man," *The American Banker,* 11 December 1936.

19. Robert T. Colwell, "The Program as an Advertisement," in Neville O'Neill, ed., *The Advertising Agency Looks at Radio* (New York: D. Appleton, 1932), 25.

20. L. Ames Brown, "Radio Broadcasting as an Advertising Medium," in O'Neill, ed., *The Advertising Agency Looks at Radio,* 7.

21. W. B. Ruthrauff, "Hard Times—Hard-Tack Copy," *Printers' Ink Monthly*, January 1933, 30.

22. Howard Angus, "Preparation of Commercial Copy Is Hardest Task of Radio Advertiser," *Broadcast Advertising*, December 1931, 8.

23. An earlier version of this research can be found in Cynthia Meyers, "Frank and Anne Hummert's Soap Opera Empire: 'Reason-Why' Advertising Strategies in Early Radio Programming," *Quarterly Review of Film and Video* 16, no. 2 (1997): 113–32.

24. Other Hummert programs that were not daytime serials for women included the juvenile dramas *Jack Armstrong, the All American Boy* (1933–51), sponsored by Wheaties; *Terry and the Pirates* (1937–48); and *Little Orphan Annie* (1931–42). Evening programs included *Dreft Star Playhouse* (1943–45), serialized adaptations of films; *Manhattan Merry-Go-Round* (1932–49), a musical hits program; *American Album of Familiar Music* (1931–51), sponsored by Bayer; and *Waltz Time* (1933–48). Jim Cox counts 125 programs in which the Hummerts were involved. Jim Cox, *Frank and Anne Hummert's Radio Factory* (Jefferson, N.C.: MacFarland & Co., 2003).

25. *Printers' Ink*, 3 May 1934, 74–75.

26. J. Walter Thompson *Newsflash*, 3 February 1937.

27. "Hummerts to Exit from B-S-H," *Advertising Age*, 16 August 1943.

28. *Tide*, May 1929, 8.

29. "Monologue by Mr. Hill Blackett of Blackett-Sample-Hummert, December 31st, 1930," Box 25, Folder 9, Rosser Reeves Papers, Wisconsin Historical Society, Madison (hereafter Reeves Papers).

30. *Printers' Ink*, 27 October 1927, 166–67. Hummert's annual salary in the 1930s was reputed to be up to $150,000.

31. Lawrence E. Doherty, "Adman Sample? He's Florida Land Tycoon," part 1, *Advertising Age*, 7 May 1962, 66.

32. Herman S. Hettinger, *A Decade of Radio Advertising* (Chicago: University of Chicago Press, 1933), 215, 226.

33. *Printers' Ink*, 7 November 1929, 133.

34. Doherty, "Adman Sample? He's Florida Land Tycoon," part 1, 66.

35. Anne Hummert explains that Frank Hummert's British accent was unintelligible to many. I am indebted to Philip F. Napoli for providing a recording of his interview with Anne Hummert, 7 June 1991, New York, New York (hereafter Hummert Interview).

36. One observer reports that their secrecy was the result of the heavy criticism of their soap operas. Thomas Whiteside, *The Relaxed Sell* (New York: Oxford University Press, 1954), 35.

37. "Hummerts to Exit from B-S-H," 2.

38. "150 Leading Radio Advertisers in 1935," *Advertising & Selling*, 16 January 1936, 29.

39. Ibid.

40. For Oxydol: *Ma Perkins, The Goldbergs, The Man I Married*; for Camay: *Pepper Young's Family, The Woman in White*; for Crisco: *Vic and Sade, Right to Happiness*; for Ivory: *Mary Marlin, The O'Neills, Against the Storm, Life Can Be Beautiful*; for Naptha: *The Guiding Light*; for Chipso: *Road of Life*; for Dreft: *Kitty Keene*; for Teel: *Midstream.* Letter from Gregory Williamson to Irna Phillips, 4 September 1940, Box 62, Pedlar & Ryan folder, Irna Phillips Papers, Wisconsin Historical Society, Madison.

41. The soap opera historian William Stedman, *The Serials: Suspense and Drama by Installment* (Norman: University of Oklahoma Press, 1971, 1977), points out that because General Mills was one of the earlier sponsors of daytime serials, the programs perhaps should have been known as "cereal dramas" rather than "soap operas" (247). For more on daytime radio serials, see Michele Hilmes, *Radio Voices* (Minneapolis: University of Minnesota Press, 1997), ch. 6; Newman, *Radio Active*, ch. 4; Jason Loviglio, *Radio's Intimate Public: Network Broadcasting and Mass-Mediated Democracy* (Minneapolis: University of Minnesota Press, 2005), ch. 3; Jennifer Hyland Wang, "Convenient Fictions: The Construction of the Daytime Broadcast Audience, 1927–1960" (PhD diss. , University of Wisconsin–Madison, 2006); and Robert C. Allen, *Speaking of Soap Operas* (Chapel Hill: University of North Carolina Press, 1985).

42. Stedman, *The Serials,* 501, 267.

43. Ibid., 306–7.

44. Harriet Corley, "Soap Opera Her Empire," *New York Sun*, 12 November 1944, n.p.

45. "Radio Serial Has Formula," *New York Times*, 31 July 1938, n.p.

46. Anne Hummert takes credit for inventing these initial basic story problems. Hummert Interview.

47. See Claude Hopkins, *My Life in Advertising* (Lincolnwood, Ill.: NTC Business Books, reprinted 1966), 242–43.

48. Michael Mok, "Radio Script-Writing Factory Outdoes Dumas Pere's Plant," *New York Post*, 30 January 1939, n.p.

49. Stedman, *The Serials*, 256.

50. "Radio Serial Has Formula," n.p.

51. James Thurber, "Soapland," *New Yorker*, 29 May 1948, 31.

52. Robert LaGuardia, *Soap World* (N.p.: Arbor House, 1983), 20.

53. Thurber, "Soapland," 31.

54. Stedman, *The Serials*, 335.

55. Quoted in Stedman, *The Serials*, 341.

56. Corley, "Soap Opera Her Empire."

57. *Ma Perkins*, broadcast on 12 December 1933.

58. Ibid.

59. Mok, "Radio Script-Writing Factory."

60. Stedman, *The Serials*, 347.

61. Cox, *Frank and Anne Hummert's Radio Factory*, 76, 104.

62. "Hummert Tells How, Why," *Variety*, 11 May 1938, 27.

63. Hilmes, *Radio Voices*, 165. For more on Irna Phillips, see Marilyn Lavin, "Creating Consumers in the 1930s: Irna Phillips and the Radio Soap Opera," *Journal of Consumer Research* 22, no. 1 (June 1995): 75–89; and Ellen Seiter, "'To Teach and to Sell': Irna Phillips and Her Sponsors, 1930–1954," *Journal of Film and Video* 41, no. 1 (Spring 1989): 21–35.

64. Mok, "Radio Script-Writing Factory."

65. "Radio Serial Has Formula." Other serials based on pre-sold characters include *David Harum*, *Our Gal Sunday*, and *Mr. Keen, Tracer of Lost Persons*.

66. Mok, "Radio Script-Writing Factory."

67. Anne Hummert admits only to assigning writers to two serials at a time. Hummert Interview.

68. Corley, "Soap Opera Her Empire"; Whiteside, *The Relaxed Sell*, 45; "The Hummerts' Super Soaps," *Newsweek*, 10 January 1944, 80.

69. "Hummert Tells How, Why."

70. Robert Landry, "Pioneer Soaper Frank Hummert, Ever the Hermit, Almost 'Sneaks' His Obit," *Variety*, 27 April 1966, n.p.

71. J. Fred MacDonald, *Don't Touch That Dial!* (Chicago: Nelson-Hall, 1979), 249.

72. However, one of their first serials was not written assembly-line style. Reporter Charles Robert Douglas Hardy Andrews churned out *Just Plain Bill* scripts single-handedly—his typing speed was legendary. See James Thurber, "Soapland."

73. Andrews later wrote a roman à clef about Anne Hummert: *Legend of a Lady: The Story of Rita Martin* (New York: Coward-McCann, 1949). The

inside flap of the dust jacket explains it as "the story of pretty, fragile Rita Martin, who beneath her charming exterior is hell-bent for success and who tramples with small, well-shod feet on all who stand in her way." Eventually, after the establishment of the American Federation of Radio Artists (AFRA), the Hummerts agreed in 1939 to allow dialogue writers' names on the covers of scripts, along with a "supervised by Frank and Anne Hummert" credit. "Frank Hummert Gives His Views," *Variety*, 25 January 1939, 26.

74. Allen, *Speaking of Soap Operas,* 53.

75. Ibid., 17. See Allen on the critical assessments that soaps could not be an art form because there are no identifiable authors, 15.

76. *Fortune*, May 1938, 14–15.

77. Ibid. Emphasis in original.

78. Hummert Interview.

79. Letter from E. M. Clasen to R. C. Patterson Jr., 21 December 1934, Box 34, Folder 39, NBC Records.

80. Memo from Roy Witmer to Lenox Lohr, 27 February 1936, Box 44, Folder 39, NBC Records.

81. Letter from Roy Witmer to Frank Hummert, 1 June 1934, Box 24, Folder 9, NBC Records.

82. Radio Broadcasting Order, 4 February 1932, Box 6, Folder 71, NBC Records.

83. Letter from Roy Witmer to Frank Hummert, 11 February 1932, Box 6, Folder 71, NBC Records.

84. Memo from Janet MacRorie to Lenox Lohr, 25 January 1939, Box 66, Folder 46, NBC Records.

85. Letter from Frank Hummert to G. F. McClelland, 25 November 1932, Box 6, Folder 71, NBC Records.

86. Letter from Roy Witmer to Frank Hummert, 25 March 1933, Box 16, Folder 7, NBC Records.

87. Letter from Roy Witmer to Frank Hummert, 14 February 1934, Box 24, Folder 16, NBC Records.

88. Letter from Frank Hummert to Roy Witmer, 16 February 1934, Box 24, Folder 16, NBC Records.

89. Telegram from Frank Hummert to Merlin Aylesworth, 1 February 1934, Box 24, Folder 16, NBC Records.

90. Memo from Roy Witmer to Lenox Lohr, 27 February 1936, Box 44, Folder 39, NBC Records.

91. Hummert Interview.

92. "Dancer-Fitzgerald-Sample Inaugurated with New York, Chicago, LA Offices," *Broadcasting & Broadcast Advertising*, 3 January 1944, 42.

93. American Business Consultants, *Red Channels: The Report of Communist Influence in Radio and Television* (New York: ABC, June 1950); Mary Jane Higby, *Tune in Tomorrow* (New York: Cowles, 1968), 139.

94. Transcript of *Young Widder Brown*, 21 July 1948, Box 25, Folder 10, Reeves Papers.

95. Stedman, *The Serials*, 346–47, 387.

96. Higby, *Tune in Tomorrow*, 213.

97. Advertisers like Procter & Gamble have owned television soap operas *As the World Turns*, *Guiding Light*, and *Another World*, just as in the radio era.

6. The Ballet and Ballyhoo of Radio Showmanship: Young & Rubicam's Soft Sell

1. John Orr Young, *Adventures in Advertising* (New York: Harper & Bros., 1949), 93.

2. Kenneth M. Goode and M. Zenn Kaufman, *Showmanship in Business* (New York: Harper & Bros., 1936).

3. Ruth Betz, "Showmanship and Salesmanship Spell Success for Strasska," *Broadcast Advertising*, January 1932, n.p.

4. Merlin Aylesworth, "Radio's Place in the Advertising Career," in Alden James, ed., *Careers in Advertising* (New York: Macmillan, 1932), 450.

5. Martin A. North, "Don't Use All of Your Showmanship in Your Program," *Broadcast Advertising*, March 1932, 13.

6. Warren B. Dygert, *Radio as an Advertising Medium* (New York: McGraw-Hill, 1939), 19.

7. JWT Staff Meeting Minutes, 26 March 1932, 4, John W. Hartman Center for Sales, Advertising and Marketing History, Duke University, Durham, North Carolina (hereafter JWT Staff Meeting Minutes).

8. For a study of how the debate over showmanship played out at NBC, see Jennifer Hyland Wang, "Convenient Fictions: The Construction of the Daytime Broadcast Audience, 1927–1960" (PhD diss., University of Wisconsin–Madison, 2007), ch. 1.

9. Goode and Kaufman, *Showmanship in Business*.

10. Ibid., 17.

11. Ibid., 5.

12. Carroll Dunn, "Radio Showmanship in Three Easy Lessons," *Advertising & Selling*, 21 October 1937, 39.

13. Mary Pickford, "Radio as Mary Sees It," *Printers' Ink*, 20 December 1934, 57.

14. "Radio—If the Stars Were Czars," Part II, *Printers' Ink Monthly*, November 1934, 46.

15. J. T. W. Martin, "Copy for the Ear," in Neville O'Neill, ed., *The Advertising Agency Looks at Radio* (New York: D. Appleton & Co., 1932), 76–77.

16. Ibid.

17. Ibid., 75.

18. Robert J. Landry, *This Fascinating Radio Business* (Indianapolis: Bobbs-Merrill, 1946), 156.

19. Howard Angus, "The Importance of Stars in Your Radio Program," *Broadcast Advertising*, February 1932, 27; John T. Flynn, "Radio: Medicine Show," *American Scholar* (Autumn 1938): 433–34. See also Peter Morrell, *Poisons, Potions and Profits: The Antidote to Radio Advertising* (New York: Knight Publishers, 1937), 9.

20. Emphasis in original. Carl Dreppert, "Success in Radio Use Can Be So Simple," *Printers' Ink Monthly*, June 1940, 57.

21. JWT Staff Meeting Minutes, 22 June 1932, 3.

22. J. Leonard McPeak, "Are We Selling Entertainment or Merchandise?" *Advertising & Selling*, 18 January 1934, 30.

23. F. B. Ryan Jr., "Copy on the Air," *Printers' Ink Monthly*, March 1934, 55.

24. Angus, "The Importance of Stars in Your Radio Program," 12.

25. L. Ames Brown, "Radio Broadcasting as an Advertising Medium," in O'Neill, ed., *The Advertising Agency Looks at Radio*, 11.

26. Tod Williams, "Selling vs. Popular Appeal," *Radio Showmanship*, January 1942, 17.

27. JWT Staff Meeting Minutes, 21 December 1932, 3.

28. William Paley, "How Radio Has Come of Age," *Advertising & Selling*, 17 June 1937, 48.

29. Elmer Wheeler, "Don't Sell the Steak . . . Sell the Sizzle!" *Radio Showmanship*, September 1940, 6.

30. Letter from Frederick Sard, 19 July 1938, Box 63, Folder 92, NBC Records, Wisconsin Historical Society, Madison (hereafter NBC Records).

31. Ellipsis added. Hubbell Robinson, "What the Radio Audience Wants," in O'Neill, ed., *The Advertising Agency Looks at Radio*, 48.

32. JWT Staff Meeting Minutes, 6 August 1929, 12.

33. Arthur F. Wertheim, *Radio Comedy* (New York: Oxford, 1979), 148.

34. Atherton W. Hobler, "The Triangle of Marketing Success," unpublished manuscript, n.d., Box 19, 98, Benton & Bowles Files, John W. Hartman Center for Sales, Advertising and Marketing History, Duke University, Durham, North Carolina (hereafter Benton & Bowles Files).

35. Susan Douglas, *Listening In: Radio and the American Imagination* (New York: Random House, 1999), 121.

36. Frank Allen Burt, *American Advertising Agencies: An Inquiry into Their Origin, Growth, Functions and Future* (New York: Harper, 1940), 18.

37. JWT Staff Meeting Minutes, 8 July 1930, 9.

38. JWT Staff Meeting Minutes, 20 October 1931, 2–3.

39. Kenneth Goode, *What about Radio?* (New York: Harper, 1937), 154.

40. Ralph M. Hower, *The History of an Advertising Agency: N. W. Ayer & Son at Work, 1869–1949*, rev. ed. (Cambridge, Mass.: Harvard University Press, 1949), 178.

41. JWT Staff Meeting Minutes, 21 December 1932.

42. Ralph E. de Castro, "Why the Wall between Radio and Other Copywriters?" *Printers' Ink*, 3 August 1945, 36.

43. Don Shaw, "The Care and Feeding of Sponsors," *Broadcasting & Broadcast Advertising*, 1 January 1937, 11.

44. Mark Woods, "Reminiscences," 1951, 65, Oral History Research Office, Columbia University, New York (hereafter Woods Reminiscences).

45. Dygert, *Radio as an Advertising Medium*, 14.

46. JWT Staff Meeting Minutes, 12 August 1930, 8.

47. JWT Staff Meeting Minutes, 2 February 1932, 4.

48. Fred Allen, "Mr. Allen Takes a Look About Him," clipping, ca. 1947, Scrapbook 3, Allen Papers, Boston Public Library. I am grateful to Kathryn Fuller-Seeley for sharing this material.

49. "Radio: A Modern Advertising Force," American Tobacco Company pamphlet, 1938.

50. Flynn, "Radio: Medicine Show," 433.

51. Ray Perkins, "Puzzled Radio Artist," *Printers' Ink Monthly*, December 1934, 38.

52. JWT Staff Meeting Minutes, 21 December 1932, 7.

53. "Lever, Lux," JWT Account Files, John W. Hartman Center for Sales, Advertising and Marketing History, Duke University, Durham, North Carolina (hereafter JWT Account Files).

54. *Lux Radio Theatre,* "To Have and Have Not," broadcast on 14 October 1946.

55. See Michele Hilmes, *Hollywood and Broadcasting: From Radio to Cable* (Urbana: University of Illinois Press, 1990), ch. 4.

56. Goode and Kaufman, *Showmanship in Business,* 195.

57. Robinson, "What the Radio Audience Wants," 42; William D. Murphy, "High Hats for Low Brows," *Printers' Ink,* 8 February 1939, 61; "Now That It Has a Sponsor," *Printers' Ink Monthly,* January 1939, 15.

58. Memo, 30 August 1928, Box 2, Folder 28, NBC Records.

59. Studs Terkel, *Hard Times* (New York: Pantheon, 1970), 63.

60. Letter from Alfred Sloan to Merlin Aylesworth, 19 November 1934, Box 27, Folder 28, NBC Records.

61. Letter from Merlin Aylesworth to Alfred Sloan, 21 December 1934, Box 27, Folder 28, NBC Records.

62. JWT Staff Meeting Minutes, 12 August 1930, 6–7.

63. Robinson, "What the Radio Audience Wants," 45.

64. Robinson's insight would serve him well as a CBS television programmer in the 1950s.

65. Dygert, *Radio as an Advertising Medium,* 12.

66. Angus, "The Importance of Stars in Your Radio Program," 12.

67. JWT Staff Meeting Minutes, 22 June 1932, 3–4.

68. Leonard Lewis, "The Play's the Thing," *Printers' Ink Monthly,* July 1935, 26.

69. Arthur Sinsheimer, "Custom Blocks the Road to Radio Progress," *Advertising & Selling,* 8 November 1934, 32.

70. Jarvis Wren, "Why Some Radio Programs Fail," *Advertising & Selling,* 5 February 1930, 23.

71. Sinsheimer, "Custom Blocks the Road to Radio Progress," 34.

72. Landry, *This Fascinating Radio Business,* 166.

73. "Radio—If the Stars Were Czars, Part I," *Printer's Ink Monthly,* October 1934, 16.

74. Eddie Cantor, "Radio Needs Showmen," *Printers' Ink,* 25 October 1934, 19.

75. Ray Perkins, "A Radio Performer Relieves His Mind," *Printers' Ink,* 5 January 1933, 24.

76. Jessica Dragonette, *Faith Is a Song* (New York: David McKay, 1951), 169.

77. Fred Allen, *Treadmill to Oblivion* (Boston: Little, Brown, 1954); "Radio—If the Stars Were Czars, Part II," 25.

78. Dale Harrison press release quoting Fred Allen, Scrapbook 3, no date, Fred Allen Papers, Boston Public Library.

79. "Radio—If the Stars Were Czars, Part II," 46.

80. JWT Staff Meeting Minutes, 21 December 1932, 9.

81. Lawrence Hughes, "Should You Hitch Your Business to a Star?" *Sales Management*, 1 March 1939, 22.

82. Victor Herbert, "Do Listeners Associate Radio Stars with the Correct Product?" *Sales Management*, 1 October 1936, 465; Victor Herbert, "Are Consumers Promptly Aware of Sponsor-Changes in Leading Radio Programs?" *Sales Management*, 1 June 1937, 1098.

83. For more on blacklisting in ad agencies, see Cynthia B. Meyers, "BBDO and US Steel on Radio and Television, 1948–52: The Problems of Sponsorship, New Media, and the Communist Threat," paper presented at "On, Archives!" Conference, Wisconsin Center for Film and Theater Research, Madison, 9 July 2010.

84. Hughes, "Should You Hitch Your Business to a Star?," 24.

85. Barbara Rosenblum, *Photographers at Work* (New York: Holmes & Meier, 1978), 81.

86. "An Advertising Man Writes to His Son," *Printers' Ink*, 19 July 1934, 81.

87. "Monologue by Mr. Hill Blackett of Blackett-Sample-Hummert," 31 December 1930, Box 25, Folder 9, Rosser Reeves Papers, Wisconsin Historical Society, Madison.

88. JWT Staff Meeting Minutes, 12 August 1930, 4; memo from Art Hungerford to Lee B. Wells, 24 May 1934, Art Hungerford Scrapbook, 1, Library of American Broadcasting, University of Maryland, College Park (hereafter Hungerford Scrapbook).

89. Memo from Hungerford to Wells, 24 May 1934, Hungerford Scrapbook, 1.

90. As Daniel Czitrom points out in *Media and the American Mind* (Chapel Hill: University of North Carolina Press, 1982), 83, 88.

91. Landry, *This Fascinating Radio Business*, 159.

92. Wertheim, *Radio Comedy*, 91.

93. Ibid., 131.

94. *Treadmill to Oblivion,* the title of radio star and former vaudevillian Fred Allen's memoir, refers to this problem directly.

95. "A Critical Appraisal of Radio Advertising" (N.p.: Crowell Publishing Co., n.d.).

96. Terkel, *Hard Times*, 64.

97. Robert T. Colwell, "The Program as an Advertisement," in O'Neill, ed., *The Advertising Agency Looks at Radio*, 29.

98. Ryan, "Copy on the Air," 17.

99. Ibid. Ellipsis added.

100. Don Gridley, "Plagiarism and Radio," *Printers' Ink Monthly*, October 1935, 32.

101. Gridley, "Plagiarism and Radio," 68.

102. Young, *Adventures in Advertising*, 65.

103. Stephen Fox, *The Mirror Makers* (New York: William Morrow, 1984), 71, 127.

104. Philip Dougherty, "Raymond Rubicam, 85, Co-Founder of Largest U.S. Ad Agency, Dies," *New York Times*, 9 May 1978, 42.

105. Young, *Adventures in Advertising*, 47.

106. Ibid., 70.

107. Fox, *Mirror Makers*, 139.

108. Young, *Adventures in Advertising*, 81.

109. Originally published in the first issue of *Fortune*, it also appeared in *Printers' Ink Monthly*, March 1938, 25.

110. Quoted in Stan Freberg, "Resisting the Usual," *Y&R and Broadcasting: Growing Up Together* (New York: The Museum of Broadcasting, n.d.), 31.

111. Dougherty, "Raymond Rubicam," 42.

112. Ibid.

113. Young, *Adventures in Advertising*, 95.

114. Draper Daniels, *Giants, Pigmies and Other Advertising People* (Chicago: Crain Communications, 1974), 39.

115. For more on George Gallup's career, see Susan Ohmer, *George Gallup in Hollywood* (New York: Columbia University Press, 2006).

116. "The Story of Young & Rubicam," *Advertising Agency and Advertising & Selling*, December 1949, 52.

117. Raymond Rubicam, "The Danger Signals Are Up," *Saturday Review*, 3 November 1951, 24.

118. Joan Hafey, "Young & Rubicam and Broadcasting: Growing Up Together," in *Y&R and Broadcasting*.

119. Young, *Adventures in Advertising*, 90. If so, whether or not Y&R or B-S-H was first to block book airtime, it was an innovation worth bragging about.

120. Emphasis in original. *Fortune*, May 1938, 93.

121. *Y&R and Broadcasting*, 24.

122. Charles Hull Wolfe, *Modern Radio Advertising* (New York: Funk & Wagnalls, 1949), 644.

123. Daniels, *Giants, Pigmies and Other Advertising People*, 44.

124. JWT Staff Meeting Minutes, 2 February 1932, 10.

125. Memo, circa 1938, Box 52, Folder 1, Thomas Brophy Papers, Wisconsin Historical Society, Madison.

126. The following analysis is based on information in *Y&R and Broadcasting*.

127. JWT Staff Meeting Minutes, 2 February 1932, 10.

128. Robinson, "What the Radio Audience Wants," 49. When Robinson later worked at CBS in the 1950s, CBS chief William Paley characterized him as having a "literary flair" that enabled him to produce programs combining "mass with class," such as *Playhouse 90*, one of the best-known television anthology dramas during the so-called golden age of television drama. William Paley, *As It Happened* (Garden City, N.Y.: Doubleday, 1979), 255.

129. Hubbell Robinson Jr., "How True Detective Mysteries, Broadcasting Dramatized Sample Stories, Won Half a Million New Readers in Less than a Year," *Broadcast Advertising*, March 1930, 12.

130. Wolfe, *Modern Radio Advertising*, 627.

131. *Y&R and Broadcasting*, 46–47.

132. Robinson, "What the Radio Audience Wants," 50.

133. "Radio—If the Stars Were Czars, Part I," 18.

134. For more on sung advertising and jingles in early radio, see Timothy Taylor, *The Sounds of Capitalism: Advertising, Music and the Conquest of Culture* (Chicago: University of Chicago Press, 2012), ch. 1–3.

135. Quoted in Wertheim, *Radio Comedy*, 148.

136. *Y&R and Broadcasting*, 46.

137. Wertheim, *Radio Comedy*, 141.

138. JWT Staff Meeting Minutes, 21 December 1932, 5.

139. "Radio—If the Stars Were Czars, Part I," 17.

140. *Ladies' Home Journal*, April 1938, n.p. Author's collection.

141. Lou Brockway, quoted in *Y&R and Broadcasting*, 23. Because of sugar shortages during the war, Jack Benny's sponsorship shifted to another General Foods brand, Grape-Nuts Flakes, in 1942. In 1944, sponsorship shifted to Lucky Strike and BBDO took over program oversight.

142. Letter from William Benton to Randolph Catlin, 7 October 1935, Box 34, Folder 34, NBC Records.

143. In his autobiography, Y&R executive Draper Daniels recalled Allen with resentment: Fred Allen "described an advertising agency as '85 percent horseshit and 15 percent commission' but not even the lowest-paid peon and Allenphile at Y&R thought it was funny." *Giants, Pigmies and Other Advertising People*, 39.

144. Allen, *Treadmill to Oblivion*, 27.

145. Memo from Janet MacRorie to John Royal, 2 February 1938, Box 59, Folder 28, NBC Records.

146. Allen, *Treadmill to Oblivion*, 90.

147. Pat Weaver with Thomas Coffey, *The Best Seat in the House: The Golden Years of Radio and Television* (New York: Knopf, 1994), 66; Allen, *Treadmill to Oblivion*, 235.

148. The version I have has been separated from the original program, but the reference to the "eagle" at the beginning of the commercial indicates this spot was probably part of the 20 March 1940 broadcast of *The Fred Allen Show*.

149. *Town Hall Tonight*, 28 June 1939 script, Box 66, Folder 55, NBC Records.

150. Memo from Bertha Brainard to E. R. Hitz, 31 August 1938, Box 65, Folder 68, NBC Records.

7. Two Agencies: Batten Barton Durstine & Osborn, Crafters of the Corporate Image, and Benton & Bowles, Radio Renegades

1. For a thoroughgoing account of how big business waged its public relations campaigns with the help of BBDO and others, see William L. Bird, *"Better Living": Advertising, Media, and the New Vocabulary of Business Leadership, 1935–1955* (Evanston, Ill.: Northwestern University Press, 1999).

2. Most of the following relies on information from the 75th Anniversary edition of the BBDO *Newsletter*, February 1966, courtesy of BBDO.

3. Ibid., 30.

4. Ibid., 1–2.

5. Ibid., 1.

6. Ibid., 31.

7. Charlie Brower, *Me, and Other Advertising Geniuses* (Garden City, N.Y.: Doubleday, 1974), 89.

8. BBDO *Newsletter*, 34.

9. Alice Payne Hackett, *70 Years of Best Sellers: 1895–1965* (New York: R. R. Bowker Co., 1967), 131–34.

10. Bruce Barton, *The Man Nobody Knows: A Discovery of the Real Jesus* (Indianapolis: Bobbs-Merrill, 1924), 37, 43.

11. Ibid., 143.

12. Ibid., 108.

13. Emphasis in original. Bruce Barton, "Human Nature in Advertising," typescript of radio talk, Box 75, Hamilton Folder, Bruce Barton Papers, Wisconsin Historical Society, Madison (hereafter Barton Papers).

14. Barton inspired a great deal of critical response. For example, see his contemporary critic James Rorty, *Our Master's Voice* (New York: The John Day Co., 1934). Academic analysis of Barton's work includes Leo Ribuffo, "Jesus Christ as Business Statesman: Bruce Barton and the Selling of Corporate Capitalism," *American Quarterly* 33 (Summer 1981): 206–31; Warren Susman, "Culture Heroes: Ford, Barton, Ruth," in *Culture as History: The Transformation of American Society in the Twentieth Century* (New York: Pantheon, 1984), 122–49; T. J. Jackson Lears, "From Salvation to Self-Realization: Advertising and the Therapeutic Roots of the Consumer Culture, 1880–1930," in R. W. Fox and T. J. J. Lears, eds., *The Culture of Consumption* (New York: Pantheon, 1983), 1–38; Edrene S. Montgomery, "Bruce Barton's *The Man Nobody Knows*: A Popular Advertising Illusion," *Journal of Popular Culture* 19 (Winter 1985): 21–34.

15. BBDO *Newsletter*, 31.

16. Ibid., 32.

17. Ibid., 8.

18. A woman with whom Barton admitted having an affair threatened to publish a roman à clef about their affair unless he paid her not to. After he accused her of blackmail, she was convicted at a trial. Stephen Fox, *The Mirror Makers* (New York: William Morrow, 1984), 111.

19. BBDO *Newsletter*, 42.

20. Ibid., 14.

21. Ibid., 42.

22. Ibid., 31.

23. Ibid., 34. Emphasis in original.

24. Elbert Hubbard (1856–1915), soap salesman, Arts and Crafts popularizer, publisher and author of magazines *The Philistine* and *The Fra*, author of *A Message to Garcia*, was another figure well known for defending the value of corporate business practice as a progressive force. See Burton Bigelow, *Elbert Hubbard: Pioneer Advertising Man* (East Aurora, N.Y.: The Roycrofters, 1931).

25. Ed Roberts, "Radio & Celebrities," unpublished manuscript, commissioned by BBDO, ca. 1966, 1. See Bruce Barton, "This Magic Called Radio," *Broadcasting*, June 1922.

26. Roberts, "Radio & Celebrities," 6–7.

27. Ibid., 5, 7.

28. Ibid., 11.

29. Emphasis in original. Roy S. Durstine, *This Advertising Business* (New York: Scribner's, 1929), 310, 312. See also Roy S. Durstine, "Function of the Agency in Broadcast Advertising," *Broadcast Advertising*, June 1929, 14ff; speech before the Association of National Advertisers, May 1929.

30. "Audible Advertising," *Advertising & Selling*, 16 April 1930, 31.

31. Roberts, "Radio & Celebrities," 14. For an in-depth analysis of *The Parade of the States*, see Bird, *"Better Living,"* ch. 2.

32. Roberts, "Radio & Celebrities," 14.

33. "Remington Rand Marches On," *Advertising & Selling*, 15 March 1934, 56ff.

34. JWT Staff Meeting Minutes, 2 February 1932, 6, John W. Hartman Center for Sales, Advertising and Marketing History, Duke University, Durham, North Carolina (hereafter JWT Staff Meeting Minutes).

35. A television version aired from 1952 to 1957.

36. Du Pont press release, 27 September 1935, Box 36, Cavalcade Folder, Public Affairs Department, Accession 1410, Du Pont Records, Hagley Museum and Library, Wilmington, Delaware (hereafter Du Pont Records).

37. For a more extensive analysis of *Cavalcade of America*, see Bird, *"Better Living,"* especially chapters 3 and 5. See also Anne Boylan, "Women's History on the Radio: The Search for a Usable Past, 1935–1953," unpublished paper presented at Hagley Museum and Library, 2010.

38. Memo from W. S. Carpenter Jr. to Crawford H. Greenewalt, 10 November 1960, Box 4, Accession 1814, Greenewalt Papers, Du Pont Records.

39. Ibid.

40. "Information for Miss Betty Vaughn," Box 35, "Slogan" Folder, Public Affairs Records, Du Pont Records; George Albee, "The Du Pont 'Cavalcade of America,'" draft manuscript, ca. 1947, Box 11, Folder 23, Advertising Department Records, Accession 1803, Du Pont Records.

41. Albee, "The Du Pont 'Cavalcade of America.'"

42. Bird, *"Better Living,"* 109.

43. "The Cavalcade of America," Box 67, Folder 81, "Du Pont," NBC Records.

44. Anne Boylan argues that the departure of Roy Durstine from BBDO coincided with a diminution of the historians' role. Personal correspondence.

45. "Famous Playwrights, Novelists, Poets Among Authors of 'Cavalcade' Scripts," March 1949, Box 11, Folder 25, Advertising Department Records, Du Pont Records.

46. Dixon Ryan Fox and Arthur M. Schlesinger, eds., *The Cavalcade of America* (Springfield, Mass.: Milton Bradley Co., 1937), ix.

47. "Stars of Stage and Screen to Be Guest Artists on Du Pont Program," October 1935, Box 3, Folder 8, and Box 3, Folder 2, Advertising Department Records, Du Pont Records.

48. Albee, "The Du Pont 'Cavalcade of America,'" 7.

49. "Nathan Hale," Box 3, Folder 1, Advertising Department Records, Du Pont Records.

50. "An Examination of Cavalcade's Present Talent Budget," 20 April 1951, Box 4, Folder 16, Advertising Department Records, Du Pont Records.

51. Albee, "The Du Pont 'Cavalcade of America,'" 1, 5, 6.

52. William H. Hamilton, "Report on 'Cavalcade of America,'" 12 June 1947, Box 11, Folder 22, 8, Advertising Department Records, Du Pont Records.

53. Bird, *"Better Living,"* 200–1.

54. Hamilton, "Report on 'Cavalcade of America,'" 4.

55. BBDO, "Recommendation for Du Pont Company Advertising on Radio and Television for 1952," May 1951, Box 4, Folder 17, Advertising Department Records, Du Pont Records.

56. *Looking in on Cavalcade*, March 1953, vol. 1, no. 2, Box 7, Folder 6, Advertising Department Records, Du Pont Records.

57. Roberts, "Radio & Celebrities," 19.

58. Chester Bowles, interview, March 1963, 29, Oral History Research Office, Columbia University, New York (hereafter Bowles Interview).

59. For more on William Benton's role in radio, see my earlier article, Cynthia B. Meyers, "From Radio Ad Man to Radio Reformer: Senator William Benton's Broadcasting Career, 1930–60," *Journal of Radio and Audio Media*, vol. 16, no. 1 (2009): 17–29.

60. Benton claims he was fired for proposing that Batten merge with the up-and-coming agency Barton Durstine & Osborn. William Benton, interview, 83, Oral History Research Office, Columbia University, New York (hereafter Benton Interview).

61. Sidney Hyman, *The Lives of William Benton* (Chicago: University of Chicago Press, 1969), 121.

62. Interview with William Benton, in Studs Terkel, *Hard Times* (New York: Pantheon, 1970), 61.

63. Benton Interview, 73.

64. Bowles Interview, 23.

65. Ibid., 25.

66. Chet Dudley, "A History of Benton & Bowles," unpublished manuscript, ca. 1938, Box 8, Benton & Bowles Files; letter from William Benton to Elma Benton, 24 May 1932, Benton & Bowles Files, John W. Hartman Center for Sales, Advertising and Marketing History, Duke University, Durham, North Carolina (hereafter Benton & Bowles Files).

67. Atherton Hobler, "The Triangle of Marketing Success," unpublished manuscript, n.d., Box 19, Benton & Bowles Files, 99.

68. In 1932, General Foods granted more accounts to Benton & Bowles on the condition that they accept a new partner in the firm, Atherton Hobler. Benton & Bowles was reincorporated with Hobler as a one-third partner who also was heavily involved in radio and who stayed at the firm much longer than either founder. Hobler, "The Triangle of Marketing Success," 83–84.

69. Bowles Interview, 31; Gordon Webber, *Our Kind of People: The Story of the First Fifty Years at Benton & Bowles* (New York: Benton & Bowles, 1979), 32.

70. Bowles Interview, 32.

71. Hobler, "The Triangle of Marketing Success," 101.

72. Dudley, "A History of Benton & Bowles," 14.

73. Hobler, "The Triangle of Marketing Success," 102.

74. Letter from William Benton to Elma Benton, 8 February 1936; letter from William Benton to Elma Benton, 11 September 1934, Benton & Bowles Files.

75. Mark Pendergrast, *Uncommon Grounds: The History of Coffee and How It Transformed Our World* (New York: Basic Books, 2000), 193.

76. Terkel, *Hard Times*, 62.

77. Ibid., 63.

78. Chester Bowles, "Agency's Responsibility in Radio," *Printers' Ink Monthly*, July 1936, 81.

79. "A Presentation of the Services of Benton & Bowles," circa 1943, Box 8, Benton & Bowles Files.

80. Hobler, "The Triangle of Marketing Success," 101.

81. Ibid., 97.

82. Ibid.

83. Ibid.

84. Ibid., 98.

85. Emphasis and ellipsis in original. Michael Varencove, "The Peeled Ear," *Advertising & Selling*, 11 April 1935, 30, 54.

86. Terkel, *Hard Times*, 62. The character in the stage and film version of *Show Boat* was named Cap'n Andy, but the name was changed to Captain Henry for the radio program, probably because the radio program was only "inspired" by Jerome Kern's *Show Boat*. Pendergrast, *Uncommon Grounds*, 193.

87. *Saturday Evening Post*, 23 March 1935, 4. Author's collection.

88. Letter from William Benton to Randolph Catlin, 7 October 1935, Box 34, Folder 34, NBC Records, Wisconsin Historical Society, Madison (hereafter NBC Records). Advertisers disliked having their agency work for a direct competitor and so routinely forced agencies to quit accounts of competitors. In this case, because Colgate's advertising appropriation was much larger than Bristol-Myers', Benton & Bowles took the financially advantageous course, despite their very publicized success with *Town Hall Tonight*.

89. Hobler, "The Triangle of Marketing Success," 111–12.

90. Fred Allen, *Treadmill to Oblivion* (Boston: Little, Brown, 1954), 29.

91. Letter from A. Hobler to Roy Witmer, 10 May 1934; memo from John Royal to Roy Witmer, 14 May 1934, Box 24, Folder 12, NBC Records.

92. Memo from L. Titterton to Ed Hitz, 8 March 1937, Box 52, Folder 36, NBC Records.

93. Letter from William Benton to M. Aylesworth, 25 August 1933, Box 16, Folder 12, NBC Records.

94. Ibid.

95. Memo from Wayne Randall to Frank E. Mason, 26 April 1933, Box 34, Folder 34, NBC Records.

96. Ibid.

97. Bowles Interview, 39.

98. Letter from William Benton to Elma Benton, 11 January 1932, Benton & Bowles Files.

99. Hyman, *The Lives of William Benton*, 153.

100. Martin Sklar, *The Corporate Reconstruction of American Capitalism, 1890–1916: The Market, the Law, and Politics* (New York: Cambridge University Press, 1988).

101. Memo from Wayne Randall to Frank E. Mason, 26 April 1933, Box 34, Folder 34, NBC Records.

102. For more on *University of Chicago Round Table*, see David Goodman, *Radio's Civic Ambition* (New York: Oxford University Press, 2011), 194–99.

103. Quoted in Hyman, *The Lives of William Benton*, 296.

104. Emphasis in original. Letter from William Benton to Editors of the *New York Times*, 28 November 1944, Box 114, Folder 39, NBC Records.

105. Ibid.

106. Bowles Interview, 29.

107. Hobler, "Triangle of Marketing Success," 85.

108. Bowles Interview, 35.

8. Madison Avenue in Hollywood: J. Walter Thompson and *Kraft Music Hall*

1. For an excellent study of the interactions of the film and broadcasting industries, see Michele Hilmes, *Hollywood and Broadcasting: From Radio to Cable* (Urbana: University of Illinois Press, 1990).

2. Ibid., 71.

3. "Advertising Agencies," *Sales Management*, 1 November 1938, 70.

4. Hilmes, *Hollywood and Broadcasting*, 62.

5. John W. Swallow, *Midwife to an Octopus* (Encino, Calif.: Garden House Press, 1964), 82.

6. Ibid., 82.

7. "Hollywood and Radio," *Business Week*, 6 November 1937, 27.

8. Robert Landry has an interesting chart comparing the strategies of the film and radio industries in *This Fascinating Radio Business* (Indianapolis: Bobbs-Merrill, 1946), 217.

9. Ibid., 216.

10. Hilmes, *Hollywood and Broadcasting*, 56.

11. Richard B. Jewell, "Hollywood and Radio: Competition and Part-nership in the 1930s," *Historical Journal of Film, Radio and Television* 4, no. 2 (1984): 127–41.

12. Ibid., 138.

13. Hilmes argues that the ban was primarily a function of the studio/distributors' placating exhibitors who were concerned that radio would siphon off box office revenues. Hilmes, *Hollywood and Broadcasting*, 56.

14. Calvin Kuhl, "The Grim Reber," unpublished reminiscence, 1971, 36–37, JWT Writings and Speeches Files, John W. Hartman Center for Sales, Advertising and Marketing History, Duke University, Durham, North Carolina (hereafter JWT Writings and Speeches Files).

15. Julian Field, "When You Hitch Your Program to a Star," *Advertising & Selling*, February 1938, 54.

16. "Hollywood and Radio," *Business Week*, 6 November 1937, 27.

17. "Advertising Agencies," 70.

18. Tom Lewis, "It's Belt-Tightening Time in Hollywood," *The Advertiser*, July–August 1947, 18.

19. "The Revolt against Radio," *Fortune*, March 1947, 103.

20. Charles Hull Wolfe, *Modern Radio Advertising* (New York: Printers' Ink Publishing Co., 1949), 21.

21. Arthur Wertheim, *Radio Comedy* (New York: Oxford University Press, 1979), 266.

22. Wolfe, *Modern Radio Advertising*, 18.

23. Lewis, "It's Belt-Tightening Time in Hollywood," 18. Tom Lewis was married to film star Loretta Young from 1940 to 1969.

24. P. H. Erbes Jr., "Hollywooden Idols," *Printers' Ink*, 18 November 1937, 18.

25. James Webb Young, *The Diary of an Ad Man* (Chicago: Advertising Publications, 1944), 199.

26. Field, "When You Hitch Your Program to a Star," 52.

27. Mr. Crampton, JWT Staff Meeting Minutes, 7 December 1932, 8, John W. Hartman Center for Sales, Advertising and Marketing History, Duke University, Durham, North Carolina (hereafter JWT Staff Meeting Minutes).

28. Ralph M. Hower, *The History of an Advertising Agency: N. W. Ayer & Son at Work, 1869–1949*, rev. ed. (Cambridge, Mass.: Harvard University Press, 1949), 191.

29. During the 1920s and into the 1930s, conscious of itself as a precedent-setting, historically significant agency, JWT took the unusual step of keeping word-for-word transcripts of its staff meetings, in which everything from strategy to radio programming to client relations was discussed. JWT also wrote up case files for each client to document its work. Consequently, much of what can be documented about advertising agencies and radio is from the JWT perspective.

30. Stephen Fox, *The Mirror Makers* (New York: William Morrow, 1984), 30. The following summary relies heavily on Fox's account.

31. Ibid., 80.

32. For an analysis of how Resor worked to turn advertising into a "science-based enterprise," see Peggy J. Kreshel, "The 'Culture' of J. Walter Thompson, 1915–1925," *Public Relations Review* 16, no. 3 (Fall 1990): 80–93.

33. Fox, *Mirror Makers*, 86–87.

34. Howard Henderson, "Some Basic Roots of the J. Walter Thompson Company," unpublished manuscript, November 1959 draft, JWT Writings and Speeches Files.

35. Reproduced in Julian Lewis Watkins, *The 100 Greatest Advertisements* (New York: Dover, 1959), 82.

36. JWT Staff Meeting Minutes, 14 January 1930, 7; JWT Staff Meeting Minutes, 2 April 1930, 11.

37. JWT Staff Meeting Minutes, 2 February 1932, 1; JWT Staff Meeting Minutes, 21 December 1932, 7.

38. JWT Staff Meeting Minutes, 13 January 1931, 5; memo from Roy Witmer to Mark Woods, 21 July 1933, Box 22, Folder 28, NBC Records, Wisconsin Historical Society, Madison (hereafter NBC Records).

39. JWT *Newsflash*, vol. 1, no. 4, 3 February 1937.

40. Kuhl, "The Grim Reber," 25.

41. ". . . Now on the Networks," JWT advertisement, *Printers' Ink*, 16 January 1936, 8–9. Programs listed included *Bakers' Broadcast* (Fleischmann's Yeast); *Buck Rogers* (Cream of Wheat); *Major Bowes' Amateur Hour* (Chase & Sanborn Coffee); *The Fleischmann Hour with Rudy Vallee* (Fleischmann's Yeast); *The Jergens Program* (Jergens); *Kraft Music Hall* (Kraft); *Lux Radio Theatre* (Lever Bros.); *N.T.G. and His Girls* (Bromo-Seltzer); *Og, Son of Fire* (Libby, McNeill & Libby); *One Man's Family* (Royal Desserts); *Roses and Drums* (Union Central Life Insurance); *Shell Chateau* (Shell); and *The Swift Studio Party* (Swift).

42. *Fortune*, [no month] 1933, 85. Author's collection.

43. "Royal Desserts: History of Radio Advertising," JWT Account Files, John W. Hartman Center for Sales, Advertising and Marketing History, Duke University, Durham, North Carolina (hereafter JWT Account Files).

44. Robert Colwell, "Chase & Sanborn Hour," no date, JWT Writings and Speeches Files.

45. JWT Staff Meeting Minutes, 22 June 1932, 5.

46. For Janet MacRorie's analysis of Fleischmann's Yeast radio advertising, see Chapter 4.

47. JWT Staff Meeting Minutes, 22 June 1932, 4.

48. JWT Staff Meeting Minutes, 14 April 1931, 4.

49. JWT Staff Meeting Minutes, 1 December 1931, 7.

50. JWT Staff Meeting Minutes, 21 December 1932, 8–10.

51. Memo from Carroll Carroll to Robert Bernstein, 5 December 1963, JWT Company History Files, John W. Hartman Center for Sales, Advertising and Marketing History, Duke University, Durham, North Carolina (hereafter JWT Company History Files).

52. Kuhl, "The Grim Reber," 9.

53. Letter from Carroll Carroll to Abel Green, 20 December 1946, Carroll Carroll Papers, John W. Hartman Center for Sales, Advertising and Marketing History, Duke University, Durham, North Carolina (hereafter Carroll Papers).

54. Rudy Vallee, *Let the Chips Fall . . .* (Harrisburg, Penn.: Stackpole Books, 1975), 184.

55. Fox, *Mirror Makers*, 89.

56. JWT *Forum*, 9 November 1937, 2.

57. For an excellent analysis of a *Lux Radio Theatre* broadcast, see Hilmes, *Hollywood and Broadcasting*, ch. 4.

58. JWT *Forum*, 9 November 1937, 2–3.

59. Carroll Carroll, *None of Your Business: Or, My Life with J. Walter Thompson (Confessions of a Renegade Radio Writer)* (New York: Cowles, 1970), 127; Sidney J. Bernstein notes, n.d., JWT Company History Files.

60. Bernstein notes, JWT Company History Files.

61. Kuhl, "The Grim Reber," 35; "Medal Award to John U. Reber," *Advertising & Selling*, 15 February 1939, 73.

62. Bernstein notes, JWT Company History Files.

63. "Kraft Radio: Account History," n.d., Box 9, 1, JWT Company History Files.

64. John H. Platt, "We Are on the Air," *Cheesekraft*, February 1929, 11.

65. Kuhl, "The Grim Reber," 14–17.

66. Carroll, *None of Your Business*, 84–85; Abel Green, "Ad Agency's V.P., Reber, Sits on Top of Jolson-Whiteman Hour on Roof," *Variety*, 8 August 1933, 34.

67. For more on Crosby and *Kraft Music Hall*, see Gary Giddens, *Bing Crosby: A Pocketful of Dreams, The Early Years, 1903–40* (Boston: Little, Brown, 2001), ch. 20.

68. John H. Platt, "52 Shows a Year," speech delivered at Chicago Federated Advertising Club, 5 May 1938, Kraft Archives, Morton Grove, Illinois.

69. Carroll Carroll, "The Kraft Music Hall Story," in T. Sennett, ed., *The Old-Time Radio Book* (New York: Pyramid Books, 1976), 70.

70. Carroll, *None of Your Business*, 160.

71. "'Crosby-isms' Win Praise as Smart Airwave Patter," *Cheesekraft*, May 1938, 25.

72. Carroll, *None of Your Business*, 139.

73. "Hail, KMH!" *Kraftsman*, October/November 1943; Platt, "52 Shows a Year"; Carroll, "The Kraft Music Hall Story," 69.

74. Letter from John Reber to Carroll Carroll, 9 February 1937, Carroll Papers.

75. Telegram from Carroll Carroll to John Reber, 5 December 1941, Carroll Papers.

76. Letter from Carroll Carroll to John Reber, 2 July 1943, Carroll Papers.

77. Letter from John Reber to Carroll Carroll, 22 July 1940, Carroll Papers.

78. "How Kraft Uses the Air: 1933–52," *Sponsor*, 5 May 1952, 26.

79. "The Kraft Mouthpiece," *Kraftsman*, March 1966, 4.

80. Platt, "52 Shows a Year."

81. Ibid.

82. *Kraft Music Hall*, broadcast on 5 June 1941.

83. *Fortune*, [no month] 1941, 107. Author's collection.

84. Ibid.

85. Crosby went on to star in a transcribed (recorded) program for Philco on ABC, which some observers believed was a "direct attack" on NBC's and CBS's insistence on live broadcasts. "Crosby's Radio Revolution," *Broadcasting/Telecasting*, 6 January 1947, 75.

86. "Bing Crosby Sued by Kraft Foods Co.," *Broadcasting/Telecasting*, 7 January 1946, 63.

87. For a thorough account of JWT's early television programming, see Michael Mashon, "NBC, J. Walter Thompson, and the Evolution of Prime-Time Television Programming and Sponsorship, 1946–58" (PhD diss., University of Maryland–College Park, 1996).

9. Advertising and Commercial Radio during World War II, 1942–45

1. Memo from Alex Osborn to Bruce Barton, 25 March 1942, Bruce Barton Papers, Wisconsin Historical Society, Madison (hereafter Barton Papers).

2. Gerd Horten, *Radio Goes to War* (Berkeley: University of California Press, 2002); Michele Hilmes, *Radio Voices: American Broadcasting, 1922–1952* (Minneapolis: University of Minnesota Press, 1997). See also Barbara Dianne Savage, *Broadcasting Freedom: Radio, War, and the Politics of Race, 1938–1948* (Chapel Hill: University of North Carolina Press, 1999).

3. Horten, *Radio Goes to War*, 7; John Morton Blum, *V Was for Victory: Politics and American Culture During World War II* (New York: Harcourt Brace Jovanovich, 1976), 38–39; Michael J. Socolow, "'News Is a Weapon': Domestic Radio Propaganda and Broadcast Journalism in America, 1939–1944," *American Journalism* 24, no. 3 (2007): 125.

4. Frank Fox, *Madison Avenue Goes to War: The Strange Military Career of American Advertising, 1941–45* (Provo, Utah: Brigham Young University Press, 1975), 26.

5. Blum, *V Was for Victory*, 122–23.

6. Fox, *Madison Avenue Goes to War*, 40.

7. Ralph M. Hower, *The History of an Advertising Agency: N. W. Ayer & Son at Work, 1869–1949*, rev. ed. (Cambridge, Mass.: Harvard University Press, 1949), 184.

8. "The History of Velveeta," February 1953, 26, JWT Account Files, John W. Hartman Center for Sales, Advertising and Marketing History, Duke University, Durham, North Carolina (hereafter JWT Account Files).

9. Fox, *Madison Avenue Goes to War*, 93.

10. BBDO *Newsletter*, February 1966, 31.

11. "Monthly Digest of Network Advertising," *Printers' Ink Monthly*, February 1941, 30.

12. Christopher Sterling and John Kittross, *Stay Tuned: A Concise History of American Broadcasting* (Belmont, Calif.: Wadsworth, 1978), 516. These numbers were calculated slightly differently from the *Printers' Ink* figures;

however, for purposes of comparison, it is clear that advertising billings almost doubled over the course of the war.

13. Fox, *Madison Avenue Goes to War*, 45–46.

14. Letter from Bruce Barton to Henry G. Weaver, 9 November 1940, Barton Papers.

15. Hower, *History of an Advertising Agency*, rev. ed., 183.

16. *Life*, 5 July 1943, 5.

17. Willard Chevalier, "Advertising in War and Postwar," speech to Advertising Federation of America, June 1943, New York, New York.

18. Letter from Bruce Barton to Henry G. Weaver, 9 November 1940, Barton Papers.

19. *Life*, 29 March 1943, 12.

20. Ibid., 113.

21. For more on prewar propaganda efforts, see Hilmes, *Radio Voices*, ch. 8.

22. Edward M. Kirby, "References and Recollections of Historic Highlights in American Broadcasting in World War II," 1964, 11–12, Wisconsin Historical Society, Madison (hereafter Kirby Recollections).

23. Ibid., 12.

24. R. A. Applegate to R. R. M. Carpenter, 14 October 1942, Box 832, Folder 16, Carpenter Papers, Du Pont Records, Hagley Museum and Library, Wilmington, Delaware.

25. Arthur Wertheim, *Radio Comedy* (New York: Oxford University Press, 1979), 273.

26. *G.I. Journal*, broadcast on 29 April 1944.

27. Letter from Elmer Davis to Carroll Carroll, 27 October 1942, Carroll Carroll Papers, John W. Hartman Center for Sales, Advertising and Marketing History, Duke University, Durham, North Carolina (hereafter Carroll Papers).

28. Carroll Carroll, *None of Your Business* (New York: Cowles Book Co., 1970), 223.

29. Ibid., 226.

30. Pat Weaver with Thomas Coffey, *Best Seat in the House: The Golden Years of Radio and Television* (New York: Knopf, 1994), 148–49.

31. Ibid., 149.

32. Ibid., 148.

33. Kirby Recollections, 16.

34. Ibid., 21.

35. Ibid., 23.

36. Ibid.

37. See Blum, *V Was for Victory;* Clayton R. Koppes and Gregory D. Black, *Hollywood Goes to War: How Politics, Profits, and Propaganda Shaped World War II Movies* (New York: Free Press, 1987); Horten, *Radio Goes to War;* Fox, *Madison Avenue Goes to War.*

38. Richard W. Steele, "The Great Debate: Roosevelt, the Media, and the Coming of the War, 1940–41," *Journal of American History* 71 (June 1984): 69–92; Allan M. Winkler, *The Politics of Propaganda: The Office of War Information, 1942–1945* (New Haven, Conn.: Yale University Press, 1978).

39. Norman Corwin, "Counting Losses," *Westways,* June 1975, 70–72.

40. See Neil Verma, *Theater of the Mind: Imagination, Aesthetics, and American Radio Drama* (Chicago: University of Chicago Press, 2012).

41. Horten, *Radio Goes to War,* 44, 62.

42. "Radio Coordination," unsigned, undated memo, Office of Facts and Figures, ca. Winter 1941–42, Box 13, 2, William B. Lewis Collection, Howard Gotlieb Archival Research Center at Boston University, Boston, Massachusetts (hereafter Lewis Collection).

43. William B. Lewis, "Radio Goes to War," speech, no date [ca. 1943], Box 9, Folder 2, 37, Lewis Collection.

44. Socolow argues that Lewis and Meservy were actually representing the interests of the networks and ultimately undermined the propaganda effort by preventing the establishment of a government-controlled broadcast network. "'News Is a Weapon': Domestic Radio Propaganda and Broadcast Journalism in America, 1939–1944," 111, 125.

45. A "curtain speech" is given at the end of a theatrical performance. William B. Lewis, speech to Advertising Council, March 1942, 9, Lewis Collection.

46. Emphasis in original. William B. Lewis, "Radio Coordination," speech, 20 January 1942, Box 9, 3, 6, Lewis Collection.

47. William B. Lewis, speech to Advertising Council, March 1942, Lewis Collection.

48. Letter from Archibald MacLeish to President Franklin Roosevelt, 8 April 1942, Lewis Collection.

49. Lewis, "Radio Goes to War."

50. William B. Lewis diary, 21 January 1942, Box 26, Lewis Collection.

51. Ellipses added; emphasis in original. OFF Radio Division War Information Fact Sheet, "Why Salvage Is Important," no date, Box 8, Lewis Collection.

52. Ibid. Ellipses in original.

53. William B. Lewis diary, 11 April 1942, Box 26, Lewis Collection.

54. William B. Lewis, speech to Advertising Council, March 1942, 8.

55. Interview of Anne Hummert by Philip F. Napoli, 7 June 1991.

56. Lewis, "Radio Goes to War," 21.

57. "Messages Assigned on Network Allocation Plan," April 1942, Lewis Collection.

58. Ferdinand Kuhn Jr., quoted in letter from William B. Lewis, 22 June 1942, Lewis Collection.

59. Letter from William B. Lewis to Ferdinand Kuhn Jr., 22 June 1942, Lewis Collection.

60. Memo from William B. Lewis to Miller McClintock, William Paley, Niles Trammell, and Mark Woods, 14 December 1942, Lewis Collection.

61. Ibid.

62. John D. Morris, "The OWI on the Domestic Radio Front," *New York Times,* 31 January 1943; Horten, *Radio Goes to War,* 7.

63. Lewis Wood, "Writers Who Quit OWI Charge It Bars 'Full Truth' for 'Ballyhoo,'" *New York Times,* 16 April 1943, 1, 13.

64. Ibid., 13.

65. Francis Brennan, quoted in Hilmes, *Radio Voices,* 249.

66. Wood, "Writers Who Quit OWI," 1.

67. Jackson Lears, *Fables of Abundance: A Cultural History of Advertising in America* (New York: Basic Books, 1994), 53; Thorstein Veblen, *The Theory of the Leisure Class* (New York: Macmillan, 1899). The concern that advertising tricks consumers with emotional appeals and associations informs the advertising critique of those who conclude advertising should include only product information. For example, see Raymond Williams, "Advertising: The Magic System," in *Problems in Materialism and Culture* (London: New Left Books, 1962, 1980), 170–95; and Inger Stole, *Advertising on Trial* (Urbana: University of Illinois Press, 2006).

68. See Horten, *Radio Goes to War*; Hilmes, *Radio Voices,* 250; Blum, *V Was for Victory,* 38–39.

69. Blum, *V Was for Victory,* 38.

70. Gardner Cowles Jr., "Advertising and the Home Front," speech, 5 February 1943, National Association of Broadcasters.

71. Charles F. McGovern, *Sold American: Consumption and Citizenship, 1890–1945* (Chapel Hill: University of North Carolina Press, 2006), 336.

72. There is no way to measure definitively the success of Lewis's policies (e.g., would the United States have won the war without them?). However, there is some evidence that specific campaigns, such as the Need for Nurses, which recruited women for nursing positions, may have been successful. Charles A. Siepmann, "American Radio in Wartime: An Interim Survey of the OWI's Radio Bureau," in Frank Stanton and Paul Lazarsfeld, eds., *Radio Research, 1942–1943* (New York: Arno Press, 1944, 1979), 129.

73. One recommendation was that the networks take control of programming away from advertisers and agencies. Lewis pointed out that radio was unlike every other advertising medium: "There is no precedent for such a wholesale surrender of editorial control." Report to William Paley, 1944, Box 4, 55, Lewis Collection.

74. For example, see Horten, *Radio Goes to War*.

75. Corwin, "Counting Losses," 71.

76. A 1945 OWI report claimed that under the Network Allocation Plan, 410 programs carried 10,920 messages to "an estimated listener-impression record of 460,000,000 per week." "OWI Issues Radio Report," *Radio Daily*, 3 January 1945, 1, 6.

77. For a more thorough discussion of how comedy programs integrated war propaganda, see Horten, *Radio Goes to War*, ch. 5.

78. *Kraft Music Hall*, broadcast on 1 April 1943.

79. *Texaco Star Theater* with Fred Allen, broadcast on 9 January 1944.

80. Fred Allen, *Treadmill to Oblivion* (Boston: Little, Brown, 1954), 103–4.

81. For a discussion of Irna Phillips's serials during the war, see Horten, *Radio Goes to War*, ch. 6.

82. Emphasis in original. Patricia Murray, "Radio Serials Transmit War Messages and Solve Problems Through Stories," *Printers' Ink*, 3 September 1943, 22.

83. Kirby Recollections, 32.

84. "Service Soap Opera," *Time*, 20 April 1942.

85. Mitchell V. Charnley, *News by Radio* (New York: Macmillan, 1948), 46.

86. G. W. Johnstone, "Commercial Wartime News Standards Are Fixed by Networks," *Printers' Ink*, 20 March 1942, 35.

10. On a Treadmill to Oblivion: The Peak and Sudden Decline of Network Radio

1. *The Best of H. T. Webster: A Memorial Collection* (New York: Simon & Schuster, 1953), 227.

2. "The Revolt against Radio," *Fortune*, March 1947, 102.

3. Robert Ruark, quoted in "The Revolt against Radio," 101.

4. Dr. Louis Berg, quoted in James Thurber, *The Beast in Me and Other Animals* (New York: Harcourt, Brace, 1948), 251.

5. "The Revolt against Radio," 101.

6. "WQXR Extends Its Ban," *New York Times*, 31 March 1944, 75.

7. Timothy Taylor, *The Sounds of Capitalism: Advertising, Music, and the Conquest of Culture* (Chicago: University of Chicago Press, 2012), 88.

8. Charles Hull Wolfe, *Modern Radio Advertising* (New York: Printers' Ink Publishing Co., 1949), 22.

9. "Blue Network Sold to Former Ad Man Edward J. Noble for $8,000,000," *Printers' Ink*, 6 August 1943, 33.

10. Laurence Bergreen, *Look Now, Pay Later: The Rise of Network Broadcasting* (Garden City, N.Y.: Doubleday, 1980), 132.

11. Federal Communications Commission, *Public Service Responsibility of Broadcast Licenses* (Washington: FCC, 7 March 1946).

12. "The Revolt against Radio," 103.

13. Ibid., 102.

14. Harry Lewis Bird, *This Fascinating Advertising Business* (Indianapolis: Bobbs-Merrill, 1947), 232; Herta Herzog and Marion Harper Jr., "The Anatomy of the Radio Commercial," *Advertising & Selling*, July 1948, 69.

15. Wolfe, *Modern Radio Advertising*, 602.

16. "The Revolt against Radio," 172.

17. John Gray Peatman, ed., *Radio and Business: Proceedings of the First Annual Conference on Radio and Business*, City College, New York, New York, 22–23 May 1945, 31.

18. Niles Trammell, "Advertising in the Public Interest," address to National Association of Broadcasters, 24 October 1946, 9.

19. David Goodman addresses this debate thoroughly, analyzing programs such as *The University of Chicago Round Table* and *America's Town Meeting of the Air. Radio's Civic Ambition: American Broadcasting and Democracy in the 1930s* (New York: Oxford University Press, 2011).

20. When asked a follow-up question of what is not a public service program, Carlin replied, "Those are the programs we don't put on the air." Peatman, ed., *Radio and Business*, 25.

21. Trammell, "Advertising in the Public Interest," 8.

22. Ibid., 12.

23. Frederic Wakeman, *The Hucksters* (New York: Rinehart & Co., 1946), 24.

24. Ibid., 25.

25. "Between the Lines," *Printers' Ink*, 26 July 1946, 79.

26. Hill articulated his advertising theory in a pamphlet, "Radio: A Modern Advertising Force: Its Proper Commercial Use," published by the American Tobacco Company, 1938.

27. One version of this story appears in Fred Allen, *Treadmill to Oblivion* (Boston: Little, Brown, 1954), 14.

28. William Paley, *As It Happened* (Garden City, N.Y.: Doubleday, 1979), 84.

29. Dan Golenpaul, interview, July 1964, 178, Oral History Research Office, Columbia University, New York.

30. Charles M. Sievert, "Reporter's Notebook," *The Advertiser*, November 1952, 2.

31. Quoted in Alan Havig, "Frederic Wakeman's *The Hucksters* and the Postwar Debate over Commercial Radio," *Journal of Broadcasting* 28, no. 2 (Spring 1984): 196.

32. "MGM's Hucksters," *Tide*, 4 July 1947, 19.

33. Memo from Charles P. Hammond to Niles Trammell, 26 June 1947, Box 115, Folder 17, NBC Records, Wisconsin Historical Society, Madison (hereafter NBC Records).

34. Memo from Syd Eiges to Niles Trammell, 1 July 1947, Box 115, Folder 17, NBC Records.

35. "The Revolt against Radio," 102.

36. For a different interpretation of *The Hucksters* phenomenon, see Kathy M. Newman, *Radio Active: Advertising and Consumer Activism, 1935–1947* (Berkeley: University of California Press, 2004), 169–74.

37. Memo from Arthur Jacobson to Niles Trammell, 28 September 1946, NBC Records; letter from John McMillan to Niles Trammell, 29 April 1940, NBC Records.

38. Wolfe, *Modern Radio Advertising*, 9.

39. Memo from Bruce Barton to Ben Duffy, 4 April 1950, Bruce Barton Papers, Wisconsin Historical Society, Madison (hereafter Barton Papers).

40. Wolfe, *Modern Radio Advertising*, 22.

41. Russ Johnston, *Marion Harper: An Unauthorized Biography* (Chicago: Crain Books, 1982), 37, 40.

42. James Playsted Wood, *The Story of Advertising* (New York: Ronald Press Co., 1958), 415; Christopher H. Sterling and John M. Kittross, *Stay Tuned: A Concise History of American Broadcasting* (Belmont, Calif.: Wadsworth, 1978), 243, 254, 533.

43. Sterling and Kittross, *Stay Tuned*, 512.

44. Ibid., 260, 516.

45. Eric Rothenbuhler and Tom McCourt, "Radio Redefines Itself, 1947–1962," in Michele Hilmes and Jason Loviglio, eds., *Radio Reader* (New York: Routledge, 2002), 367–87.

46. Michael Mashon, "NBC, J. Walter Thompson, and the Evolution of Prime-Time Television Programming and Sponsorship, 1946–58" (PhD diss., University of Maryland–College Park, 1996), 115.

47. Sterling and Kittross, *Stay Tuned*, 516.

48. Alexander Russo, *Points on the Dial* (Durham, N.C.: Duke University Press, 2010), ch. 4.

49. Weston Hill, "All Through the Day," *Radio Showmanship*, November 1943, 369; Wolfe, *Modern Radio Advertising*, 18.

50. Frederic Ziv, "Twenty Years—Past and Future," *The Advertiser*, October 1950, 66.

51. Ziv's production company would soon become a top packager of television programs.

52. For a discussion of the importance of transcriptions throughout the radio era, see Russo, *Points on the Dial*, ch. 3.

53. Patricia Murray, "Cooperative Radio Programs," *Printers' Ink*, 21 December 1945, 44.

54. Tom Lewis, "It's Belt-Tightening Time in Hollywood," *The Advertiser*, July–August 1947, 32; JWT *Newsletter*, 11 August 1947, 2, John W. Hartman Center for Sales, Advertising and Marketing History, Duke University, Durham, North Carolina.

55. Correspondence among Ozzie Nelson, Sidney Strotz, and Niles Trammell, December 1948, Box 115, Folder 38, NBC Records.

56. Sally Bedell Smith, *In All His Glory: The Life of William S. Paley* (New York: Simon & Schuster, 1990), 259.

57. Memo from F. Silvernail to Bruce Barton, 22 September 1943, Barton Papers.

58. Sterling and Kittross, *Stay Tuned*, 535.

59. JWT Staff Meeting Minutes, 11 July 1928, 5; JWT Staff Meeting Minutes, 12 August 1930, 1, John W. Hartman Center for Sales, Advertising and Marketing History, Duke University, Durham, North Carolina (hereafter JWT Staff Meeting Minutes).

60. Edgar Felix, "Predicts Television Will Be Greatest Advertising Medium," *Broadcast Advertising*, September 1931, 21.

61. Bird, *This Fascinating Advertising Business*, 237.

62. Memo from Carroll Carroll to Danny Danker et al., 28 April 1944, Carroll Carroll Papers, John W. Hartman Center for Sales, Advertising and Marketing History, Duke University, Durham, North Carolina (hereafter Carroll Papers).

63. JWT *Newsletter*, 20 December 1946, 2; JWT *Newsletter*, 18 November 1946; Kraft Account History, Box 9, JWT Account Files, John W. Hartman Center for Sales, Advertising and Marketing History, Duke University, Durham, North Carolina.

64. Bob Foreman, "Listening and Looking," *Advertising Agency and Advertising & Selling*, September 1949, 21.

65. Bill Hendricks and Montgomery Orr, *Showmanship in Advertising* (New York: Showmen's Trade Review, 1949), 217.

66. Fred Coe, "A Program Producer Evaluates Commercials," *Television Magazine*, September 1949, 13.

67. Edgar Kobak, Television Seminars, 8 June 1944, 7, Radio Executives Club Papers, Wisconsin Historical Society, Madison.

68. Victor Armstrong, "Obstacles Facing Television," *Printers' Ink Monthly*, October 1936, 50.

69. Roy T. Ragatz, "Television—A Revolution or a Gadget?" *Advertising & Selling*, 20 May 1937, 38.

70. Douglas Stapleton, "Television Audience Will Be Smaller But More Attentive," *Printers' Ink*, 4 August 1944, 20.

71. Ibid.

72. Jack Miller, "The Effect of Television on Advertising," speech at Radio Executives Club, 17 August 1944, 7.

352 | Notes to pages 269–74

73. James S. Tyler, "Is Advertising Ready for Television?" *Advertising & Selling*, 12 September 1935, 23.

74. Emphasis in original. E. P. H. James, "How Will Television Affect Other Advertising Media?" *Printers' Ink*, 13 August 1948, 30.

75. Charles Durban, "The Advertiser's View of Television," speech at Radio Executives Club, 13 November 1947.

76. Emphasis in original. Fred Fidler, "Television May Lead to Revolution in Selling," *Advertising Agency and Advertising & Selling*, June 1949, 53.

77. Lawrence R. Samuel, *Brought to You By: Postwar Television Advertising* (Austin: University of Texas Press, 2001), 19, 20, 36.

78. *The Goldbergs*, broadcast on 12 September 1949. Accessed at http://archive.org/details/theGoldbergs-12September1949 on 12 January 2013.

79. Mashon, "NBC, J. Walter Thompson, and the Evolution of Prime-Time Television Programming," 123.

80. Ned Midgley, *The Advertising and Business Side of Radio* (New York: Prentice-Hall, 1948), 95.

81. Memo from W. W. Crider to Bruce Barton, 30 August 1948, Barton Papers.

82. Charlie Brower, *Me, and Other Advertising Geniuses* (Garden City, N.Y.: Doubleday, 1974), 213.

83. Mashon, "NBC, J. Walter Thompson, and the Evolution of Prime-Time Television Programming," 84.

84. Thomas F. Harrington, "Can an Advertising Agency Handle Television at a Profit?" *Advertising Agency and Advertising & Selling*, May 1949, 49ff.

85. Ibid., 51.

86. Memo from Tax Cumings to Ben Duffy, 23 August 1949, Barton Papers.

87. Ellipsis in original. *Television Magazine*, February 1949, 4.

88. Armstrong, "Obstacles Facing Television," 71–72.

89. Leslie Pearl, "I Remember Madison Avenue," *Advertising & Selling*, 4 July 1935, 22, 40.

90. "Outline for Wm. A. Hart Talk to DuPont Circle, Atlanta, March 13, 1953," Box 12, Folder 6, 8, Advertising Department Records, Accession 1803, Du Pont Records, Hagley Museum and Library, Wilmington, Delaware (hereafter Du Pont Records).

91. Letter from J. Warren Kinsman to Crawford H. Greenewalt, 12 April 1949, Box 4, Folder 1, Crawford Greenewalt Papers, Accession 1814, Du Pont Records.

92. Mashon, "NBC, J. Walter Thompson, and the Evolution of Prime-Time Television Programming," 101; letter from Robert Colwell to Carroll Carroll, 10 February 1946, 5, Carroll Papers.

93. Untitled article, *Variety*, ca. May 1947, copy in NBC Records.

94. Mashon, "NBC, J. Walter Thompson, and the Evolution of Prime-Time Television Programming," 114–15.

95. "The Development of the Packager," undated, unsigned memo, N. W. Ayer Archives.

96. Ibid.

97. So, for example, packager-produced quiz shows such as *$64,000 Question*, *21*, *What's My Line*, and *Dotto* dominated network schedules by the end of the 1950s—a reign ended only by the quiz show scandals of 1958 when it became public that many contests were prearranged for maximum dramatic effect.

98. My analysis of Weaver's role also appears in Cynthia B. Meyers, "The Problems with Sponsorship in Broadcasting, 1930s–50s: Perspectives from the Advertising Industry," *Historical Journal of Film, Radio and Television* 31, no. 3 (September 2011): 355–72.

99. Pat Weaver with Thomas M. Coffey, *The Best Seat in the House: The Golden Years of Radio and Television* (New York: Knopf, 1994), 81.

100. Ibid., 165.

101. Ibid., 164.

102. Pat Weaver, "Discussion of Television," speech, NBC Convention, 7–9 September 1949, Box 118, Folder 30, NBC Records.

103. Memo from Pat Weaver, 26 September 1949, Box 118, Folder 5, 1, NBC Records.

104. Weaver, "Discussion of Television," 9.

105. Memo from Pat Weaver, 26 September 1949, Box 118, Folder 5, 2, NBC Records.

106. The head of Foote Cone & Belding (the agency descended from Lord & Thomas) wrote David Sarnoff in 1953 suggesting that television programming should be a network function and that advertising be placed as in magazines. Letter from Fairfax Cone to David Sarnoff, 28 July 1953, NBC Records. A letter from Young & Rubicam head Raymond Rubicam to William Benton similarly objected to sponsor control of programming as undermining the broadcast medium. Letter from Raymond Rubicam to William Benton, 3 October 1951, Box 7, Barton Papers. See also "Can TV Survive Advertising? A

Debate by Raymond Rubicam and Maurice B. Mitchell," *Saturday Review of Literature*, 3 November 1951, 24ff.

107. Weaver, *Best Seat in the House*, 180.

108. Letter from A. J. McGinness to Walter E. Myers, 29 September 1949, Box 118, Folder 11, NBC Records.

109. Unsent letter from Pat Weaver to A. J. McGinness, 11 October 1949, Box 118, Folder 11, 5, NBC Records.

110. Weaver, *Best Seat in the House*, 190–91.

111. Michele Hilmes has questioned the notion that Weaver was the "author" of the magazine plan, pointing out the use of participating sponsorship in daytime radio. Hilmes, *Radio Voices*, 277–87. Alexander Russo likewise documents the history of multiple sponsorship and interstitial advertising on radio well before their use on networks, *Points on the Dial*, ch. 4. Robert I. Garver, *Successful Radio Advertising with Sponsor Participation Programs* (New York: Prentice-Hall, 1949).

112. Memo from Pat Weaver, 26 September 1949, Box 118, Folder 5, 1, NBC Records.

113. James L. Baughman, *Same Time, Same Station: Creating American Television, 1948–1961* (Baltimore: Johns Hopkins University Press, 2007), 301.

Conclusion

1. Emphasis in original. David Potter, *People of Plenty: Economic Abundance and the American Character* (Chicago: University of Chicago Press, 1954), 167–68.

2. James Livingston, *Against Thrift: Why Consumer Culture Is Good for the Economy, the Environment, and Your Soul* (New York: Basic Books, 2011), 125.

3. For more on this, see Cynthia B. Meyers, "The Problems with Sponsorship in Broadcasting, 1930s–50s: Perspectives from the Advertising Industry," *Historical Journal of Film, Radio and Television* 31, no. 3 (September 2011): 355–72.

4. See Charles McGovern, *Sold American* (Chapel Hill: University of North Carolina Press, 2006).

5. Roland Marchand, *Advertising the American Dream* (Berkeley: University of California Press, 1985), 41.

6. Key scholarship on the transition to television includes William Boddy, *Fifties Television* (Urbana: University of Illinois Press, 1990); James L.

Baughman, *Same Time, Same Station* (Baltimore: Johns Hopkins University Press, 2007); Michael Mashon, "NBC, J. Walter Thompson, and the Evolution of Prime-Time Television Programming and Sponsorship, 1946–58" (PhD diss., University of Maryland–College Park, 1996).

7. I explore some of the post-radio developments in advertising and television in Cynthia B. Meyers, "From Sponsorship to Spots: Advertising and the Development of Electronic Media," in Jennifer Holt and Alisa Perren, eds., *Media Industries: History, Theory, and Method* (Oxford: Wiley-Blackwell, 2009): 69–80.

8. Chris Anderson, *Hollywood TV: The Studio System in the Fifties* (Austin: University of Texas Press, 1994).

9. Christopher Sterling and John Kittross, *Stay Tuned: A Concise History of American Broadcasting* (Belmont, Calif.: Wadsworth, 1978), 516, 518.

10. Barry Shanks, "Network Television: Advertising Agencies and Sponsors," in J. W. Wright, ed., *The Commercial Connection* (New York: Dell Publishing, 1979), 96.

11. Sterling and Kittross, *Stay Tuned*, 394.

12. Jonathan Price, *The Best Thing on TV: Commercials* (New York: Penguin, 1978), 165.

13. Current advertising awards include the Clios, the Addys, the Effies, and the Golden Lions, among others.

14. John Battelle, "Gone in 30 Seconds," *Business 2.0*, November 2003, 68.

15. Arto Joensuu, "Owned, Bought, Earned Media Evolves," accessed at http://artojoensuu.wordpress.com/2011/02/06/own-bought-earned-media-evolves/ on 26 March 2012.

16. Claire Cain Miller, "Ad Agencies Fashion Their Own Horn, and Toot It," *New York Times*, 31 December 2008.

17. Ibid.

Bibliography

Archival Collections

Howard Gotlieb Archival Research Center, Boston University, Boston, Massachusetts
    William B. Lewis

Hagley Library and Museum, Wilmington, Delaware
    E. I. Du Pont de Nemours and Co.
        Advertising Department
        Walter S. Carpenter
        Crawford Greenewalt

John H. Hartman Center for Sales, Advertising and Marketing History, Duke University Library, Durham, North Carolina
    Benton & Bowles
    Carroll Carroll
    J. Walter Thompson

Kraft Archives, Morton Grove, Illinois

Library of American Broadcasting, University of Maryland–College Park
    William Hedges
    Art Hungerford
    Oral Histories

N. W. Ayer Archives, New York

Oral History Research Office, Columbia University, New York
    Frank A. Arnold
    William Benton
    Chester Bowles

Edgar Felix
Roy Durstine
Dan Golenpaul
E. P. H. James
Mark Woods

Wisconsin Historical Society, Madison
Bruce Barton
Thomas Brophy
Dorothy Dignam
Edward Hitz
E. P. H. James
Edward M. Kirby
Irna Phillips
NBC Records
Radio Executives Club
Rosser Reeves

Trade Publications
The Advertiser
Advertising Age
Advertising Agency
Advertising Agency and Advertising & Selling
Advertising & Selling
Broadcast Advertising
Broadcast Merchandising
Broadcasting
Printers' Ink
Printers' Ink Monthly
Radio Broadcast
Radio Digest
Radio Showmanship
Sales Management
Television Magazine
Tide
Variety

Books and Articles

Allen, Fred. *Treadmill to Oblivion*. Boston: Little, Brown, 1954.

Allen, Robert C. *Speaking of Soap Operas*. Chapel Hill: University of North Carolina Press, 1985.

American Business Consultants. *Red Channels: The Report of Communist Influence in Radio and Television*. New York: ABC, June 1950.

American Tobacco Company. *Radio: A Modern Advertising Force*. American Tobacco Company, 1938.

Anderson, Christopher. *Hollywood TV: The Studio System in the Fifties*. Austin: University of Texas Press, 1994.

Andrews, Robert Hardy. *Legend of a Lady: The Story of Rita Martin*. New York: Coward-McCann, 1949.

Arcenaux, Ronald J. "Noah." "Department Stores and the Origins of American Broadcasting, 1910–31." PhD diss., University of Georgia, 2007.

Archer, Gleason. *History of Radio to 1926*. New York: The American Historical Company, 1938.

———. *Big Business and Radio*. New York: The American Historical Company, 1939.

Atwan, Robert, Donald McQuade, and John W. Wright. *Edsels, Luckies, and Frigidaires: Advertising the American Way*. New York: Dell, 1979.

Banning, William Peck. *Commercial Broadcasting Pioneer: The WEAF Experiment, 1922–26*. Cambridge, Mass.: Harvard University Press, 1946.

Baran, Paul, and Paul Sweezy. *Monopoly Capital*. New York: Monthly Review Press, 1966.

Barnouw, Erik. *A Tower in Babel: A History of Broadcasting in the United States, Vol. 1—to 1933*. New York: Oxford University Press, 1966.

———. *The Golden Web: A History of Broadcasting in the United States, Vol. 2—1933 to 1953*. New York: Oxford University Press, 1968.

———. *The Image Empire: A History of Broadcasting in the United States, Vol. 3—from 1953*. New York: Oxford University Press, 1970.

———. *The Sponsor: Notes on a Modern Potentate*. New York: Oxford University Press, 1978.

Barton, Bruce. *The Man Nobody Knows: A Discovery of the Real Jesus*. Indianapolis: Bobbs-Merrill, 1924.

Baughman, James L. *Same Time, Same Station: Creating American Television, 1948–1961*. Baltimore: Johns Hopkins University Press, 2007.

Bergreen, Laurence. *Look Now, Pay Later: The Rise of Network Broadcasting*. Garden City, N.Y.: Doubleday, 1980.

The Best of H. T. Webster: A Memorial Collection. New York: Simon & Schuster, 1953.

Bigelow, Burton. *Elbert Hubbard: Pioneer Advertising Man.* East Aurora, N.Y.: The Roycrofters, 1931.

Bird, Harry Lewis. *This Fascinating Advertising Business.* Indianapolis: Bobbs-Merrill, 1947.

Bird, William L. *"Better Living": Advertising, Media, and the New Vocabulary of Business Leadership, 1935–55.* Evanston, Ill.: Northwestern University Press, 1999.

Blum, John Morton. *V Was for Victory: Politics and American Culture During World War II.* New York: Harcourt Brace Jovanovich, 1976.

Boddy, William. *Fifties Television: The Industry and Its Critics.* Urbana: University of Illinois Press, 1990.

Bogart, Michele. *Artists, Advertising, and the Borders of Art.* Chicago: University of Chicago Press, 1995.

Borden, Neil H. *The Economic Effects of Advertising.* Chicago: Irwin, 1942.

Boylan, Anne. "Women's History on the Radio: The Search for a Usable Past, 1935–53." Paper presented at Hagley Museum and Library, 2010.

Brower, Charlie. *Me, and Other Advertising Geniuses.* Garden City, N.Y.: Doubleday, 1974.

Browne, Nick. "The Political Economy of the Television (Super) Text." In Horace Newcomb, ed., *Television: The Critical View, 4th ed.* New York: Oxford University Press, 1987, 585–99.

Burt, Frank Allen. *American Advertising Agencies: An Inquiry into Their Origin, Growth, Functions and Future.* New York: Harper & Brothers, 1940.

Caldwell, John Thornton. *Production Culture.* Durham, N.C.: Duke University Press, 2008.

———. "Cultures of Production: Studying Industry's Deep Texts, Reflexive Rituals, and Managed Self-Disclosure." In Jennifer Holt and Alisa Perren, eds., *Media Industries: History, Theory, and Method.* Malden, Mass.: Wiley-Blackwell, 2009, 199–212.

Carroll, Carroll. *None of Your Business: Or, My Life with J. Walter Thompson (Confessions of a Renegade Radio Writer).* New York: Cowles, 1970.

Charnley, Mitchell V. *News by Radio.* New York: Macmillan, 1948.

Chevalier, Willard. "Advertising in War and Postwar." In *Advertising's War Task and Post-War Responsibility*, War Advertising Conference, Advertising Federation of America, 28–30 June 1943, New York.

Connell, Ian. "Fabulous Powers: Blaming the Media." In L. Masterman, ed., *Television Mythologies.* London: Boyars, 1984.

Cox, Jim. *Frank and Anne Hummert's Radio Factory.* Jefferson, N.C.: McFarland & Co., 2003.

Cruikshank, Jeffrey L., and Arthur W. Schultz. *The Man Who Sold America: The Amazing but True Story of Albert D. Lasker and the Creation of the Advertising Century.* Boston: Harvard Business Review Press, 2010.

Czitrom, Daniel. *Media and the American Mind.* Chapel Hill: University of North Carolina Press, 1982.

Daniels, Draper. *Giants, Pigmies and Other Advertising People.* Chicago: Crain Communications, Inc., 1974.

Doerksen, Clifford J. *American Babel: Rogue Radio Broadcasters of the Jazz Age.* Philadelphia: University of Pennsylvania Press, 2005.

Doherty, Thomas. *Hollywood's Censor: Joseph I. Breen and the Production Code Administration.* New York: Columbia University Press, 2007.

Douglas, Susan. *Inventing American Broadcasting, 1899–1922.* Baltimore: Johns Hopkins University Press, 1987.

———. *Listening In: Radio and the American Imagination.* New York: Random House, 1999.

Dragonette, Jessica. *Faith Is a Song: The Odyssey of an American Artist.* New York: David McKay Co., 1951.

Durstine, Roy S. *This Advertising Business.* New York: Scribner's, 1929.

Dygert, Warren B. *Radio as an Advertising Medium.* New York: McGraw-Hill, 1939.

Ely, Melvin Patrick. *The Adventures of Amos 'n' Andy: A Social History of an American Phenomenon.* New York: Free Press, 1991.

Ewen, Stuart. *Captains of Consciousness: Advertising and the Social Roots of the Consumer Culture.* New York: McGraw-Hill, 1976.

Federal Communications Commission. *Public Service Responsibility of Broadcast Licenses.* Washington: FCC, 7 March 1946.

Federal Radio Commission. *Second Annual Report of the Federal Radio Commission,* 1 October 1928.

Flynn, John T. "Radio: Medicine Show." *American Scholar* (Autumn 1938): 430–37.

Forty, Adrian. *Objects of Desire: Design and Society since 1750.* London: Thames and Hudson, 1986.

Fox, Dixon Ryan, and Arthur M. Schlesinger Sr., eds. *The Cavalcade of America.* Springfield, Mass.: Milton Bradley Co., 1937.

Fox, Frank W. *Madison Avenue Goes to War: The Strange Military Career of American Advertising, 1941–45*. Provo, Utah: Brigham Young University Press, 1975.

Fox, Richard Wightman, and T. J. Jackson Lears, eds. *The Power of Culture*. Chicago: University of Chicago Press, 1993.

Fox, Stephen. *The Mirror Makers: A History of American Advertising and Its Creators*. New York: William Morrow, 1984.

Frederick, J. George, ed. *Masters of Advertising Copy*. New York: Frank-Maurice, Inc., 1925.

Friedman, Walter A. *Birth of a Salesman: The Transformation of Selling in America*. Cambridge, Mass.: Harvard University Press, 2004.

Friedrich, Carl Joachim, and Jeannette Sayre. "The Development of the Control of Advertising on the Air." *Studies in the Control of Radio*, no. 1, November 1940.

Garver, Robert I. *Successful Radio Advertising with Sponsor Participation Programs*. New York: Prentice-Hall, 1949.

Garvey, Ellen Gruber. *The Adman in the Parlor: Magazines and the Gendering of Consumer Culture, 1880s to 1910s*. New York: Oxford University Press, 1996.

Giddens, Gary. *Bing Crosby: A Pocketful of Dreams, The Early Years, 1903–1940*. Boston: Little, Brown, 2001.

Gledhill, Christine. "Pleasurable Negotiations." In E. Deidre Pribram, ed., *Female Spectators: Looking at Film and Television*. New York: Verso, 1988, 68–89.

Goode, Kenneth M. *How to Turn People into Gold*. New York: Harper, 1929.
———. *What about Radio?* New York: Harper & Brothers, 1937.

Goode, Kenneth M., and M. Zenn Kaufman. *Showmanship in Business*. New York: Harper & Brothers, 1936.

Goodman, David. *Radio's Civic Ambition: American Broadcasting and Democracy in the 1930s*. New York: Oxford University Press, 2011.

Hackett, Alice Payne. *70 Years of Best Sellers: 1895–1965*. New York: R. R. Bowker Co., 1967.

Hartley, John. "From the Consciousness Industry to the Creative Industries." In Jennifer Holt and Alisa Perren, eds., *Media Industries: History, Theory, and Method*. Malden, Mass.: Wiley-Blackwell, 2009, 231–44.

Havig, Alan. "Frederic Wakeman's *The Hucksters* and the Postwar Debate over Commercial Radio." *Journal of Broadcasting* 28, no. 2 (Spring 1984): 187–99.

Hendricks, Bill, and Montgomery Orr. *Showmanship in Advertising*. New York: Showmen's Trade Review, 1949.

Hettinger, Herman S. *A Decade of Radio Advertising*. Chicago: University of Chicago Press, 1933.

Higby, Mary Jane. *Tune in Tomorrow*. New York: Cowles, 1968.

Hilmes, Michele. "Beating the Networks at Their Own Game: The Hollywood/Ad Agency Alliance of the 1930s." Unpublished paper.

———. *Hollywood and Broadcasting: From Radio to Cable*. Urbana: University of Illinois Press, 1990.

———. *Radio Voices: American Broadcasting, 1922–1952*. Minneapolis: University of Minnesota Press, 1997.

———. "The Kraft Music Hall Story." In T. Sennett, ed., *The Old-Time Radio Book*. New York: Pyramid Books, 1976.

———. "Nailing Mercury." In Jennifer Holt and Alisa Perren, eds., *Media Industries: History, Theory, and Method*. Malden, Mass.: Wiley-Blackwell, 2009.

———. *Network Nations: A Transnational History of British and American Broadcasting*. New York: Routledge, 2011.

Hilmes, Michele, ed. *NBC: America's Network*. Berkeley: University of California Press, 2007.

Holt, Jennifer, and Alisa Perren, eds. *Media Industries: History, Theory, and Method*. Malden, Mass.: Wiley-Blackwell, 2009.

Hoover, Herbert. Address. *Recommendations for the Regulation of Radio Adopted by the Third National Radio Conference*, 6–10 October 1924.

Hopkins, Claude. *My Life in Advertising; Scientific Advertising*. Lincolnwood, Ill.: NTC Business Books, reprinted 1966.

Horkheimer, Max, and Theodor Adorno. "Culture Industry: Enlightenment as Mass Deception. In Meenakshi Gigi Durham and Douglas Kellner, eds., *Media and Cultural Studies: Keyworks,* 2nd ed. Boston: Blackwell, 2006, 41–72.

Horowitz, Daniel. *The Morality of Spending: Attitudes toward the Consumer Society in America, 1875–1940*. Baltimore: Johns Hopkins University Press, 1985.

Horten, Gerd. *Radio Goes to War: The Cultural Politics of Propaganda during World War II*. Berkeley: University of California Press, 2002.

Hower, Ralph M. *The History of an Advertising Agency: N. W. Ayer & Son at Work, 1869–1939*. Cambridge, Mass.: Harvard University Press, 1939.

————. *The History of an Advertising Agency: N. W. Ayer & Son at Work, 1869–1949*, rev. ed. Cambridge, Mass.: Harvard University Press, 1949.

Hyman, Sidney. *The Lives of William Benton*. Chicago: University of Chicago Press, 1969.

James, Alden, ed. *Careers in Advertising: And the Jobs Behind Them*. New York: Macmillan, 1932.

Jewell, Richard B. "Hollywood and Radio: Competition and Partnership in the 1930s." *Historical Journal of Film, Radio and Television* 4, no. 2 (1984): 127–41.

Jhally, Sut. *The Codes of Advertising: Fetishism and the Political Economy of Meaning in the Consumer Society*. New York: St. Martin's Press, 1987.

Johnston, Russ. *Marion Harper: An Unauthorized Biography*. Chicago: Crain Books, 1982.

Kallet, Arthur, and Frederick J. Schlink. *100,000,000 Guinea Pigs*. New York: Grosset and Dunlap, 1933.

Koppes, Clayton R. "The Social Destiny of Radio: Hope and Disillusionment in the 1920s." *South Atlantic Quarterly* 68, no. 3 (1969): 363–76.

Koppes, Clayton R., and Gregory D. Black. *Hollywood Goes to War: How Politics, Profits, and Propaganda Shaped World War II Movies*. New York: Free Press, 1987.

Kreshel, Peggy J. "The 'Culture' of J. Walter Thompson, 1915–1925." *Public Relations Review* 16, no. 3 (Fall 1990): 80–93.

LaGuardia, Robert. *Soap World*. n.p.: Arbor House, 1983.

Laird, Pamela Walker. *Advertising Progress: American Business and the Rise of Consumer Marketing*. Baltimore: Johns Hopkins University Press, 1998.

Landry, Robert J. *This Fascinating Radio Business*. Indianapolis: Bobbs-Merrill, 1946.

Lasker, Albert Davis. *The Lasker Story: As He Told It*. Chicago: Advertising Publications, Inc., 1963.

Lavin, Marilyn. "Creating Consumers in the 1930s: Irna Phillips and the Radio Soap Opera." *Journal of Consumer Research* 22, no. 1 (June 1995): 75–89.

Leach, William. *Land of Desire: Merchants, Power, and the Rise of a New American Culture*. New York: Pantheon, 1993.

Lears, T. J. Jackson. "From Salvation to Self-Realization: Advertising and the Therapeutic Roots of the Consumer Culture, 1880–1930." In R. W. Fox and T. J. J. Lears, eds., *The Culture of Consumption*. New York: Pantheon, 1983, 1–38.

———. "Some Versions of Fantasy: Toward a Cultural History of Advertising, 1880–1930." *Prospects* 9 (1984): 349–405.

———. "The Concept of Cultural Hegemony: Problems and Possibilities." *American Historical Review* 90, no. 3 (June 1985): 567–93.

———. *Fables of Abundance: A Cultural History of Advertising in America.* New York: Basic Books, 1994.

Leiss, William, Stephen Kline, Sut Jhally, and Jackie Botterill. *Social Communication in Advertising: Consumption in the Mediated Marketplace,* 3d ed. New York: Routledge, 2005.

Livingston, James. *Against Thrift: Why Consumer Culture Is Good for the Economy, the Environment, and Your Soul.* New York: Basic Books, 2011.

Loviglio, Jason. *Radio's Intimate Public: Network Broadcasting and Mass-Mediated Democracy.* Minneapolis: University of Minnesota Press, 2005.

MacDonald, J. Fred. *Don't Touch That Dial! Radio Programming in American Life, 1920–1960.* Chicago: Nelson-Hall, 1979.

Mander, Mary S. "The Public Debate About Broadcasting in the Twenties: An Interpretive History." *Journal of Broadcasting* 20 (Spring 1984): 167–85.

Marchand, Roland. *Advertising the American Dream: Making Way for Modernity, 1920–1940.* Berkeley: University of California Press, 1985.

———. *Creating the Corporate Soul: The Rise of Public Relations and Corporate Imagery in American Big Business.* Berkeley: University of California Press, 1998.

Mashon, Michael. "NBC, J. Walter Thompson, and the Evolution of Prime-Time Television Programming and Sponsorship, 1946–58." PhD diss., University of Maryland–College Park, 1996.

McChesney, Robert. *Telecommunications, Mass Media, and Democracy: The Battle for the Control of U.S. Broadcasting, 1928–1935.* New York: Oxford University Press, 1993.

McGovern, Charles F. *Sold American: Consumption and Citizenship, 1890–1945.* Chapel Hill: University of North Carolina Press, 2006.

Meehan, Eileen. "Conceptualizing Culture as Commodity: The Problem of Television." *Critical Studies in Mass Communication* 3 (1986): 448–57.

Meyer, Donald. *The Positive Thinkers.* Rev. ed. Middletown, Conn.: Wesleyan University Press, 1988.

Meyers, Cynthia. "Frank and Anne Hummert's Soap Opera Empire: 'Reason-Why' Advertising Strategies in Early Radio Programming." *Quarterly Review of Film & Video* 16, no. 2 (1997): 113–32.

———. "From Radio Ad Man to Radio Reformer: Senator William Benton's Broadcasting Career, 1930–60." *Journal of Radio and Audio Media* 16, no. 1 (2009): 17–29.

———. "From Sponsorship to Spots: Advertising and the Development of Electronic Media." In Jennifer Holt and Alisa Perren, eds., *Media Industries: History, Theory, and Method*. Malden, Mass.: Wiley-Blackwell, 2009: 69–80.

———. "The Problems with Sponsorship in Broadcasting, 1930s–50s: Perspectives from the Advertising Industry." *Historical Journal of Film, Radio and Television* 31, no. 3 (September 2011): 355–72.

Midgley, Ned. *The Advertising and Business Side of Radio*. New York: Prentice-Hall, 1948.

Mills, C. Wright. *White Collar: The American Middle Classes*. New York: Oxford University Press, 1951.

Montgomery, Edrene S. "Bruce Barton's *The Man Nobody Knows*: A Popular Advertising Illusion." *Journal of Popular Culture* 19 (Winter 1985): 21–34.

Morrell, Peter. *Poisons, Potions and Profits: The Antidote to Radio Advertising*. New York: Knight Publishers, 1937.

Murray, Matthew. "Broadcast Content Regulation and Cultural Limits, 1920–1962." PhD diss., University of Wisconsin–Madison, 1997.

Newman, Kathy M. *Radio Active: Advertising and Consumer Activism, 1935–1947*. Berkeley: University of California Press, 2004.

Ohmann, Richard. *Selling Culture: Magazines, Markets and Class at the Turn of the Century*. London, New York: Verso, 1996.

Ohmer, Susan. *George Gallup in Hollywood*. New York: Columbia University Press, 2006.

O'Neill, Neville, ed. *The Advertising Agency Looks at Radio*. New York: D. Appleton & Co., 1932.

Paley, William. *As It Happened*. Garden City, N.Y.: Doubleday, 1979.

Parkin, Katherine J. *Food Is Love: Advertising and Gender Roles in Modern America*. Philadelphia: University of Pennsylvania Press, 2006.

Pease, Otis. *The Responsibilities of American Advertising: Private Control and Public Influence, 1920–40*. New Haven, Conn.: Yale University Press, 1958.

Peatman, John Gray, ed. *Radio and Business: Proceedings of the First Annual Conference on Radio and Business*. New York: City College, 22–23 May 1945.

Pendergrast, Mark. *Uncommon Grounds: The History of Coffee and How It Transformed Our World*. New York: Basic Books, 2000.

Pope, Daniel. *The Making of Modern Advertising.* New York: Basic Books, 1983.

Potter, David M. *People of Plenty: Economic Abundance and the American Character.* Chicago: University of Chicago Press, 1954.

Presbrey, Frank. *The History and Development of Advertising.* New York: Greenwood Press, 1929, 1968.

Price, Jonathan. *The Best Thing on TV: Commercials.* New York: Penguin, 1978.

Proceedings of the Fourth National Radio Conference, and Recommendations for the Regulation of Radio, 9–11 November 1925.

Ribuffo, Leo. "Jesus Christ as Business Statesman: Bruce Barton and the Selling of Corporate Capitalism." *American Quarterly* 33 (Summer 1981): 206–31.

Rorty, James. *Our Master's Voice.* New York: The John Day Co., 1934.

Rosenblum, Barbara. *Photographers at Work.* New York: Holmes and Meier, 1978.

Rothenbuhler, Eric, and Tom McCourt. "Radio Redefines Itself, 1947–1962." In Michele Hilmes and Jason Loviglio, eds., *Radio Reader.* New York: Routledge, 2002, 367–87.

Rotzoll, K., J. Haefner, and C. Sandage. *Advertising and Society: Perspectives towards Understanding.* Columbus, Ohio: Copywright Grid, 1976.

Rowsome, Frank Jr. *They Laughed When I Sat Down: An Informal History of Advertising in Words and Pictures.* New York: Bonanza Books, 1959.

Russo, Alexander. *Points on the Dial: Golden Age Radio beyond the Networks.* Durham, N.C.: Duke University Press, 2010.

Sahlins, Marshall. *Culture and Practical Reason.* Chicago: University of Chicago Press, 1976.

Samuel, Lawrence. *Brought to You By: Postwar Television Advertising.* Austin: University of Texas Press, 2001.

Savage, Barbara Dianne. *Broadcasting Freedom: Radio, War, and the Politics of Race, 1938–1948.* Chapel Hill: University of North Carolina Press, 1999.

Schudson, Michael. *Advertising, the Uneasy Persuasion: Its Dubious Impact on American Society.* New York: Basic Books, 1984.

Seiter, Ellen. "'To Teach and to Sell': Irna Phillips and Her Sponsors, 1930–1954." *Journal of Film and Video* 41, no. 1 (Spring 1989): 21–35.

Shanks, Barry. "Network Television: Advertising Agencies and Sponsors." In J. W. Wright, ed., *The Commercial Connection.* New York: Dell Publishing, 1979, 94–107.

Siepmann, Charles A. "American Radio in Wartime: An Interim Survey of the OWI's Radio Bureau." In Frank Stanton and Paul Lazarsfeld, eds., *Radio Research, 1942–1943.* New York: Arno Press, 1944, 1979.

Sklar, Martin. *The Corporate Reconstruction of American Capitalism, 1890–1916: The Market, the Law, and Politics.* New York: Cambridge University Press, 1988.

Smith, Sally Bedell. *In All His Glory: The Life of William S. Paley.* New York: Simon & Schuster, 1990.

Smulyan, Susan. *Selling Radio: The Commercialization of American Broadcasting, 1920–1934.* Washington: Smithsonian Institution Press, 1994.

Socolow, Michael J. "'Always in Friendly Competition': NBC and CBS in the First Decade of National Broadcasting." In Michele Hilmes, ed., *NBC: America's Network.* Berkeley: University of California Press, 2007, 25–43.

———. "'News Is a Weapon': Domestic Radio Propaganda and Broadcast Journalism in America, 1939–44." *American Journalism* 24, no. 3 (2007): 109–31.

Spears, Timothy B. *100 Years on the Road: The Traveling Salesman in American Culture.* New Haven, Conn.: Yale University Press, 1995.

Stanton, Frank, and Paul Lazarsfeld, eds. *Radio Research, 1942–1943.* New York: Arno Press, 1944, 1979.

Stedman, William. *The Serials: Suspense and Drama by Installment.* Norman: University of Oklahoma Press, 1971, 1977.

Steele, Richard W. "The Great Debate: Roosevelt, the Media, and the Coming of the War, 1940–41." *Journal of American History* 71 (June 1984): 69–92.

Sterling, Christopher, and John Kittross. *Stay Tuned: A Concise History of American Broadcasting.* Belmont, Calif.: Wadsworth, 1978.

Stole, Inger. *Advertising on Trial: Consumer Activism and Corporate Public Relations in the 1930s.* Urbana: University of Illinois Press, 2006.

Strasser, Susan. *Satisfaction Guaranteed: The Making of the American Mass Market.* New York: Pantheon, 1989.

Street, Sean. *Crossing the Ether: British Public Service Radio and Commercial Competition, 1922–1945.* Eastleigh, UK: John Libbey Publishing, 2006.

Streeter, Thomas. *Selling the Air: A Critique of the Policy of Commercial Broadcasting in the United States.* Chicago: University of Chicago Press, 1996.

Susman, Warren. *Culture as History: The Transformation of American Society in the Twentieth Century.* New York: Pantheon, 1984.

Swallow, John W. *Midwife to an Octopus.* Encino, Calif.: Garden House Press, 1964.

Taylor, Timothy D. *The Sounds of Capitalism: Advertising, Music, and the Conquest of Culture.* Chicago: University of Chicago Press, 2012.

Terkel, Studs. *Hard Times: An Oral History of the Great Depression.* New York: Pantheon, 1970.

Thurber, James. "Soapland." *New Yorker,* 29 May 1948, 30ff.

———. *The Beast in Me and Other Animals.* New York: Harcourt, Brace, 1948.

Trade-Ways, Inc. *Selling Broadcast Advertising: A Handbook for NBC Salesmen.* New York: NBC, 1933.

Trammell, Niles. "Advertising in the Public Interest." Address to National Association of Broadcasters, Chicago, Illinois, 24 October 1946.

Vallee, Rudy. *Let the Chips Fall . . .* Harrisburg, Penn.: Stackpole Books, 1975.

Veblen, Thorstein. *The Theory of the Leisure Class.* New York: Macmillan, 1899.

Verma, Neil. *Theater of the Mind: Imagination, Aesthetics, and American Radio Drama.* Chicago: University of Chicago Press, 2012.

Wakeman, Frederic. *The Hucksters.* New York: Rinehart & Co., 1946.

Wang, Jennifer Hyland. "Convenient Fictions: The Construction of the Daytime Broadcast Audience, 1927–1960." PhD diss., University of Wisconsin–Madison, 2006.

Watkins, Julian Lewis. *The 100 Greatest Advertisements.* New York: Dover, 1959.

Weaver, Pat, with Thomas Coffey. *The Best Seat in the House: The Golden Years of Radio and Television.* New York: Knopf, 1994.

Webber, Gordon. *Our Kind of People: The Story of the First Fifty Years at Benton & Bowles.* New York: Benton & Bowles, 1979.

Wertheim, Arthur F. *Radio Comedy.* New York: Oxford University Press, 1979.

Whiteside, Thomas. *The Relaxed Sell.* New York: Oxford University Press, 1954.

Wicke, Jennifer. *Advertising Fictions: Literature, Advertisement, and Social Reading.* New York: Columbia University Press, 1988.

Williams, Raymond. *Problems in Materialism and Culture.* London: New Left Books, 1962, 1980.

———. *Television: Technology and Cultural Form.* New York: Schocken Books, 1977.

Williamson, Judith. *Decoding Advertisements: Ideology and Meaning in Advertising.* London: Marion Boyars, 1978.

Winkler, Allan M. *The Politics of Propaganda: The Office of War Information, 1942–1945.* New Haven, Conn.: Yale University Press, 1978.

Wolfe, Charles Hull. *Modern Radio Advertising.* New York: Printers' Ink Publishing Co., Inc., 1949.

Wood, James Playsted. *The Story of American Advertising.* New York: Ronald Press Co., 1958.

Wu, Tim. *The Master Switch: The Rise and Fall of Informational Empires.* New York: Knopf, 2010.

Y&R and Broadcasting: Growing Up Together. New York: Museum of Broadcasting, n.d.

Young, James H. *The Toadstool Millionaires.* Princeton, N.J.: Princeton University Press, 1961.

Young, James Webb. *The Diary of an Ad Man: The War Years, June 1, 1942– December 31, 1943.* Chicago: Advertising Publications, Inc., 1944.

———. *How to Become an Advertising Man.* Chicago: Advertising Publications, Inc., 1963.

Young, John Orr. *Adventures in Advertising.* New York: Harper & Bros., 1949.

Index

Network Allocation Plan, 239–40,
    241, 242, 246
networks, 64, 78–102, 148; advertis-
    ers and agencies, wooing of,
    42–53; advertising standards
    of, 94–101; and agencies, 83–
    90, 123, 194, 209; competition
    between, 42, 81–82, 92–93;
    and criticism of radio, 256–57,
    261; formation of, 38–42; and
    postwar radio, 263–67; and
    programming, 57, 60, 62, 93,
    195–96, 266–67, 277–80, 286,
    288; revenues of, 64, 78, 83,
    205, 227; and television, 254,
    274–76, 278–80, 288–90; in
    World War II, 227, 231, 237,
    242. *See also* NBC; CBS; Mu-
    tual Broadcasting System
New York Sun (periodical), 172
New York Telephone (firm), 174
New York Times, 197
New York Tribune (periodical), 172
New Yorker (periodical), 113, 279
Newman, Kathy, 4
News-Scope (program), 168
Niven, David, 219
Noble, Edward J., 256
Norwich Pharmacal (firm), 153
Nye Hearings, 180

Oboler, Arch, 183
Office of Facts and Figures (OFF),
    235–40
Office of War Information (OWI), 10,
    226, 233, 235, 239–46, 286
Old Gold (brand), 149, 220
Old Gold Hollywood Screen Scoops
    (program), 205

Olsen & Johnson (act), *212*, 214
O'Meara, Walter, 189
One Man's Family (program), 211, 212
Osborn, Alex, 172, 225
Our Gal Sunday (program), 112, 119
Ovaltine (brand), 108, 122, 123, *124*
Oxydol (brand), 110, 116 117, 122,
    124

P. Lorillard (firm), 168
Packard (brand), 153
Painted Dreams (program), 119
Paley, William S., 41, 45, 48, 81, 195,
    238, 246–47, 256, 259, 266
Pall Mall (brand), 159
Palmolive (brand), 89, 108, 194. *See
    also* Colgate–Palmolive
Palmolive Beauty Box Theater (pro-
    gram), 186, 189
Parade of the States, The (program),
    179
Paramount (firm), 81, 202
Paramount Decrees, 288
Parsons, Louella, 205, 217
Passing Parade (program), 205
patent medicines, 16, 19, 23, 61, 77,
    106, 134, 169
Patterson, John, 187
Pearl, Jack, 194, 212
Peck (agency), 87, 145
Penner, Joe, 211, *212*, 213
People Look at Radio, The (book), 256
Pepsi-Cola (brand), 255
Pepsodent (brand), 68–69, 110, 187,
    312*n*80
Pepto-Bismol (brand), 231
Perkins, Ray, 146–47
Perren, Alisa, 3